terrorist assemblages

NEXT WAVE: NEW DIRECTIONS IN WOMEN'S STUDIES

A series edited by Inderpal Grewal, Caren Kaplan, and Robyn Wiegman

TERRORIST

ASSEMBLAGES

homonationalism in queer times

JASBIR K. PUAR

duke university press ⟡ durham and london 2007

© 2007 Duke University Press
All rights reserved
Printed in the United States
of America on acid-free paper ∞
Designed by Katy Clove
Typeset in Cycles by Keystone Typesetting, Inc.
Library of Congress Cataloging-in-Publication
Data appear on the last printed page of this book.

An earlier version of chapter 1 appeared as "Mapping U.S. Homonormativities,"
in *Gender, Place, and Culture: A Journal of Feminist Geography* 13, no. 1 (2006): 67–88.

An earlier version of chapter 2 appeared as "Abu Ghraib: Arguing against
Exceptionalism," in *Feminist Studies* 30, no. 2 (2004): 522–34.

FOR SANDEEP SINGH PUAR

MAY 8, 1970–FEBRUARY 20, 2003

contents

If we think of tactics as the art of assembling men and weapons in order to win battles, and of strategy as the art of assembling battles in order to win wars, then logistics could be defined as the art of assembling war and the agricultural, economic, and industrial resources that make it possible. If a war machine could be said to have a body, then tactics would represent the muscles and strategy the brain, while logistics would be the machine's digestive and circulatory systems: the procurement and supply networks that distribute resources throughout an army's body.—Manuel De Landa, *War in the Age of Intelligent Machines*

Do not build on the good old days, but on the bad new ones.—Walter Benjamin, *Reflections*

What do lives of privilege look like in the midst of war and the inevitable violence that accompanies the building of empire?—M. Jacqui Alexander, *Pedagogies of Crossing*

preface:

tactics, strategies, logistics

July 19, 2006, was declared the International Day of Action against Homophobic Persecution in Iran by two lesbian, gay, bisexual, transgender, intersex, and queer (LGBTIQ) organizations, the self-proclaimed militant British-based OutRage!, and the Paris-based group IDAHO (an acronym for International Day against Homophobia). Marking the one-year anniversary of the public hangings in the city of Mashad of two male Iranian youths, Mahmoud Asgari and Ayaz Marhoni, the two groups initiated a call for global protests that resulted in actions in dozens of cities across the United States, Canada, and Europe. Demonstrations in San Francisco, New York, London, Amsterdam, Moscow, Dublin, and Stockholm were joined by less predictable locales, such as Salt Lake City, Sioux Falls, Tulsa, Warsaw, Marseille, Mexico City, and Bogotá.[1] The call was also endorsed by numerous organizations, including the International Lesbian and Gay Association and the Dutch gay organization, Center for Culture and Leisure; scores of LGBTIQ activists, artists, academics, politicians, and celebrities (for example, the writer-activist Larry Kramer, the founder of the Center for Lesbian and Gay Studies and CUNY professor Martin Duberman, and New York State Senator Tom Duane); the Persian Gay and Lesbian Organization, a gay Iranian group with European and Canadian secretariats; the website Gay Egypt; and the editors of *MAHA*, a "clandestine gay zine in Iran," who wrote that "international LGBT pressure on the Iranian authorities, in solidarity with Iranian LGBT people, is most vital and welcome."[2] The French activist and founder of IDAHO Louis-George Tin hailed the executions as the genesis of an international gay solidarity movement, regarding the International Day of Action as "something special [that] has happened since 19 July 2005."[3]

There was, however, plenty of discord among LGBTIQ organizations regarding the call for international protests. The culmination of a year-long argument regarding the facts of the execution, these disputes involved Peter Tatchell's OutRage!; the director of the International Gay and Lesbian Human Rights Commission (IGLHRC) Paula Ettelbrick; Scott Long, director of the Lesbian, Gay, Bisexual and Transgender Rights Project of Human Rights Watch (HRW); the *Gay City News* writer Doug Ireland; Al-Fatiha's founder, Faisal Alam; and the usual suspects among gay commentators, such as Andrew Sullivan.[4] In the wake of the London bombings, photos of the hangings circulating on the Internet drew international outrage. A posting about and three photos of the execution were initially released on the website of the Iranian Students' News Agency. A translation of this article in an OutRage! press release qualified the hangings as "honor killings" of gay youth, and the story spread rapidly across LGBTIQ listservs, websites, and blogs. The scholar and LGBTIQ activist Richard Kim, however, in a meticulously detailed chronology of the events, writes in *The Nation* that it quickly became unclear whether the two had had consensual sex (with each other or others) and were the victims of antigay persecution, or if the teenagers were convicted of gang raping a 13-year-old boy.[5] On July 22, 2005, the Human Rights Campaign, the largest lesbian and gay organization in the United States, issued a statement demanding that Secretary of State Condoleezza Rice condemn the killings. Sweden and the Netherlands temporarily suspended deportations of gay Iranians and OutRage! called for the EU to institute trade sanctions against Iran at a time, Kim notes, "when the EU was engaged in delicate negotiations with Iran over its nuclear capacity."[6] By July 23, according to Kim, both IGLHRC and HRW were concerned that "gay rights" were being co-opted at the expense of a broader social justice issue: execution of minors.

Whether the complex case at hand is one of "juvenile execution," the persecution of gays, or both, many commentators note that the United States continues to resist a growing consensus that capital punishment is inhumane, having only just recently outlawed executions of those under 18 in March 2005. As Faisal Alam notes, that three Nigerian "homosexual" men were sentenced to be stoned to death earlier that summer elicited no such global indignation.[7] Nor have these abuses elicited so much response from LGBTIQ groups in the past. Along these lines, there were no protests in May 2004 when the circulation of photos of the torture practices at Abu Ghraib exhumed the revolting homophobia of the U.S. military. As IGLHRC's director Paula Ettelbrick asks, "Why now? Why just Iran?"[8]

Hailed as a member of the "axis of evil" by the Bush administration, and with evidence of planned U.S. military action mounting during the summer of 2005, it seems pretty clear why now, and why Iran. Further, the 2006 anniversary protests took place during the second month of the Israeli invasion of Lebanon, amid escalating pressure to consider military strikes against Syria and Iran for their support of Hezbollah. The frenzied fixation on the homophobia of Iran's state regime is thus perpetuated, in many instances, by the very same factions who are responsible for the global proliferation of protests against a future invasion of Iran. At this historical moment, this bizarre conjuncture functions as nothing less than the racism of the global gay left and the wholesale acceptance of the Islamophobic rhetoric that fuels the war on terror and the political forces pushing for an Iranian invasion, if not a tacit acceptance of the pending occupation itself.

Terrorist Assemblages: Homonationalism in Queer Times is an invitation to deeper exploration of these connections among sexuality, race, gender, nation, class, and ethnicity in relation to the tactics, strategies, and logistics of war machines. This project critiques the fostering, managing, and valorizing of life and all that sustains it, describing the mechanisms by which queerness as a process of racialization informs the very distinctions between life and death, wealth and poverty, health and illness, fertility and morbidity, security and insecurity, living and dying. Race, ethnicity, nation, gender, class, and sexuality disaggregate gay, homosexual, and queer national subjects who align themselves with U.S. imperial interests from forms of illegitimate queerness that name and ultimately propel populations into extinction.[9] *Terrorist Assemblages* foregrounds the proliferation, occupation, and suppression of queernesses in relation to patriotism, war, torture, security, death, terror, terrorism, detention, and deportation, themes usually imagined as devoid of connection to sexual politics in general and queer politics in particular. Impelled not only by this folding of queer and other sexual national subjects into the biopolitical management of life, but by the simultaneous folding out of life, out toward death, of queerly racialized "terrorist populations," biopolitics delineates not only which queers live and which queers die—a variable and contestable demarcation—but also *how* queers live and die. The result of the successes of queer incorporation into the domains of consumer markets and social recognition in the post–civil rights, late twentieth century, these various entries by queers into the biopolitical optimization of life mark a shift, as homosexual bodies have been historically understood as endlessly cathected to death. In other words, there is a transition under way in how queer subjects are relating to nation-states, particularly the United States, from being figures of death (i.e., the AIDS epidemic) to becoming tied to ideas of life and productivity (i.e., gay marriage and families). The politics of recognition and incorporation entail that certain—but certainly not most—homosexual, gay, and queer bodies may be the temporary recipients of the "measures of benevolence" that are afforded by liberal discourses of multicultural tolerance and diversity.[10] This benevolence toward sexual others is contingent upon ever-narrowing parameters of white racial privilege, consumption capabilities, gender and kinship normativity, and bodily integrity. The contemporary emergence of homosexual, gay, and queer subjects—normativized through their deviance (as it becomes surveilled, managed, studied) rather than despite it—is integral to the interplay of perversion and normativity necessary to sustain in full gear the management of life. In making this argument, I deploy "racialization" as a figure for specific social formations and processes that are not necessarily or only tied to what has been historically theorized as "race."

The emergence and sanctioning of queer subjecthood is a historical shift condoned only through a parallel process of demarcation from populations targeted for segregation, disposal, or death, a reintensification of racialization through queerness. The cultivation of these homosexual subjects folded into life, enabled through "market virility" and "regenerative reproductivity," is racially demarcated and paralleled by a rise in the targeting of queerly raced bodies for dying. If the "turn to life" for queer subjects is now possible, how queerness folds into racialization is a crucial factor in whether and how that turn to life is experienced, if it is experienced at all. Further, the rise of these nonnormative national subjects is linked in no uncertain terms to the racialized populations that come into being through the assignment of queerness, an assignment disavowed by the queer subject embraced by biopolitical incitement to life. *Terrorist Assemblages* thus attends to the connectivities that generate queer, homosexual, and gay disciplinary subjects while concurrently constituting queerness as the optic through which perverse populations are called into nominalization for control. That is, this recasting of queerness as that optic—and the operative technology—in the production, disciplining, and maintenance of populations drives the analyses in this book. This disjuncture of the regulating and regulated queer, homosexual, gay disciplinary subjects and the queered darkening of terrorists marks the surprising but not fully unexpected flowering of new normativities in these queer times.

In *Terrorist Assemblages*, my primary interest is in this process of the management of queer life at the expense of sexually and racially perverse death in relation to the contemporary politics of securitization, Orientalism, terrorism, torture, and the articulation of Muslim, Arab, Sikh, and South Asian sexualities. I argue that during this historical juncture, there is a very specific production of terrorist bodies against properly queer subjects. The questions that have fueled this project include but are not limited to the following: What are the historical linkages between various periods of national crisis and the pathologizing of sexuality, the inflation of sexual perversions? What are the heteronormative assumptions still binding the fields and disciplines of security and surveillance analyses, peace and conflict studies, terrorism research, public policy, transnational finance networks, human rights and human security blueprints, and international peacekeeping organizations such as the United Nations? How do we conceptualize queer sexualities in Afghanistan, Iraq, and other parts of the "Middle East"—a term I hesitate to use given its area studies origins— without reproducing neocolonialist assumptions that collude with U.S. missionary and savior discourses? Given the mechanics of scapegoating sexual minorities as well as South Asians, Arab Americans, and Muslim Americans, what kinds of discursive and material strategies are queer Muslims and queer Arabs using to resist state and societal violence?[11]

The import of these questions is suggested by the changing demographics of HIV transmission, prevention funding, and pharmaceutical industry exploitation; the decriminalization of sodomy in the United States; the global (albeit uneven) incorporation of various versions of legalized gay

[handwritten margin note: Management of Queer life]

marriage and domestic partnership; the rise of a global gay right wing anchored in Europe and attaining credibility very pointedly through Islamophobic rhetoric; flourishing gay and lesbian representation (in the U.S. mainstream) such as *The L Word* and *Queer Eye for the Straight Guy*; normativizing gay and lesbian human rights frames, which produce (in tandem with gay tourism) gay-friendly and not-gay-friendly nations; the queer "market virility" that can simulate heteronormative paternity through the purchase of reproductive technology; the return to kinship and family norms implicit in the new lesbian "global family," complete with transnational adoptee babies; and market accommodation that has fostered multibillion-dollar industries in gay tourism, weddings, investment opportunities, and retirement. In large part, the conversation that has dominated sexuality studies of the post-civil rights era is a fatigued debate about the advances and merits of civil legitimation—legalization of sodomy, gay marriage, and gay adoption—in contrast to the sold-out politics embedded within market interpellations of LGBTIQ subjects, with the question of resistance always at the core of this polarity. Rather than emphasizing the resistant or oppositional, I seek to exhume the *convivial* relations between queernesses and militarism, securitization, war, terrorism, surveillance technologies, empire, torture, nationalism, globalization, fundamentalism, secularism, incarceration, detention, deportation, and neoliberalism: the tactics, strategies, and logistics of our contemporary war machines.

Tactics: A Word on Method

The correspondence between nonnormative sexualities, race, and pathologized nationality has been examined and interrogated by theorists working on transnational sexualities and queer diasporic identities, sexual citizenship, consumption practices in relation to legislative gains and civil liberties, the workings of global LGBTIQ nongovernmental organizations and sexual rights, and the reproduction of kinship and normative familial structures in globalization.[12] Reflective of an ongoing push to articulate queer theories beyond their origins in literary studies, as well as a challenge to unprobed assumptions of whiteness and citizenship privilege, the import of this work remains relatively unaddressed in contemporary political dialogues. *Terrorist Assemblages* continues this critical mandate to disrupt certain dialogues when they refuse to take into account feminist, queer, and transnational contributions to these conversations by highlighting heteronormative framings and absent analytics.

In the spirit of such disruptions, *Terrorist Assemblages* engages a range of different theoretical paradigms, textual materials, and tactical approaches that are reflective of a queer methodological philosophy. Queerness irreverently challenges a linear mode of conduction and transmission: there is no exact recipe for a queer endeavor, no a priori system that taxonomizes the linkages, disruptions, and contradictions into a tidy vessel. The texts I have assembled are governmental texts on counterterrorism technologies; films, documentaries, and television shows; print media (especially LGBTIQ regional, national, and international newspapers and magazines); organizational press releases and manifestos; and ethnographic data (including participant-observation at numerous pivotal LBGTIQ political events and meetings and interviews with prominent LGBTIQ community organizers and activists). I have also examined what might be constituted as circuits of alternative press (postings from listservs such as professorsforpeace.org and portside.org, and numerous websites and news services such as the Pacifica News Service and opendemocracy.net) and representational and cultural artifacts (photos, consumables, visual depictions). Assembling these varied and often disjunctive primary sources is crucial to countering the platitudinous and journalistic rhetoric that plagues those public discourses most readily available for consumption. By considering those sources within the frame of this study, I hope to contribute to the building of an alternative historical record, archive, and documentation of our contemporary moments. However, I veer away from the instinctual, the natural, or the commonsensical as the basis of a queer sensibility. On the contrary, I am interested in the unexpected, the unplanned irruptions, the lines of flight, the denaturalizing of expectation through the juxtaposition of the seemingly unrelated, working to undo the naturalized sexual scripts of terror that become taken-for-granted knowledge formations.

My analyses draw upon more than five years of research conducted in New York, New Jersey, and Connecticut involving community-based organizations, activist events, meetings, protests, teach-ins, and panels, as well as pamphlets, educational materials, propaganda, and press releases from both alternative and mainstream media. The methodologies employed in this work involve formal interviews, participant-observation at meetings and events, discursive analyses of mainstream and alternative media, and readings of legal decisions. A film project on which I am currently working, about the participation since the early 1990s of South Asian progressive organizations in the annual New York City India Day Parade, titled *India Shining*, also forms the backdrop of this manuscript and informs my analyses. More than 150 hours of footage for the film, including interviews with over sixty South Asian community activists, artists, and community members, visually portray the political conundrums written about here.

This book spans South Asian, Arab American, and Muslim racial formations, centering what are currently being termed West Asian formations as well as Arab American and Muslim identities in the study of Asian American and South Asian American historical and contemporary processes of racialization and sexualization, promoting a linking of Arab American and Asian American studies. While there is a clear focus on U.S. sexual exceptionalisms, I draw together discrete state projects that radiate outward, tracing other national sexual exceptionalisms—in Britain and, to a lesser extent, the Netherlands—via the growing cohesion of a global gay Islamophobia. Clearly the scales of place and space in this project are unruly and perhaps at times too specific: New York City, for example, and the tristate area beyond it (New York, New Jersey, Connecticut) are a key focus of some of the LGBTIQ organizing and news coverage. Nevertheless, the expansive geographical boundaries of this project, both real and imagined, reflect both an unhomed interdisciplinarity as well as mediated tensions and deliberate blurring between area studies knowledge formations and ethnic, diaspora, and transnational studies. In the age of what Rey Chow hails as the "world target"—the world as an object to be destroyed—the mandate to envision alternatives to "target fields" (the conventional organization of postwar military area studies geographies that are "fields of information retrieval and dissemination . . . necessary for the perpetuation of the United States' political and ideological hegemony") only intensifies. This project may fail in fully displacing the self-referential eye/I that Chow argues is the crux of U.S. practices of targeting the world. By not playing by the disciplinary rules, however, I can offer alternative and submerged geographies—the United States from decidedly underresourced, nonnormative vantage points—exposing the United States not only as targeting but also as the target, as targeted.[13]

Strategies: On Speed—Hauntings, Timings, Temporalities

The present as an experience of a time is precisely the moment when
different forms of absence become mixed together: absence of those
presences that are no longer so and that one remembers (the past),
and absence of those others that are yet to come and are anticipated
(the future).—Achille Mbembe, *On the Postcolony*

The accelerated state tends to be exuberant in invention and fancy, leaping rapidly from one association to the next, carried along by the force of its own impetus. Slowness, in contrast, tends to go with care and caution, a sober and critical stance, which has its uses no less than the "go" of effusion.—Oliver Sacks, "Speed: Aberrations of Time and Movement"

The time is out of joint. The world is going badly. It is worn but its wear no longer counts. Old age or youth—one no longer counts in that way. The world has more than one age. We lack the measure of the measure. We no longer realize the wear, we no longer take account of it as of a single age in the progress of history. Neither maturation, nor crisis, nor even agony. Something else. What is happening is happening to age itself, it strikes a blow at the teleological order of history. What is coming, in which the untimely appears, is happening to time but it does not happen in time. Contretemps. *The time is out of joint.*—Jacques Derrida, *Specters of Marx*

The tempo of always-becoming is in part what Achille Mbembe, writing about Africa as an anachronistic void, elucidates in his usage of "emerging time," "time that is appearing," "passing time," and "the time of entanglement." In his critique of telos, unilateral directionality, and the cyclical pattern of stability and rupture, Mbembe wants not only to claim time as nonlinear, an always already apropos move, but insufficient, he argues, given that nonlinearity has been embraced as chaos. Ultimately, he seeks to destabilize the opposition between stability and chaos, such that chaos is discharged from its semiotic resonance with violence, upheaval, anarchy.[14] It is not to normativize chaos per se, nor to mark its production as aberrant, but to allow for what might issue forth from it, what it might produce, rather than to seek the antidote that would suppress it. It is also to disentangle political and social chaos from the terms of its conventional response, that of political urgency.

This notion of political urgency, a temporality that problematically resuscitates state of exception discourses, suggests a particular relationship to temporality and change, inasmuch as it cuts across or runs against the grain of the ideal of laborious, ponderous, leisurely production of intellectual scholarship that can thrive only in the stable confines of a "room of one's own" or a political climate that is not disruptive or tumultuous. No doubt this is, or was, a western concept of intellectual labor, mired in modernist yearnings for and fantasies about work, leisure, temporality, and spatiality. If we say that events are happening fast, what must we slow down in order to make such a pronouncement? If we delineate time as having a steady rhythm, what disjunctures must we smooth out or over in order to arrive at that conclusion? If we feel that things are calm, what must we forget in order to inhabit such a restful feeling?

Foregrounding the political urgency of this project reifies certain events: in this case, September 11, 2001, commonly 9/11, as a particular turning point or a central generator of desires for expediency, rapidity, political innovativeness, caught in a binary debate of rupture versus continuity.[15] As metaphor, 9/11 reflects particular spatial and temporal narratives and also produces spatializing and temporalizing discourses.[16] September 11, when invoked, is done so cautiously, as an event in the Deleuzian sense, privileging lines of flight, an assemblage of spatial and temporal intensities, coming together, dispersing, reconverging. The event-ness of September 11 refuses the binary of watershed moment and turning point of radical change, versus intensification of more of the same, tethered between its status as a "history-making moment" and a "history-vanishing moment."[17] On behalf of his conceptualization of September 11 as a "snapshot"—a break and an explosion—Nilüfer Göle argues that "understanding September 11th requires building a narrative starting from the terrorist moment as an instance, that is an exemplary incident which, in one moment, allows different temporalities to emerge, and with them, a range of issues hitherto suppressed." For Göle, the snapshot encompasses the temporalities of the instant and the image, of fast-forwarding, rewinding, and shuttering, rather than being strictly anchored to the past, present and future.[18] Less wedded to visual metaphor is David Kazanjian's reworking of Walter Benjamin's thoughts on memory and history in relation to flashes, aufblitz, "flashpoints," what he defines as a "burst[ing] into action and being, not out of nothing, but transformed from one form to another; and . . . the powerful effects of that transformation or emergence."[19] Flashpoints signal a procedural becoming-time for Kazanjian, a centripetal turbulence of illumination so powerful that it may blind the past even as it spotlights the present and lights up the future.

Terrorist Assemblages emerges as a story about various events that operate as both snapshots and flashpoints: of September 11, torture at Abu Ghraib, the decriminalization of sodomy in the United States, the spate of racial backlash crimes against Muslims and Sikhs, the detention and deportation of suspected terrorists, and post-9/11 organizing. But both frames—snapshot, through its relation to history making and history vanishing, and flashpoint, as a concretized movement from one incarnation of being to another—rely on the paradigms of past, present, and future, a before and an after, even if their inherent periodizations spill over, foreshadow and stalk each other, loop back recursively, return and relay, and scramble their attendant spatializing effects. As with all narratives of telos and periodization, such as those embedded in and endemic to modernity, to heterosexuality, to adulthood, temporal qualifications work to determine the intelligible sphere of scholarly legitimacy. How, then, to reassess the valuation of scholarly production emergent from apparent notions of stability, longevity, depth? Such a rethinking of the assumed shapes·and temporalities of the labor of thinking and writing contributes to a broader global vision that does not erase profoundly uneven materialities of production in their manifold constellations. This is not to advocate a postmodern fetishization of anything quick, fleeting, and superficial, nor to deny that there is stillness in this writing. I have struggled to situate becoming-time as a collapsing of the binary frame of urgency, expediency, and politicality versus stability and calm, and move to a notion of becoming-time that allows for the force of the present in the ways of which Mbembe speaks, embracing the heteroglossia of public intellectual and intellectual activist modalities.

The futures are much closer to us than any pasts we might want to return to or revisit. What does it mean to be examining, absorbing, feeling, reflecting on, and writing about the archive as it is being produced, rushing at us— literally, to entertain an unfolding archive? This question may lend an immediacy to the work, or it may emit a hollow ringing of the past that no longer feels pertinent; even more bizarrely, it may mean that the present is still unrecognizable to us. So while this is not a historical project, it is indeed a historicization of the contemporary moment, historicizing biopolitics of the now. This has meant in part less emphasis on historicization, or on the historicity of the biopolitical modes of surveillance, terror, war, securitization, torture, empire, and violence examined in this text, and a move toward collecting, shaping, and interrogating an archive that will be available for future historicization.

This project is thus profoundly impelled by an anticipatory temporality, a modality that seeks to catch a small hold of many futures, to invite futurity even as it refuses to script it, distinct from an anticipatory "paranoid temporality" that Eve Kosofsky Sedgwick critiques. Sedgwick writes of paranoia, "No time could be too early for one's having-already-known, for its having-already-been-inevitable, that something bad would happen. And no loss could be too far in the future to need to be preemptively discounted."[20] Paranoid temporality is thus embedded in a risk economy that attempts to ensure against future catastrophe. This is a temporality of negative exuberance—for we are never safe enough, never healthy enough, never prepared enough—driven by imitation (repetition of the same or in the service of maintaining the same) rather than innovation (openness to disruption of the same, calling out to the new).

A paranoid temporality therefore produces a suppression of critical creative politics; in contrast, the anticipatory temporalities that I advocate more accurately reflect a Spivakian notion of "politics of the open end,"[21] of positively enticing unknowable political futures into our wake, taking risks rather than guarding against them. In that sense it is also ensconced in an antedating temporality, an example of which is as follows: "The runner's belief that he consciously heard the gun and then, immediately, exploded off the blocks is an illusion made possible . . . because the mind antedates the sound of the gun by almost half a second."[22] This book is an attempt at antedating the sound of the gun—that is, not only or primarily anticipating the future, but also recording the future that is already here, yet unknown but for a split second. Writing that "haunting is a constituent element of modern social life," Avery Gordon asks us to contemplate "the paradox of tracking through time and across all those forces which makes its mark by being there and not being there at the same time, cajoling us to reconsider . . . the very distinctions between there and not there, past and present, force and shape."[23]

Here, "ghostly matters" signal the primacy of the past and our inheritance of the past: its hauntings, its demands, its present absences and absent presences. However, in part what I mean to highlight through an antecedent temporality are the ghosts of the future that we can already sniff, ghosts that are waiting for us, that usher us into futurities. Haunting in this sense defuses a binary between past and present—because indeed the becoming-future is haunting us—while its ontological debt to that which once was nevertheless cautions against an easy privileging of the fetish of innovation, of what might otherwise be demeaned as an unthinking reach for that which is trendy or cutting-edge. Haunting, as Gordon implies, is also a methodological approach that keeps an eye out for shadows, ephemera, energies, ethereal forces, textures, spirit, sensations: "Haunting is a very particular way of knowing what has happened or is happening. Being haunted draws us affectively, sometimes against our will and always a bit magically, into the structure of feeling of a reality that we come to experience, not as cold knowledge, but as a transformative recognition."[24]

To understand how we experience such transformative recognition, I turn to the neurologist Oliver Sacks, who has brilliantly written on the "wild range of speeds" experienced by the human brain. In his exposition he details other ways of measuring time outside of the past-present-future triad and their scrambling, as an intensification or de-intensification of the experience of time, as one of "registering larger or smaller numbers of events in a given time." Relationships between speed (how fast or slow time feels), pace (the tempo, rate, or intervals of registering events within time), and duration (the length of time within which these events are registered) alter and are altered. Sacks quotes William James: "Our judgment of time, our speed of perception, depends on how many 'events' we can perceive in a given unit of time." The speeding up of time involves "a foreshortening, a telescopy of time," a contraction or compression of time whereby less is registered in shorter time units but time is lived faster. Slowing down time enables an "enlargement, a microscopy of time," an expansion of time during which more is registered, but time is lived as slow, or slowed, "increased speed of thought and an apparent slowing down of time" resulting in an "enlarged and spacious timescape." As Sacks explains, "The apparent slowing of time in emergencies . . . may come from the power of intense attention to reduce the duration of individual frames."[25] So, in the midst of the frenetic speeds of crisis and urgency, a slowing of time happens, and with it, a deeper scrutiny of every single experienced moment. Like an enlarged timescape, this text is also a slowing down of a particular historical moment of crisis, a matching of increased speed of thought that accompanies responses to crisis with the slowing down of individual frames necessary to really comprehend and attend to that crisis. History, at least what one might conventionally think of as history, is secondary to the enlarged timescape—that is, the time of entanglement—of this book.

In proposing what Elizabeth Freeman calls a "deviant chronopolitics," one that envisions "relations across time and between times" that upturn developmentalist narratives of history,[26] I would add that time must be conjured not only as nonlinear, but also as nonmetric. Manuel De Landa describes metric temporality as that which "take[s] for granted the flow of time already divided into identical instants bearing such close resemblance to one another that the flow may regarded as essentially homogenous." Nonmetric time deconstructs the naturalization of the administrative units of measurement of the "familiar, divisible, and measurable time of everyday experience" and challenges the assumption that the repetition of these units, these "stable oscillators" at different scales, is "composed of identical instants."[27] Quite simply, one second is not the same as another second. Following both De Landa and Sacks, the chronopolitics of any text must also be seen to be resonant with affective modalities of speed, duration, and pace. Excavating the schisms between clock time and personal time, "not constrained by external perception or reality,"[28] Sacks suggests that speed, pace, and duration are ontological properties rather than temporal qualifications, raising the following questions: What kinds of times are we living? How are we living time in these times? That is, what is the relation of historical time to lived time, to temporalities of living? Each work has its own time, and times within itself: the time of its writing, the time of its release (times to which it belongs), and the time of the text, of the words themselves, of times and temporalities that intersect with its audience's times (times that it impels); that is, temporalities of production and absorption. There are a multitude of times embedded in any enunciation, act, or articulation. The time of any text remains a mystery, a chance encounter with a moment, a reader, an assemblage of all of these converging; to borrow from Shakespeare (like Derrida), the time is out of joint: something is happening *to* time, not *in* time, revamping an encounter with time. And so this book is an assemblage of temporalities and movements—speed, pace, duration—which is not strictly bound to developmentalist or historical telos or their disruption, and an assemblage of theoretical interests, meaning that there is not one or several main strands that thread through this book, but rather ideas that converge, diverge, and merge. For example, the book takes a turn in the middle: the introduction and chapters 1 and 2 focus primarily on representational problematics and subject formation, while the last two chapters take up complications of the efficacy of representational praxis with issues of affect, ontology, and biopolitical control, foregrounding population construction. Proliferating here are multiple and layered temporalities, multiple histories and futures, within all these of these: snapshots, flashpoints, and assemblages.

Logistics: Mapping the Text

José Esteban Muñoz's writing on the "terrorist drag" of the Los Angeles–based performance artist Vaginal Davis bizarrely harks to another political era, as if it were long ago, when the notion of the terrorist had a trenchant but distant quality to it. Muñoz argues that Davis's drag performances, encompassing "cross-sex, cross-race minstrelsy," are terrorist on two levels. Aesthetically, Davis rejects glamour-girl feminine drag in favor of "ground level guerilla representational strategies" such as white supremacist militiamen and black welfare-queen hookers, what Muñoz calls "the nation's most dangerous citizens." This alludes to the second plane of meaning, the re-enactment of the "nation's internal terrors around race, gender, and sexuality."[29] It is imperative to note that guerrillas and terrorists have vastly different national and racial valences, the former bringing to mind the phantasmatic landscapes of Central and South America, and the latter, the enduring legacy of Orientalist imaginaries. In the context of these geographies it is notable that Davis as the white militiaman astutely brings terrorism home—to Oklahoma City, in fact—and in doing so dislodges, at least momentarily, the Orientalist legacy of terrorism.

Muñoz's description of this terrorist drag appropriately points to the historical convergences between queers and terror: homosexuals have been traitors to the nation, figures of espionage and double agents, associated with communists during the McCarthy era, and, as with suicide bombers, have brought on and desired death through the AIDS pandemic (both suicide bomber and gay man always figure as already dying, a decaying or corroding masculinity). More recent exhortations place gay marriage as "the worst form of terrorism" and gay couples as "domestic terrorists."[30] Clearly, one can already ask: What is terrorist about the queer? But the more salient and urgent question is: What is queer about the terrorist? And what is queer about terrorist corporealities? The depictions of masculinity most rapidly disseminated and globalized at this historical juncture are terrorist masculinities: failed and perverse, these emasculated bodies always have femininity as their reference point of malfunction, and are metonymically tied to all sorts of pathologies of the mind and body—homosexuality, incest, pedophilia, madness, and disease. We see, for example, the queer physicality of terrorist monsters haunting the U.S. State Department counterterrorism website.[31] With the unfurling, viruslike, explosive mass of the terrorist network, tentacles ever regenerating despite efforts to truncate them, the terrorist is concurrently an unfathomable, unknowable, and hysterical monstrosity, and yet one that only the exceptional capacities of U.S. intelligence and security systems can quell. This unknowable monstrosity is not a casual bystander or parasite; the nation assimilates this effusive discomfort with the unknowability of these bodies, thus affectively producing new normativities and exceptionalisms through the cataloguing of unknowables. Concomitantly, masculinities of patriotism work to distinguish, and thus discipline or incorporate and banish, terrorist from patriot. It is not that we must engage in the practice of excavating the queer terrorist, or queering the terrorist; rather, queerness is always already installed in the project of naming the terrorist; the terrorist does not appear as such without the concurrent entrance of perversion, deviance. The strategy of encouraging subjects of study to appear in all their queernesses, rather than primarily to queer the subjects of study, provides a subject-driven temporality in tandem with a method-driven temporality. Playing on this difference, between the subject being queered and queerness already existing within the subject (and thus dissipating the subject as such), allows for both the temporality of being (ontological essence of the subject) and the temporality of always-becoming (continual ontological emergence, a Deleuzian *becoming without being*).

The introduction, "Homonationalism and Biopolitics," details three pertinent frames of the book project: sexual exceptionalism, regulatory queerness, and the ascendancy of whiteness. These frames act as an interlocking nexus of power grids that map the various demarcations of race, gender, class, nation, and religion that permeate constructions of terror and terrorist bodies. I argue that in the United States at this historical juncture an opportunity for forms of LGBTIQ inclusion in the national imaginary and body politic rests upon specific performances of American sexual exceptionalism vis-à-vis perverse, improperly hetero- and homo- Muslim sexualities. To elucidate forms of regulatory queerness, I discuss forms of queer secularity that attenuate constructions of Muslim sexuality. In particular, sites of queer struggle in Europe—Britain, the Netherlands—have articulated Muslim populations as an especial threat to LGBTIQ persons, organizations, communities, and spaces of congregation. Finally, I review the emergence of a global political economy of queer sexualities that—framed through the notion of the "ascendancy of whiteness"—repeatedly coheres whiteness as a queer norm and straightness as a racial norm.

Chapter 1, "The Sexuality of Terrorism," elaborates on the rise of U.S. homonationalism, the dual movement in which certain homosexual constituencies have embraced U.S. nationalist agendas and have also been embraced by nationalist agendas. I argue that discourses of counterterrorism are intrinsically gendered, raced, and sexualized and that they illuminate the production of imbricated normative patriot and terrorist corporealities that cohere against and through each other. I survey the schizophrenic domestication and expulsion of queer sexualities via the normalizing im-

pulses of patriotism after September 11, 2001. I examine the field of terrorism studies, and its growth over the last several decades, to narrate its
investments in a western romance of the heteronormative family coupled
with the assumed sexual pathologies of terrorists. I highlight the propensity
for recent feminist and queer theorizing on terrorist subjectivities to unwittingly reproduce these investments. Using Edward Said's *Orientalism* to
read various episodes of the satirical cartoon comedy show *South Park*, I
demonstrate that the U.S. formation of the homonational subject of rights
discourses works in conjunction with patriotic propaganda to produce populations of "queer terrorists." Through an assessment of these multiple
texts, I argue that the contemporary U.S. heteronormative nation actually
relies on and benefits from the proliferation of queerness, especially in
regard to the sexually exceptional homonational and its evil counterpart,
the queer terrorist of elsewhere. These fleeting invitations into nationalism
indicate that U.S. nation-state formations, historically reliant on heteronormative ideologies, are now accompanied by—to use Lisa Duggan's term—
homonormative ideologies that replicate narrow racial, class, and gender
national ideals.

Building on this frame of U.S. homonationalism, in chapter 2, "Abu
Ghraib and U.S. Sexual Exceptionalism," I demonstrate homonationalism's
deployment in a transnational frame, whereby a claim is made to a proper
modern homosexual exceptional identity in relation to an Orientalist version of Muslim male sexuality. Surveying the critical commentary generated by feminist and queer theorists—such as Barbara Ehrenreich, Patrick
Moore, Zillah Eisenstein, and Slavoj Žižek—during the aftermath of the
release of the Abu Ghraib photos in May 2004, I maintain that Muslim
masculinity is simultaneously pathologically excessive yet repressive, perverse yet homophobic, virile yet emasculated, monstrous yet flaccid. This
discourse serves to rearticulate the devitalization of one population sequestered for dying—Iraqi detainees accused of terrorist affiliations—into
the securitization and revitalization of another population, the American
citizenry. Effectively, this is a biopolitical reordering of the negative register
of death transmuted into the positive register of life, especially for U.S.
homonormative subjects who, despite the egregious homophobic, racist,
and misogynist behavior of the U.S. military prison guards, benefit from the
continued propagation of the United States as tolerant, accepting, even
encouraging of sexual diversity. America is narrated by multiple progressive
sectors as embodying an exceptional multicultural heteronormativity, one
that is also bolstered by homonormativity.

While the first two chapters foreground conservative homonormative formations, chapter 3, "Intimate Control, Infinite Detention: Rereading the *Lawrence* Case," continues the examination of the proliferation of sexual exceptionalism through queer liberal subject formations. The historic *Lawrence and Garner v. Texas* ruling decriminalized sodomy between consensual adults in the United States in June 2003. The language of the *Lawrence* decision imagines the homosexual subject as a queer liberal one, invested in consumption, property ownership, and intimate, stable sexual relationships, relying on an archaic formulation of public/private divides that has little utility for daily living. It also assumes that being accorded the right to the private realm is adequate compensation for the intrusions of public surveillance. Finally, the ruling posits the capacity for intimacy as the barometric measure of which sexual actors, more so than sexual acts, are worthy of protection.

Through a deconstruction of the celebratory readings of the ruling, I argue that such readings are only possible through the erasure of the contemporary politics of surveillance, racial profiling, detention, and deportation. I reread the privacy and intimacy debates of *Lawrence* through a different set of optics: the 1996 Immigration and Welfare Reform Act, the USA PATRIOT Act (Uniting and Strengthening America by Providing Appropriate Tools Required to Intercept and Obstruct Terrorism Act), and the subsequent spatial politics and practices of detention and deportation. The *Lawrence* decision is emblematic of legislative incorporation for queer liberal and homonormative subjects. Further, intimacy for queerly racialized populations (demarcated for neglect, disposal, and death), rather than residing in the private or mismanaged in the public, appears as circulating points of exchange and contact within a biopolitical control economy. This economy is mediated by surveillance, systems of information gathering and monitoring, and aggregations of statistics, such that the spatial and representational public and private domains of liberal personhood remain meaningful only insofar as they demarcate subjects of privilege. Thus I rearticulate intimacy as a register beyond the disciplinary subject, embedded in control societies as a mode of population disaggregation between those incited to life and those consigned to death.

Chapter 4, " 'The Turban Is Not a Hat': Queer Diaspora and Practices of Profiling," extends this analysis of queer liberal formations to queer diasporic subjects. Ironically, South Asian queer diasporic subjects are under even greater duress to produce themselves as exceptional American subjects, not necessarily as heteronormative but as homonormative, even as the queernesses of these very bodies are simultaneously used to pathologize populations of terrorist look-alike bodies. As contagions that trouble the exceptionalisms of queer South Asian diasporas, male turbaned Sikh bodies, often mistaken for Muslim terrorist bodies, are read as patriarchal by queer diasporic logics and placed within heteronormative victimology narratives by Sikh American advocacy groups focused on redressing the phenomenon of "mistaken identity." Both queer diasporic and Sikh American logics are indebted to visual representations of corporeality. Hence, I reread these bodies as affectively troubling—generating affective confusion and interdeterminancy—in terms of ontology, tactility, and the combination of organic and nonorganic matter. Reading turbans through affect challenges both the limits of queer diasporic identity that balks at the nonnormativity of the turbaned body (even as it avows the pathological racial and sexual renderings of terrorist bodies) while simultaneously infusing the "mistaken identity" debates with different methods of comprehending the susceptibility of these bodies beyond heteronormative victimology narratives.

In the conclusion, "Queer Times, Terrorist Assemblages," I survey the chapters to argue for new directions in cultural studies that critically reassess the use of intersectional models. I turn to affective, ontological, and assemblage paradigms to challenge the limits of identity-based narratives of queerness, especially those reliant on visibility politics. Thus the book concludes with a strong political and intellectual mapping for the futurity of queer critique and its relevance to global forces of securitization, counterterrorism, and nationalism.

Terrorist Assemblages: Homonationalism in Queer Times offers a new paradigm for the theorization of race and sexuality. The book marks the powerful emergence of the disciplinary queer (liberal, homonormative, diasporic) subject into the bountiful market and the interstices of state benevolence— that is, into the statistical fold that produces appropriate digits and facts toward the population's optimization of life and the ascendancy of whiteness: full-fledged regulatory queer subjects and the regularization of deviancy. Further, this sexually exceptional subject is produced against queer*ness*, as a process intertwined with racialization, that calls into nominalization abject populations peripheral to the project of living, expendable as human waste and shunted to the spaces of deferred death. Reflective of my desire for responsive political and pedagogical strategies that, in Gayatri Chakravorty Spivak's words, produce an "uncoercive rearrangement of desires,"[32] this book is my modest contribution to that mandate. I hope it will spur more questions and dilemmas than it necessarily resolves, spark debate, and invite such uncoercive rearrangements rather than situate itself or be situated as masterly, correcting, or prescriptive. The guiding question for this endeavor remains: Can we keep our senses open to emergent and unknown forms of belonging, connectivity, intimacy, the unintentional and indeterminate slippages and productivities of domination, to signal a futurity of affective politics?

"People are now coming out of the closet on the word empire," said the conservative columnist Charles Krauthammer. "The fact is no country has been as dominant culturally, economically, technologically and militarily in the history of the world since the Roman Empire." The metaphor of coming out is striking, part of a broader trend of appropriating the language of progressive movements in the service of empire. How outrageous to apply the language of gay pride to a military power that demands that its soldiers stay in the closet.—Amy Kaplan, "Violent Belongings and the Question of Empire Today"

introduction:

homonationalism and biopolitics

Both Krauthammer and his critic, the American studies scholar Amy Kaplan, highlight the confluence of American sexuality and politics.[1] The coming out metaphor, which Kaplan later states is invoked incessantly by U.S. neocons to elaborate a burgeoning ease with the notion of the United States as an empire, is striking not only for its appropriative dissemination, but for what the appropriation indexes. On the one hand, the convergence marks a cultural moment of national inclusion for homosexuality, alluding to a particular kind of parallel possibility for the liberated nation and the liberated queer. This sanctioning of the lingua franca of gay liberation hints that the liberation of American empire from its closets—an empire already known but concealed—will and should result in pride, a proud American empire. In this incisive piece, Kaplan astutely points to the necessary elisions of Krauthammer's pronouncement, but unfortunately enacts another effacement of her own. From a glance at the demographics, one could deduce that those most likely to be forced into closeting by the "Don't Ask, Don't Tell" policy, given their disproportionate percentage of enlistment in the U.S. military, are men and women of color.[2] Thus, any affinity with nonnormative sexual subjects the nation might unconsciously intimate is vigilantly circumscribed by a "military power that demands that its soldiers stay in the closet." This proviso is implicitly racially inflected, demarcating the least welcome entrants into this national revelation of pride to be queer people of color. Moreover, in this reclamation of exceptionalism, both Krauthammer and Kaplan execute a troubling affirmation of the teleological investments in "closeting" and "coming out" narratives that have long been critiqued by poststructuralist theorists for the privileged (white) gay, lesbian, and queer liberal subjects they inscribe and validate.

National recognition and inclusion, here signaled as the annexation of homosexual jargon, is contingent upon the segregation and disqualification of racial and sexual others from the national imaginary. At work in this dynamic is a form of sexual exceptionalism—the emergence of national homosexuality, what I term "homonationalism"—that corresponds with the coming out of the exceptionalism of American empire. Further, this brand of homosexuality operates as a regulatory script not only of normative gayness, queerness, or homosexuality, but also of the racial and national norms that reinforce these sexual subjects. There is a commitment to the global dominant ascendancy of whiteness that is implicated in the propagation of the United States as empire as well as the alliance between this propagation and this brand of homosexuality. The fleeting sanctioning of a national homosexual subject is possible, not only through the proliferation of sexual-racial subjects who invariably fall out of its narrow terms of acceptability, as others have argued, but more significantly, through the simultaneous engendering and disavowal of *populations* of sexual-racial others who need not apply.

In what follows I explore these three imbricated manifestations—sexual exceptionalism, queer as regulatory, and the ascendancy of whiteness—and their relations to the production of terrorist and citizen bodies. My goal is to present a dexterous portrait, signaling attentiveness to how, why, and where these threads bump into each other and where they weave together, resisting a mechanistic explanatory device that may cover all the bases. In the case of what I term "U.S. sexual exceptionalism," a narrative claiming the successful management of life in regard to a *people*, what is noteworthy is that an exceptional form of national heteronormativity is now joined by an exceptional form of national homonormativity, in other words, homonationalism. Collectively, they continue or extend the project of U.S. nationalism and imperial expansion endemic to the war on terror. The terms of degeneracy have shifted such that homosexuality is no longer a priori excluded from nationalist formations. I unearth the forms of regulation implicit in notions of queer subjects that are transcendent, secular, or otherwise exemplary as resistant, and open up the question of queer re/production and regeneration and its contribution to the project of the optimization of life. The ascendancy of whiteness is a description of biopolitics proffered by Rey Chow, who links the violence of liberal deployments of diversity and multiculturalism to the "valorization of life" alibi that then allows for rampant exploitation of the very subjects included in discourses of diversity in the first instance. I elucidate how these three approaches to the study of sexuality, taken together, suggest a trenchant rereading of biopolitics with regard to queerness as well as the intractability of queerness from biopolitical arrangements of life and death.

U.S. Sexual Exceptionalism

One mapping of the folding of homosexuals into the reproductive valorization of living—technologies of life—includes the contemporary emergence of "sexually exceptional" U.S. citizens, both heterosexual and otherwise, a formation I term "U.S. sexual exceptionalism." Exceptionalism paradoxically signals distinction from (to be unlike, dissimilar) as well as excellence (imminence, superiority), suggesting a departure from yet mastery of linear teleologies of progress. Exception refers both to particular discourses that repetitively produce the United States as an exceptional nation-state and Giorgio Agamben's theorization of the sanctioned and naturalized disregard of the limits of state juridical and political power through times of state crisis, a "state of exception" that is used to justify the extreme measures of the state.[3] In this project, this double play of exception speaks to Muslim and Sikh "terrorist" corporealities as well as to homosexual patriots. The "sexual torture scandal" at Abu Ghraib is an instructive example of the interplay between exception and exceptionalism whereby the deferred death of one population recedes as the securitization and valorization of the life of another population triumphs in its shadow. This double deployment of exception and exceptionalism works to turn the negative valence of torture into the positive register of the valorization of (American) life, that is, torture in the name of the maximization and optimization of life.

As the U.S. nation-state produces narratives of exception through the war on terror, it must temporarily suspend its heteronormative imagined community to consolidate national sentiment and consensus through the recognition and incorporation of some, though not all or most, homosexual subjects. The fantasy of the permanence of this suspension is what drives the production of exceptionalism, a narrative that is historically and politically wedded to the formation of the U.S. nation-state. Thus, the exception and the exceptional work in tandem; the state of exception haunts the proliferation of exceptional national subjects, in a similar vein to the Derridean hauntology in which the ghosts, the absent presences, infuse ontology with a difference.[4]

Through the transnational production of terrorist corporealities, homosexual subjects who have limited legal rights within the U.S. civil context gain significant representational currency when situated within the global scene of the war on terror. Taking the position that heterosexuality is a necessary constitutive factor of national identity, the "outlaw" status of homosexual subjects in relation to the state has been a long-standing theoretical interest of feminist, postcolonial, and queer theorists. This outlaw status is mediated through the rise during the 1980s and 1990s of the gay consumer, pursued by marketers who claimed that childless homosexuals had enormous disposable incomes, as well as through legislative gains in civil rights, such as the widely celebrated 2003 overturning of sodomy laws rendered in the *Lawrence and Garner v. Texas* decision. By underscoring circuits of homosexual nationalism, I note that some homosexual subjects are complicit with heterosexual nationalist formations rather than inherently or automatically excluded from or opposed to them. Further, a more pernicious inhabitation of homosexual sexual exceptionalism occurs through stagings of U.S. nationalism via a praxis of sexual othering, one that exceptionalizes the identities of U.S. homosexualities vis-à-vis Orientalist constructions of "Muslim sexuality." This discourse functions through transnational displacements that suture spaces of cultural citizenship in the United States for homosexual subjects as they concurrently secure nationalist interests globally. In some instances these narratives are explicit, as in the aftermath of the release of the Abu Ghraib photos, where the claims to exceptionalism resonated on many planes for U.S. citizen-subjects: morally, sexually, culturally, "patriotically." This imbrication of American exceptionalism is increasingly marked through or aided by certain homosexual bodies, which is to say, through homonationalism.

What is nascent is not the notion of exceptionalism, nor of a gender exceptionalism that has dominated the history of western feminist theoretical production and activism. Current forms of exceptionalism work or are furthered by attaching themselves to, or being attached by, nonheterosexual, homonormative subjects. Exceptionalism is used not to mark a break with

A double insertion: State of Exception reinforces the exceptional

Representational Currency

Queer Muslims

historical trajectories or a claim about the emergence of singular newness. Rather, exceptionalism gestures to narratives of excellence, excellent nationalism, a process whereby a national population comes to believe in its own superiority and its own singularity—"stuck," as Sara Ahmed would say, to various subjects.[5] Discourses of American exceptionalism are embedded in the history of U.S. nation-state formation, from early immigration narratives to cold war ideologies to the rise of the age of terrorism. These narratives about the centrality of exceptionalism to the formation of the United States imply that indoctrination à la exceptionalism is part of the disciplining of the American citizen (as it may be to any nationalist foundation).[6] Debates about American exceptionalism have typically mobilized criteria as far ranging as artistic expression, aesthetic production (literary and cultural), social and political life, immigration history, liberal democracy, and industrialization and patterns of capitalism, among others.[7] However, discussions of American exceptionalism rarely take up issues of gender and sexuality. While for the past forty years scholars have been interrogating feminist practices and theorizations that explicitly or implicitly foster the consolidation of U.S. nationalism in its wake, a growing cohort is now examining queer practices and theorizations for similar tendencies. Forms of U.S. gender and (hetero)sexual exceptionalism from purportedly progressive spaces have surfaced through feminist constructions of "other" women, especially via the composite of the "third world woman."[8]

Inderpal Grewal, for example, argues against the naturalization of human rights frames by feminists, noting that the United States routinely positions itself "as the site for authoritative condemnation" of human rights abuses elsewhere, ignoring such abuses within its borders. Grewal alludes to the American exceptionalism that is now requisite common sense for many feminisms within U.S. public cultures: "Moral superiority has become part of emergent global feminism, constructing American women as saviors and rescuers of the 'oppressed women.' "[9] The recent embrace of the case of Afghani and Iraqi women and Muslim women in general by western feminists has generated many forms of U.S. gender exceptionalism. Gender exceptionalism works as a missionary discourse to rescue Muslim women from their oppressive male counterparts. It also works to suggest that, in contrast to women in the United States, Muslim women are, at the end of the day, unsavable. More insidiously, these discourses of exceptionalism allude to the unsalvageable nature of Muslim women even by their own feminists, positioning the American feminist as the feminist subject par excellence.[10]

One pertinent example is culled from the interactions of the Revolution-ary Association of the Women of Afghanistan (RAWA) with the Feminist Majority Foundation, which ended with an accusation of appropriation and erasure of RAWA's efforts by the foundation. A letter written on April 20, 2002 condemns the foundation's representation of its handiwork as having "a foremost role in 'freeing' Afghan women" while failing to mention RAWA's twenty-five-year presence in Afghanistan (indeed, failing to men-tion RAWA at all), as if it had "single-handedly freed the women of Afghani-stan from an oppression that started and ended with the Taliban." Calling the Feminist Majority Foundation "hegemonic, U.S.-centric, ego driven, corporate feminism," RAWA notes that it has "a longer history than the Feminist Majority can claim" and cites multiple instances of the founda-tion's erasure of RAWA's political organizing. RAWA also berates the Feminist Majority for its omission of the abuse of women by the Northern Alliance, atrocities that at times were more egregious than those committed by the Taliban, stating that "the Feminist Majority, in their push for U.S. political and economic power, are being careful not to anger the political powers in the U.S."[11]

The ranks of "hegemonic, U.S.-centric" feminists enamored with the plight of Afghan women under Taliban rule included the Feminist Majority Foundation, which had launched "Our Campaign to Stop Gender Apart-heid in Afghanistan" in 1996.[12] This campaign arguably led to commodity fetishes such as Eve Ensler's V-Day benefit with her "tribute to Afghan women," a monologue entitled "Under the Burqa" performed by Oprah Winfrey at New York City's largest arena, Madison Square Garden, to a sold-out audience in February 2001.[13] The event also promoted the pur-chase, in remembrance of Afghan women, of a "burqa swatch," meant to be worn on one's lapel to demonstrate solidarity with Afghan women through the appropriation of a "Muslim" garment. While these forms of celebrity feminism might provide us momentary sardonic amusement, they are an integral part of U.S. feminist public cultures and should not be mistaken as trivial. Their agendas are quite conducive to that of serious liberal feminists in the United States such as those in the ranks of the Feminist Majority, and in the age of professionalized feminism these purportedly divergent circuits divulge their imbrication through various modes of commodification. These feminists, having already foregrounded Islamic fundamentalism as the single greatest violent threat to women, were perfectly poised to capital-ize on the missionary discourses that reverberated after the events of Sep-tember 11. Despite their active stance against the invasion of Afghanistan, they were caught in a complicitous narrative of U.S. exceptionalism in regard to the removal of the Taliban.[14] As Drucilla Cornell notes, the silence of the Feminist Majority Foundation on the replacement of the Taliban by the Northern Alliance "forces us to question whether the humanitarian-intervention discourse of the U.S. government was not a particularly cynical effort to enlist U.S. feminists in an attempt to circumscribe the definition of what constitutes human rights violations—to turn the Feminist Majority into an ideological prop that delegitimizes the political need for redressing human-rights violations." Cornell basically implies that mainstream U.S. feminists traded RAWA's stance against punitive state laws penalizing women who refuse to wear the burqa (but not against women wearing burqas, an important distinction) for the celebratory media spectacle of unveiling rampant in the U.S. media after the "successful" invasion of Afghanistan.[15] Under the burqa indeed. But as a final comment, it is worth heeding Gayatri Chakravorty Spivak's observation, "We will see, every time, the narrative of class mobility." Complicating any indigenous positioning of RAWA, she writes, "It is the emergence of [the] middle class that creates the possibility for the kind of feminist struggle that gives us a RAWA. And this middle class, the agent of human rights all over the world, is altogether distant from the subaltern classes in 'their own culture,' epistemically."[16] Despite RAWA's feud with the Feminist Majority, invariably they remain complicit with a displacement of other Afghan women's organizations that cannot so easily enter the global feminist stage. Spivak's caution is a reminder that the dominant reception of feminist discourses on Muslim women is a tokenistic liberal apology that often leaves uninterrogated a west/Islam binary.

With the United States currently positioning itself as the technologically exceptional global counterterrorism expert, American exceptionalism feeds off of other exceptionalisms, particularly that of Israel, its close ally in the Middle East. The exceptional national security issues of Israel, and the long-term "existential" threat it faces because of its sense of being "entangled in a conflict of unparalleled dimensions," for example, proceeds thus: "exceptional vulnerability" results in "exceptional security needs," the risks of which are then alleviated and purportedly conquered by "exceptional counterterrorism technologies."[17] In this collusion of American and Israeli state interests, defined through a joint oppositional posture toward Muslims, narratives of victimhood ironically suture rather than deflate, contradict, or nullify claims to exceptionalism. In other words, the Israeli nation-state finds itself continuously embroiled in a cycle of perceived exceptional threats of violence that demand exceptional uses of force against the Palestinian population, which is currently mirrored by U.S. government officials' public declarations of possible terror risks that are used to compel U.S. citizens to support the war on terror.

Reflecting upon contemporary debates about the United States as empire, Amy Kaplan notes, "The idea of empire has always paradoxically entailed a sense of spatial and temporal limits, a narrative of rising and falling, which U.S. exceptionalism has long kept at bay." Later, she states, "The denial and disavowal of empire has long served as the ideological cornerstone of U.S. imperialism and a key component of American exceptionalism."[18] Thus, for Kaplan the distancing of exceptionalism from empire achieves somewhat contradictory twofold results: the superior United States is not subject to empire's shortcomings, as the apparatus of empire is unstable and ultimately empires fall; and the United States creates the impression that empire is beyond the pale of its own morally upright behavior, such that all violences of the state are seen, in some moral, cultural, or political fashion as anything but the violence of empire. U.S. exceptionalism hangs on a narrative of transcendence, which places the United States above empire in these two respects, a project that is aided by what Domenico Losurdo names as "the fundamental tendency to transform the Judeo-Christian tradition into a sort of national religion that consecrates the exceptionalism of American people and the sacred mission with which they are entrusted ('Manifest Destiny')."[19] Kaplan, claiming that current narratives of empire "take American exceptionalism to new heights," argues that a concurrent "paradoxical claim to uniqueness and universality" are coterminous in that "they share a teleological narrative of inevitability" that posits America as the arbiter of appropriate ethics, human rights, and democratic behavior while exempting itself without hesitation from such universalizing mandates.[20]

Whether one agrees that American exceptionalism has attained "new heights," Kaplan's analysis perfectly illustrates the intractability of state of exception discourses from those of exceptionalism. Laying claim to uniqueness (exception = singularity) and universality (exceptional = bequeathing teleological narrative) is not quite as paradoxical as Kaplan insists, for the state of exception is deemed necessary in order to restore, protect, and maintain the status quo, the normative ordering that then allows the United States to hail its purported universality. The indispensability of the United States is thus sutured through the naturalized conjunction of singularity and telos, the paradox withered away.[21] State of exception discourses rationalize egregious violence in the name of the preservation of a way of life and those privileged to live it. Giorgio Agamben, noting that biopolitics continually seeks to redefine the boundaries between life and death, writes, "The state of exception is neither external nor internal to the juridical order, and the problem of defining it concerns precisely a threshold, or a zone of indifference, where inside and outside do not exclude each other but rather blur with each other."[22] The temporality of exception is one that seeks to conceal itself; the frenzied mode of emergency is an alibi for the quiet certitude of a slowly normativized working paradigm of liberal democratic government, an alibi necessary to disavow its linkages to totalitarian governments. The state of exception thus works to hide or even deny itself in order to further its expanse, its presence and efficacy, surfacing only momentarily and with enough gumption to further legitimize the occupation of more terrain. Agamben likens the externally internal space of the state of exception to a Möbius strip: at the moment it is cast outside it becomes the inside.[23] In the state of exception, the exception insidiously becomes the rule, and the exceptional is normalized as a regulatory ideal or frame; the exceptional is the excellence that exceeds the parameters of proper subjecthood and, by doing so, redefines these parameters to then normativize and render invisible (yet transparent) its own excellence or singularity.

Sexual exceptionalism also works by glossing over its own policing of the boundaries of acceptable gender, racial, and class formations. That is, homosexual sexual exceptionalism does not necessarily contradict or undermine heterosexual sexual exceptionalism; in actuality it may support forms of heteronormativity and the class, racial, and citizenship privileges they require. The historical and contemporaneous production of an emergent normativity, homonormativity, ties the recognition of homosexual subjects, both legally and representationally, to the national and transnational political agendas of U.S. imperialism. Homonormativity can be read as a formation complicit with and invited into the biopolitical valorization of life in its inhabitation and reproduction of heteronormative norms. One prime mechanism of sexual exceptionalism is mobilized by discourses of sexual repression—a contemporary version of Foucault's repressive hypothesis—that are generative of a bio- and geopolitical global mapping of sexual cultural norms. Unraveling discourses of U.S. sexual exceptionalism is vital to critiques of U.S. practices of empire (most of

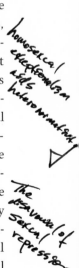

which only intermittently take up questions of gender and rarely sexuality) and to the expansion of queerness beyond narrowly conceptualized frames that foreground sexual identity and sexual acts.

Given that our contemporary political climate of U.S. nationalism relies so heavily on homophobic demonization of sexual others, the argument that homosexuality is included within and contributes positively to the optimization of life is perhaps a seemingly counterintuitive stance. Nonetheless, it is imperative that we continue to read the racial, gender, class, and national dimensions of these vilifying mechanisms. So I proceed with two caveats. First, to aver that some or certain homosexual bodies signify homonormative nationalism—homonationalism—is in no way intended to deny, diminish, or disavow the daily violences of discrimination, physical and sexual assault, familial ostracism, economic disadvantage, and lack of social and legal legitimacy that sexual others must regularly endure; in short, most queers, whether as subjects or populations, still hover amid regimes of deferred or outright death. What I am working through in this text are the manifold trajectories of racialization and un-nationalization of sexual others that foster the conditions of possibility for such violent relegation to death. The spectral resistances to gay marriage, gay adoptive and parental rights, "Don't Ask, Don't Tell" policies, and the privatization of sexuality entail that the protection of life granted through national belonging is a precarious invitation at best. Second, there is no organic unity or cohesion among homonationalisms; these are partial, fragmentary, uneven formations, implicated in the pendular momentum of inclusion and exclusion, some dissipating as quickly as they appear. Thus, the cost of being folded into life might be quite steep, both for the subjects who are interpellated by or aspire to the tight inclusiveness of homonormativity offered in this moment, and for those who decline or are declined entry due to the undesirability of their race, ethnicity, religion, class, national origin, age, or bodily ability. It also may be the case, as Barry D. Adams argues, that the United States is exceptional only to the degree to which, globally speaking, it is unexceptional, another angle that stresses the contingency of any welcome of queer life. In terms of legal recognition of gay and lesbian relationships, Adams notes ironically that to some extent the United States lags behind most European countries, as well as Canada, Brazil, Colombia, New Zealand, Australia, and South Africa—a "backwardness" that the United States often ascribes to others in comparison to itself.[24] We can also say that the United States has investments in being exceptionally heteronormative even as it claims to be exceptionally tolerant of (homosexual) difference. But Adams's reliance on lag reinscribes a troubling teleology of modernity that, despite situating exceptionalism as a narrative that masks or fuzzes over regional differences, impels like-minded countries in a unilateral itinerary rather than multidirectional flows. Some efforts to determine whether the United States is indeed exceptional, efforts that have dominated various debates in history, American studies, and political science, among other fields, have focused on comparative empirical studies that do little to challenge or even question this telos.[25] With the range of discussion on American exceptionalism in mind, my intent is not to determine whether the United States is indeed exceptional—exceptionally good or ahead, or exceptionally behind or different—but to illustrate the modes through which such claims to exceptionalism are loaded with unexamined discourses about race, sexuality, gender, and class. Furthermore, exceptionalisms rely on the erasure of these very modalities in order to function; these elisions are, in effect, the ammunition with which the exception, necessary to guard the properties of life, becomes the norm, and the exceptional, the subjects upon whom this task is bestowed, becomes the normal.

Queer as Regulatory

U.S. sexual exceptionalism has its European counterparts, especially in Britain and the Netherlands, which expand, intersect, contrast, and often fuel U.S. homonormative formations. The echoes and divergences among locations are crucial to keep in mind because of the varied colonial histories, distinct migration trajectories, and class differences between U.S. Muslims and European Muslims.[26] In Figure 1, what could such a pronouncement—"I am a homosexual also"—signify and imply? What kinds of representational currency, cultural capital, and affective resonance does this statement, in our contemporary political landscapes, create and dispel? In this incredible photograph by Poulomi Desai, surfacing in a collection of British South Asian queer photography published in 2003, we have a Muslim cleric staging terrorist drag.[27] This provocative image of a figure in Osama bin Laden drag sets us anew on a disruptive queer epistemology and ontology. I use the term "drag" provisionally: despite the makeup, dress, faux beard and moustache, and the contexts (both the political landscape of Britain and the queer documentation angle of the book project itself), the term might reiterate the normative understanding of the radical incommensurability of the two subject positions staged together and graft a normative modernist gendered binary frame onto an otherwise far more complexly

FIGURE 1. Poulomi Desai, *I Am a Homosexual Also*. From Poulomi Desai and Parminder Sekhon, *Red Threads: The South Asian Queer Connection in Photographs*. London: Diva Books, 2003. Reprinted with the artist's permission.

related sex-gender-desire triad. The garb of Muslim clerics is both naturalized as the fundamentalist dress of Osama bin Laden and reclaimed as a site of queer desires and queerly desiring subjects, interrupting both conventional epistemological and ontological renderings of this body.

The image is startling, to say the least, to the queer liberal imaginary at play in contemporary discourses of terrorism and counterterrorism: resolutely secular, unforgiving in its understanding of (irrational, illogical, senseless) religion, faith, or spirituality as the downfall of any rational politics. Queer secularity demands a particular transgression of norms, religious norms that are understood to otherwise bind that subject to an especially egregious interdictory religious frame. The queer agential subject can only ever be fathomed outside the norming constrictions of religion, conflating agency and resistance.

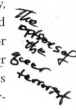

To Muslims and queers who disavow the practices of queer religiosity, the sign conveys: I too am you, and I am within you. Queer Arabs and Muslims, doubly indicted for the fundamentalist religion they adhere to or escape from and for the terrorist bodies that religion produces, are either liberated (and the United States and Europe are often the scene of this liberation) or can only have an irrational, pathological sexuality or queerness. These entanglements, debatably avoidable to an extent for queers from other traditions such as Judeo-Christian, plague Muslim queers because of the widespread conflation of Muslim with Islamic and Arab: Muslim = Islam = Arab. Religion, in particular Islam, has now supplanted race as one side of the irreconcilable binary between queer and something else. For queer Arabs and Muslims the either/or plight thickens: queer secularity understands observance of religious creed, participation in religious public spaces and rituals, devotion to faith-based or spiritual practices, and simply residence within an Islamic nation-state (floating upon the supposition of the separation of church and state in non-Islamic nation-states; for example, the denial of Christian fundamentalism as a state practice in the United States) as marks of subjugated and repressed sexuality void of agency. But regardless of complex affinities with Islam, Arab nation-states, and Muslim identity, the agency of all queer Muslims is invariably evaluated through the regulatory apparatus of queer liberal secularity.[28] This further contributes to apolitical readings typically ascribed to the refusals of western modernity that may be enacted by Islamic followers. Finally, queer secularity most virulently surfaces in relation to Islam because Islam, the whole monolith of it, is often described as unyielding and less amenable to homosexuality than Christianity and Judaism, despite exhortations by some queer Muslims who "insist their religious and family struggles are not much different from those of their Christian or Jewish counterparts."[29] As with the question of exceptionalism, my interest is not to determine the truth or falsity of these claims, but to examine the resilience and stranglehold of this discourse, its operating logic, the myths and realities it manufactures.

Why "homosexual," a clinical term that resonates with the medicalization of homosexuality in the west and intimates an immature version of queerness in an anthropological sense as well as within universal rights discourses? The secular gay and lesbian human rights framing of Islamic sexual repression mistakes or transposes state repression for sexual repression, essentially denying any productive effects of juridical structures (replaying again the repressive hypothesis Foucault warns against). This contemporary version of repression does not contradict colonial fantasies of Orientalist sexual excess, perversity, and pedophilia. Working in tandem, the proper modern gay or lesbian Muslim subject is foreclosed, while the terrorist is forever queer, improperly sexual, embedded in an "always already homosexualized population."[30] In this rendition, male homosociality is linked to pedophilia, ascribed to the perceived lack of sexual contact with women, or continually misread as faggotry or homosexuality. In contrast, female homosociality, sequestered out of view, is presumed to signal gender and sexual oppression.[31] The claim to homosexuality counters two tendencies: the colloquial deployment of Islamic sexual repression that plagues human rights, liberal queer, and feminist discourses, and the Orientalist wet dreams of lascivious excesses of pedophilia, sodomy, and perverse sexuality. At the intersection of the body and the population, Desai's image challenges the perverse pathological sexualization of terrorist lookalike populations by claiming a modernist subject identity—through religion, not despite it—that is typically reserved for homonormative (white, western or westernized) bodies. While the claim to modernist sexual subjecthood is enacted, a subjecthood often credited to the homogenizing forces of globalization, the unsettling, monstrous terrorist corporeality that inhabits this sexual subjecthood challenges the terms upon which it is policed.

Visually, the body reclaims the faggotry, the effeminacy, the failed masculinity, always already installed in the naming of the terrorist, staging further defiance in the face of such easily rendered accusations of being a terrorist. The (white) secular norms by which queerness abides contributes greatly to (racist) Islamo- and homophobic representations of terrorists. That is, the queer transgressive subject accrues its legitimacy and currency at this historical juncture through an inability to disentangle these representations via a broader articulation of queer religiosity. Queer secularity is constitutive of and constituted by the queer autonomous liberal subject against and through the reification of the very pathological irrational sexualities that are endemic to discourses of terrorist culpability.

The "also" of "I am a homosexual also," a sort of "deal with it" kind of insistence, signals to multiple audiences the conjuncture of Muslim and queer identities, thus challenging the mutually exclusive Orientalist versions of Muslim and homosexual. The singularity of the Muslim or gay binary has been amplified, in the United States as well as globally, since September 11, 2001. Groups such as the U.S.-based LGBTIQ Al-Fatiha Foundation (from the first line of the Koran, meaning "the beginning") have been probed like curious specimens, a queer anomaly.[32] The queer Muslim filmmaker Parvez Sharma, currently working on a documentary titled *In the Name of Allah*, flags a particularly emblematic example of this trend by pointing to the following description of his work and activism: "In the wake of Sept. 11th . . . [Sharma's work] seemed hard to imagine for many U.S. commentators: Muslim, sexual diversity, community, voice, and rights."[33] Mubarak Dahir reports on queer Muslim lives after the attacks: " 'It's bad enough to be hated for being gay,' says Mahmoud, a Muslim living in Pittsburgh who asked that his real name not be used. 'But now I'm also hated for being Muslim. That mistrust seems to emanate from all Americans too. I'd hoped that my gay friends—themselves the target of so much prejudice—would be more likely to question the stereotypes. But my gay friends are no better than anyone else.' " Later in the article Mahmoud says, "Since September 11, I've had to lean more than ever on my religious community for strength."[34] Ifti Nazim from SANGAT/Chicago ("a gay, lesbian, bisexual, and transgender organization and support group for people from India, Pakistan, Bangladesh, Sri Lanka, Nepal, Afghanistan, Iran, Burma, and rest of the South Asian countries") concurs, saying that many heterosexual Muslims in Chicago became more willing to view him as a community leader: "A lot of conservative Muslim leaders are reaching out to mainstream gay organizations now. . . . I am very happy about this and shocked because I never knew they would be like this. It's all due to September 11th."[35] These comments are significant at the very least because queer secularity, and queer transgressive subjecthood in general, is also underpinned by a powerful conviction that religious and racial communities are more homophobic than white mainstream queer communities are racist. Those caught in the interstices, queers of color, presumably engage with white mainstream queer folks, politics, social spaces, erotic entanglements, and community events with vastly greater ease than they do in their respective religious or racial communities, families, churches, rituals, celebrations, weddings (where the liberal coming-out telos functions as the barometer of acceptance). By implication, a critique of homophobia within one's home community is deemed more pressing and should take precedence over a critique of racism within mainstream queer communities. (One interpretation of the "Fight Racism and the [British National Party]" sticker is that it functions as an explicit challenge to the white and citizenship privileges implicit within queer liberalism.)

A prime conundrum demonstrating this point is the debate over the decision to hold World Pride 2006 in Jerusalem. "No Pride without Palestinians," a queer coalition based in New York City, sought to move World Pride to another location, arguing that Palestinian queers (and many Arabs from neighboring countries) would be banned from the celebrations, and those already present risked intensified surveillance, policing, harassment, and deportation. The organizers called for "moving World Pride to a place where all queers can celebrate real freedom" and noted that the Israeli state has on many occasions deported "queer human rights activists working to end the occupation of Palestine." Their website declared, "World Pride is supposed to be a celebration of queer freedom. Holding World Pride in Jerusalem—a city under occupation, a party hosted by the violent occupier —is a slap in the face to freedom. . . . It's not 'World' Pride without Palestinian and Arab queers, and we refuse to pit our queer celebrations against Palestinians' freedom."[36] InterPride, the organization that coordinates World Pride, is based in the United States and run predominantly by North Americans and some Europeans. Israel's decision to host World Pride was irritatingly strategic, as the event would showcase Israel as a tolerant, diverse, and democratic society, further submerging its dismal human rights record. (The violence and tensions between ultra-Orthodox, other conservative Jewish sects, and queer Jews that are typically effaced was highlighted by the June 2005 stabbing of three gay pride parade participants by "a man in ultra-Orthodox attire.")[37] From the circuits of "transnational queerdom," this decision covertly impelled collusion with oppressive Israeli state policy toward Palestinians while also encouraging and sanctioning overt anti-Palestinian sentiments.[38] It also reiterated that Israeli queers can be legitimated by the Israeli state as well as by transnational queerdom through the quest for and right of sovereignty, while Palestinian queers are teleologically read through the fanatic lens of Islamic fundamentalism rather than the Palestinian struggle for self-determination and statehood, an interest in progressive queer politics, or even a liberal humanist exegesis of desire.[39] It is utterly important that queer Jewish and queer Palestinian activists, among others, lobbied together to cancel or alter the location of World Pride 2006.[40] It is also imperative that these coalitional efforts reject queer missionary, liberatory, or transcendent paradigms that might place Palestinian queers in a victim narrative parallel to that propagated by the Israeli state they are battling against.

Another trap lies in the valorization of victims as vanguard by elevating them to heroism. The activities of the British-based queer group OutRage! border dangerously on this thin line. Calling for a "queer fatwa" (a rather moronic appropriation of the term "fatwa") against the United Kingdom's "Islamic fundamentalist" leader Omar Bakri Mohammed during a rally in London on International Women's Day (March 8, 2005), OutRage!'s posters claimed "Solidarity with Islamic Women" and mandated "No Islamic State No Shar'ia Law."[41] This latter conviction reflects queer secularity; it is inconceivable that women or queers could negotiate or have agency within an Islamic state. At the Free Palestine rally in London on May 21, 2005, OutRage! carried placards commanding "Israel: stop persecuting Palestine! Palestine: stop persecuting queers!" and "Stop 'honour' killing women and gays in Palestine." This seemingly innocuous and politically correct messaging, stemming from the group's commitment to protest "Islamophobia and homophobia," unfortunately reaffirms the modernity of Israel and Judaism and the monstrosity of Palestine and Islam. Delineating Palestine as the site of queer oppression—oppression that is equated with the occupation of Palestine by Israel—effaces Israeli state persecution of queer Palestinians. Israeli state persecution of queer Israelis—because Israel is hardly exempt from homophobic violence toward its own citizens regardless of religious or ethnic background—is erased in this trickle-down model of sloganeering. This dialectical analogy, whereby the persecution of Palestinians by Israel is "like" Palestinian persecution of queers, does a tremendous disservice to the incommensurate predicaments at stake and refuses any possible linkages between the two, indeed refuses that one form of oppression might sustain or even create the conditions of possibility for the other. Further, this analogy eviscerates vital connections: between the disciplinary liberationist paradigms of gay and lesbian human rights and escalating Islamic state repression of nonnormative sexualities, the solidification of gender binaries in modernity and its imposition on differently gendered societies,[42] and the histories of economic and cultural domination of colonialism and neocolo-

FIGURE 2. OutRage! founder Peter Tatchell with "Queer Fatwa" sign. Photograph by Piers Allardyce (for OutRage!). Reprinted with the artist's permission.

nialism and the endless navigation of these power networks by colonized peoples. Ironically, the very logic that feeds the Israeli state's rationalization and justification of its occupation of Palestine and its horrific treatment of Palestinians—the purported barbarity and unhumanness of the backward, fundamentalist Muslim-Palestinian suicide-bomber-terrorist—is reinscribed by OutRage!'s messaging at a Free Palestine rally. The differential treatment of queers in these transnational contexts is heavily dependent on national and racial belonging and dis/enfranchisement.

OutRage! has been accused of using a queer platform to propagate anti-Muslim rhetoric, not an unfounded fear given the evidence.[43] OutRage!'s most prominent activist, Peter Tatchell, warned of Islamic fundamentalism in 1995, saying its ascendancy "has ushered in an era of religious obscurantism and intolerance," which he refers to as the "New Dark Ages."[44] Exemplary of paranoia as well as the ubiquitous polarization of Muslim and gay subjectivities, in 1998 he wrote, "The political consequences for the gay community could be serious. As the fundamentalists gain followers, homophobic Muslim voters may be able to influence the outcome of elections in 20 or more marginal constituencies."[45] In regard to OutRage!'s protests against "Islamic fundamentalist" Yusuf al-Qaradawi's visit to Britain in summer 2004, the mayor of London Ken Livingstone writes that a "wave of Islamophobia" has overshadowed the purpose of al-Qaradawi's trip, a conference on the rights of women to choose to wear the Muslim headscarf (motivated by the ban on headscarves in French schools). A second letter, signed by the National Assembly against Racism, the National Union of Students Black LGB, the Lesbian and Gay Coalition against Racism, and Operation Black Vote, echoes similar sentiments ("We must express our concern at the tenor and pitch of the campaign by OutRage! and others, in relation to Yusuf al-Qaradawi, which we believe fits in with what is a rising wave of anti-Muslim hysteria"), citing "a powerful and dangerous campaign to insist that Muslim fundamentalism is the most serious threat facing the world" emanating from Western Europe and the United States.[46] OutRage!, for its part, points out that Dr. al-Qaradawi's website, Islamonline, sanctions the burning and stoning to death of homosexuals and violence against women.[47]

My intent is not to delve into the intricate political organizing history of OutRage!, nor to berate its multifaceted work: coalitions with the Black Gay Men's Advisory Group, the Queer Youth Alliance, and the Green Party; rallies against the same-sex marriage ban, the Vatican and the Catholic religion, the homophobic lyrics of Caribbean musicians Beenie Man, Vybz Kartel, Bounty Killer, Elephant Man, and Buju Banton, the torture and execution of gays in Saudi Arabia, the deportation of gay asylum seekers Algerian Ramzi Isalam and Belorussian Vadim Selyava, and Mugabe's dictatorship in Zimbabwe; and vigils for murdered Jamaican gay activist Brian Williamson and Sierra Leonean lesbian activist Fannyann Eddy—and surely the list goes on.[48] Rather, the Free Palestine rally serves as an example of displays of solidarity with other queers, often well-intentioned gestures of inclusion and acknowledgment of multicultural diversity, that may unwittingly replicate the very neocolonial assumptions OutRage! seeks to dislodge.

But there is something more insidious going on here. The Muslim or gay binary mutates from a narrative of incommensurate subject positionings into an "Islam versus homosexuality" tug of populations war: a mutation that may reveal the contiguous undercurrents of conservative homonormative ideologies and queer liberalism. For example, the gay Dutch politician Pim Fortuyn of the Netherlands pledged to terminate immigration and asylum and used anti-Muslim rhetoric to propel his political party, Lijst Pim Fortuyn, to a twenty-six-seat presence in Parliament; he was murdered by an animal rights activist nine days before the victory.[49] Yoshi Furuhashi comments, "The rise of Pim Fortuyn . . . signaled a new era of white gay male politics. By promoting anti-immigrant politics vigorously and marketing it with anti-Muslim prejudice demagogically, Fortuyn showed that right-wing populism can very well be gay and enormously popular to boot." Unlike right-wing white gay male politicians working "against their own interests," who have faced ostracization and banishment by fellow right-wingers, Furuhashi implies that the right to marry will accord even more credibility and legitimacy to these gay politicians.[50] In the aftermath of the July 7, 2005 London bombings, the perpetrators of which were not sleeper-cell terrorists from some remote country who had infiltrated the sacred homeland but home-grown British Muslims, Sandip Roy notes that Europe is symbolically bifurcated into one arena where legalizing same-sex marriage is a priority (Netherlands, Belgium, Spain, the United Kingdom) and another where Islamic fundamentalism, responsible for the death of the filmmaker Theo van Gogh, for instance, purportedly reigns.

Gay marriage, "less about gay rights and more about codifying an ideal of European values,"[51] has become a steep but necessary insurance premium in Europe, whereby an otherwise ambivalent if not hostile populace can guarantee that extra bit of security that is bought by yet another marker in the distance between barbarism and civilization, one that justifies further targeting of a perversely sexualized and racialized Muslim population (pedophilic, sexually lascivious and excessive, yet perversely repressed) who refuse to properly assimilate, in contrast to the upright homosexuals engaged in sanctioned kinship norms. Gay marriage reform thus indexes the racial and civilizational disjunctures between Europeans and Muslims, while effacing the circuits of political economy (class, immigration) that underpin such oppositions. While the conflict is increasingly articulated as one between queers and Muslims, what is actually at stake is the policing of rigid boundaries of gender difference and the kinship forms most amenable to their maintenance.[52]

Shortly after the bombings, OutRage! claimed that it had received death threats from various Muslim organizations.[53] Among other groups, Out-Rage! is codifying, for Europeans but also implicitly for Americans, that Muslims are an *especial threat* to homosexuals, that Muslim fundamentalists have deliberately and specifically targeted homosexuals, and that the parameters of this opposition correlate with those of the war on terror: civilization versus barbarianism. As with both Fortuyn and OutRage!, we are witnessing, from vastly different corners, the rise of homonormative Is-

FIGURE 3. Imaan float at EuroPride 2006, London. Photograph by Liz Van Gerven. Reprinted with the artist's permission.

lamophobia in the global North, whereby homonormative and queer gay men can enact forms of national, racial, or other belongings by contributing to a collective vilification of Muslims.[54]

To return once more, for a moment, to our photograph of the Muslim fundamentalist-cum–perverse terrorist–cum-homosexual, this oscillation from an individuated dilemma of subjectivity—Are you Muslim, or are you gay?—to a war of mutually exclusive populations confirms the absolute sense of the irreconcilably stubborn natures of unassimilating and unas-similatable (working-class European) Muslims. The disciplined homosex-ual subject and the sexually pathological terrorist figure wedded to its pop-ulace remain suspended together, refusing to condone conflation of the two, a collapsing of one into the other or the shunting into one over the other. The text modifies image, directs our interpretation of it, but cannot fully domesticate the saturation of Orientalist tropes endowed to this body.

Some may strenuously object to the suggestion that queer identities, like their "less radical" counterparts, homosexual, gay, and lesbian identities, are also implicated in ascendant white American nationalist formations, preferring to see queerness as singularly transgressive of identity norms. This focus on transgression, however, is precisely the term by which queerness narrates its own sexual exceptionalism. While we can point to the obvious problems with the emancipatory, missionary pulses of certain (U.S., western) feminisms and of gay and lesbian liberation, queerness has its own exceptionalist desires: exceptionalism is a founding impulse, indeed the very core of a queerness that claims itself as an anti-, trans-, or uniden-tity. The paradigm of gay liberation and emancipation has produced all sorts of troubling narratives: about the greater homophobia of immigrant communities and communities of color, about the stricter family values and mores in these communities, about a certain prerequisite migration from home, about coming-out teleologies. We have less understanding of queerness as a biopolitical project, one that both parallels and intersects with that of multiculturalism, the ascendancy of whiteness, and may collude with or collapse into liberationist paradigms. While liberal underpinnings serve to constantly recenter the normative gay or lesbian subject as exclusively libera-tory, these same tendencies labor to insistently recenter the normative queer subject as an exclusively transgressive one.

Queerness here is the modality through which "freedom from norms" becomes a regulatory queer ideal that demarcates the ideal queer. Arguing that "more reflection on queer attachments might allow us to avoid positing assimilation or transgression as choices," Sara Ahmed notes, "The idealization of movement, or transformation of movement into a fetish, depends on the exclusion of others who are already positioned as *not free in the same way*."[55] Individual freedom becomes the barometer of choice in the valuation, and ultimately, regulation, of queerness.

Ahmed's post-Marxian frame focuses on the material, cultural, and social capital and resources that might delimit "access" to queerness, suggesting that queerness can be an elite cosmopolitan formulation contingent upon various regimes of mobility. Ironically, "those that have access" to such cultural capital and material resources may constitute the very same populations that many would accuse of assimilation, living out queerness in the most apolitical or conservatively political ways. I am thinking of queerness as exceptional in a way that is wedded to individualism and the rational, liberal humanist subject, what Ahmed denotes as "attachments" and what I would qualify as deep psychic registers of investment that we often cannot account for and are sometimes best seen by others rather than ourselves. "Freedom from norms" resonates with liberal humanism's authorization of the fully self-possessed speaking subject, untethered by hegemony or false consciousness, enabled by the life/stylization offerings of capitalism, rationally choosing modern individualism over the ensnaring bonds of family. In this problematic definition of queerness, individual agency is legible only as resistance to norms rather than complicity with them, thus equating resistance and agency. Both Saba Mahmood and Ahmed critique this conflation and redirect their attention to agency that supports and consolidates norms, but even this turn presupposes some general universal understanding of what counts as norm, resistance, and complicity. As Mahmood asks, "[Is it] possible to identify a universal category of acts—such as those of resistance—outside of the ethical and political conditions within which such acts acquire their particular meaning?"[56] The rhetoric of freedom is also of course a mainstay in philosophies of liberal democracy and is indeed a foundational tenet of American exceptionalism. But finally, queerness as transgression (which is one step ahead of resistance, which has now become a normative act) relies on a normative notion of deviance, always defined in relation to normativity, often universalizing. Thus deviance, despite its claims to freedom and individuality, is ironically cohered to and by regulatory regimes of queerness—through, not despite, any claims to transgression.

While Ahmed also looks to queerness as a challenge predominantly to heteronorms, queer theorists such as Cathy Cohen implicate queer politics in an intersectional model that should also ideally challenge race and class norms as they intersect with heteronorms.[57] Other queer theorists might articulate queerness as a poststructuralist endeavor that deconstructs not only heteronorms, but the very logic of identity itself. In the first version of queerness, resistance to heteronorms may be privileged in a way that effaces the effects of this resistance in relation to possible complicities with other norms, such as racial, class, gender, and citizenship privileges. Queer intersectional analyses challenge this regulatory queerness, but in doing so may fail to subject their own frames to the very critique they deploy. In this second formulation, queer of color and queer immigrant communities (not to mention queer of color critique) are always beyond reproach, an untenable position given the (class, religious, gender-queer, national, regional, linguistic, generational) tensions within, among, and between queer diasporic, immigrant, and of color communities, thus obfuscating any of their own conservative proclivities. Conversely, it also holds queer of color organizing and theorizing to impossible standards and expectations, always beholden to spaces and actions of resistance, transgression, subversion. In the last instance, all (of one's) identities (not just gender and sexual) must be constantly troubled, leading to an impossible transcendent subject who is always already conscious of the normativizing forces of power and always ready and able to subvert, resist, or transgress them. It is precisely by denying culpability or assuming that one is not implicated in violent relations toward others, that one is outside of them, that violence can be perpetuated. Violence, especially of the liberal varieties, is often most easily perpetrated in the spaces and places where its possibility is unequivocally denounced.

What is at stake in defusing queer liberal binaries of assimilation and transgression, secularity and religiosity? If we are to resist resistance, reading against these binaries to foreground a broader array of power affiliations and disaffiliations that are often rife with contradiction should not provide ammunition to chastise, but rather generate greater room for self-reflection, autocritique, and making mistakes. It is easy, albeit painful, to point to the conservative elements of any political formation; it is less easy, and perhaps much more painful, to point to ourselves as accomplices of certain normativizing violences. In sum, what we can say about the mechanics of queerness as a regulatory frame of biopolitics includes the following:

1. Queerness as automatically and inherently transgressive enacts specific forms of disciplining and control, erecting celebratory queer liberal subjects folded into life (queerness as subject) against the sexually pathological and deviant populations targeted for death (queerness as population).

2. Within that orientation of regulatory transgression, queer operates as an alibi for complicity with all sorts of other identity norms, such as nation, race, class, and gender, unwittingly lured onto the ascent toward whiteness.

3. Allowing for complicities signals not the failure of the radical, resistant, or oppositional potential of queernesses, but can be an enabling acknowledgment.

4. But conundrums abound even with the fluidity of resistances and complicities, for intersectional models cannot account for the simultaneous or multifarious presences of both or many.

The Ascendancy of Whiteness

Rey Chow, drawing on Foucault's work in *The Order of Things*, proposes that "Foucault's discussion of biopower can be seen as his approach, albeit oblique, to the question of the ascendancy of whiteness in the modern world." Engendered through scientific observation, classification and taxonomy, the production of data, detail, and description, leading to the micromanagement of information and bodies, all attempt to "render the world a knowable object." This objectification and honing for the purposes of management and domestication is paralleled, according to Chow, by an increasing mystification and obscuring of the primary beneficiaries of this epistemological project: European subjectivities. This simultaneity of specification and abstraction is the very basis of distinctions between subjects and objects (and populations), or, for Chow, between those who theorize and those who are theorized about.[58]

For Chow, in contemporary times, the "ascendancy of whiteness" in biopower incorporates the multiplication of appropriate multicultural ethnic bodies complicit with this ascendancy. Part of the trappings of this exceptional citizen, ethnic or not, is the careful management of difference: of difference within sameness, and of difference containing sameness. We can note, for example, that the multicultural proliferation of the cosmopolitan ethnic à la Chow has some demanding limitations in terms of class, gender, and especially sexuality. That is, what little acceptance liberal diversity proffers in the way of inclusion is highly mediated by huge realms of exclusion: the ethnic is usually straight, usually has access to material and cultural capital (both as a consumer and as an owner), and is in fact often male. These would be the tentative attributes that would distinguish a tolerable ethnic (an exceptional patriot, for example) from an intolerable ethnic (a terrorist suspect). In many cases, heteronormativity might be the most pivotal of these attributes, as certain Orientalist queernesses (failed heteronormativity, as signaled by polygamy, pathological homosociality) are a priori ascribed to terrorist bodies. The twin process of multiculturalization and heterosexualization are codependent in what Susan Koshy denotes as the "morphing of race into ethnicity," a transmogrification propelled by the cultivation of "white privilege as color-blind meritocracy." (This morphing has also inspired the politicization of the designation "people of color.") While Chow does not explicitly discuss why racial frames lose their salience (and retain denigrated status) in relation to market-driven ethnicity, Koshy adds "the accommodation of new immigrants and the resurgence of white ethnicity" as compelling factors that "obscure the operations of race and class" in transnational contexts.[59]

These "operations" involve what Koshy describes as "class fraction projected as the model minority" produced through "changed demographics, class stratifications, new immigration, and a global economy . . . thereby enabling opportunistic alliances between whites and different minority groups as circumstances warrant . . . project[ing] a simulacrum of inclusiveness even as it advances a political culture of market individualism that has legitimized the gutting of social services to disadvantaged minorities in the name of the necessities of the global economy." Koshy argues that fractioning allows "an ethnic particularist position" to "escape scrutiny" because the distance it impels from whiteness in cultural terms is abrogated through its proximity to "whiteness as power through . . . class aspirations," enabling "a seemingly more congenial dispensation that allows for cultural difference even as it facilitates political affiliations between whites and some nonwhites on certain critical issues such as welfare reform, affirmative action, and immigration legislation."[60] Thus, for the ethnic with access to capital, both in terms of consumption and ownership, the seduction by global capital is conducted through racial amnesia, among other forms of forgetting. This fractioning, or disassembly into fractals, is contiguous with state racism in that it too promotes "caesuras within the biological continuum" necessary to simultaneously particularize and homogenize populations for control.[61]

Racial / Amnesia

The ascendancy of whiteness for Koshy, as for Chow, is ensconced in (neo)liberal ideologies of difference—market, cultural, and convergences of both—that correspond to "fitness-within-capitalism" and ultimately promise "incorporation into the American Dream."[62] That this promise always appears almost on the verge of fulfillment, but is never quite satisfied, is what Sara Ahmed alludes to in her claim that "love may be especially crucial in the event of the failure of the nation to deliver its promise for the good life." For Ahmed, national love is a form of waiting, a lingering that registers a "stigma of inferiority" that epitomizes the inner workings of multiculturalism.[63] Unrequited love keeps multicultural (and also homonormative) subjects in the folds of nationalism, while xenophobic and homophobic ideologies and policies fester. Through this dynamic the benevolence of the state (and also of the market) can appear boundless while still committed to the anti–gay marriage amendment and the USA PATRIOT Act, as just two examples. Furthermore, the market is a foil for the state, producing consumer subjects (as well as highly skilled laborers) that simulate (and experience simulated) affective modes of belonging to the state, modes that assuage the angst of unrequited love. Thus the nation-state maintains its homophobic and xenophobic stances while capitalizing on its untarnished image of inclusion, diversity, and tolerance. Concomitantly, multicultural (and homonormative) subjects reorient their loyalty to the nation through market privileges, a remasculinization that Heidi Nast terms "market virility,"[64] that

Unrequited Love

masquerade as forms of belonging to the nation and mediate the humiliation of waiting for national love. Multiculturalism is the accomplice to the ascendancy of whiteness, reproducing the biopolitical mandate to live through the proper population statistics; channeled through the optics of gender and class are their attendant attributes and valuations of longevity, illness, health, environment, fertility, and so on. Through the pining for national love, the temporality of multicultural model minority discourses is one of futurity, an endlessly deferred or deflected gratification, mirroring biopower's constant march forward, away from death, where the securitization for today funnels back through guarantees of the quality of life for tomorrow. This requires gender and sexual normativity and the reproduction of the hybrid multicultural body politic in exchange for lucrative possibilities within the global economy.

But is multiculturalization unequivocally heteronormativization? What are the stakes in rigid sexual and gendered dynamics of this multiculturalism, for those who can sustain this unrequited love, and for those who cannot, dare not, begin to imagine its possibility? A foregone conclusion might be that multiculturalism as heteronormativization works to police sexual and gender relations and embodiments similar to its classist gatekeeping logic. But the history of capitalist developments and kinship forms (the move from subsistence labor to waged labor in the late 1800s and early 1900s that allowed for gay male urban subcultures) intimates that capitalism is ambivalent: the very workings of capital that instantiate the heterosexual nuclear family as pivotal for the reproduction of the labor force, the relegation of women to free labor in the house or as underwaged surplus workers, and the family as the basic social unit of intimacy that mediates the brutalities of the working world are factors that have freed (predominantly white male) workers to form alternative sexual and kinship communities and networks.[65] Both consolidation and rupturing of traditional heterosexual family forms are possible, but in our present-day global economy the prerequisite mobility is, as it was before, constrained by race, ethnicity, gender, class, and citizenship. As Ann Pellegrini writes, "The invention of homosexuality was also, then, the invention of heterosexuality, and family has shifted from site of production to site of consumption."[66]

If we follow Koshy's lead on the "political culture of market individualism," access to capital—"market virility"—mediates national belonging and the folding into life for multicultural ethnic subjects, homonormative subjects, and possibly even some of those subjects positioned at the intersection of the two.[67] For the ethnic, heteronormativity is mandated by the nation-state yet negotiable through the market, that is, conspicuous consumption and high-skilled labor; for the homonormative, whiteness is mandated by the state but negotiable through the market, again both for labor and consumption. The figure of the queer or homonormative ethnic is crucial for the appearance of diversity in homonormative communities (arriving as the difference of culture rather than as the simulacra of capital) and tolerance in ethnic and racialized immigrant communities (marked as an entrance of alternative lifestyle rather than through the commonalities of capital). Ironically, the queer ethnic is also a marker of the homophobia (and the claim that homosexuality reflects the taint of the west) of his or her racial/ethnic/immigrant community while in homonormative spaces, perhaps more so than a marker of the racism of homonormative communities while in one's home community. (This might be so because the benevolent [U.S] state has to date made more concessions to the ethnics—a folding into life—than to the homos, at least in terms of civil rights and its historical trajectory.)

The factioning, fractioning, and fractalizing of identity is a prime activity of societies of control, whereby subjects (the ethnic, the homonormative) orient themselves as subjects through their disassociation or disidentification from others disenfranchised in similar ways in favor of consolidation with axes of privilege. The queer or homonormative ethnic is a crucial fractal in the disaggregation of proper homosexual subjects, joining the ranks of an ascendant population of whiteness, from perversely sexualized populations. As with the class fraction that projects a model minority, we have here a class, race, and sexual fraction projected to the market as the homonormative gay or queer consumer. This is a consumer without kin, the best kind, projected to the state as a reproducer of heteronorms, where associations with white national hetero- and homonormative bodies trump the desire for queer alliances across class, race, and citizenship. But what of racialized immigrants or people of color who fall outside the class parameters of the model minority ethnic, of the homonormative, or who inhabit the intersection of the two: the queer (immigrant) of color? As Lisa Duggan reminds us, neoliberalism's privatizing agenda from the 1970s onward has dismantled an already minimal welfare state.[68] She notes that welfare downsizing nearly mandates heterosexual conjugal marriage; this downsizing, epitomized by the 1996 Welfare Reform Act, also resulted in a number of policies that linked the promotion of heterosexual marriage through welfare reform as it sought to produce more stable traditional kinship configurations, the "politics of privatization" of heterosexual marriage.[69]

Duggan argues that aside from the moralizing agendas of the "family values" cohort, there are obvious economic benefits for the state in pushing heterosexual marriage. Further, moralizing arguments, entrenched within the rubric of culture, obscure economic exploitation: "The effort to promote marriage among low-income populations works at the rhetorical level to shift blame for economic hardship onto the marital practices of the poor rather than on the loss of jobs, employment benefits or government services,"[70] those marital practices coded as problematic cultural and racial anomalies (polygamy, matriarchy, gender segregation) or coded as failures due to cultural and racial attributes (black welfare queen). Likewise, immigration policies hinge on family reunification and sponsorship from family members, not to mention reliance on family for opportunities for employment, housing, language, and vital community and religious networks that aid in acculturation and cushion against racist and classist state practices and everyday racism.

We have here all the makings of the discourse attached to immigrant populations and communities of color about a more overt disapproval of homosexuality and a more deeply entrenched homophobia, this homophobia cast as properly conservative and traditional when it serves the political right and the state, cast as uncosmopolitan and hopelessly provincial when it can fuel anti-immigrant, counterterrorist, and antiwelfare discourses. But also, heteronormative multiculturalism and gay and lesbian liberation are frames that are indebted to the understanding of immigrant families and communities of color as more homophobic than white mainstream American families. The descriptor "homophobic culture" elides the workings of economic disparities and the differentiation between cosmopolitan ethnicity and pathological racialization, a feature of neoliberalism's reproduction of the separation of economic justice from identity politics.[71] Where it appears palpable or deemed locatable, empirically and experientially, the designation of homophobia produces a geopolitical mapping of neoliberal power relations in the guise of cultures of sexual expression and repression. Debates regarding which communities, countries, cultures, or religions are more, less, equally, similarly, or differently homophobic miss a more critical assessment regarding the conditions of its possibility and impossibility, conditions revolving around economic incentives, state policies on welfare and immigration, and racial hierarchy, rather than some abstracted or disengaged notion of culture per se. Gay marriage, for example, is not simply a demand for equality with heterosexual norms, but more importantly a demand for reinstatement of white privileges and rights—rights of property and inheritance in particular —while for others, gay marriage and domestic partnership are driven by dire needs for health care. For George W. Bush during the 2004 election season, opposition to gay marriage spawned otherwise elusive photo ops in African American churches, supplementing right-wing forays into churches in communities of color.[72] The right wing relies on poor immigrant labor for its hegemonic ideological base—family values, faith-based initiatives, anti–gay marriage, anti–gay adoption rights, antichoice—and reproduces the economic and political conditions of compulsory heterosexuality and thus is the breeding ground for homophobia.

Most critiques of homonormative political formations observe the complicity of heteronorms of gender and kinship without noting their reproduction of racial and national norms (if another norm is noticed, it is often class). Through the ascendancy of heteronormativity there are implicit and increasingly explicit interests in the ascendancy to whiteness and attendant citizenship privileges (gay marriage is the most pertinent example of this), a variant of which Heidi Nast terms "queer white patriarchy."[73] In a highly contentious essay, Nast maintains that "there is substantial room for discussion about white patriarchal privilege outside heterosexual confines." She expounds on a trenchant point about the displacement of white heterosexual male beneficiaries of capitalism by white gay males who "hold a competitive edge: With no necessary ideological-material ties to biologically based house-holding and the attendant mobility frictions these entail, they share the potential for considerable, if ironic, patriarchal advantage that is relational and cuts across lines of class."[74] While Lisa Duggan refuses the paralleling or equalizing of homonormativity to heteronormativity, pointing out that dominant heteronormative social, political, and economic structures are ultimately impossible to trump regardless of homonormative privilege,[75] from a neo-Marxist approach Nast marks the privileges of queer patriarchy through "market virility" and the paternal control of "the products of reproduction." Folded into life and reproducing life, an aspirant class of wealthy white gay males who can simulate the biopolitical mandate to reproduce and regenerate may actually have it better than their hetero counterparts, perhaps even significantly so.[76]

Implicating white lesbians as part of this scenario (of paternity?) via the global circuits of transnational adoption, David Eng writes, "[Transnational adoption] is becoming a popular and viable option not only for heterosexual but also—and increasingly—for homosexual couples and singles seeking to (re)consolidate and (re)occupy conventional structures of family and kinship." Noting a historical and political shift from discourses and practices of disaffiliation from homophobic families to modes of assembling homosexual kinship norms, he states, "Gays and lesbians today are no longer eccentric to structures of family and kinship." Further, through a reading of a John Hancock commercial featuring two white American lesbians at a major U.S. airport ushering their newly adopted Chinese baby girl through immigration and customs, Eng contends that white American lesbians with capital are "an emerging consumer niche group." Querying the "ethics of multiculturalism," not to mention flexible accumulation, global capital, and exploitation immanent to the contemporary emergence of the "new global family," Eng ponders, "How is this respectable lesbian couple with money being positioned as the idealized inhabitants of an increasingly acceptable gay version of the nuclear family?"[77] His argument intimates that Chinese adoptees (and other nationalities and ethnicities that are not black) have become, and need to be turned into, surrogate white children.

Queer liberalism embraces these spaces of diversity through what Chow names the "white liberalist alibi." Paraphrasing Robyn Wiegman, she writes of "the particular formation of the contemporary, politically correct white subject, who imagines that he has already successfully disaffiliated from his culture's previous, more brutal forms of racism."[78] To be excused from a critique of one's own power manipulations is the appeal of white liberalism, the underpinnings of the ascendancy of whiteness, which is not a conservative, racist formation bent on extermination, but rather an insidious liberal one proffering an innocuous inclusion into life.[79] These two examples from Nast and Eng suggest that the capitalist reproductive economy (in conjunction with technology: in vitro, sperm banks, cloning, sex selection, genetic testing) no longer exclusively demands heteronormativity as an absolute; its simulation may do.

To summarize, the ascendancy of whiteness, rendering both disciplinary subjects and population norms, is not strictly delimited to white subjects, though it is bound to multiculturalism as defined and deployed by whiteness. The ethnic aids the project of whiteness through his or her participation in global economic privileges that then fraction him or her away from racial alliances that would call for cross-class affinities even as the project of multiculturalism might make him or her seem truly and authentically representative of his or her ethnicity. Neither is the ascendancy of whiteness strictly bound to heterosexuality, though it is bound to heteronormativity. That is to say, we can indeed mark a specific historical shift: the project of whiteness is assisted and benefited by homosexual populations that participate in the same identitarian and economic hegemonies as those hetero subjects complicit with this ascendancy. The homonormative aids the project of heteronormativity through the fractioning away of queer alliances in favor of adherence to the reproduction of class, gender, and racial norms. The ascendancy of heteronormativity, therefore, is not tethered to heterosexuals; neither is it discretely delimited to white people, though it is bound to whiteness. This is where the good ethnic comes in. While the good (straight) ethnic has been a recipient of "measures of benevolence,"[80] that is, folded into life, for several decades now, the (white) homonormative is a more recent entrant of this benevolence (civil rights and market) that produces affective be/longing that never fully rewards its captives yet nonetheless fosters longing and yearning as affects of nationalism. I belabor these stiff emplotments, well aware of the dangerous communion of descriptive and prescriptive narrative, to elucidate the manufacture of figures (and communities) and their attendant mythologies. Taken together, these figures play and are played off each other to cohere a pernicious binary that has emerged in the post–civil rights era in legislative, activist, and scholarly realms: the homosexual other is white, the racial other is straight.

Queer Necropolitics

In 1992, Judith Butler, faulting Foucault's *The History of Sexuality* for his "wishful construction: death is effectively expelled from Western modernity, cast *behind* it as a historical possibility, surpassed or cast *outside* it as a non-Western phenomenon," asks us to revaluate biopolitical investment in fostering life from the vantage point of homosexual bodies that have been historically cathected to death, specifically queer bodies afflicted with or threatened by the HIV pandemic.[81] For Foucault, modern biopower, emerging at the end of the eighteenth century, is the management of life—the distribution of risk, possibility, mortality, life chances, health, environment, quality of living—the differential investment of and in the imperative to live. In biopower, propagating death is no longer the central concern of the state; staving off death is. Cultivating life is coextensive with the sovereign right to kill, and death becomes merely reflective, a byproduct, a secondary effect of the primary aim and efforts of those cultivating or being cultivated for life. Death is never a primary focus; it is a negative translation of the imperative to live, occurring only through the transit of fostering life. Death becomes a form of collateral damage in the pursuit of life.

This distancing from death is a fallacy of modernity, a hallucination that allows for the unimpeded workings of biopolitics. In *"Society Must Be Defended"* Foucault avers, "Death was no longer something that suddenly swooped down on life, as in an epidemic. Death was now something permanent, something that slips into life, perpetually gnaws at it, diminishes it and weakens it."[82] Butler, transposing the historical frame of Foucault's elaboration of biopower onto the context of contemporary politics of life and death, notes the irony of Foucault's untimely death in 1984 due to causes related to AIDS, at that time an epidemic on the cusp of its exponential detonation.[83] Thus, Butler's 1992 analysis returns bodies to death, specifically queer bodies afflicted with or threatened by the HIV virus.[84]

With a similar complaint, albeit grounded in the seemingly incongruous plight of colonial and neocolonial occupations, Achille Mbembe redirects our attention from biopolitics to what he terms "necropolitics." Mbembe's analysis foregrounds death decoupled from the project of living—a direct relation to killing that renders impossible any subterfuge in a hallucinating disavowal of death in modernity—by asking, "Is the notion of biopower sufficient to account for the contemporary ways in which the political, under the guise of war, of resistance, or of the fight against terror, makes the murder of its enemy its primary and absolute objective?"[85] For Foucault, massacres are literally vital events;[86] for Mbembe, they are the evidence of the brutality of biopower's incitement to life.

For a millisecond, we have an odd conflation and complicity, rendering necropolitical death doubly displaced: first by biopolitical antennae of power, and second by the theorist who describes them. Laboring in the service of rational politics of liberal democracy, biopolitical scopes of power deny death within itself and for itself; indeed, death is denied through its very sanction. In *The History of Sexuality*, Foucault, himself ensnared in the very workings of biopolitics, a disciplinary subject of biopolitics, denies death within biopolitics too. However, in *"Society Must be Defended,"* he contends that the "gradual disqualification of death" in biopolitical regimes of living stigmatizes death as "something to be hidden away. It has become the most private and shameful thing of all (and ultimately, it is now not so much sex as death that is the object of a taboo)." This privatization of death, Foucault indicates, signals that in the quest to optimize life, "power no longer recognizes death. Power literally ignores death."[87]

Mbembe's "death-worlds" of the "living dead," on the other hand, may cohere through a totalizing narrative about the suffocation of life through the omnipotent forces of killing.[88] In the face of daily necropolitical violence, suffering, and death, the biopolitical will to live plows on, distributed and redistributed in the minutiae of quotidian affairs not only of the capacity of individual subjects but of the capacity of populations: health, hygiene, environment, medicine, reproduction and birthrates (and thus fertility, child care, education), mortality (stalling death, the elongation of life), illness ("form, nature, extension, duration, and intensity of the illnesses prevalent in a population" in order to regulate labor production and productivity), insurance, security. These "technologies of security" function to promote a reassuring society, "an overall equilibrium that protects the security of the whole from internal dangers," and are thus implicated in the improvement of the race through purification, and the reignition and regeneration of one's race.[89]

While questions of reproduction and regeneration are central to the study of biopolitics, queer scholars have been oddly averse to the Foucauldian frame of biopolitics, centralizing instead *The History of Sexuality* through a focus on the critique of psychoanalysis and the repressive hypothesis, implicitly and often explicitly delegating the study of race to the background. Rey Chow notes the general failure of scholars to read sexuality through biopower as symptomatic of modernist inclinations toward a narrow homosexual/heterosexual identitarian binary frame that favors "sexual intercourse, sex acts, and erotics" over "the entire problematic of the reproduction of human life that is, in modern times, always racially and ethnically inflected."[90] I would add to this observation that the rise of the centrality of *The History of Sexuality* in queer studies has been predominantly due to interest in Foucault's disentanglement of the workings of the "repressive hypothesis" and his implicit challenge to Freudian psychoanalytic narratives that foreground sexual repression as the foundation of subjectivity. (In other words, we can trace the genealogic engagements of *The History of Sexuality* as a splitting: scholars of race and postcoloniality taking up biopolitics, while queer scholars work with dismantling the repressive hypothesis. These are tendencies, not absolutes.)[91] It is also the case, however, that scholars of race and postcoloniality, despite studying the intersections of race and sexuality, have only recently taken up questions of sexuality beyond the reproductive function of heterosexuality.[92] While Chow's assessment of western proclivities toward myopic renditions of sexuality is persuasive, the relegation of the sexual purely to the realm of (heterosexual) reproduction seems ultimately unsatisfactory. In the case of Chow's project, it allows her to omit any consideration of the heteronorms that insistently sculpt the parameters of acceptable ethics. Moreover, nonnormative sexualities are rarely centered in efforts elaborating the workings of biopolitics, elided or deemed irrelevant despite the demarcation of perversion and deviance that is a key component of the very establishment of norms that drive biopolitical interests.[93]

Many accounts of contemporary biopolitics thus foreground either race and state racism or, as Judith Butler does, the ramification of the emergence of the category of "sex," but rarely the two together.[94] In this endeavor I examine the process of disaggregating exceptional queer subjects from queer racialized populations in contemporary U.S. politics rather than proffer an overarching paradigm of biopolitical sexuality that resolves these dilemmas. By centering race and sexuality simultaneously in the reproduction of relations of living and dying, I want to keep taut the tension between biopolitics and necropolitics. The latter makes its presence known at the limits and through the excess of the former; the former masks the multiplicity of its relationships to death and killing in order to enable the proliferation of the latter. The distinction and its attendant tensions matter for two reasons. First, holding the two concepts together suggests a need to also attend to the multiple spaces of the deflection of death, whether it be in the service of the optimization of life or the mechanism by which sheer death is minimized. This bio-necro collaboration conceptually acknowledges biopower's direct activity in death, while remaining bound to the optimization of life, and necropolitics' nonchalance toward death even as it seeks out killing as a primary aim. Following Mbembe, who argues that necropolitics entails the increasingly anatomic, sensorial, and tactile subjugation of bodies—whether those of the detainees at Guantánamo Bay or the human waste of refugees, evacuees, the living dead, the dead living, the decaying living, those living slow deaths—it moves beyond identitarian and visibility frames of queerness to address questions of ontology and affect.[95]

Second, it is precisely within the interstices of life and death that we find the differences between queer subjects who are being folded (back) into life and the racialized queernesses that emerge through the naming of populations, thus fueling the oscillation between the disciplining of subjects and the control of populations. Accountable to an array of deflected and deferred deaths, to detritus and decay, this deconstruction of the poles of bio- and necropolitics also foregrounds regeneration in relation to reproduction. We can complicate, for instance, the centrality of biopolitical reproductive biologism by expanding the terrain of who reproduces and what is reproduced, dislodging the always already implicit heterosexual frame, interrogating how the production of identity categories such as gay, lesbian, and even queer work in the service of the management, reproduction, and regeneration of life rather than being predominantly understood as implicitly or explicitly targeted for death. Pressing Butler on her focus on how queers have been left to die, it is time to ask: How do queers reproduce life, and Which queers are folded into life? How do they give life? To what do they give life? How is life weighted, disciplined into subjecthood, narrated into population, and fostered for living? Does this securitization of queers entail deferred death or dying for others, and if so, for whom?

People often say that modern society has attempted to reduce sexuality to the couple—the heterosexual and, insofar as possible, legitimate couple. There are equal grounds for saying that it has, if not created, at least outfitted and made to proliferate, groups with multiple elements and a circulating sexuality: a distribution of points of power, hierarchized and placed opposite to one another; "pursued" pleasures, that is, both sought after and searched out; compartmental sexualities that are tolerated or encouraged; *proximities that serve as surveillance procedures*, and function as mechanisms of intensification; contacts that operate as inductors.—Michel Foucault, *The History of Sexuality, Volume 1*, emphasis mine

The Empire Strikes Back . . . So you like skyscrapers, huh, bitch? —The legend on posters that appeared in midtown Manhattan only days after September 11, depicting a turbaned caricature of Osama bin Laden being anally penetrated by the Empire State Building

the sexuality of terrorism

There has been a curious and persistent absence of dialogue regarding sexuality in public debates about counterterrorism, despite its crucial presence in American patriotism, warmongering, and empire building. Without these discourses of sexuality (and their attendant anxieties)—heterosexuality, homosexuality, queerness, metrosexuality, alternative and insurgent sexuality—the twin mechanisms of normalization and banishment that distinguish the terrorist from the patriot would cease to properly behave. At this historical juncture, the invocation of the terrorist as a queer, nonnational, perversely racialized other has become part of the normative script of the U.S. war on terror. One need only reflect upon the eager proliferation of homophobic-racist images (reactivated from the 1991 Gulf War, the Israel-Palestine conflict, and eighteenth-, nineteenth-, and twentieth-century Orientalist histories) of terrorists since September 11, 2001. Take the case of Osama bin Laden, who was portrayed as monstrous by association with sexual and bodily perversity (versions of both homosexuality and hypertrophied heterosexuality, or failed monogamy, that is, an Orientalist version of polygamy, as well as disability) through images in popular culture (also the case with Saddam/Sodom Hussein).[1] Recall, as an example, a website where weapons are provided to sodomize Osama bin Laden to death. Or even spy novelist John le Carré's pronouncement in *The Nation* that Osama bin Laden's manner in his video was akin to a "man of narcissistic homoeroticism," which can provide Americans with hope as "his barely containable male vanity, his appetite for self-drama and his closet passion for the limelight . . . will be his downfall, seducing him into a final dramatic act of self-destruction, produced, directed, scripted and acted to death by Osama bin Laden himself."[2]

Sexual deviancy is linked to the process of discerning, othering, and quarantining terrorist bodies, but these racially and sexually perverse figures also labor in the service of disciplining and normalizing subjects worthy of rehabilitation *away from* these bodies, in other words, signaling and enforcing the mandatory terms of patriotism. In this double deployment, the emasculated terrorist is not merely an other, but also a barometer of ab/normality involved in disciplinary apparatuses. Leti Volpp suggests, "September 11 facilitated the consolidation of a new identity category that groups together persons who appear 'Middle Eastern, Arab, or Muslim.' This consolidation reflects a racialization wherein members of this group are identified as terrorists, and are dis-identified as citizens."[3] This disidentification is a process of sexualization as well as of a racialization of religion. But the terrorist figure is not merely racialized and sexualized; the body must appear improperly racialized (outside the norms of multiculturalism) and perversely sexualized in order to materialize as the terrorist in the first place. Thus the terrorist and the person to be domesticated—the patriot—are not distant, oppositional entities, but "close cousins."[4]

Through this binary-reinforcing "you're either with us or against us" normativizing apparatus, the war on terror has rehabilitated some—clearly not all or most—lesbians, gays, and queers to U.S. national citizenship within a spatial-temporal domain I am invoking as "homonationalism," short for "homonormative nationalism." Homonormativity has been theorized by Lisa Duggan as a "new neo-liberal sexual politics" that hinges upon "the possibility of a demobilized gay constituency and a privatized, depoliticized gay culture anchored in domesticity and consumption." Building on her critique of gay subjects embroiled in "a politics that does not contest dominant heteronormative forms but upholds and sustains them,"[5] I am deploying the term homonationalism to mark arrangements of U.S. sexual exceptionalism explicitly in relation to the nation. Foucault notes that the legitimization of the modern couple is complicit with, rather than working against, the "outfitting" and proliferation of compartmental, circulating, and proximity-surveillance sexualities, pursued pleasures and contacts. We see simultaneously both the fortification of normative hetero-sexual coupling and the propagation of sexualities that mimic, parallel, contradict, or resist this normativity. These proliferating sexualities, and their explicit and implicit relationships to nationalism, complicate the di-chotomous implications of casting the nation as only supportive and pro-ductive of heteronormativity and always repressive and disallowing of homosexuality. I argue that the Orientalist invocation of the terrorist is one discursive tactic that disaggregates U.S. national gays and queers from racial and sexual others, foregrounding a collusion between homosexuality and American nationalism that is generated both by national rhetorics of patri-otic inclusion and by gay and queer subjects themselves: homonationalism. For contemporary forms of U.S. nationalism and patriotism, the production of gay and queer bodies is crucial to the deployment of nationalism, insofar as these perverse bodies reiterate heterosexuality as the norm but also because certain domesticated homosexual bodies provide ammunition to reinforce nationalist projects.

Mapping forms of U.S. homonationalism, vital accomplices to Oriental-ist terrorist others, instructively alludes to the "imaginative geographies" of the United States. Derek Gregory, reworking Edward Said's original fram-ing, describes these geographies as fabrications, "combin[ing] 'something fictionalized' and 'something made real' because they are imaginations given substance."[6] What I take from this definition is that certain desired truths become lived as truths, as if they were truths, thus producing mate-rial traces and evidences of these truths, despite what counterevidence may exist. In other words, Gregory argues, imaginative geographies are perfor-mative: they produce the effect that they name and describe. Importantly, imaginative geographies endeavor to reconcile otherwise irreconcilable truths; they are mechanisms of, in Freudian terms, disavowal. It is through imaginative geographies produced by homonationalisms, for example, that the contradictions inherent in the idealization of the United States as a properly multicultural heteronormative but nevertheless gay-friendly, tol-erant, and sexually liberated society can remain in tension. Despite the obvious unevenness of sexual and racial tolerance across varied U.S. spaces and topographies of identity, it nonetheless exists as a core belief system about liberal mores defined *within* and *through* the boundaries of the United States.

I begin with a survey of the multiple activations of anxious multicultural heteronormativity that surfaced after the attacks on the World Trade Center and the Pentagon, noting the fissures and disruptions where gay and queer discourses intervene. I then explore multiple sites and genealogies of homonationalism, focusing less on conservative LGBTIQ discourses, which, though horrifically xenophobic, are hardly surprising and have been well-documented. Instead, I foreground three less apparent lineages of homonationalism: the analyses of terrorist corporealities by feminist, queer, and other scholars; the consumer habits of the gay and lesbian tourism industry, which consciously defines itself as a progressive industry that seeks social change through the disruption of "straight space"; and the liberal multicultural discourses of tolerance and diversity portrayed in the cable television cartoon *South Park*. These three sites, enmeshed in vastly differing homonationalisms, suggest both the radical contingency of any nationalist homosexual formation and the potency of their potential consolidation; thus, they may craft new critical cartographies as much as they may reify hegemonic dominant terrains.

Hetero- and Homonationalisms

We're told to go on living our lives as usual, because to do otherwise is to let the terrorists win, and really, what would upset the Taliban more than a gay woman wearing a suit in front of a room full of Jews?
—Ellen DeGeneres, hosting the 2001 Emmy Awards, twice postponed, on November 4, 2001; cited in Besen, "A True American Hero"

Heteronormativity is, as it always has been, indispensable to the promotion of an aggressive militarist, masculinist, race- and class-specific nationalism. In the United States, the aftermath of September 11 entailed the daily bombardment of reactivated and reverberating white (*and multicultural*, in cases where people of color and certain immigrant groups are properly patriotic, or serve symbolic or material needs, for example, Condoleezza Rice, the U.S. military) heteronormative imagery, expectations, and hegemonies. From the images of grieving white widows of corporate executives to the concern about white firemen leaving their families to console widows of former coworkers to the consolidation of national families petitioning for bereavement funds to more recent images of broken military homes, the preservation of white American heteronormative families has been at stake. But events such as the National Day of Mourning (where multicultural families gathered together to grieve national loss), the work of numerous national advocacy groups for Arab, Muslim, and Sikh Americans who presented their communities as established by upright, *proper* citizens, and the ubiquitous appearance of American flags in immigrant communities, indicate the extent to which normative multiculturalism helped actively produce this renewed nationalism. The narration of sexual practices after the attacks iterated September 11 as a trauma of national sexual violation, proffering predictions as well as advice about "terror sex." Worried that the "nation's sexual health could spiral," Judy Kuriansky and other sex therapists discouraged "maladaptive" behavior, that is, sex outside of primary, intimate relationships, insinuating that nonmonogamous and other nonnormative sexual scenarios were not helping or were disrupting the nation's healing process.[7] Conservative Christian right-wingers such as Jerry Falwell and Pat Robertson predictably blamed abortionists, feminists, and gays and lesbians for the attacks, while George W. Bush used them as yet another alibi for his pro-family agenda through federal programs to fund research and education on "healthy marriages."[8] Same-sex surviving partners petitioning for bereavement funds were initially subjected to plans to have the families of deceased partners account for and validate their relationship, infuriating many LGBTIQ advocates.[9] Additionally, gay and bisexual men continued to be broadly excluded from donating blood.[10]

However, even as patriotism immediately after September 11 was inextricably tied to a reinvigoration of heterosexual norms for Americans, progressive sexuality was championed as a hallmark of U.S. modernity. For despite this reentrenchment of heteronormativity, the United States was also portrayed as "feminist" in relation to the Taliban's treatment of Afghani women (a concern that had been previously of no interest to U.S. foreign policy) and gay-safe in comparison to the Middle East.[11] While Americans lauded "gay heroes" such as Mark Bingham, who attempted to divert one of the hijacked planes, and Father Mychal Judge, a gay New York Fire Department chaplain who perished in 1 World Trade Center, the *New York Times* published obituaries of gay and lesbian victims focusing on their bereaved partners and commemorating their long-term relationships.[12] For a brief moment there was talk of a retraction or suspension of the "Don't Ask, Don't Tell" policy in the face of the need for greater recruitment.[13] (The exercising of this policy has resulted in the dismissal of at least twenty-two gay or lesbian military linguists specializing in Arabic, Korean,

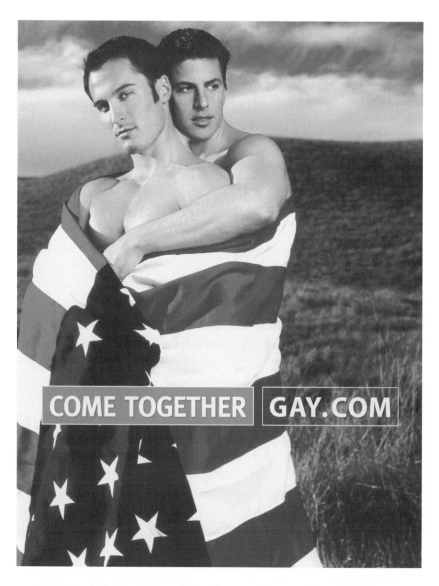

FIGURE 4. *Embody* (from Gay.com's "Come Together" advertising campaign).
©2006. PlanetOut Inc. All rights reserved. Produced by PlanetOut Creative Services
Group; Christy Shaefer, Creative Director.

and Farsi. The Pentagon's latest statistics show that the number of discharges since September 11, 2001, have declined by half and are at their lowest level from the time the figures were first tallied in 1997.)[14]

Paralleling an uneasy yet urgent folding in of homosexuality into the "us" of the "us-versus-them" nationalist rhetoric, LGBTIQ constituencies took up the patriotic call in various modalities.[15] Gay conservatives such as Andrew Sullivan came out in favor of bombing Afghanistan and advocated "gender patriotism": butching up and femme-ing down to perform the virility of the American nation,[16] a political posture implying that emasculation is unseemly and unpatriotic. The American flag appeared everywhere in gay spaces, in gay bars and gay gyms, and gay pride parades became loaded with national performatives and symbolism: the pledge of allegiance, the singing of the national anthem, and floats dedicated to national unity.[17] (As with the case of communities of color, these flags and other patriotic symbolism may function as both defensive and normalizing gestures.) Many gays and queers identified with the national populous as "victims of terrorism" by naming gay and queer bashing a form of terrorism;[18] some claimed it was imperative to support the war on terror in order to "liberate" homosexuals in the Middle East. Mubarak Dahir angrily challenges this justification of the war and calls on gays and lesbians who support the war in Iraq to "stop using the guise of caring about the plight of gay Arabs to rationalize their support."[19] National LGBTIQ organizations such as the National Gay and Lesbian Task Force (NGLTF) and the Human Rights Campaign had little political reaction to the invasion of Afghanistan (and subsequently have been more preoccupied with gay marriage campaigns and gays in the military than the occupation of Iraq).[20] One exception was the protest of homophobic graffiti on an army missile, "High Jack This Fags," by the Gay and Lesbian Alliance against Defamation (GLAAD). Their press release quotes Executive Director Joan M. Garry: "If U.S. military property had been defaced with a racial, ethnic or religious slur against any other group— including against the targeted terrorists—I doubt the Associated Press would have found such a photo acceptable for publication."[21] Interesting in this passage is that the epithet "fags" is de-linked from any racist connotations, comprehended only as a homophobic slur; the "targeted terrorists" are naturalized as the appropriate mark for this missile, thus implying support for the invasion of Afghanistan. Presumably, the word "fags" refers to the Afghanis, a racist epithet that GLAAD did not question.

Opposition to the war from various queer quarters also took bizarre forms. The decrease of funding for HIV/AIDS research was proffered as one rationale not to go to war.[22] An even more egregious example is the equating of victims of homophobia with victims of the Iraq invasion; note, for example, the statement released by the Metropolitan Community Church:

> We call upon all people of faith and people of goodwill everywhere, especially our sisters and brothers in the lesbian, gay, bisexual and transgender communities who know first hand what it means to be vilified, labeled and violently attacked, and who also know how difficult it is to survive under such circumstances, to join with the friends and members of Metropolitan Community Churches to oppose any further acts of aggression against Iraq.[23]

Positive exceptions to these homonationalist discussions came from Al-Fatiha, the international Muslim LGBTIQ association, and the Audre Lorde Project, an LGBTQ of color community-based organization in Brooklyn; both issued statements condemning the attacks and hate crimes and opposing retaliatory measures against Afghanistan.[24] The Audre Lorde Project created a nationwide coalition of antiwar LGBTIQ groups, as did Queers for Peace and Justice.[25] Many queer of color groups, mostly located in major urban locales, reported that immediately after the events of September 11, 2001, their lines of solidarity fell toward their respective nonqueer mainstream racial and immigrant advocacy groups rather than with mainstream queer organizations.[26] Additionally, Surina Khan (a Pakistani Muslim), then the director of the International Gay and Lesbian Human Rights Commission, stated that IGLHRC took a "clear position against the bombing of Afghanistan." Citing the Cairo-52 (raids against homosexuals in Cairo in May 2001) as casualties of the war on terrorism, Khan noted that the United States had already begun to relax pressure on other countries committing human rights abuses. She and IGLHRC have received heavy criticism for their antiwar statement.[27]

Unwittingly enacting this split between queers of color and white and mainstream queers, the *Village Voice* executive editor and journalist Richard Goldstein claimed that there had been a transference of national stigma from one group, queers, to another, Arabs. In relegating the queer and the Arab to mutually exclusive realms, Goldstein articulates a primary facet of homonationalism: that of the whiteness of gay, homosexual, and queer bodies, and the attendant presumed heterosexuality of colored bodies. While this cleaving of race and sexuality resonates historically, the legal theorist Muneer Ahmad explains why such transference of stigma appears acceptable:

FIGURE 5. American flag at Chicago's gay pride parade, 2005.
Photograph by Sara Antunovich. Reprinted with the artist's permission.

The killings of people like James Byrd and Matthew Shepard were deemed incomprehensible. In contrast, the killing of Balbir Singh Sodhi, Waqar Hasan, and
others, while deplored as wrong, have been understood as the result of displaced
anger, that underlying anger being one with which the vast majority of Americans sympathize and agree. The perpetrators of these crimes, then, were guilty
not of malicious intent, but of expressing a socially appropriate emotion in
socially inappropriate ways. To borrow from criminal law, the hate killings before September 11 were viewed as crimes of moral depravity, while the hate
killings since September 11 have been understood as crimes of passion.[28]

Hate crimes against gays and lesbians are still rationalized through these
very same terms: is not the expression of "a socially appropriate emotion in
socially inappropriate ways" the crux of the "gay panic" defense? Historical
amnesia prevails. In the sway from crimes of moral depravity to crimes of
passion, Ahmad argues, it is not only that the targets of attack have altered,

but that the entire mechanism of scapegoating is now rife with sentiment that is attached to the gendered, sexualized, and racial codings of these bodies. It is notable that white, middle- to upper-class, kind-and-gentle college student Matthew Shepard became the quintessential poster boy for the U.S.-based LGBTIQ antiviolence movement, one that has spawned a stage production (*The Laramie Project*) among other consumables.[29] Indeed, exemplary of this transference of stigma, positive attributes were attached to Mark Bingham's homosexuality: butch, masculine, rugby player, white, American, hero, gay patriot, called his mom (i.e., homonational), while negative connotations of homosexuality were used to racialize and sexualize Osama bin Laden: feminized, stateless, dark, perverse, pedophilic, disowned by family (i.e., fag).[30] What is at stake here is not only that one is good and the other evil; the homosexuality of Bingham is converted into acceptable patriot values, while the evilness of bin Laden is more fully and efficaciously rendered through associations with sexual excess, failed masculinity (i.e., femininity), and faggotry.

While I have briefly highlighted the most egregious examples of the collusions between homosexuality and U.S. nationalism—gay conservatives such as Andrew Sullivan being the easiest and prime target—I am actually more compelled by progressive and liberal discourses of LGBTIQ identity and how they might unwittingly use, rely upon, or reinscribe U.S. nationalisms, U.S. sexual exceptionalisms, and homonormative imaginative geographies. The proliferation of queer caricatures in the media and popular culture (such as *Queer Eye for the Straight Guy* and, more recently, *Queer Eye for the Straight Girl*), the Massachusetts Supreme Court ruling upholding same-sex marriage (2004), and the overturning of sodomy regulations through the *Lawrence and Garner v. Texas* ruling (2003) all function as directives regarding suitable and acceptable kinship, affiliative, and consumption patterns, consolidating a deracialized queer liberal constituency that makes it less easy to draw delineations between assimilated gay or lesbian identities and ever-so-vigilant and -resistant queer identities. Even the acronym LGBTIQ suggests the collapsing into or the analogizing of multiple identity strands. In homonormative narratives of nation, there is a dual movement: U.S. patriotism momentarily sanctions some homosexualities, often through gendered, racial, and class sanitizing, in order to produce "monster-terrorist-fags"; homosexuals embrace the us-versus-them rhetoric of U.S. patriotism and thus align themselves with this racist and homophobic production.[31] Aspects of homosexuality have come within the purview of normative patriotism, incorporating aspects of queer subjectivity into the body of the normalized nation; on the other hand, terrorists are quarantined through equating them with the bodies and practices of failed heterosexuality, emasculation, and queered others. This dual process of incorporation and quarantining involves the articulation of race with nation. Nation, and its associations with modernity and racial and class hierarchies, becomes the defining factor in disaggregating between upright, domesticatable queernesses that mimic and recenter liberal subjecthood, and out-of-control, untetherable queernesses.

Queer theory has contributed to the analysis of the heteronormative constructions of nation as well as of citizenship. M. Jacqui Alexander claims that the "nation disallows queerness"; V. Spike Peterson locates "nationalism as heterosexism"; Lauren Berlant and Michael Warner have elaborated upon "national heterosexuality."[32] But heteronormative penetration paradigms continue to inform feminist and progressive theorizing of globalization conquest and war—the land is female and virgin territory, the invader masculine—epitomized by heterosexual rape as the ultimate violation of the nation through its emasculating force, a normative colonial genealogy. As Frantz Fanon's work symptomatizes so well, the concern about heterosexual rape functions doubly: it attends, importantly, to violence against women, but it also forcefully masks triangulated desire, whereby the fear—and fantasy—of the penetrated male is displaced onto the safer figure of the raped female. Thus rape itself, as a weapon of war or as a metaphor for economic exploitation, is emptied of its might without this suturing of heteronormative ideologies and homoerotically charged audiences. In the persuasive rethinking of the discursive and hermeneutic qualities of capitalism by J. K. Gibson-Graham (pseudonym for Julie Graham and Katherine Gibson), rape as a metaphor of the penetration of globalization is differently articulated. This is a noteworthy poststructuralist feminist intervention seeking to denaturalize Marxist economic theories. By asking how globalization might "lose its erection," Gibson-Graham seek to overturn the "phallocentric heterosexism (in which the act of penetration, whether called rape or intercourse, defines sexual difference)" of this story of capitalism: "The globalization script normalizes an act of non-reciprocal penetration. Capitalist social and economic relations are scripted as penetrating 'other' social and economic relations but not vice versa. (The penis can penetrate or invade a woman's body, but a woman cannot imprint, invade, or penetrate a man.)"[33]

Following Sharon Marcus's work on the rape script, Gibson-Graham suggest a two-pronged deconstructive approach: diminish the power of the perpetrator by refusing the victim role and challenge discourses of sexuality within which such scripts garner their potency. While Gibson-Graham dismantle to some extent the coherency of male bodies "as hard, thrusting and powerful," as well as scramble the market-commodity-capital trajectory of capitalism, they are less successful in their attempt to destabilize the sex-gender-sexuality triad that secures heteronormativity. A reversal of positions is conceded and masculine-masculine penetration acknowledged, but feminine-feminine penetration (fists, fingers, dildos, to name but a few projectiles) appears unfathomable. Furthermore, a lack of engagement with postcolonial theory leaves racial dynamics unexplored (for, as Fanon reveals, the subordinate position of the feminine is always perversely racialized). In short, the act of penetration itself is categorically naturalized, not only as part of a heterosexuality that, through the intent to destabilize it, is cast as the same everywhere regardless of geopolitical locale. Left undeconstructed, the penetration narrative reproduces racial subordination as inevitable within a natural ordering, precisely the qualifications of the rape script that Gibson-Graham seek to dislodge. They mess around with gender, but at the expense of race, which must remain transparent and stable, a hallmark of much feminist Marxist scholarship. Thus the script is mainly inverted, not subverted. The reliance on binaried positionalities lingers;[34] even analyses that do center sexuality tend to be restricted by their articulation of whiteness as a queer norm.

In a similar vein, Shane Phelan's book *Sexual Strangers* argues that "lesbians, gays, bisexuals, and transgendered people in the United States are strangers," defined as "neither us nor clearly them, not friend and not enemy, but a figure of ambivalence who troubles the border between us and them. The enemy is the clear opposite of the citizen, but the stranger is more fraught with anxiety."[35] Yet it is certainly the case that within a national as well as a transnational frame, some queers are better than others. While this body of work collectively underscores heteronormativity as a prerequisite for both legal and cultural citizenship, some of it also fails to theorize the class-, race-, and gender-specific dimensions of this heteronormativity; heteronormativity is held as temporally and spatially stable, uninflected, and transparent. An uninterrogated positioning of white racial privilege and a single, rather than intersectional, axis of identity is assumed. There are indeed multiple figures of ambivalence, many strangers who trouble and destabilize the nation's boundaries, suggesting a more complex imaginative geography of the United States than is envisioned with the notion of lesbians and gays as the quintessential strangers of the nation.

While queering the nation has impelled politically salient dialogue regarding reproduction of racial and national lineages and norms, nationalizing queerness has primarily served to reiterate discourses of American sexual exceptionalism. As nationhood and queerness are both indebted to modernity, and modern sexual identities are built on the histories of colonialism, nation formation and empire, and racialization, the nation is founded on the (homo)sexual other. As mentioned earlier, Fanon's corpus of work is luminously suggestive of the homosexual fantasies and fears that found nationalism, whereby his anxieties about interracial heterosexual relations filter out homoerotic charges and antagonisms between colonized and colonizing men (and by inference, colonized and colonizing women).[36] The figures of the raped colonized woman and the lynched black colonized man and even the conquered (by the black man) white woman work to deflect the gaze away from other, less tolerable figures and subsequent lines of affinity, such as the penetrated (raped?) male and the woman-desiring female. Thus one could argue that homosexual desires, and their redirection, are foundational to the project of nationalism, as is the strict policing of the homo-hetero binary, and nations are heteronormative because of, rather than despite, homosexuality.

Thus, my interest in theorizing U.S. national homosexuality, or homonationalism, is to map out the intersections, confluences, and divergences between homosexuality and the nation, national identity, and nationalism —the convivial, rather than antagonistic, relations between presumably nonnormative sexualities and the nation. If we follow V. Spike Peterson's theorization of nationalism as heterosexism, in which she situates the nation not only as familial, but also as fraternal, we see that the fraternal nation-state is organized to promote political homosocial relations among men in order to discourage and prohibit homosexual relations between men. While homosexuality is considered incompatible with serving in the military, it nevertheless is a prime example of "how heterosexist premises underpin hegemonic masculinity. As a site of celebrated homosocial bonding the military affords men a unique opportunity to experience intimacy and interdependence with men."[37] Debatable is her assertion of the sheer uniqueness of this opportunity, given the preponderance of fraternities, sports teams and events, male-only clubs, firehouses, the upper echelons of corporate spaces, and so on. This is an outdated description of the U.S. military given the large proportion of men of color and of female recruits, especially women of color, building the American face of the diverse, progressive national normativity. Nonetheless, Peterson's trenchant point remains. If we are to take seriously the proposition that the nation is at once familial *and* fraternal, homosocial fraternal relations exist both to reiterate the centrality of the heteronormative family and to act as a stopgap preventative measure—a consolation for the prohibition of homosexual relations. To invert this trajectory, familial structures of the nation work both to consolidate heterosexuality as indispensable to national belonging and homosexuality as inimical to it. Heterosexuality works to secure the uninterrogated, unremarked upon access to homosocial spaces; through its prohibition of homosexuality, heterosexuality sanctions homosociality while naming and producing the disallowed homosexuality. Thus the (western) homosexual-heterosexual binary is a primary rather than secondary facet of the project of nationalism. Furthermore, theorizations of nationalism and sexuality need to attend to the multiplicity of the others of heteronormativity and, in turn, the multiple figures of the others of homonationalism. As Alexander has demonstrated, "Heterosexuality is at once necessary to the state's ability to constitute and imagine itself, while simultaneously marking a site of its own instability."[38] If, according to binaried sex-gender-desire logic, homosexuality is that which shadows the instability of the nation's heterosexuality, then that shadow itself is not constituted outside of nationhood, but rather within it, around it, hovering over it. Through the prescription of heteronormative stability, or security, the matter of the insecure becomes highlighted: the shadow that is within and outside, the internally disciplined and the externally quarantined and banished.

Returning to Foucault's sketch of flourishing sexualities as a "circulating sexuality: a distribution of points of power, hierarchized and placed opposite to one another," the shadow is imagined, felt, feared, desired, and in some instances, envisioned, to effectively function as a threat.[39] Queer bodies may be disallowed, yet there is room for the absorption and management of homosexuality—temporally, historically, and spatially specific—when advantageous for the nation. As homonormativity is one of a range of "compartmental sexualities that are tolerated or encouraged," this management is not consistent and is often directed only toward certain audiences. As a "proximity that serves as surveillance procedures," homonormativity is both disciplined by the nation and its heteronormative underpinnings and also effectively surveils and disciplines those sexually perverse bodies that fall outside its purview. Thus the nation not only allows for queer bodies, but also actually disciplines and normalizes them; in other words, the nation is not only heteronormative, but also homonormative. Reading nonnormative gay, homosexual, and queer bodies *through* the nation, not against it, is to acknowledge that (some) nations are productive of nonnormative sexualities, not merely repressive of them. There are at least three deployments of homonationalism that bolster the nation. First, it reiterates heterosexuality as the norm; for example, the bid for gay marriage accords an "equal but different" status (equal to the heterosexual norm of marriage for gay and queer monogamous relationships). Second, it fosters nationalist homosexual positionalities indebted to liberalism (through normative kinship forms as well as through consumption spheres that set up state/market dichotomies), which then police (through panopticon and profile) nonnationalist nonnormative sexualities. Third, it enables a transnational discourse of U.S. sexual exceptionalism vis-à-vis perversely racialized bodies of pathologized nationalities (both inside and outside U.S. borders), as the violence in Abu Ghraib (chapter 2) horrifically lays bare.

Genealogies of Terrorism

As our enemies exploit the benefits of our global environment to operate around the world, our approach must be global as well. When they run, we will follow. When they hide, we will find them. Some battlefields will be known, others unknown. The campaign ahead will be long and arduous. In this different kind of war, we cannot expect an easy or definitive end to the conflict.—White House, *National Strategy for Combating Terrorism*

One of the subtler trajectories of homonationalism emerges in critical scholarly commentary on the causal links between terrorism and subjectivity. These efforts, launched in part to redress the absence of gender and sexuality in analyses of terrorism and to disrupt dominant narratives about pathology and trauma, nonetheless reproduce some of the very assumptions they seek to dismantle. Government renditions of the causes of terrorism and the field of terrorism studies are highly dependent on such assumptions. For example, the *National Strategy for Combating Terrorism* lays out the U.S. blueprint for a global surveillance network headed by an international police and interrogation force trained and led by the United States. A list of terrorist attacks on the United States excludes the Oklahoma City bombing, relegating terrorism to the unknowable and inchoate nonwhite outside and evading the knowledge of an internal threat.[40] In this document the stated goal of U.S. policy is to "Return Terrorism to the 'Criminal Domain'" through a disciplining—"squeeze, tighten, and isolate" is the phrase used—of diffuse and global terrorist cells in order to "localize the threat," that is, to quarantine that which is ostensibly beyond the criminal domain (the perversion and pathology of the stateless, uncivilized, unrecognizable) into

the realm of the domestic space of the feminized, state-contained, ineffectual. The lexicon of contagion and disease suture the etymological and
political links of terrorist infiltration and invasion to queerness and the
AIDS virus. The two models of terrorism used by the State Department
vacillate between pyramid structure and network structure. The former
(also present as a terrorist structure, along with the "tapeworm metaphor,"
in the *Battle of Algiers*, viewed by the Pentagon in August 2003) represents a
known rational administrative format: phallic, and hence castratable. The
latter can be read as the monstrosity of perverse projectiles and chaotic
presences.[41] The yearning to castrate that which eludes castration is a potent prophylactic and, as such, hardly tangential. As a productive narrative,
it provides the justification for heightened surveillance, border control, and
interrogation mandates and sets the stage for the scapegoating and attack of
sexualized and racialized terrorist look-alikes.

The anxiety of managing rhizomic, cell-driven, nonnational, transnational terrorist networks that have no self-evident beginning or finite end
point is often sublimated (against the foil of the western liberal rational
subject) through the story of individual responsibility and individuated
pathology. In her attention to discursivity, Judith Butler notes that these
speculations about the terrorists' "personal pathology" are one of only a
few narrative options if one is to start the story prior to September 11, 2001.
Such stories are necessary because they displace other pre-9/11 stories of
U.S. foreign policy and global capital (for example, in relation to the rise of
the Taliban in Afghanistan). As Butler points out, "It works as a plausible
and engaging narrative in part because it resituates agency in terms of a
subject, something we can understand, something that accords with our
idea of personal responsibility, or with the theory of charismatic leadership
that was popularized with Mussolini and Hitler in World War II."[42] The
fully individuated psyche, one centered in conventional psychoanalytic theory and praxis, is without a context, history, or politics.

The counterpart to this obsessive pathologizing of the individual is the
deep narcissism implied in the query "Why do they hate us?" (the intonation of which usually implies something different: How *could* they hate
us?). Edward Said, tracing the shift from cold war to terrorist anxieties,
turns the psychoanalytic metanarrative gaze back upon the terrorized:

> Past and future bombing raids aside, the terrorism craze is dangerous because it
> consolidates the immense, unrestrained pseudopatriotic narcissism we are nour-
> ishing. Is there no limit to the folly that convinces large numbers of Americans

that it is now unsafe to travel, and at the same time blinds them to all the pain and violence that so many people in Africa, Asia, and Latin America must endure simply because we have decided that local oppressors, whom we call freedom fighters, can go on with their killing in the name of anticommunism and antiterrorism?[43]

Situating terrorism as a pseudo-patriotic narcissistic discourse provides an opportunity to examine what is at stake for the terrorist in this inversion. It is exactly this reversal that is enacted in the narrative of the United States as the victim of terrorism. Commenting on this deployment of "the culture industry of 'trauma' [which] leads to a mystification of history, politics, and cultural critique," the authors of a statement titled "Transnational Feminist Practices against War" write, "Signs of the current trauma discourse's ethnocentricity come through in media depictions staged within the therapeutic framework that tend to afford great meaning, significance, and sympathy to those who lost friends and family members in the attacks on the World Trade Center and the Pentagon. By contrast, people who have lost loved ones as a consequence of US foreign policy elsewhere are not depicted as sufferers of trauma or injustice."[44] However, it is not only that psychic distress is allowed to exist for those in the United States but not for others, but that the one narrative of trauma that does appear to apply to the terrorist—the deranged product of the failed (western) romance of the heteronormative nuclear family—stands nearly alone as the pathological force behind terrorism.

Such recitations of individual pathology plague the field of terrorism studies as well, and its accomplice, counterterrorism studies; both academic endeavors are fueled by private security trade corporations and "neoconservative Israeli or Washington think-tanks."[45] In September 1999, the Federal Research Division of the Library of Congress prepared a comprehensive manuscript, "The Sociology and Psychology of Terrorism: Who Becomes a Terrorist and Why?," to survey the literature on terrorism studies. In this policy document, causality is divided into five purportedly distinct approaches: political (driven by university environments, a "major recruiting ground for terrorists," where "Marxist-Leninist ideology or other revolutionary ideas" are learned); organizational (group versus individual leader dynamics); physiological (the media acts as a contagion factor in the stimulation of potential terrorists who "become aroused in a violence-accepting way by media presentations of terrorism"); psychological (the subdivisions of which include the frustration-aggression hypothesis, the negative identity hypothesis—"a vindictive rejection of the role regarded as desirable and proper by an individual's family and community," and the narcissistic rage hypothesis, mental illness induced by psychological damage during childhood); and finally, multicausal (a combination of the above).[46] The "terrorist mindset" is thus qualified by two standard theories: the terrorist as mentally ill, or the terrorist as fanatic—a "rational, logical, planning individual" ("this approach takes into account that terrorists are often well-educated and capable of sophisticated, albeit highly biased, rhetoric and political analysis").[47] Terrorist psychologists have developed certain models, which are described in the report: Eric Shaw's personal pathway model declares, "The underlying need to belong to a terrorist group is symptomatic of an incomplete or fragmented psychosocial identity" (25); Jerrold Post has developed the notion of "terrorist psycho-logic," which evacuates intentional choice from a terrorist's actions, stating that psychological forces drive the terrorist to violence (28). Overall, however, the report concedes, "There is considerable evidence . . . that international terrorists are generally quite sane," and "the careful, detailed planning and well-timed execution that have characterized many terrorist operations are hardly typical of mentally disturbed individuals" (30). Citing "Social Psychology of Terrorist Groups" by C. R. McCauley and M. E. Segal, who assert, "Terrorists do not show any striking psychopathology," the report concludes, "Terrorists are recruited from a population that describes most of us" (30–31). Terrorism expert Martha Crenshaw concurs, alleging, "The outstanding common characteristic of terrorists is their normality" (thus the concept of normality is not reassessed nor altered).[48] In making that statement, Crenshaw is also pointing to the details of the sociological terrorist composite or profile, which Robin Morgan also enumerates: 80 percent are male, average age between 22 and 25, unmarried, and more than two-thirds are from the middle to upper classes and have university training, if not an advanced degree.[49]

Despite the Federal Research Division's cautious evaluation of the most conservative elements of terrorism studies, the realm of the anti-U.S., anti-western imperialist political is nonetheless cast as misguided, irrational, and archaic, a mainstay of modernity's failures. Throughout the report, while political motivations for terrorist acts are alluded to, the urgency and import of the political critique is discounted or deemed inconsequential. The report regularly employs metonymic strings to uncivilized barbarism; terms and phrases such as *subjective interpretation, narrow lens, cultural, extreme end of a continuum, delusional and biased, moral imperatives*, and "distorting lens of their religious beliefs" (43), as well as statements like "their worldviews differ in critical ways from western worldviews" (43), are littered throughout. Although Osama bin Laden is hailed as "the prototype of a new breed of terrorist—the private entrepreneur who puts modern enterprise at the service of a global terrorist network" (6), religion—not politics, not economics—is figured as the reason behind terrorist activity. Religion is understood in these documents through the lens of liberal secularism as the antithesis to modernity and rationality. In a section entitled "New Types of Cold War Terrorists," the report argues for recognition of a shift in terrorist action:

> When the conventional terrorist groups and individuals of the early 1970's are compared with terrorists of the early 1990's, a trend can be seen: the emergence of religious fundamentalist and new religious groups espousing the rhetoric of mass-destruction terrorism. . . . These groups have a *different attitude towards violence*—one that is *extranormative* and seeks to maximize violence against the perceived enemy. . . . Their outlook is one that divides the world simplistically into "them" and "us." (6) (emphasis mine)

Religious belief is thus cast, in relation to other factors fueling terrorism, as the overflow, the final excess that impels monstrosity—the "different attitude towards violence" signaling these uncivilizable forces. Difference itself is pathological. In the liberal-secular imaginary, religion is also *always already* pathological. Later, the document highlights that the most dangerous terrorist is the Islamic fundamentalist, quoting Jerrold M. Post, who claims that "the most dangerous terrorist is likely to be the religious terrorist": "Unlike the average political or social terrorist, who has a defined mission that is somewhat measurable in terms of media attention or government reaction, the religious terrorist can justify the most heinous acts 'in the name of Allah,' for example."[50] Apparently, a critique of western neo-imperialist economic domination or U.S. foreign policy or Christian and Jewish fundamentalisms and hegemonies does not constitute a legitimate raison d'être for political or social terrorism, nor does the establishment and observation of religion itself qualify as a mode of political or social criticism, dissent, or resistance. Ironically, the secular model that purports to protect politics from religion functions in this case to efface this very realm. Furthermore, the entrenchment of Islamophobia in terrorism studies is structural as well as ideological; as Kevin Toolis observes, "Israel . . . remains the model of the counter-terrorist state. Almost all western counter-terrorist academic centers are closely linked to Israeli institutions such as the International Policy Institute for Counter Terrorism."[51] Note that this assessment of Islam is easily rendered through the blatant omission in this report of "right-wing terrorists": "A fifth typology [the others are nationalist-separatist, religious fundamentalist, new religious, and social revolutionary], for right-wing terrorists, is not listed because right-wing terrorists were not specifically designated as being a subject of this study. In any case, there does not appear to be any significant right-wing group on the U.S. Department of State's list of foreign terrorist organizations" (15). That is to say, the only terrorists not examined in this document are white supremacists and Christian fundamentalists such as Timothy McVeigh and Matt Hale and their organizations; in absentia they are sanctioned and rendered on par with other uncommented upon variables such as the state terrorisms of Israel and the United States. Toolis notes, "Counter-terrorism remains a study by the state, in the form of selected academics and a few police and military figures, of the enemies of the states. The objects of study—'terrorists' or their political representatives . . . are never invited to contribute."[52]

These proclivities do not lie within terrorism studies alone. Remarking on the "interesting overlap between pronouncements by career militarists and reductive analyses by pseudo-scientists," Robin Morgan argues, "The 'terrorist psychology' concept is a convenient way of evading complexities, including political ones. Some of its advocates have solemnly announced that terrorists are created by 'inadequate or absent mothering' that has resulted in depression, hypochondria, dysphoria, and destructiveness. When in doubt, blame mothers." Critical of terrorism studies experts like Jerrold Post, who favor the western heteronormative nuclear family structure as they zero in on psychic childhood dysfunction, Morgan's attempts at theorizing the relationships between patriarchy and violence, though perhaps feminist in intent, also have reductive tendencies. Her analysis of patriarchy as the backbone of terrorism, in typical radical feminist fashion, suggests that terrorism functions as sex, what she terms "ejaculatory politics."[53] Unsurprisingly, she borders on advocating lesbianism and a women-centered world as the antidote to terrorism.

Claiming that "it is in the crucible of all-male intensity that the bonds of terrorist commitment and self-denial are formed," anthropologist Lionel Tiger offers up the conventional and overstated male-bonding thesis:

> The terrorism of Bin Laden harnesses the chaos of young men, uniting the energies of political ardor and sex in a turbulent fuel. The structure of al-Qaida—an all-male enterprise, of course—appears to involve small groups of relatively young men who maintain strong bonds with each other, bonds whose intensity is dramatized and heightened by the secrecy demanded by their missions and the danger of their projects.[54]

Tiger foregrounds the prominence of gender-segregated spaces and polygamy in Muslim communities, arguing that these are the fodder for the same-sex intimacy necessary for the intensity of terrorist bonding. Later, however, he avers that bin Laden's troops "have no choice but to accustom themselves to relatively monastic lives," at once overlooking the possibility of same-sex liaisons while also rendering any homosociality, indeed homosexuality, as mere defaults due to the apparent impossibility of approximating fulfilling heterosexual relations. According to Joseph Massad, this is a common Orientalist discourse propagated by what he dubs the "Gay International": gay and lesbian liberationist and missionary NGOs, supplemented by purportedly queer anthropological and ethnographic accounts of Arab male same-sex sexuality.[55] Perhaps the most damning aspect of Tiger's psychological analysis is its foreclosure of any kind of political, economic, or material critique immanent to terrorist motivations. A final quote: "The danger of belonging to [bin Laden's troops] enhances their excitement and feeds their sense of worthwhile enterprise. Their comrades provide them an emotional haven and a clear focus for the turbulent energies at the intersection of youth and despair. Their basic weapons are intensity and extreme commitment, not the usual visible armament of warriors."[56] Tiger's focus on the erotic rush colludes with an insinuation floating about in conservative discourses that the legalization of homosexuality in Arab countries would delimit the recruitment of isolated young men into terrorist organizations. The emotive affect of Tiger's piece, presumably intended to stress the psychic and mental desperation of the young men he writes about, serves only to further mock the possibility of politically motivated (rather than emotional, sexual, theological, irrational, or moral—all excessive and feminized attributes within Tiger's explanatory devices) dissent.[57]

Zillah Eisenstein reminds us that while narratives of the Taliban's problematic womenless world abounded, no such failure was ascribed to the "very manly moment" of the post-9/11 white world of rugged firefighters, policemen, ground zero workers, and corporate suits. The point is well taken, but Eisenstein goes on to quote Ahmed Rashid writing on the Taliban, who says that "most of these men grew up in refugee camps without the love or camaraderie of mothers or sisters."[58] Here we see the over-reliance on a type of heteronormative psychoanalytic explanatory framework of patriarchy that evacuates politics, global capital, even poverty from the range of potential origin narratives. In an inverse move, Ros Petchesky also claims that the normality of patriarchy is what terrorist networks and the global capitalism of the United States have in common.[59] One claims abnormality, the other normality; both of these ahistorical and aspatial explanations portend amnesia of the presence of same-sex, gender-segregated realms and cogendered arenas of domestic and public life in the many varied Middle Eastern, Muslim, and Arab contexts.

The sociologist Michael Kimmel also argues that normative gender regimes contribute to the humiliation of damaged psyches: "What is relevant is not the possible fact of . . . [Mohamed] Atta's gayness, but the shame and fear that surround homosexuality in societies that refuse to acknowledge sexual diversity"—ironic, given that (indeed) the United States is such a society.[60] Claiming that, for the Taliban, terrorism offers the "restoration of their masculinity," Kimmel focuses on class: "Central to their political ideology is the recovery of manhood from the emasculating politics of globalization and the westernization of Afghanistan as humiliations." While Kimmel's emphasis on processes of gendering rather than sexual object choice is laudable, he conjures globalization as an overwhelming and overarching force that depletes all resistance, with the distinguished exception of retribution: "The terrors of emasculation experienced by lower-middle-class men all over the world will no doubt continue, as they struggle to make a place for themselves in shrinking economies and inevitably shifting cultures. They may continue to feel a seething resentment against women, whom they perceive as stealing their rightful place at the head of the table, and against the governments that displace them."[61]

Comparing the Taliban to white supremacists in the United States and Mohammed Atta to Timothy McVeigh, Kimmel universalizes the plight of emasculated manhood through essentializing a global heteromasculine identity and presuming the global hegemony of a normative sex-gender-desire triad, not to mention a crude Marxist version of class affinity. Once again, there is a misreading of gender in Afghanistan as strictly heteronormative, as distinct from a mixture of homosocial and heterosocial milieus. Massad argues, "Efforts to impose a European heterosexual regime on Arab men have succeeded only among the upper classes and the increasingly Westernized middle-classes."[62] The question that must be posed before such comparisons can be proffered is this: What constitutes normative gender regimes in Arab contexts? (This, of course, does not even begin to attend to Atta's time in Germany, nor his upbringing in Cairo.) Furthermore, naming fiasco after fiasco of Hitler's, Atta's, and McVeigh's—"all three failed at their chosen profession"—Kimmel's analysis insinuates that the inability of entitled men to assimilate themselves into the downwardly mobile economic rescaling of globalization is somehow a malfunction of personal character, thus mirroring the "negative identity hypothesis" of psychological terrorist profiles. Citing Arlie Hochschild on the "global masculinity crisis," this depiction of globalization is also proffered by Barbara Ehrenreich, who otherwise rightly suggests that the linkages among misogyny, masculinity, and terrorism need further probing.[63] But like Eisenstein's, Ehrenreich's assessment that gender-segregated spaces are the product of Islamic fundamentalist misogyny (veiling is usually cited as the most egregious example of oppression by liberal feminists) ignores decades (centuries even, per Fatima Mernissi's work) of Muslim feminist work arguing the contrary.[64] As Saba Mahmood argues, this myopia is due to the inability of secular liberal feminism to conceptualize the agency of religious women unless it appears as resistance to the nonsecular.[65] A final example of this feminist propensity should suffice: "Long-term warriors have a tendency to see women as a corrupting and debilitating force. Hence, perhaps, the all-male *madrassas* in Pakistan, where boys as young as six are trained for jihad, far from the potentially softening influence of mothers and sisters. Or recall terrorist Mohamed Atta's specification, in his will, that no woman handle his corpse or approach his grave."[66]

Interestingly, and this is a point not attended to by those attempting to ascribe something specific to the Muslim terrorist, the discourses of gender shaming and humiliation are endemic to conceptualizations (and self-presentations) of right-wing terrorists as well. The terrorism expert Jessica Stern's research spans a range of terrorist organizations, from Muslim, Hindu, and Sikh to Jewish, Christian, and white supremacist neo-Nazi:

> While the terrorists I met described a variety of grievances, almost every one talked about humiliation. The Identity Christian cultist told me he suffered from chronic bronchitis as a child and his mother discouraged him from exerting himself. He had been forced to attend the girls' physical education classes because he couldn't keep up with the boys. "I don't know if I ever got over the shame and humiliation of not being able to keep up with the other boys—or even with some of the girls," he said. The first time he felt strong was when he was living on an armed compound, surrounded by armed men.
>
> A man involved in the violent wing of the anti-abortion movement told me he was "vaginally defeated," but now he is "free," by which he meant celibate and beyond the influence of women.[67]

In these supposedly politically progressive efforts, many of them feminist, to de-pathologize the individual in favor of contextualizing socialization and the social, the victim status of the (always male) terrorist is resuscitated, this time not through the failures of the dysfunctional nuclear family but rather through the inescapable brutalities of global capital and heteronormativity. What is gained through these narrative devices? To summarize, through the consideration of gender and sexuality, these explanatory frames and models serve to (1) resurrect feminist constructions of "patriarchy," which homogenize and universalize heteronormative and nuclear familial and sexual relations, inferring that heterosexuality is the same everywhere; (2) posit the causal foci of terrorism within either the individual or within an undifferentiated social; in both cases, the nonsecular victim or defect model prevails, evacuating and nullifying political critiques and insurgent nonstate forms of resistance; (3) foreclose a serious evaluation of female terrorists by positing a failed masculinity and an investment in patriarchy as compulsory for the growth of terrorism; women are posited as either victims of patriarchy or as emasculating forces vis-à-vis globalization, and sometimes both concomitantly; (4) swerve from, if not avoid altogether, the conundrum of translating gender across geopolitical locations, in particular through the erasure of histories of gender-segregated space and a misreading of homosociability as engendered chiefly through the failure to secure "proper" heterosexuality, thus lending to the production of U.S. sexual exceptionalism; (5) preempt a serious, complicated dialogue about homosexuality in Arab societies that acknowledges the historical and spatial complexities of gender-segregated realms as well as the uneven processes of queer globalization, again rendering homonormativity as an exclusively western affair; and (6) conquer the unknown resistant possibilities of political dissent by resorting to the banality of nomenclature and of a narrative structure, thus obfuscating critical thinking through these containment strategies.

These stories about the consequences and punishments of nonnormative gender and kinship formations—that is, what these western feminists and scholars ensconced in liberal secularism understand as nonnormative—function to circumvent the transnational framings and translations of circuitry and reference points to favor a singular, national, and even cultural frame of appropriate subjecthood. In doing so, these feminist accounts unwittingly dovetail with those of the most conservative terrorist experts in the field, who similarly ascribe myopic, monocausal, psychological, and affective explanations to the phenomenon of terrorist violence, thus privatizing and evacuating the critiques of political economies that the terrorists themselves often articulate. But perhaps the most devastating insight meticulously avoided by all explanations regardless of source or intent is of "the terrorist imagination that (without our knowing it) dwells within us all." In "The Mind of Terrorism," Jean Baudrillard writes:

> In the end, it was they who did it but we who wished it. If we do not take this fact into account, the event loses all symbolic dimension; it becomes a purely arbitrary act, the murderous phantasmagoria of a few fanatics we need only repress. But we know well that such is not the case. Without our profound complicity the event would not have reverberated so forcefully, and in their strategic symbolism the terrorists knew they could count on this unconfessable complicity.[68]

Thus it is not through the rhetoric of externality, of difference—cultural, economic, political, religious, psychological, or otherwise—that terrorism must be evaluated; what is needed is a theory of proximity that allows at once for both specificity and interiority, the interiority of familiarity and complicity.[69]

Homonational Spending

Another specific genealogy of homonationalism can be discerned in the long-standing debate about the relations between gay and lesbian civil liberties and queer consumer recognition. Janet Jakobsen argues that through the nation's reinvestment of "family values," the apparent contradiction between value-free markets and the restrictive, repressive policies of the nation-state can be manipulated to the nation's benefit. (How does the nation benefit? Jakobsen says precisely through the way the family is then reintegrated "at a different level into the transnational economy."):

> The market may not care if individuals are gay in the way lawmakers apparently do, but the appeal to market-niche status as site of gay liberation seriously underestimates the intertwining of the value-free with values and of the market and the state. Even apparent conflicts may enact the intertwining of the two. For example, if lesbian and gay politics just turns to the market over and against the dominative values of the state, such efforts will produce the most limited of "benefits." If family values are simply the site of stability over against flexible capital, then, we would read, for example, the Defense of Marriage Act as a contestation between market and the state, with the state articulating values and the market acting in a value-free manner. Fair enough. But what this reading does not include is the intertwining of the two, the ways these values also work for capitalism, the ways even when incorporated into the state as resistances to "diversity" and "transnationalization" in the economic sector, family values can

operate to remake the nation as family that can work in the "new world order." Constructing the family as nation allows the state to be relatively autonomous from the nation in such a way as to work for corporations, and since corporations don't really care whether "gays" who are not of the type eligible for employment can get married or not, the contradiction is not in any way disabling to the management of diversity in both the workforce and the nation. . . . Conflicts between the state and the market, thus, need to be understood as structured by complicity.[70]

We thus do not have an opposition here between civil liberties for queers and the offerings of the marketplace. That is to say, we are not stuck between the conservative claim that market entry is reflective of social equality and the assimilationist accusations from queer left factions. Rather, the nation benefits from the liberalization of the market, which proffers placebo rights to queer consumers who are hailed by capitalism but not by state legislation. Therefore, the familial- and kinship-delineating heteronormativity of the nation and the "value-free" homonationalism of the market are convivial and complicitous rather than oppositional entities. For this reason, my genealogy of homonationalism embraces both the emphasis of queer liberalism on the queer subject before the law and the coterminous and, in some cases, preceding presence of queer consumer citizenship offered by the market.

An example of how the nation benefits by homonationalism can be found in the history of the gay and lesbian tourism industry. As national identity is being reoriented toward excellence in consumption rather than public civic political participation, gay tourists are representative of a form of U.S. exceptionalism expressed through patriotic consumption designed to recover the American nation's psychic and economic health. Constituting more than 10 percent of the overall U.S. travel industry, the multibillion-dollar gay and lesbian tourist sector is characterized by consumers with high discretionary income, better education, and fewer children (and hence more leisure time) and who travel to more international locations than other tourists (compared to a national average of 29 percent, 89 percent of gay and lesbian tourists hold passports).[71] Thomas Roth, director of Community Marketing, states that while gay and lesbian travelers constitute about 10 percent of the market in terms of actual numbers, it is more than 10 percent of the market monetarily speaking. (As a gay and lesbian marketing firm, Community Marketing has to date generated the most statistical and demographic information about the gay and lesbian tourism industry.)

About this interest in international travel, Roth insists, "If there's one statistic that says something about gay and lesbian tourists, that's the one."[72] Their 2001 survey confirms the high discretionary income of gay and lesbian tourists due to the absence of children and attendant financial responsibilities, claiming that this group is about 50 percent dual income with no kids. The report goes on to state that, compared to the national average, gay and lesbian travelers travel more frequently and further, spend more money per trip, and have revitalized a flagging cruise industry (20 percent took a cruise, compared to the national average of 2 percent).[73] As might be expected, the industry (private companies as well as national, regional, and city tourist bureaus) centralizes the white middle- to upper-class gender-normative gay male traveler as its ideal tourist.[74] Emergent trends include "giving back to the community," the expansion of lesbian-oriented tourism, and the materialization of the gay and lesbian family travel market. While the original political impetus of the gay and lesbian travel industry was the disruption and dismantling of heterosexual space so that innovative visions of gay and lesbian spaces could emerge, a new social and political agenda has emerged in the push to "give back" in the form of charitable contributions and volunteer services to the nonprofit social, political, and health organizations that have supported gay and lesbian communities. The booming lesbian transnational adoption market has spurred the growth of both the lesbian tourism and the gay and lesbian family tourism market; the circuitry of these adoption networks are likewise cohered and impelled through the gay and lesbian tourism industry.

In *Selling Out: The Lesbian and Gay Movement Goes to Market*, Alexandra Chasin writes, "Advertising to gay men and lesbians has played on ideas about national identity in two significant ways. First, such advertising has often appealed to gays on the basis of their identification as Americans. Second, advertising to gay men and lesbians has often promised that full inclusion in the national community of Americans is available through personal consumption." Chasin's astute analysis of the role of U.S. nationalism in the creation and maintenance of the gay and lesbian marketing demographic is especially relevant to current homonormative imaginative geographies. Noting that in the early decades of the twentieth century advertising in the United States was one vehicle for uniting white immigrant submarkets into a "single—and American, or at least Americanizable —mass," Chasin demonstrates that this historical precedent sets up the promise of American belonging through consumption for nonwhite ethnic immigrants and later, in the early 1990s, for gays and lesbians. Moreover, she argues that, since the 1970s, the increasing pressure to create "new classes of consumers" led to the demand for the "national" and the "niche" to coexist: "So at the same time that producers have needed national markets, they have also needed specialized markets, and it is in this context that 'diversity' has become both a social value (however superficially) and an economic imperative."[75] This history of Americanization through consumption practices, clearly tied to the rise of discourses of multiculturalism and diversity, foreshadows the mandate to mark forms of U.S. nationalism and patriotism in the context of the war on terror, a mandate that the gay and lesbian tourism industry fully embraced.

Terrorism has long been articulated as the foe of tourism, the former breeding intolerance and hatred, while the latter is constituted as a democratizing and liberalizing venture that embraces pluralism.[76] Immediately after the attacks, Robert Wilson, executive director of the International Gay and Lesbian Travel Association (IGLTA) wrote, "IGLTA headquarters has been rather quiet of late due to the current situation that's developed from the tragedy of September 11th. Members from as far away as Turkey and New Zealand are reporting a rather sharp decline in inquires and new business, with other members advising that they have received many cancellations." This assessment was quickly revised a month later; these cautionary missives were rapidly replaced by narratives of recovery that contrasted sharply with the overall assessments of the tourism industry at the time: "Two G & L travel surveys have recently been published and these too are reflecting real increases and that our community is in the forefront of 'business as usual' with travel plans and holiday reservations being maintained and the commitment to not allow the present climate to disrupt business travel or vacations." Already distinct from the broader tourism industry, claiming the greater affluence and greater mobility of its constituency as well as a political disruption of heteronormative travel practices and spaces, the gay and lesbian tourism industry niche market immediately began staging its defense against the general slowdown of travel after 9/11.[77] Two examples follow:

> What a rough time. Your friends at Community Marketing know that you/we are all hurting on many levels: emotional, spiritual and financial. Our best "therapy" is to move ahead, and not let these *outside interests* paralyze us for too long. I flew on an AA flight Thursday 9/20, and it was good to see more activity, more security, more confidence. (Community Marketing newsletter, October 2001, emphasis mine)

For most of us, travel = freedom and we value that right. (Community Marketing e-mail, October 2001)

In positing the events of September 11 as "outside interests," the gay and lesbian tourism industry sought to recuperate itself as distinct and exceptional. Therapeutic healing through consumption is proffered by further distancing itself from the broader tourism industry, as well as through a disavowal of any connection to the political ramifications of the attacks.[78] Encouragement of patriotic consumption allows participation in the national grieving psyche and allows for queer subjects to embrace as well as be embraced by the nation. Furthermore, the equation "travel = freedom" references both the notion that travel can function as an escape from heteronormativity and the promotion of U.S. exceptionalism regarding freedom and democracy. Claiming greater opportunities for travel for gay and lesbian consumers, advertising missives stated that unlike the "general public," gay and lesbian travelers planned to take no fewer vacations in the next twelve months as a result of the terrorist attacks. They also correctly predicted a record turnout for the annual International Gay and Lesbian World Travel Expo held in New York City in October 2001. In an e-mail circulated days after the attacks, Community Marketing stated, "While the mainstream travel industry is stagnating and trying to find a direction, research shows that gay and lesbian travelers plan no decrease in future vacations." According to an online survey of 446 gay and lesbian travelers conducted at the end of September 2001, 65 percent planned to take at least three vacations in the coming twelve months, nearly unchanged from the previous twelve months. Nine percent of domestic vacations and 10 percent of international vacations had been postponed as a result of the attacks and the economic downturn, but it was claimed that few gay and lesbian tourists had canceled their travel plans. Furthermore, the report revealed that among the motivations for choosing destinations, 50 percent cited "gay-friendly" locations, 42 percent "more affordable," and 29 percent "safer."

Similarly, in an editorial for *Passport Magazine* written in response to her research on the impact of the September 11 attacks on the gay and lesbian tourism industry, Reed Ide declared, "Gays and lesbians, in greater numbers than the population at large, will not be driven easily from the values and pleasures they hold dear."[79] Echoing this sentiment, Celso A. Thompson, president of IGLTA, stated in their November 2001 newsletter, "The terrorist attacks on 9-11 continue to have a devastating impact in the travel industry. Travel agents are losing 50 million dollars per day worldwide.

Economists predict a decrease of 1.8% in the American economy and no recovery until the fourth quarter of 2002. . . . The good news is that gay and lesbian travel is still a leading niche in the travel industry. Tour operators and specialized travel agents experience a different reality to the industry norm. The booking pace seems to be recovering."[80]

Notably, lesbian tourism overall was not a beneficiary of these statistical claims. Many lesbian tour operators reported significant booking losses in the wake of September 11 and the following months, reflecting divergent gendered relationships to mobility, space, place, and nation rarely commented on by industry frontrunners. Given the general lack of debate on race and racial diversity within the gay and lesbian travel industry, it is feasible to claim that the industry constructs itself as outside the effects of racial profiling and travel surveillance technologies. Therefore, these discourses of patriotic resilience work in tandem with an overt effacement of the racialized and gendered aspects of the gay and lesbian tourism industry (and the fact that many queers live with the threat of violence in the United States daily). Further, it is important to iterate, as M. V. Lee Badgett does, that such statistical profiles, also produced by the Simmons Marketing Research Bureau and Overlooked Opinions, not only misrepresent gays and lesbians as affluent, progeny-free consumers,[81] but historically they have also been used as ammunition for state and county antigay ballot initiative campaigns, often in rural locales (in Colorado, Oregon, Idaho, Maine, and Florida). Since the early 1990s "economic misinformation" has been used by the right wing to argue against "special rights" for gays and lesbians.[82] The rhetoric of touristic exceptionalism is thus reliant on an urban-rural dichotomy as well as demographics that then serve to further marginalize those the industry leaders would otherwise characterize as part of their community. Ironically, rural constituencies are a prime source of potential tourists wanting to travel to urban gay meccas.

What fuels this rhetoric of queer touristic exceptionalism? And what are the relationships between this exceptionalism and U.S. nationalism and patriotism? Chasin points to the compatibility of U.S. nationalism with a "kind of gay nationalism" through a shared discourse of "by our people and for our people," suggesting a "friendly and close, if not identical, relation between the gay community and U.S. national foundations . . . enact[ing] the convergence of market and state, reinforcing the equation between citizens and consumers."[83] In the case of gay and lesbian tourists, the purported demonstration of a commitment to mobility and travel signals far more than merely a set of consumption practices. It also highlights a commitment to U.S. nationalism and patriotism, responding to pleas to revive the psychic and economic health of the U.S. nation devastated by the terrorist attacks, and suggests a convergence of consumption and politics: you are what you buy, politically speaking. If you are not a terrorist, you are a patriot, as demonstrated by an excellence in consumption, and the act of consumption is a statement about one's political belief in the democratic machinery of the United States. Thus the exceptionalism presented in these narratives about gay and lesbian consumption contains not only the gay or lesbian consumer as a consumer par excellence, but also marks this homonational consumer as an American patriot par excellence. Homonationalism is sustained not only via privileged relations to capital, but also through replicating discourses of nationalism and its attendant fantasies of racial harmony and gender normativity. The homonational is mobilized against the immobile terrorist look-alike. Furthermore, the transnational circuits of capital entail that homonationalism circulates both through nationalism and beyond it. U.S. exceptionalisms may well be articulated by homonationalism globally, and homonationalism is increasingly immanent to some strands of U.S. exceptionalism, especially in the realms of consumption and human and sexual rights discourses.

South Park *and the Pakistani Leather Bottom*

I turn now to *South Park*, cable channel Comedy Central's popular cartoon show directed at adults and known for its dark celebration of perversity and excess.[84] Always ridiculing the contradictions of politically correct liberalism, the show's satirical storylines regularly produce social and political commentaries about contemporary race, gender, and class politics with a focus on that which is uncomfortable, uncanny, or shunned. While its audience is clearly international, as demonstrated by the variety of fans conversing about the show in chat rooms and on listservs, *South Park* is very much about the mockery of so-called American mores and values. However, I am interested in *South Park* not because of the size or location of its audience, nor because of its potential or perceived cultural impact. Rather, what intrigues me is the reflection of and continuities with critiques of the war on terror and the pathologization of terrorist bodies that is surfacing in popular culture. Thus *South Park* itself, as perhaps a minor cultural artifact, may appear superfluous, but the implications of its representational praxis and approaches are not. The trivial must be attended to precisely because marking it as such may mask or obfuscate its deeper cultural relevance.

South Park immediately took on the imbrications of nonnormative sexualities and perverse and pathological nationalities in the post-9/11 context. First aired on November 7, 2001, episode 509, "Osama bin Laden Has Farty Pants" had originally been titled "Osama bin Laden Has a Small Penis"—a title much more to the point. A frenzied plot finds three friends, Cartman (the pudgy boy), Stan (the average American kid), and Kyle (the brainy Jew), held in captivity in bin Laden's cave in Afghanistan. In one scene Cartman inexplicably pulls bin Laden's pants down (presumably to thwart him?), only to reveal one magnifying glass after another, for a total of nine, until finally his small penis is discernable. A sign appears, "Tiny, ain't it?," and Cartman asks, "So *that's* what this is all about?" Pointing to the popular obsessions with the sexuality of criminality, especially in the tabloid press, Cartman's observation, as reductive as it may be, mimics, mirrors, and isn't so far off from radical feminist interpretations of contemporary conflict, for example, Robin Morgan's conceptualization of "ejaculatory politics." A more astute reading of the fascination with bin Laden's small package is offered by Mark Driscoll, who opines, "Although there are other possible readings, I want to argue that the identification of lack with Osama bin Laden is isomorphic with the inscription of modernization shortcomings in capitalist developmental discourse. That is, the coercion of one single model of development and sociohistorical progress onto the semi-periphery and periphery of the world system consolidated a structure where lack was naturalized for places outside the North."[85] The lack in penis size signals the lack of modernity; thus the space of the traditional is feeble, flaccid, weak. Later in the episode, Cartman once again tries to distract bin Laden, this time by masquerading as a Muslim woman in a purple chador sitting on a camel. In the display of bin Laden's dysfunctional heterosexuality—his eyes bugging out, falling on the floor, tongue lolling on the ground, howling like a wild animal—it turns out that he is more interested in fornicating with the camel, whom he then proceeds to woo with wine. Now the lack of modernity (a perverse modernity) this time figured by the veiled Muslim woman (whose lack, unlike bin Laden's, cannot even be seen, but is hidden by the veil), is coupled with Orientalist imageries of animalistic excess and bestiality.

More recently, *South Park* continues to press against the parameters of national homosexualities, fragmenting sexual spaces to such an extent that even queerness, as a critique of identity, cannot account for the multiplicity of contradictions. In the October 2003, much-chattered about "South Park Is Gay" episode, the school kids of South Park have jumped on the metrosexual fad with a vengeance. Sporting freshly highlighted hair and trendy new clothing and dishing in the latest lingo about fabrics, fashion, and hygiene, Stan, Cartman, and Kenny deride Kyle for wearing his regular polyester jacket. "You gotta get with the times, girlfriend," claims Stan. Adds Cartman, "Yeah, that jacket is so September 10th."

In this U.S.-based context, metrosexuality, a modality seeped in metro and urban referents (though in *South Park* the setting is not urban) that tentatively queers (and to some extent, effeminizes and emasculates) straight men, is a symptom of the pervasiveness of homonationalism, in that queerness has already been assimilated into the homonational. As a marker of that which is passé, tedious, and tired, September 10 delineates an age of old-fashioned American innocence and ignorance (an advertising line nostalgically capitalized on by many, for example, Kenneth Cole, whose clothing ad uses September 12 as a moment of lingering normalcy: "On September 12th, we used protection in the bedroom, not in the mailroom"). Outdated as well are normative hetero-homo divides. As a "contact" that operates as a "conductor" (Foucault), metrosexuality both caves in to this binary and implodes it. Metrosexuality entails contact with queerness and conducts the appropriation of stereotypically queer attributes by heterosexual men. As a response to the age of terrorism, and the war on terror, metrosexuality in its American incarnation stages its own form of terrorism, manifested through penetrating and all-encompassing queer aesthetics, even as it capitulates to the regime of homonationalism though the dilution of queer politics: queerness is now something spectacular to be had, to covet, rather than to reject and revile. In this imaginative geography, the dovetailing of two claims of U.S. exceptionalism—of superior counterterrorism intelligence and technology and of the greatest sexual freedom and tolerance—come together in the demarcation of September 10 as part of a prior era. In taking a jab at the glib and facile use of September 11 as a significant moment of change in global history, the scene both displaces this usage—how often is reference made to September 10?—but also, through its allusion to an article of clothing, made of polyester no less, the iconic and even traumatic standing of September 11 is mocked. As a counterpart to the age of U.S. new imperialism, metrosexuality triumphantly hails American modernity as the space of sexual exceptionalism and promotes a union between queerness and patriotism, albeit one that most profitably hails from cosmopolitan cityscapes. Thus, this imaginative geography of the United States, privileging a cosmopolitan, urban (*metro*) formation of sexual laissez fair, smoothes the cracks and fissures of a highly uneven national terrain of sexual and racial differences across spaces, fore-grounding at once the presumed centrality of urban spaces to queer cultures (an urban-rural dichotomy that elides other forms of dissident sexualities that emerge elsewhere) and the desire to repress a metropole-periphery model in favor of a unified singular impression of American tolerance. As a nascent homonational thread, the *metro* of metrosexuality suggests that these threads are most readily apparent in cosmopolitan cityscapes. Critiquing the unmarked privileging of urban spaces to queer theorizing, Judith Halberstam defines "metronormativity" as a tendency that problematically "reveals the rural to be the devalued term in the urban/rural binary governing the spatialization of modern U.S. sexual identities."[86] Read through this particular exchange in *South Park*, we can signal urban spaces as rife with virulent homonationalist fodder while at the same time acknowledging that rural places and spaces, despite their general characterization as intolerant of queer cultures, should not be underestimated as they might provide greater or different opportunities for parallel or contrasting homonational formations. Further, propping up urban scapes as optimal for the proliferation of homonationalisms both effaces the varied topography of cities (in New York City, for example, the difference between Chelsea and Jackson Heights) and functions as a displacement of urban queer bashing in favor of fetishistic renderings of violences encountered in small towns and rural areas.[87]

The rest of the episode features the "Fab Five" from *Queer Eye for the Straight Guy*, a television show that solidified the metrosexual phenomenon in the United States, radiating out from its European (predominantly British) roots. The boys' fathers define metrosexuality in various interlocking ways. Skeeter, refuting the charge that he has turned gay, claims, "Just because a guy cares about how he looks and is in touch with his feminine side doesn't mean he's gay anymore." Stuart chimes in, "Yeah. Metrosexual means you're straight, but you appreciate the gay culture." "It's super-fabulous," adds Randy. As the Fab Five metrosexualize everything in their wake and plans are made for a metrosexual pride parade to combat metrophobia, the gay schoolteacher Mr. Garrison, fed up with the selling out of gay culture and identity, calls the metrosexual fad to a halt.

For the most part, these and other examples are surface treatments of sexual politics that pale in comparison to one episode in particular.[88] In the midst of a U.S. military buildup to an imminent invasion of Iraq and massive global antiwar protests, an especially bizarre *South Park* episode titled "The Death Camp of Tolerance" first aired on November 20, 2003. Discovering that he could sue his employers for millions of dollars if fired from his position because of his sexual orientation, Mr. Garrison uses sexual performativity to escalate discomfort and elicit disgust from his fourth-grade students. One day in class Mr. Garrison introduces a new teacher's assistant, Mr. Slave (who appears white), otherwise called the "Teacher's Ass." Mr. Slave, typifying a leather bottom, is a large strapping white man with a dark moustache, clad in a pink shirt, blue jeans, black leather chaps, vest, and boots, and a police cap. As a leather bottom, Mr. Slave is not only a gay or queer character, as represented by Mr. Garrison, but also a figure of sexual transgression and perversity referencing S/M sexual practices, the sexual promiscuity of gay male culture, and its attendant pathologized recreational drug usage. After his introduction Mr. Slave moves toward his seat, but not before being spanked by Mr. Garrison. As Mr. Slave sits down, Cartman and Craig, two white students in the classroom, confer about Mr. Slave. Cartman, whispering to Craig while glancing around furtively, states, "Dude, I think that Mr. Slave guy might be a . . . Pakistani."

This significant moment is swift and quickly overridden by a return to the classroom antics of Mr. Garrison and his slave. The comment reflects a curious suturing of racial and sexual difference: the perverse leather bottom, unrecognized as such by the students, is instead mistaken for another historically salient figure of perversion, the Muslim other of Orientalist fame. This other is of course perversely sexualized as well: the Pakistani is recognized through, not against, his sexual excesses, as well as through Mr. Slave's feminized gender positioning as the recipient of a spanking, and later, of being anally penetrated by a gerbil. If one juxtaposes the queer (leather, S/M) body with the Pakistani (Muslim, fundamentalist, terrorist) body, the commonality of perversion becomes clearer, in that both bodies represent pathological spaces of violence that are constituted as sexually excessive, irrational, and abnormal, taking us back to the figure of the terrorist in Orientalist, public policy, and feminist archives.

One can open up this analysis to the level of geopolitics as well. It is notable that Cartman did not wonder if Mr. Slave was an Afghani or an Iraqi. By naming him a Pakistani, the show astutely points to an understated complexity in the war on terror, that of the liminal position of the nation of Pakistan. Since September 11, 2001, Pakistan's conundrum has been about the question of its own state-sanctioned and unsanctioned terrorism: caught between U.S. expectations of assistance in reining in terrorist cells (this assistance rewarded by the lifting of trade sanctions and greater access to IMF loans) and India's wrath as a supposed victim of

Pakistan's terrorist activities. One could read the referencing of Pakistan as the hailing of the unaddressed terrorist (in that sense, it is a covert acknowledgment of the status of Saudi Arabia as well). More pointedly, the scene alludes to the complicity of the United States and the CIA with the buildup of Pakistan's terrorist industrial complex: military dictators, opium markets, terrorist training centers set up to fight the Soviets. Arundhati Roy writes of post-9/11 relations between the United States and Pakistan, "Now the U.S. government is asking (asking?) Pakistan to garrote the pet it [the United States] has hand-reared in its backyard for so many years."[89] Pakistan, in Roy's estimation, has been the pilfered bottom to the United States' imperialist topping.

The anally penetrated Mr. Slave tempts the viewer into another association: that of the suicide bomber. In his seminal article "Is the Rectum a Grave?," Leo Bersani complicates the feminized posture of those receiving anal sex. In its close association with AIDS, Bersani argues, anal sex has come to figure, for heterosexuals, as a destructive self-annihilation, a dark side ascribed to the *jouissance* of ecstatically forsaken bodily boundaries during sexual exchange.[90] Judith Butler, summarizing Jeff Nunokawa, writes that the male homosexual is "always already dying, as one whose desire is a kind of incipient and protracted dying." This kind of sex not only kills oneself, but also, through the demolition of the self, kills others. Butler further elaborates the multiplicity of death: "The male homosexual is figured time and time again as one whose desire is somehow structured by death, either as the desire to die, or as one whose desire is inherently punishable by death."[91] Likewise, the suicide bomber, always already dying, is not only consumed with perverted desires of the deaths of self and others, but also focused on the exact target of technologies of death. This incorporation of death, as Fanon argues, saturates every stratum of being: "The terrorist, from the moment he undertakes an assignment, allows death to enter his soul."[92] The ghost of the suicide bomber haunts Mr. Slave, interpellated here as the sexually deviant Pakistani.

Thus, the effeminate and emasculated status of Pakistan, as symbolized through the anally penetrated Mr. Slave, is signified as a nation that is decomposing and deteriorating. Cast into the politics of the South Asian diaspora, Pakistan, through an erasure of the huge number of Muslims in India, represents the Muslim other, an association from which normative Hindu Americans and Sikh Americans must distance themselves. This distancing requires an ever-narrowing South Asian model minority positioning as it seeks to separate from terrorist look-alikes. But most important,

Pakistan is used, in the dual movement of disciplining and quarantining, to separate the nationally sanctioned space of U.S. queerness, the homonormative Mr. Garrison, from the banished, perverse, external Muslim other.

Back to *South Park*, where the students complain to their parents that Mr. Garrison and his assistant are "totally gay" and "super gay." The parents chastise them and immediately take them to the Museum of Tolerance. Inside the Hall of Stereotypes, the group walks through the Tunnel of Prejudice, where they hear "queer, beaner, chink, nigger, heeb, faggot, cracker, slope, jap." "Queer" and "faggot" are the only nonracial and nonethnic epithets, analogizing race with sexuality and once again producing the white queer as split off from the perverse racial other. After surveying and challenging a number of stereotypes, they come across the Arab as terrorist. The tour guide promptly says, "But of course, we know that all Arabs aren't terrorists, don't we kids?" (Note an interesting slippage: in the official transcript of the show, the text reads otherwise: "But of course, we know that all Arabs are terrorists, don't we kids?")

The next day in class, Mr. Garrison proceeds to insert the class gerbil, Lemmiwinks, into Mr. Slave's anus, after the paddling and gagging of the hospitable leather bottom results in no disciplinary action whatsoever from the school's administration. Lemmiwinks disappears into Mr. Slave's anus; after encountering a skeleton of another gerbil in Mr. Slave's lower intestine, Lemmiwinks turns around, only to find that Mr. Slave's anus is now closed. In a bizarre subplot that tempts even the critical bounds of *South Park*, Lemmiwinks embarks on a journey to traverse Mr. Slave's large intestine in hopes of finding another opening. A folk song dictates his voyage: "Lemmiwinks! Lemmiwinks! You must escape the gay man's ass or your tale can not be told." Encouraged by the spirits of the Frog King, the Sparrow Prince, and the Catfish—the remains of other small animals shoved into Mr. Slave's anus (called the "ass of doom")—Lemmiwinks and the three spirits are eventually coughed up by Mr. Slave, and Lemmiwinks is crowned the Gerbil King. In the meantime, Mr. Garrison's failed efforts to get fired land him and Mr. Slave in Tolerance Camp, where they've been sent by the school principal to learn to tolerate their own behavior.

As a team, Mr. Garrison and Mr. Slave embody the sliding relationship between the pyramid structural model and the network model. Mr. Garrison speaks to the civilizational projects at hand: as both the object of tolerance and the tolerant subject, he disciplines the monstrosity of Mr. Slave even as he manipulates this monstrosity. Mr. Slave is a convenient conduit or foil for Mr. Garrison's own reticent perverse proclivities. We see also that such binary characterizations are part of the history of sexuality as written by the west. Let us take a look at Foucault's performative and pedagogical rendering of the Orient, which, as Janet Afary and Kevin B. Anderson argue, "was not a geographical concept; rather, it included the Greco-Roman world, as well as the modern Middle East and North Africa,"[93] in the form of the *ars erotica* that he ascribes to "the societies" of China, Japan, India, Rome, and the Arabo-Moslem:

> In the erotic art, truth is drawn from pleasure itself, understood as a practice and accumulated as experience; pleasure is not considered in relation to an absolute law of the permitted and the forbidden, nor by reference to a criterion of utility, but first and foremost in relation to itself; it is experienced as pleasure, evaluated in terms of its intensity, its specific quality, its duration, its reverberations in the body and the soul. Moreover, this knowledge must be deflected back into the sexual practice itself, in order to shape it as though from within and amplify its effects. In this way, there is formed a knowledge that must remain secret, not because of an element of infamy that might attach to its object, but because of the need to hold it in the greatest reserve, since, according to tradition, it would lose its effectiveness and its virtue by being divulged. Consequently, the relationship to the master who holds the secret is of paramount importance; only he, working alone, can transmit this art in an esoteric manner and as the culmination of an initiation in which he guides the disciple's progress with unfailing skill and severity. The effects of this masterful art, which are considerably more generous than the spareness of its prescriptions would lead one to imagine, are said to transfigure the one fortunate enough to receive its privileges: an absolute mastery of the body, a singular bliss, obliviousness to time and limits, the elixir of life, the exile of death and its threats.[94]

As distinct from *scientia sexualis*, *ars erotica* signals the perverse modernity (but is it modern?) outside of science, outside of the domestication of sex through the confessional and through the clinical practices of psychoanalysis. Mr. Garrison, through the disclosure of his affinities in his confessional classroom performances, occupies the realm of *scientia sexualis* as representative of that which can be told. Within Foucault's "act to identity" telos, one that suggests an incomplete continuum with multiple slippages and ruptures but nonetheless posits temporal progression, the *ars erotica*, embodied here by Mr. Slave, functions as a prediscursive space of sexual acts and the return of surges of unrestricted and unregulated desire (one which Foucault contests via a critique of psychoanalysis). In short, as an "art of initiation and the masterful secret," *ars erotica* is not simply outside of, but is opposed to, the knowledge-power configuration of the telling of sex in the Christian west.[95]

Thus, the perverse and the primitive collide in the figure of Mr. Slave: the violence of homophobia is shown to be appropriate when directed toward a pathological nationality, while the violence of racism is always already caught in the naming of the queer. The show works to demonstrate the unevenness of liberal forms of diversity and tolerance, noting, as Edward Said does in *Orientalism*, that the Arab terrorist is a stereotypical category which nonetheless exceeds the normative boundaries of deconstructing the Other. In reading the *ars erotica* through the lens of Said's *Orientalism*, one deeply attentive to the imaginative geographies of the Orient and the Occident yet myopically resistant to the omnipresent homoerotics of colonialism, we see perversion and primitivity coalesce in the figure of the queer terrorist: guided from above, subsumed to the will of a master, death-seeking and death-defying, unable to comprehend rational structures of temporality and space, drunk with pleasure. Sexuality in *ars erotica* is both prediscursive and beyond discourse, what Afary and Anderson describe as Foucault's "Romantic Orientalism" and "what he regarded as the open homoeroticism of the Arab Mediterranean."[96] The Orient, as interpreted from the Occident, is the space of illicit sexuality, unbridled excess, and generalized perversion, "dangerous sex and freedom of intercourse," and afflicted with nonnormative corporeal practices.[97] Mr. Slave exemplifies what Foucault names "pursued pleasures"—bodies, practices, and energies both "sought after and searched out"—fascinating pleasures simultaneously abhorred and coveted. Said writes that "the Orient was a place where one could look for sexual experiences unobtainable in Europe" and procure "a different type of sexuality." As a regenerative discourse—"the Orient is a form of release, a place of original opportunity"—prolific reproduction of the sexual norms of the Occident is made possible through the sexual excesses of the Orient, available through the travel and conquest of colonialism. Seen as the space of spirituality and sensuality, the Orient helps the Occident to maintain the rigidity of the rational while partaking in the secret pleasures of the illicit. As with other processes of colonial extraction and production, the raw materials of the Orient—in this case, the "raw novelty" of sexual perversion—are imported to sustain the prolific consumption habits, fertility, and reproduction of the Occident.[98] Foucault also points to the Orient as regenerative, stating that the *scientia sexualis* may actually be the *ars erotica* par excellence. In this statement the premodern and the postmodern converge. Mr. Garrison extracts a differential value from Mr. Slave to reorganize his status within his place of employment; as both in opposition to (dichotomy) and an extension of (continuum), Mr. Garrison and Mr. Slave work through complementarity as well as (Derridean) supplementarity. Mr. Slave personifies the raw materials extracted and imported for Mr. Garrison's regenerating usage and ultimate gain. As the queer terrorist, Mr. Slave functions to regenerate the U.S.-based homonormativity of Mr. Garrison; the whiteness of gay, homosexual, and even queer is normativized through this pairing.

The ritualized acts of sex performed by Mr. Garrison and Mr. Slave also demarcate a queer temporality of sorts: the incommensurability of the perceived queer Pakistani terrorist and the white gay schoolteacher is at once the management of the crisis of modernity—the traditional and the modern woven together—and a reaching beyond the typical prescriptions of the past informing the present and the present reverberating back to the past, undermining the temporality of fear that aims to secure the present-future through the future, to a certain kind of futurity, the queer times of now and beyond. Mr. Slave embodies a harking back in time that projects both the future that must be conquered and the future that cannot be overcome—the future and the antifuture. The singularity of each figure lies not only in what they represent—tradition/modernity, white/brown, patriot/terrorist, assimilated/monstrous—but in what they perform, in the temporalities they issue forth. As Mbembe argues, "What connects terror, death, and freedom is an ecstatic notion of temporality and politics. The future, here, can be authentically anticipated, but not in the present. The present itself is but a moment of vision—vision of the freedom not yet come."[99]

Terror/Sex

How does the queer terrorist function to regenerate the heteronormative or even homonormative patriot, elaborated in the absurd but tangible play between the terrorist and the patriot? In the never-ending displacement of the excesses of perverse sexualities to the outside, a mythical and politically and historically overstated externality so fundamental to the imaginative geographies at stake, the (queer) terrorist regenerates the civilizational missives central to the reproduction of racist-heterosexist U.S. and homonormative nationalisms, apparent in public policy archives, feminist discourses, and media representations, among other realms. Discourses of

terrorism are thus intrinsic to the management not only of race, as is pain-
fully evident through the entrenching modes of racial profiling and hate
crime incidents. Just as significantly, and less often acknowledged, discourses of terrorism are crucial to the modulation and surveillance of sexuality, indeed a range of sexualities, within and outside U.S. parameters.
Unfortunately (or fortunately—this story has not been fully written yet),
U.S. nationalisms no longer a priori exclude the homosexual; it is plausible
perhaps, given the generative and constitutive role that homosexuality
plays in relation to heteronormativity as well as homosociality, that the
heteronormativity so necessary to nationalist discourse has been a bit overstated or has functioned to overshadow the role of homosexual and homonormative others in the reproduction of nation.

I have elaborated upon three threads of homonationalism: feminist
scholarly analysis that, despite its progressive political intent, reproduces
the gender-sex nonnormativity of Muslim sexuality; gay and lesbian tourists who perform U.S. exceptionalisms, reanimated via 9/11, embedded in
the history of LGBTIQ consumer-citizens; and the inclusion of gay and queer
subjectivities that are encouraged in liberal discourses of multiculturalism
and diversity but are produced through racial and national difference. As
reflected by the debates on gay marriage in the United States, these are
highly contingent forms of nationalism and arguably accrue their greatest
purchase through transnational comparative frames rather than debates
within domestic realms; sustaining these contradictions is perhaps the
most crucial work of imaginative geographies of nationalism. Produced in
tandem with the "state of exception,"[100] the demand for patriotic loyalty to
the United States merely accelerates forms of sexual exceptionalism that
have always underpinned homonormativities. Furthermore, there is nothing inherently or intrinsically antination or antinationalist about queerness,
despite a critical distancing from gay and lesbian identities. Through the
disaggregating registers of race, kinship, and consumption, among others,
queerness is also under duress to naturalize itself in relation to citizenship,
patriotism, and nationalism. While many claim September 11 and the war
on terror as scotomatous phenomena, the demand for patriotic loyalty
merely accelerates forms of queer exceptionalism that have always underpinned the homonational. In a climate where President Bush states that gay
marriage would annihilate "the most fundamental institution of civilization" and the push for a constitutional amendment to defend heterosexual
marriage is called "the ultimate homeland security" (equating gay marriage
with terrorism, by former Pennsylvania Republican senator Rick San-

torum), homonationalism is also a temporal and spatial illusion, a facile construction that is easily revoked, dooming the exceptional queers to insistent replays and restagings of their exceptionalisms.[101]

Thus the "gains" achieved for queers, gains that image the United States in sexually exceptional terms, media, kinship (gay marriage), legality (sodomy), consumption (queer tourism) and so forth, can be read in the context of the war on terror, the USA PATRIOT Act, the Welfare Reform Act, and unimpeded U.S. imperialist expansion, as conservative victories at best, if at all. It is not only that a history of race is produced through sexuality that renders white heterosexuality proper in contrast to (black, slave) colored heterosexuality as improper, and as always in the teleological progressive space of mimicry. The history of Euro-American gay and lesbian studies and queer theory has produced a cleaving of queerness, always white, from race, always heterosexual and always homophobic. But now we have the split between proper, national (white) homosexuality (. . . queerness?) and improper (colored) nonnational queerness. Therefore, the proliferating sexualities of which Foucault speaks (the good patriot, the bad terrorist, the suicide bomber, the married gay boy, the monster-terrorist-fag, the effeminate turbaned man, the Cantor Fitzgerald wives, the white firefighters, the tortured Iraqi detainee . . .) must be studied not as analogous, dichotomous, or external to each other, but in their singularities, their relatedness, their lines of flight, their internalities to and their complicities with one another.

We called it just another night in the desert.—Sergeant First Class
Scott McKenzie, discharged for mistreatment of Iraqi prisoners at
Camp Bucca, quoted in Douglas Jehl and Eric Schmitt, "The Military"

abu ghraib and u.s. sexual exceptionalism

The torture of Iraqi prisoners at Abu Ghraib is neither exceptional nor
singular, as many (Secretary of Defense Donald Rumsfeld and the George
W. Bush administration, the U.S. military establishment, and even good
liberals) would have us believe. We need think only of the fact that so many
soldiers who faced prosecution for the Iraqi prisoner situation came from
prison guard backgrounds (reminding us of the incarceration practices
within the U.S. prison industrial complex), let alone the treatment of Palestinian civilians by the Israeli army guards, or even the brutal sodomizing of
Abner Louima by New York City police. Neither has it been possible to
normalize the incidents at Abu Ghraib as "business as usual" even within
the torture industry. As public and governmental rage alike made clear, a
line had been crossed. Why that line is demarcated at the place of so-called
sexual torture—specifically, violence that purports to mimic sexual acts
closely associated with deviant sexuality or sexual excess such as sodomy
and oral sex, as well as S/M practices of bondage, leashing, and hooding—
and not, for example, at the slow starvation of millions due to UN sanctions
against Iraq, the deaths of thousands of Iraqi civilians since the U.S. invasion in April 2003, or the plundering and carnage in Falluja, is indeed a
spectacular question. The reaction of rage, while to some extent laudable,
misses the point entirely, or perhaps more generously, upstages a denial of
culpability. The violence performed at Abu Ghraib is not an exception to
nor an extension of imperialist occupation. Rather, it works in concert with
proliferating modalities of force, an indispensable part of the "shock and
awe" campaign blueprinted by the Israelis upon the backs of Palestinian
corpses. Bodily torture is but one element in a repertoire of techniques of

occupation and subjugation that include assassinations of top leaders; house-to-house roundups, often involving interrogations without interpreters; the use of tanks and bulldozers in densely populated residential areas; helicopter attacks; the trashing and forced closure of hospitals and other provisional sites; and other violences that frequently go against international legal standards.

The sexual humiliation and ritual torture of Iraqi prisoners enabled the Bush administration to forge a crucial distinction between the supposed depravity of Abu Ghraib and the "freedom" being built in Iraq. Days after the photographs from Abu Ghraib had circulated in the domestic and foreign press, President George W. Bush stated of the abused Iraqi prisoners, "Their treatment does not reflect the *nature* of the American people."[1] Not that I imagine the American president to be so thoughtful or profound (though perhaps his speechwriters are), but his word choice is intriguing. Which one, exactly, of the acts perpetrated by American soldiers is inimical to the "natural" tendencies of Americans? Is it the behavior of the U.S. soldiers conducting the abuse? The ones clicking the digital shutter? Or is it the perverse behaviors forcibly enacted by the captured prisoners? What *exactly* is it that is "disgusting"—a word commonly used during the first few days of the prison scandal—about these photos? The U.S. soldiers grinning, stupidly waving their thumbs in the air? The depicted "sex acts" themselves, simulated oral and anal sex between men? Or the fact that the photos were taken at all? And why are these photos any more revolting than pictures of body parts blown apart by shards of missiles and explosives, or the scene of Rachel Corrie's death by bulldozer?[2] Amid Bush's claims to the contrary, the actions of the U.S. military in Saddam's former torture chambers certainly narrows the gap between us and them—between the patriot and the terrorist; the site, the population, and nearly sequential time periods all overlie quite nicely to drive this point home.[3] But not without attempts to paint the United States as the victim: in response to the photos, Thomas Friedman frets, "We are in danger of losing something much more important than just the war in Iraq. We are in danger of losing America as an instrument of moral authority and inspiration in the world. I have never known a time in my life when America and its president were more hated around the world than today."[4]

Bush's efforts to refute the idea that the psychic and fantasy lives of Americans are depraved, sick, and polluted by suggesting instead that they remain naturally free from such perversions—not only would one never enjoy the infliction of such abuse, but one would never even have the mindset or capacity to think of such acts—reinstantiates a liberal regime of multicultural heteronormativity intrinsic to U.S. patriotism. Building on the critique of national homosexual subjects in chapter 1, in this chapter I argue that homonationalism is consolidated through its unwitting collusions with nationalist sentiment regarding "sexual torture" in general and "Muslim sexuality" in specific. I also argue that this homonationalism works biopolitically to redirect the devitalizing incident of torture toward a population targeted for death into a revitalizing life-optimizing event for the American citizenry for whom it purports to securitize. Following Giorgio Agamben, state of exception discourses surrounding these events is produced on three interrelated planes. The first is the rarity of this particular form of violence: we are overtaken by the temporality of emergency, portrayed as excessive in relation to the temporality of regularity. The second is the sanctity of "the sexual" and of the body: the sexual is the ultimate site of violation, portrayed as extreme in relation to the individual rights of privacy and ownership accorded to the body within liberalism. The third is the transparency of abuse: the torture at Abu Ghraib is depicted as clear overkill in relation to other wartime violence and as defying the normative standards that guarantee the universality of the human in human rights discourses. Here is an extreme example, but indicting on all three counts nonetheless, of how these discourses of exceptionalism work in tandem. In May 2004, Rev. Troy Perry of the Metropolitan Community Church, an LGBTIQ religious organization, circulated a press release in reaction to incidents at Abu Ghraib in which he condemned "the use of sexuality as an instrument of torture, shame, and intimidation," arguing that the fact "that prisoners were forced to perform sexual acts that violate their religious principles and personal consciences is particularly heinous." The press release concluded by declaring, "MCC pledges to continue to work for a world in which all people are treated with dignity and equality and where sexuality is celebrated, respected and used for good."[5]

Hardly exceptional, as Veena Das argues, violence is not set apart from sociality, nor is sociality resistant to it: "Violence is actually embedded in sociality and could itself be a form of sociality."[6] Rita Maran, in her study of the application of torture in the French-Algerian war, demonstrates that torture is neither antithetical nor external to the project of liberation; rather, it is part and parcel of the necessary machinery of the civilizing mission. Torture is the underside, indeed the accomplice of the civilizing mission. Furthermore, Maran, citing Roger Trinquier, notes that "torture is the particular bane of the terrorist" and that the "rational equivalency" plays out as follows: "As the terrorist resorts to extremes of violence that cause grievous individual pain, so the state replies with extremes of violence that, in turn, cause grievous individual pain."[7] Any civilizing mission is marked precisely by this paradox: the civilizing apparatus of liberation is exactly that which delimits the conditions of its possibility. Thus torture is at the very least doubly embedded in sociality: it is integral to the missionary and savior discourse of liberation and civilizational uplift, and it constitutes apposite punishment for terrorists and the bodies that resemble them. Neither is the practice and propagation of torture antithetical to modernity. Noting that "all major accounts of punishment subscribe to the view that as societies modernize, torture will become superfluous to the exercise of power," Darius M. Rejali argues that even Foucault, despite arguing that penal reform actually reflected a more efficacious mode of control (and moved punishment out of public domains), falls into this trap by assuming that torture dissipated as disciplinary regimes of society developed. Rejali counters:

> Does the practice of modern torture today indicate a return to the past? One might be tempted to believe this because modern torture is so severely corporeal. But it would be a mistake to let corporal violence be the sole basis for one's judgment. Modern torture is not mere atavism. It belongs to the present moment and arises out of the same notions of rationality, government, and conduct that characterize modernity as such.[8]

As Agamben demonstrates so well, state of exception discourses labor in the service of historical discontinuities between modernizing and liberalizing modalities and the regressive forces they purport to transform or overcome. As I argue in this chapter, deconstructing U.S. exceptionalism, in particular sexual exceptionalism, and contextualizing the embeddedness of torture—rather than taking refuge in state of exception pretenses—entails attending to discourses and affective manifestations of sexuality, race, gender, and nation that activate torture's corporeal potency.

The Production of the Muslim Body as Object of Torture

"Such dehumanization is unacceptable in any culture, but it is especially so in the Arab world. Homosexual acts are against Islamic law and it is humiliating for men to be naked in front of other men," Bernard Haykel, a professor of Middle Eastern studies at New York University, explained. "Being put on top of each other and forced to masturbate, being naked in front of each other—it's all a form of torture," Haykel said.—Seymour Hersh, "Torture at Abu Ghraib," May 10, 2004

Those questioned for their involvement, tacit and explicit, in torture at Abu Ghraib cited both the lack-of-training and the cultural-difference arguments to justify their behavior: "If we had known more about them, about their culture and their way of life," whines one soldier plaintively on the U.S. news, "we would have been better able to handle the situation." The monolith of Muslim culture constructed through this narrative (performatively reiterated by Bush's tardy apology for the Abu Ghraib atrocities, bizarrely directed at the token Muslim visiting at the time, King Abdullah of Jordan) aside, the cultural-difference line has also been used by conservative and progressive factions alike to comment on the particularly intense shame with which Muslims experience homosexual and feminizing acts. For this, the prisoners receive vast sympathy, for a split second, from the general public. The taboo of homosexuality in Islamic cultures figures heavily in the equation for why the torture has been so "effective"; this interpretation of sexual norms in the Middle East—sexuality is repressed, but perversity is just bubbling beneath the surface—forms part of a centuries-long Orientalist tradition, an Orientalist phantasm that certainly informed photographs of the torture at Abu Ghraib. In "The Gray Zone," Seymour Hersh delineates how the U.S. military made particularly effective use of anthropological texts to determine effective torture methods:

> The notion that Arabs are particularly vulnerable to sexual humiliation became a talking point among pro-war Washington conservatives in the months before the March 2003 invasion of Iraq. One book that was frequently cited was *The Arab Mind*, a study of Arab culture and psychology, first published in 1973, by Raphael Patai, a cultural anthropologist who taught at, among other universities, Columbia and Princeton, and who died in 1996. The book includes a twenty-five-page chapter on Arabs and sex, depicting sex as a taboo vested with shame and repression. "The segregation of the sexes, the veiling of the women . . . and all the other minute rules that govern and restrict contact between men and women, have the effect of making sex a prime mental preoccupation in the Arab world," Patai wrote. Homosexual activity, "or any indication of homosexual leanings, as with all other expressions of sexuality, is never given any publicity. These are private affairs and remain in private." The Patai book, an academic told me, was "the bible of the neocons on Arab behavior." In their discussions, he said, two themes emerged—"one, that Arabs only understand force and, two, that the

biggest weakness of Arabs is shame and humiliation." The government consultant said that there might have been a serious goal, in the beginning, behind the sexual humiliation and the posed photographs. It was thought that some prisoners would do anything—including spying on their associates—to avoid dissemination of the shameful photos to family and friends. The government consultant said, "I was told that *the purpose of the photographs was to create an army of informants, people you could insert back in the population.*" The idea was that they would be motivated by fear of exposure, and gather information about pending insurgency action, the consultant said. If so, it wasn't effective; the insurgency continued to grow.[9]

I quote this passage at length to display how the intricate relations among Orientalist knowledge production, sexual and bodily shame, and espionage informed the torture at Abu Ghraib. As Yoshie Furuhashi astutely points out, Patai's *The Arab Mind* actually surfaced in Edward Said's *Orientalism* as an example of contemporary conduits of Orientalism, which also include the knowledge formations of foreign and public policy, terrorism studies, and area studies.[10] (We should add to Said's list the interrogation and intelligence gathering industry: Titan Corporation and CACI International, two U.S.-based security firms, have been accused of "outsourcing torture" to Iraq and refining, honing, and escalating torture techniques in order to demonstrate proven results, thus winning lucrative U.S. government contracts and ultimately directing the illegal conduct at Abu Ghraib.)[11] Patai, who also authored *The Jewish Mind*, writes of the molestation of the male baby's genitals by doting mothers, the routine beatings and stabbings of sons by fathers, the obsession with sex among Arab students (as compared to American students), and masturbation: "Whoever masturbates . . . evinces his inability to perform the active sex act, and thus exposes himself to contempt." *The Arab Mind* constitutes a mainstay text in diplomatic and military circles, and the book was reissued in November 2001 with an introduction by Norvell B. De Atkine, director of Middle East studies at the JFK Special Warfare Center and School at Fort Bragg in North Carolina.[12] Clearly, not only is the lack of knowledge with respect to cultural difference irrelevant (would knowing have ended or altered the use of these torture tactics?), but it is precisely through this knowledge that the U.S. military has been diplomatically instructed. It is exactly this unsophisticated notion of Arab/Muslim/Islamic cultural difference—in the singular—that military intelligence capitalized on to create what it believed to be a culturally specific and thus "effective" matrix of torture techniques. Furthermore, though originally the photographs at Abu Ghraib had a specific information-retrieval purpose (i.e., for blackmail), they clearly took on a life of their own, informed by what Slavoj Žižek recalls as the " 'unknown knowns'—the disavowed beliefs, suppositions and obscene practices we pretend not to know about, even though they form the background of our public values."[13]

In another example of the transfer of information, the model of terrorism used by the State Department swerves between a pyramid structure and a network structure. The former represents a known, rational administrative format, one that is phallic and hence castratable; the latter represents chaotic and unpredictable alliances and forces. The pyramid form also appears in the *Battle of Algiers* (1967, English subtitles), viewed for brainstorming purposes by the Pentagon in September 2003; in the film the French describe the rebels by stating, "They don't even know each other. To know them we can eliminate them." It is not, however, important to discern if it is mere coincidence that in several of the Abu Ghraib photos, Iraqi prisoners are arranged naked in human pyramids, simulating both the feminized prone position, anus in the air, necessary to receive anal sex, and the "activo" mounting stance of anal sex. Should the sexual connotations of the pyramid be doubted, Adel L. Nakhla, an Arabic translator working for the U.S. security firm Titan Corporation, stated of the pyramid in the Taguba report:

> They made them do strange exercises by sliding on their stomach, jump up and down, throw water on them and made them some wet, called them all kinds of names such as "gays" do they like to make love to guys, then they handcuffed their hands together and their legs with shackles and started to stack them on top of each other by insuring that the bottom guy's penis will touch the guy on top's butt.[14]

What is significant here, however, is not whether the meaning of the pyramid has been understood and translated from one context to another, but that the transfer of information and its mimicry does not depend on contextual meaning to have symbolic and political effect. As an assemblage of entities, the pyramid simultaneously details fusion and hierarchy, singularity and collectivity.

Such transnational and transhistorical linkages—including unrelated but no less relevant examples drawn from Israeli surveillance and occupation measures (indeed, there are reports that at least one Israeli interrogator was working at Abu Ghraib), the behavior of the French in Algeria, and even the 2002 Gujarat pogrom in India—surge together to create the Muslim body as a particular typological object of torture.[15] During the Algerian war, for instance, one manner of torture of Arabs "consisted of suspending them, their hands and feet tied behind their backs . . . with their head upwards. Underneath them was placed a trestle, and they were made to swing, by fist blows, in such a fashion that their sexual parts rubbed against the very sharp pointed bar of the trestle. The only comment made by the men, turning towards the soldiers present: 'I am ashamed to find myself stark naked in front of you.' "[16] This kind of torture directed at "the supposed Muslim terrorist" is subject to the normativizing knowledges of modernity that mark him (or her) both as sexually conservative, modest and fearful of nudity (and it is interesting how this conceptualization is rendered both sympathetically and as a problem), as well as queer, animalistic, barbarian, and unable to control his (or her) urges. Thus the shadow of homosexuality is never far. In *Brothers and Others in Arms: The Making of Love and War in Israeli Combat Units*, Danny Kaplan, looking at the construction of hegemonic masculinity and alternative sexual identities in the Israeli military, argues that sexualization is neither tangential nor incidental to the project of conquest but, rather, is central to it: "[The] eroticization of enemy targets . . . triggers the objectification process." This eroticization always inhabits the realm of perversion:

> An instance where the image of mehablim [literally, "saboteurs," a general term for terrorists, guerrilla soldiers, or any Arab groups or individuals that operate against Israeli targets]—in this case, Palestinian enemy men—merges with another image of subordination, that of actual homosexual intercourse. It seems that the sexual-targeting drive of masculiary [*sic*] soldier could not resist such a temptation. This is one way to understand Shaul's account of one of the brutalities he experienced in the Lebanon War. During the siege on Palestinian Liberation Organization forces in Beirut, he was stationed next to a post where Israeli snipers observed PLO activity in city houses. Suddenly, something unusual appeared in the sniper's binoculars:
>
> "One of them said to me, 'Come here; I want you to see something.' I looked, and I saw two mehablim, one fucking the other in the ass; it was pretty funny. Like real animals. The sniper said to me, 'And now look.' He aims, and puts a bullet right into the forehead of the one that was being fucked. Holy shit, did the other one freak out! All of a sudden his partner died on him. It was nasty. We were fucking cruel. Cruelty—but this was war. Human life didn't matter much in a case like this, because this human could pick up his gun and fire at you or your buddies at any moment."

Kaplan concludes this vignette by remarking that despite the episode's brutal ending, the gender position of the active partner is what was ultimately protected: "It is striking that even in this encounter it is the passive partner who gets the bullet in his ass, while the active partner remains unscathed."[17] Violence is naturalized as the inexorable and fitting response to nonnormative sexuality.

But not only is the Muslim body constructed as pathologically sexually deviant and as potentially homosexual, and thus read as a particularized object for torture, but the torture itself is constituted on the body as such: as Brian Axel has argued, "The performative act of torture produces its object."[18] The object, the tortured Muslim body, spins out repetitively into folds of existence, cohering discourse, politics, aesthetics, affectivity. Thus, the body informs the torture, but the torture also forms the body. That is, the performative force of torture not only produces an object but also proliferates that which it names.[19] This sutures the double entrenchment of perversion into the temporal circuitry of always-becoming. I question whether it is politically astute to denote the acts of torture as simulating gay sex acts, a conundrum I discuss later in this chapter. But the veracity of this reading nonetheless indicates, in the eyes of the perpetrators and in our own, that the torture performs an initiation into or confirmation of what is already suspected of the body, or even, in moments, breaking with the double temporality at play, a telling conversion. Furthermore, the faggot Muslim as torture object is splayed across five continents, predominantly in Arab countries, through the "transnational transfer of people" in a tactic called "renditions,"[20] the U.S. practice of transporting terrorist suspects to third country locations, such as Uzbekistan, Pakistan, Saudi Arabia, Egypt, Morocco, Jordan, and, most recently, Syria, where practices of torture may be routine and systemic. Thus the tortured Muslim body sustains a "worldwide constellation of detention centers," which renders these citizenship-stripped bodies, about whom the United States can deny having any knowledge, "ghost detainees."[21]

As the space of "illicit and dangerous sex,"[22] the Orient is the site of carefully suppressed animalistic, perverse, homo- and hypersexual instincts. This paradox is at the heart of Orientalist notions of sexuality that are reanimated through the transnational production of the Muslim terrorist as torture object. Underneath the veils of repression sizzles an indecency waiting to be unleashed. The most recent invocation of the perverse deranged terrorist and his naturalized proclivities is found in this testimony by one of the prisoner guards at Abu Ghraib: "I saw two naked detainees, one masturbating to another kneeling with its mouth open. . . . I saw [Staff Sergeant] Frederick walking towards me, and he said, 'Look what these animals do when you leave them alone for two seconds.' I heard PFC England shout out, 'He's getting hard.' "[23] Note how the mouth of the Iraqi prisoner, the one in fact kneeling in the submissive position, is referred to not as "his" or "hers," but "its." The use of the word "animals" signals both the cause of the torture and its effect. Identity is performatively constituted by the very evidence—here, getting a hard-on—that is said to be its results. (Because you are an animal you got a hard-on; because you got a hard-on you are an animal.) Contrary to the recent public debate on torture, which foregrounds the site of detention as an exemplary holding cell that teems with aggression, this behavior is hardly relegated to prisons, as an especially unnerving moment in Michael Moore's documentary *Fahrenheit 9/11* (2004) reveals. A group of U.S. soldiers are shown loading a dead Iraqi, presumably recently killed by them, covered with a white sheet onto a stretcher. Someone yells, "Look, Ali Baba's dick is still hard!," while others follow in disharmonized chorus, "You touched it, eeewww you touched it." Even in death the muscular virility of the Muslim man cannot be laid to rest in some humane manner; not only does the Orientalist fantasy transcend death, but the corpse's sexuality does too; it rises from death, as it were. Death here becomes the scene of the ultimate unleashing of repression.

Whither Feminism?

Despite the recurring display of revulsion for attributes associated with the feminine, the United States apparently still regards itself as the arbiter of feminist civilizational standards. For example, Kelly Cogswell worries about homophobic and misogynist backlash, as if the United States had not already demonstrated its capacity to perpetuate their most extreme forms. Writing in *The Gully*, an LGBTQ political news forum, she states:

> Images of men forced to wear women's underwear over their faces and engage in homosexual activity will also inflame misogyny and homophobia. Forget about Bush's anti-gay marriage stand in the United States. By tolerating this behavior in Iraq and elsewhere, his administration has made homosexuality abhorrent world-wide. The image of an American woman holding a prisoner's leash will be used as a potent argument against modernization and the emancipation of women.[24]

Barbara Ehrenreich expresses comparable concerns:

It was England we saw with a naked Iraqi man on a leash. If you were doing PR for Al Qaeda, you couldn't have staged a better picture to galvanize misogynist Islamic fundamentalists around the world. Here, in these photos from Abu Ghraib, you have everything that the Islamic fundamentalists believe characterizes Western culture, all nicely arranged in one hideous image—imperial arrogance, sexual depravity, and gender equality.[25]

It is surely wishful thinking to assume that U.S. guards, female or not, having forced prisoners to wear women's underwear, among other derogatory "feminizing" acts, would then be perceived by the non-west as a product of the west's gender equality. In fact, misogyny is perhaps the one concept most easily understood by both captor and captive. Former prisoner Dhia al-Shweiri notes, "We are men. It's OK if they beat me. Beatings don't hurt us; it's just a blow. But no one would want [his] manhood to be shattered. They wanted us to feel as though we were women, the way women feel, and this is the worst insult, to feel like a woman."[26]

The picture of Lynndie England, dubbed "Lynndie the Leasher," leading a naked Iraqi on a leash (also referred to as "pussy whipping") has now become a surface on which fundamentalism and modernization, apparently dialectically opposed, can wage war. The image is about both the victories of liberal feminism, which argues that women should have equal opportunities within the military, and its failures to adequately theorize power and gender beyond male-female dichotomies that situate women as less prone to violence and as morally superior to men. Writes Zillah Eisenstein, "When I first saw the pictures of the torture at Abu Ghraib I felt destroyed. Simply heart-broken. I thought 'we' are the fanatics, the extremists; not them. By the next day as I continued to think about Abu Ghraib I wondered how there could be so many women involved in the atrocities?"[27] Why is this kind of affective response to the failures of Euro-American feminisms, feminisms neither able to theorize gender and violence nor able to account for racism within its ranks, appropriate to vent at this particular moment— especially when it works to center the (white) Euro-American feminist as victim, her feminism having fallen apart? Another example: brimming with disappointment, Ehrenreich pontificates, "Secretly, I hoped that the presence of women would over time change the military, making it more respectful of other people and cultures, more capable of genuine peacekeeping. . . . A certain kind of feminism, or perhaps I should say a certain kind of feminist naiveté, died in Abu Ghraib."[28] Patrick Moore articulates the death of a parallel yearning, as if gay male sexuality had never chanced upon its own misogyny: "The idea that female soldiers are as capable as men of such atrocities is disorienting for gay men who tend to think of women as natural allies."[29] Nostalgically mourning the loss of the liberal feminist subject, this emotive convergence of white liberal feminists and white gay men unwittingly reorganizes the Abu Ghraib tragedy around their desires.

But the sight of England with her leash also hints at the sexual perversions associated with S/M, something not mentioned at all in the popular press. The comparisons proffered between the depraved, cigarette-toting, dark-haired, pregnant and unmarried, racialized England (now implicated in making a pornographic film with another guard), and the heroic girl-next-door Jessica Lynch, informed by their working-class similarities but little else, speak also of the need to explain away the presence of female Abu Ghraib torturers as an aberration.[30] While the presence of women torturers may at least initially give us pause, it is a mistake to exceptionalize these women; the pleasure and power derived from these positions and actions cannot be written off as some kind of false consciousness or duping by the military, nor as the work of what Eisenstein refers to as "white female decoys."[31] If, as Veena Das argues, violence is a form of sociality, then women are not only the recipients of violence, but are actually connected to and benefit from forms of violence in myriad ways, regardless of whether or not they are the perpetrators of violence themselves.[32] That is to say, the economy of violence produces a circulatory system whereby no woman is strictly an insider or outsider. Women can be subjects of violence but also agents of it, whether it is produced on their behalf or perpetuated directly by them.[33] In this regard three points are at stake: How do we begin to understand the literal presence of women, and possibly of gay men and lesbians, in both the tortured and the torturer populations? How should one explore the analytic of gender positionings and sexual differentiation beyond masculine and feminine? And finally, what do we make of the participation of U.S. guards in the photos, behind the cameras, and in front of computer screens, and ourselves, as curious and disturbed onlookers?

Gay Sex?

Male homosexuality is deeply shameful in Arab culture; to force naked Arab prisoners to simulate gay sex, taking pictures you could threaten to show, would be far worse than beating them.—Gregg Easterbrook, "Whatever It Takes"

Deploying a parallel homophobic logic, conservative and progressive pundits have both claimed that the illegal status of homosexual acts in Islamic law demarcates sexual torture in relation to the violence at Abu Ghraib as especially humiliating. Republican senator Susan Collins of Maine, for example, was skeptical that the U.S. guards elected to inflict "bizarre sexual humiliations that were specifically designed to be particularly offensive to Muslim men," while others remarked that sexual humiliation is constituted as "a particular outrage in Arab culture."[34] But from a purely military security perspective, the torture was very effective and therefore completely justified.[35] The Bush administration claims that the torture was particularly necessary and efficacious for interrogation because of the ban against homosexuality in Islam. That "nakedness, homosexuality and control by a woman might be particularly humiliating in Arab culture" has been a sentiment echoed by many.[36]

Madhi Bray, the executive director of the Muslim American Society, a nonprofit Islamic organization located in Virginia, says that Islam calls for "modesty in dress," "being seen naked is a tremendous taboo and a tremendous humiliation in Muslim culture," and that homosexuality, considered a sin, "only becomes a problem when it is flaunted, affecting the entire society." Faisal Alam, founder and former director of the international Muslim LGBTIQ organization Al-Fatiha, issued a press release stating, "Sexual humiliation is perhaps the worst form of torture for any Muslim." The press release continues, "Islam places a high emphasis on modesty and sexual privacy. Iraq, much like the rest of the Arab world, places great importance on notions of masculinity. Forcing men to masturbate in front of each other and to mock same-sex acts or homosexual sex, is perverse and sadistic, in the eyes of many Muslims." In another interview Alam reiterates that the torture of the prisoners is an "affront to their masculinity."[37]

I want to underscore the complex dance of positionality that Muslim and Arab groups such as the Muslim American Society and especially Al-Fatiha must perform in these times, during which a defense of "Muslim sexuality" through the lens of culture easily becomes co-opted into racist agendas. The gay conservative Andrew Sullivan, for example, capitalizes on the cultural difference discourse, nearly claiming that the repressive culture of Muslim extremism is responsible for the potency of the torture, in effect blaming the victims. Islamophobia has become central to the subconscious of homonormativity.[38] I do take issue with Al-Fatiha's statements, as they, along with many others', relied on an Orientalist notion of Muslim sexuality that foregrounded sexual repression and upheld versions of normative masculinity; that is, being in the feminized "passivo" positioning is naturalized as humiliating, producing a muscular nationalism of sorts. In displays of solidarity, Al-Fatiha's comments were uncritically embraced by various queer sectors: the Center for Lesbian and Gay Studies newsletter used them to authenticate its perspective through that of the native informant, while the U.S. gay press endlessly reproduced the appropriate masculinity and sexual conservatism lines. However, given their place at the crossroads of queerness and Arabness, Al-Fatiha was, and still is, under the most duress to authenticate Orientalist paradigms of Muslim sexuality, thus reproducing narratives of U.S. sexual exceptionalism. Reinforcing a homogeneous notion of Muslim sexual repression vis-à-vis homosexuality and the notion of modesty works to resituate the United States, in contrast, as a place free of such sexual constraints, thus confirming the now-liberated status of the formerly repressed diasporic Muslim. This captive/liberated transition is reflected in what Rey Chow terms "coercive mimeticism—a process (identitarian, existential, cultural, or textual) in which those who are marginal to mainstream Western culture are expected . . . to resemble and replicate the very banal preconceptions that have been appended to them, a process in which they are expected to objectify themselves in accordance with the already seen and thus to authenticate the familiar imaginings." Unlike a (Bhabhaian) version of mimesis that accentuates the failed attempts of the Other to imitate the Self, Chow's account claims that "the original that is supposed to be replicated is no longer the white man or his culture but rather an image, a stereotyped view of the ethnic." The ethnic as a regulatory device sustains the fictive ideals of multicultural pluralism.[39] For Al-Fatiha to have elaborated on the issues of Islam and sexuality more complexly would have not only missed the Orientalist resonance so eagerly awaited by the mass media; that is, there is almost no way to get media attention unless this mimetic resonance is met. It would have also considerably endangered a population already navigating the pernicious racist effects of the USA PATRIOT Act: surveillance, deportations, detentions, registrations, preemptive migrations and departures. Thus Al-Fatiha's performance of a particular allegiance with American sexual exceptionalism is the result of a demand, not a suggestion. The proliferation of diverse U.S. subjects, such as the Muslim American and even the queer Muslim American, and their epistemological conditions of existence are mandates of homeland security, ones that produce and regulate homonationalism.

In a very different context, Patrick Moore, author of *Beyond Shame: Reclaiming the Abandoned History of Radical Gay Sex*, opines:

Because "gay" implies an identity and a culture, in addition to describing a sexual act, it is difficult for a gay man in the West to completely understand the level of disgrace endured by the Iraqi prisoners. But in the Arab world, the humiliating techniques now on display are particularly effective because of Islam's troubled relationship with homosexuality. This is not to say that sex between men does not occur in Islamic society—the shame lies in the gay identity rather than the act itself. As long as a man does not accept the supposedly female (passive) role in sex with another man, there is no shame in the behavior. Reports indicate that the prisoners were not only physically abused but also accused of actually being homosexuals, which is a far greater degradation to them.[40]

The Foucauldian "act to identity" telos spun out by Moore delineates the west as the space of identity (disregarding the confusion of act-identity relations at the heart of U.S. homosexualities), while the Arab world is relegated, apparently because of "Islam's troubled relationship to homosexuality," to the backward realm of acts. The fiction of identity, one based on the concept of progressive coherence, effaces, for example, men who have sex with men, or those on the down low, so that the presence of gay- and lesbian-identified Muslims in the "Arab world" becomes inconceivable. Dare one mention Christianity's troubled relationship with homosexuality? But let us follow Moore's logic to its conclusion: since the acts are allegedly far more morally neutral for Muslims than they are for men in the west, being forced to do them in the obvious absence of an avowed identity should actually prove not so humiliating. Given the lack of any evidence that being called a homosexual is much more degrading than being tortured, Moore's rationalization reads as an Orientalist projection that conveys much more about the constraints and imaginaries of identity in the west than anything else.

These accounts by LGBTIQ progressives are perhaps an unintended side effect of the focus on homosexuality, which, in the effort to disrupt homophobia, tends to reproduce misogyny, the erasure of women, and the demeaning of femininity. Any singular-axis identity analysis will reiterate the most normative versions of that identity, in this case, those that center privileged (white) gay men. Furthermore, we see the trenchant replay of what Foucault termed the "repressive hypothesis": the notion that a lack of discussion or openness regarding sexuality reflects a repressive, censorship-driven apparatus of deflated sexual desire. In the face of the centrality of Foucault's *The History of Sexuality* to the field of queer studies, it is somewhat baffling that some queer theorists have accepted at face value the discourse of Muslim sexual repression. That is not to imply that Foucault's work should be transparently applied to other cultural and historical contexts, especially as he himself perpetuates a pernicious form of Orientalism in his formulation of the *ars erotica*. Rather, Foucault's insights deserve evaluation as a methodological hypothesis about discourse. Thus the point to be argued is not how to qualify the status of homosexuality across the broad historical and geographical, not to mention religious, regional, class, national, and political variances of the Middle East. We must consider instead how the production of homosexuality as taboo is situated within the history of encounters with the western gaze. While in Said's *Orientalism* the illicit sex found in the Orient was sought out in order to liberate the Occident from its own performance of the repressive hypothesis, in the case of Abu Ghraib, conversely, it is the (perverse) repression of the Arab prisoners that is highlighted in order to efface the rampant hypersexual excesses of the U.S. prison guards. The Orient, once conceived in Foucault's *ars erotica* and Said's deconstructive work as the place of original release, unfettered sin, and acts with no attendant identities or consequences, now symbolizes the space of repression *and* perversion, and the site of freedom has been relocated to western identity.

Given the unbridled homophobia (among other phobias) demonstrated by the U.S. guards, it is indeed ironic, yet predictable, that the United States nonetheless emerges as sexually exceptional: less homophobic and more tolerant of homosexuality (and less tainted by misogyny and fundamentalism) than the repressed, modest, nudity-shy Middle East. Through feminist, queer, and even conservative reactions to the violence at Abu Ghraib, we have a clear view of the performative privileges of Foucault's "speaker's benefit": an exemplar of sexual exceptionalism whereby those who are able to articulate sexual knowledge (especially of themselves) then appear to be freed, through the act of speech, from the space of repression. Foucault describes it thus: "There may be another reason that makes it so gratifying for us to define the relationship between sex and power in terms of repression: something that one might call the speaker's benefit. If sex is repressed, that is, condemned to prohibition, nonexistence, and silence, then the mere fact that one is speaking about it has the appearance of a deliberate transgression."[41] As Sara Ahmed notes, this hierarchy between open (liberal democracy) and closed (fundamentalist) systems obscures "how the constitution of open cultures involves the projection of what is closed onto others, and hence the concealment of what is closed and contained 'at home.' "[42] Thus those who appear to have the speaker's benefit not only reproduce, through a geopolitical mapping of homophobia and where it is most virulent (a mapping that mirrors open/closed, tolerant/repressed dichotomies), the hegemonic ideals of U.S. exceptionalism; the projection of homophobia onto other spaces enacts a clear disavowal of homophobia at "home."

What, then, is closed and what is contained at home? In the American gay press, the Abu Ghraib photos are continuously hailed as "evidence of rampant homophobia in the armed forces;" Aaron Belkin decries "the most base, paranoid, or extreme elements of military homophobia;" Paula Ettelbrick, the executive director of the International Gay and Lesbian Human Rights Commission, maintains that "this sort of humiliation" becomes sanctioned through the operation of Don't Ask, Don't Tell, as if therein lies the brunt of the military establishment's cruelty, and not in the murders of thousands of civilian Iraqis.[43] Humiliation becomes sanctioned because the military functions as a reserve for what is otherwise seen as socially unacceptable violence, sanitizing all aggression in its wake under the guise of national security. In these accounts, the homophobia of the U.S. military is pounced upon, with scarce mention of the linked processes of racism and sexism. Patrick Moore, who himself says the photos "evoked in me a deep sense of shame as a gay man," in particular sets up the (white) gay male subject as the paradigmatic victim of the assaulting images, stating that "for closeted gay men and lesbians serving in the military, it must evoke deep shame."[44] Is it really prudent to unequivocally foreclose the chance that there might be a gay man or lesbian among the perpetrators of the torture at Abu Ghraib? To foreground homophobia over other vectors of shame—this foregrounding functioning as a key symptom of homonormativity—is to miss that these photos are not merely representative of the homophobia of the military; they are also racist, misogynist, and imperialist. To favor the gay male spectator—here, presumably white—is to negate the multiple and intersectional viewers implicated by these images, and oddly, is also to privilege as victim the identity (as fictional progressive coherence) of white gay male sexuality in the west (and those closeted in the military) over the signification of acts, not to mention the bodies of the tortured Iraqi prisoners themselves. In another interview Moore complicates this audience vectorship: "I felt the government had found a way to use sexuality as a tool of humiliation both for Arab men and for gay men here." The drawing together of (presumably straight) Arab men and (presumably white) gay men is yet another moment where the sexuality of Arab men is qualified as repressed and oriented toward premodern acts, the precursor to the identity-solidified space of "here," thus effacing the apparently unfathomable presence of queer Arabs (particularly those in the United States).[45]

Mubarak Dahir, writing for the *New York Blade*, intervenes in a long-standing debate among LGBTIQ communities about whether the war on terrorism is a gay issue by underscoring gay sex as central to the images: "The claim by some members of the gay and lesbian community that the invasion and occupation of Iraq is not a 'gay' issue crumbled last week when photos emerged of hooded, naked Iraqi captives at the Abu Ghraib prison near Baghdad being forced to simulate gay sex acts as a form of abuse and humiliation." And later: "As a gay man and as a person of Arab descent, I felt a double sting from those pictures. Looking at the blurred-out photos of hooded Iraqi prisoners being forced to perform simulations of gay oral sex on one another, I had to wonder what it was that my fellow Americans in uniform who were directing the scene found the most despicable: the fact that the men were performing gay sex, or that they were Arabs."[46] If we return to the construction of the faggot Muslim body as object of torture and the performative force of torture, the answer to Dahir's query would be both. Of course, the attention that Dahir draws to the intersectional vectors of Arab and gay is also an important intervention in the face of widespread tendencies to construct homosexuality and Muslim sexuality as mutually exclusive. Given the resounding silence of national and mainstream LGBTIQ organizations, currently obsessed by the gay marriage agenda, the political import of Dahir's response on the war on terror in general and on Abu Ghraib in particular should not be dismissed. In fact, on May 28, 2004, in the midst of furious debate regarding sexual torture, the Human Rights Campaign, the Servicemembers Legal Defense Network, and the American Veterans for Equal Rights jointly released "Fighting for Freedom," a press statement highlighting brave and patriotic "LGBT" soldiers in the military and announcing the release of *Documenting Courage*, a book on LGBT veterans. Driven by "stories [that] go unmentioned," both the statement and the book privilege the testimonial voice of authenticity. In the absence of any commentary about or position on Abu Ghraib, this might be read as a defensive move to restore honor to U.S. soldiers while reminding the public of the struggles LGBT soldiers face in the military, thus shifting the focus of victimhood away from Iraqi prisoners.[47]

Declaring that the acts are simulations of gay sex, however, invites other consequences, such as the response from Egyptian protestors in Cairo calling for the removal of the "homosexual American executioners,"[48] which reaffirmed that homosexuality is an unwanted import from the west. Such an accusation feeds nicely into Bush's antigay marriage agenda and reflects a curious tryst between the gay marriage debate and the discussion about homosexuality and the Abu Ghraib photos, both of which send a very clear message about the desires of the Bush administration to sanction and disseminate homophobia. Right-wing organizations such as Concerned Women for America have similarly condemned the torture as a direct result of homosexual cultural depravity. But are the acts specifically and only referential of gay sex (and here, "gay" means "sex between men")? And is it the case that, as Patrick Moore argues, homosexuality has been employed as the "ultimate tool of degradation" and as a "military tactic [that] reaches new levels of perversity"?[49] Certainly this rendition evades a conversation about what exactly constitutes the distinction between gay sex and straight sex and also presumes some static normativity about gender roles. Saying that the simulated and actual sex scenes replicate gay sex is an easy way for all—mass media, Orientalist anthropologists, the military establishment, LGBTIQ groups and organizations—to disavow the supposedly perverse proclivities inherent in heterosexual sex and the gender normativity immanent in some kinds of gay sex. It should be noted that Amnesty International is among the few that did not mention homosexuality, homosexual acts, or same-sex sexuality in its press release condemning the torture.[50]

These readings reproduce what Gayle Rubin calls the "erotophobic fallacy of misplaced scale." "Sexual acts," Rubin argues, "are burdened with an excess of significance";[51] this excess produces a misreading and perhaps even an exaggeration of the scale by which the significance of sex is measured, one that continually privileges humiliation (mental, psychic, cultural, social) over physical pain. In fact, it may well be that these responses by westerners reveal what we might deem the worst form of torture—that is, sexual torture and humiliation rather than extreme pain—more than any comprehension of the experiences of those tortured. The simulated sex acts must be thought of in terms of gendered roles rather than through a universalizing notion of sexual orientation. But why talk about sex at all? Was anyone having sex in these photos? One could argue that in the photos, the torturers were turned on, erotically charged, and looked as one does when having sex. As Trishala Deb and Rafael Mutis point out:

> Women's rights advocates in the U.S. have made the distinction between sex and rape for a long time. By defining rape and sexual assault as an act of violence and not sex, we are placing the validity in the voice of the assaulted, and accepting

their experience as central to the truth of what happened. . . . What we understand by centering the perspective of the assaulted people is that there was no sex happening regardless of the act.[52]

The focus on gay sex also preempts a serious dialogue about rape, both the rape of Iraqi male prisoners but also, more significantly, the rape of female Iraqi prisoners, the occurrence of which appears neither news- nor photograph-worthy. Indeed, there has been a complete underreporting of the rapes of Afghani and Iraqi women both inside and outside of detention centers. Major General Anthony Taguba's report notes that among the eighteen hundred digital photos there are unreleased pictures of females being raped and women forced at gunpoint to bare their breasts, as well as videotape of female detainees forced to strip and rumors of impregnated rape victims.[53] Why are there comparatively few photos of women, and why have they not been released? Is it because the administration found the photos of women even more appalling? Or has the wartime rape of women become so unspectacular, so endemic to military occupation as to render its impact moot? Or could these photos finally demolish the line of reasoning that the United States is liberating Muslim women, a fantasy so crucial to the tenets of American sexual exceptionalism? How, ultimately, do we begin to theorize the connections and disjunctures between male and female tortured bodies, and between masculinities and femininities?

Although feminist postcolonial studies have typically theorized women as the bearers of cultural continuity, tradition, and national lineage, in the case of terrorism, the line of transmission seems always to revert to the male body. The locus of reproductive capacity is, momentarily, expanded from the female body to include the male body. This expansion does not mark a shift away from women as the victims of rape and pawns between men during wartime. But the principal and overriding emphasis on rape of women as a weapon of war can displace the importance of castrating the reproductive capacities of men; furthermore, this line of inquiry almost always returns us to an uninterrogated heteronormative frame of penetration and conduction. In this particular case, it is precisely masculinity, the masculinity of the terrorist, that threatens to reproduce itself. Writing about the genital and anal torture of Sikh men in Punjab, Brian Keith Axel argues that torture produces sexual differentiation not as male and female, but rather what he calls national-normative sexuality and antinational sexuality:

> I propose that torture in Punjab is a practice of repeated and violent circumscription that produces not only sexed bodies, but also a form of sexual differentia-

tion. This is not a differentiation between categories of male and female, but between what may be called national-normative sexuality and antinational sexuality. . . . National-normative sexuality provides the sanctioned heterosexual means for reproducing the nation's community, whereas antinational sexuality interrupts and threatens that community. Torture casts national-normative sexuality as a fundamental modality of citizen production in relation to an antinational sexuality that postulates sex as a "cause" of not only sexual experience but also of subversive behavior and extraterritorial desire ("now you can't be married, you can't produce any more terrorists"). The form of punishment corresponds to the putative source of transgression: sexual reproduction, identified as a property of masculine agency within the male body.[54]

It is important to emphasize, of course, that there exist multiple national-normative sexualities and likewise, multiple antinational sexualities, as well as entities that make such distinctions fuzzy. It is equally important to recognize that, for all of its insights, Axel's formulation cannot be entirely and neatly transposed onto the Abu Ghraib situation, as Punjabi Sikh detainees form part of the Indian nation and are also branded as the religious fundamentalist terrorists that threaten to undo that nation. In other words, for Punjabi detainees, torture works to finalize expulsion from the nation-state. What I find most compelling is Axel's formulation of national differentiation as sexual differentiation. However, I argue that it is precisely feminizing (and thus not the categories of male and female, as Axel notes), and the consequent insistence on mutually exclusive positions of masculine and feminine, that strips the tortured male body of its national-normative sexuality. This feminizing divests the male body of its virility and thus compromises its power not only to penetrate and reproduce its own nation (our women), but to contaminate the other's nation (their women) as well. Furthermore, the perverted sex of the terrorist is a priori cast outside the domain of normative national sexualities: "the form of punishment," that is, meddling with penis and anus, "corresponds to the putative source of transgression" not only because of the desire to truncate the terrorist's capacity to sexually reproduce, but also because of the (homo)sexual deviancy always already attached to the terrorist body. These two attributes, the fertility of the terrorist (in the case of Muslim men, interpreted through polygamy) and the (homo)sexual perversions of the terrorist, are rendered with extra potency given that the terrorist is also a priori constituted as stateless, lacking national legitimization and national boundaries. In the political imagination, the terrorist serves as the monstrous excess of the nation-state.

Torture, to compound Axel's formulation, works not merely to disaggregate national from antinational sexualities—for those distinctions (the stateless monster-terrorist-fag) are already in play—but also, in accordance with nationalist fantasies, to reorder gender and, in the process, to corroborate implicit racial hierarchies. The force of feminizing lies not only in the stripping away of masculinity, the faggotizing of the male body, or in robbing the feminine of its symbolic and reproductive centrality to national-normative sexualities; it is the fortification of the unenforceable boundaries between masculine and feminine, the rescripting of multiple and fluid gender performatives into petrified sites of masculine and feminine, the regendering of multiple genders into the oppressive binary scripts of masculine and feminine, and the interplay of it all within and through racial, imperial, and economic matrices of power. This is the real force of the torture.

Axel writes, "Torture casts national-normative sexuality as a fundamental modality of citizen production." But we can also flip these terms around: *national-normative sexuality casts torture as a fundamental modality of citizen production.* One could scramble this line further still: citizen production casts national-normative sexuality as a fundamental modality of torture—and so on. The point is that in the metonymic chain linking torture, citizen production, and national-normative sexualities, torture surfaces as an integral part of a patriotic mandate to separate the normative-national genders and sexualities from the antinational ones. Joanna Bourke elaborates:

> It is hard to avoid the conclusion that, for some of these Americans, creating a spectacle of suffering was part of a bonding ritual. Group identity as victors in an increasingly brutalised Iraq is being cemented: this is an enactment of comradeship between men and women who are set apart from civilian society back home by acts of violence. Their cruel, often carnivalesque rites constituted what Mikhail Bakhtin called "authorised transgression."[55]

The bonding ritual, culminating in an authorized transgression, is authorized not from above but between actors seeking to redirect animosity toward each other. In this sense the bonding ritual of the carnival of torture —discussing it, producing it, getting turned on by it, recording it, disseminating the proof of it, gossiping about it—is the ultimate performance of patriotism. As Sara Ahmed so incisively expounds, (torture-as-) patriotism is driven not merely by hatred of the Other, but also by love: "Hate is renamed as love, a renaming that 'conceals' the ambivalence that it exercises (we love *rather than* hate)." As a nascent arena of multicultural nationalist normativity, the military is a prime site of this love for the nation, a love that, for those who fail to meet the standards of the ideal citizen (i.e., working classes, people of color, immigrants), remains unrequited. Ahmed theorizes this "national love as a form of waiting," whereby the *"failure of return extends one's investment."*[56] One can only imagine what this failure of return entails for those being prosecuted for these crimes.

It is likewise horrifically telling that Lynndie England and Charles A. Graner became romantically involved while in Iraq; sharing torture functions to instigate and heighten sexual chemistries or release them or both. What is the relationship between the kinds of sex they were having with each other and the kind of corporeal experiences of sexual domination they were jointly having with the prisoners? While torture elevates the erotic charge and intensity for those already ready to fuck each other, it externalizes the hatred between those ready to kill each other. Here all internal tensions and hostilities (the working-class, "white trash" Lynndie, the African American sergeant Ivan Frederick, and so forth) are defused outward, toward the hapless bodies in detention, so that a united front of American multicultural heteronormativity can be not only performed, but, more important, affectively felt. Within the interstices of what is seen and what is felt, how it looks and how it feels, the photos emanate most powerfully the patriotic ties that bind.

Technologies of Simulacrum

As voyeur, conductor, dictator, dominatrix, those orchestrating these acts, several of whom appear erotically riled in the photos, are part of, not external to, the torture scenes themselves, sometimes even explicitly so. For example, Specialist Jeremy Sivits in his testimony states, "Staff Sergeant Frederick would take the hand of the detainee and put it on the detainee's penis, and make the detainee's hand go back and forth, as if masturbating. He did this to about three of the detainees before one of them did it right."[57] This is hardly indicative of a detached, objective, distanced observer behind the camera, positioned only to capture the events via the click of the shutter. Reports of sodomizing with chemical light sticks and broomsticks and of Americans inserting fingers into prisoners' anuses also fully implicate the U.S. guards and raise specters of interracial and intercultural sex. Al Jazeera has reported the American journalist Seymour Hersh's claim that there are videotapes of American soldiers sodomizing, that is, raping Iraqi "boys."[58] Less overtly, the separation of participant from voyeur becomes infinitely complicated by the pleasures of taking, posing for, and looking at pictures, especially as the use of cameras and videos inform varied practices (watching porn, nudie pics, to name a few) between partners of all genders in all kinds of sex.

Many of the photos, originally cropped for damaged-controlled consumption, are now revealing multiple spectators, bystanders, and participants; in the case of the widely disseminated and discussed photo of a hooded man made to stand on a box with wires attached like appendages to his arms, legs, and penis—a classic torture pose known predominantly to interrogation experts as "the Vietnam"—a U.S. guard is on the periphery, nonchalantly examining his digital camera. The Vietnam, explains Darius Rejali, derives from an amalgamation of the forced standing technique used by torturers in the British army (where it was known as "the crucifixion"), the French army (where it was known as "the Silo"), armies in the early twentieth century, U.S. police, Stalin's People's Commissariat for Internal Affairs (NKVD), the Gestapo in the 1930s, and South African and Brazilian police (who added the electrical supplement) in the 1970s.[59] In fact, it is this image, deemed by many to be the least sexually explicit and therefore less horrifying to view, that has been most reproduced around the world, its simulacra taking shape on billboards and murals and parodied in antiwar protest attire worn on the streets of Tehran, London, and New York and in fake iPod adverts done in hot pink, lime green, electric blue, and neon yellow. Performance artists, such as the New York City–based Hieronymus Bang, use the American flag as a substitute for the black cloak.[60] In Salah Edine Sallat's mural in Baghdad, the hooded prisoner on the box is paired with a shrouded Statue of Liberty holding up an electric gadget connected to the circuit breaker that threatens to electrocute them both. A brilliant painting by Richard Serra uses the silhouette of the covered prisoner to demand "Stop Bush." The Berkeley artist Guy Colwell's painting, titled *Abuse*, depicts hooded prisoners with wires sprouting from their bodies as American soldiers stand by with lightsticks (see figures 6–8b).[61]

To what can we attribute the now iconic status of this image? For starters, it is the only released photo to date that exposes almost no skin; only the legs and shins of the victim can be seen, preserving an anonymity of body that simultaneously incriminates the viewer less than some of the more pornographic images. It also radiates a distressing mystique; the hood harks back to the white hoods of the Ku Klux Klan but also resembles a veil. Indeed, the cloaking of nearly the entire body references another iconic image, that of the oppressed Muslim woman in her burqa, covered head

FIGURE 6. Iraqi artist Salah Edine Sallat finishes a mural in Baghdad, May 23, 2004. Photograph by Razmi Haidar. Reprinted with permission from Razmi Haidar/AFP/Getty Images.

FIGURE 7. Richard Serra, *Stop Bush*, 2004. Lithocrayon on mylar, 59¼ in. x 48 in. Reprinted with permission from Trina McKeever.

to toe in black and in need of rescue. It is plausible that this image of the Vietnam resonates as yet another missionary project in the making. It is the male counterpart to the Muslim-woman-in-burqa that liberal feminist organizations (like the National Organization for Women and the Feminist Majority Fund), the Bush administration (especially Laura Bush), and the conservative right-wingers who tout rhetorics of democracy and freedom love so well.

There is another, more sinister reason why the photo echoes so acutely. Called "stealth torture that leaves no marks," the Vietnam is traceless, leaving the bodies of its victims undifferentiated from unscathed ones. As happens with cloaking, the body remains both untroubled and unseen, and "if it were not for the photographs, no one would know that [torture] had been practiced."[62] The only evidence of the Vietnam comes in the form of the photograph. Its mass multiplication and mutations may speak to the need to document and inscribe into history and our optic memories that which otherwise leaves no visual proof. As Susan Sontag proclaimed, "The pictures will not go away."[63] Noting that "soldiers trained in stealth torture take these techniques back into civilian life as policemen and private security personnel," Rejali claims that the Vietnam is found throughout U.S. policing and imprisonment tactics, another likely rationale for the intense reverberations of this photo.[64]

Claiming that "theatricality leads us to the crux of the matter," Slavoj Žižek argues that the pictures "suggest a theatrical staging, a kind of tableau vivant, which brings to mind American performance art, [Antonin Artaud's] 'theatre of cruelty,' the photos of [Robert] Mapplethorpe or the unnerving scenes in David Lynch's films."[65] The facile comparison of the evidence of brutal wartime violence to spaces of artistic production might put the reader on edge. Indeed, the right wing is concocting similar conjectures: in *The American Spectator* George Neumayr writes, "Had Robert Mapplethorpe snapped the photos at Abu Ghraib, the Senate might have given him a government grant."[66] But the point, as I understand it, is not so much that these photos resemble works of art, but that the pictures look indeed as if the U.S. guards felt like they were on stage, hamming it up for the proud parents nervously biting their lips in the audience. The affect pouring from these photos is one of exaggerated theatricality; jovial and void of any somberness, they repulsively invite the viewer to come and jump on stage as well. As Richard Goldstein points out, "One reason why these photos are such a sensation is that they are stimulating."[67] The word "stimulating" pinpoints affect as the limit of representation; these photos matter beyond

FIGURE 8A. Forkscrew Graphics, image from *iRaq* series, yellow version, 2004. Courtesy of Forkscrew Graphics.

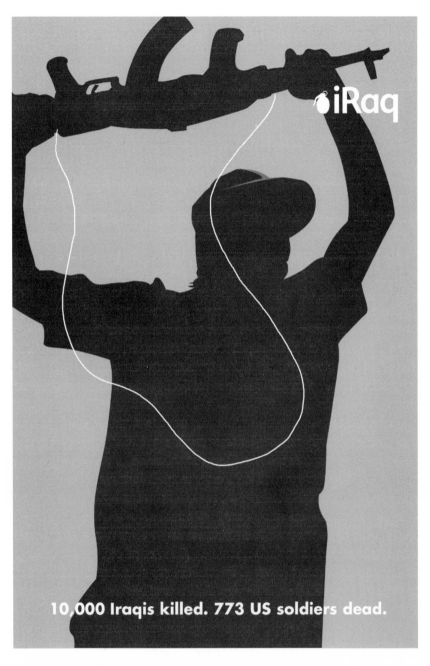

FIGURE 8B. Forkscrew Graphics, image from *iRaq* series, blue version, 2004.
Courtesy of Forkscrew Graphics.

what one can see in them, suggestive of haptic space: a way of seeing that is distinct from optical space, which renegotiates the tactile through the optical—"the eye itself may fulfill this non-optical function," such that one can feel touch through vision.[68] This is the collapsing of production and consumption, image and viewer onto the same vectors, the same planes. There is no inside or outside here; there are only movement, circulation, contingent temporalities, momentary associations and disassociations.

These photos not only depict the techniques of the torture; they also depict how both process (the photographing) and product (the pictures) are shaming technologies and function as a vital part of the humiliating, dehumanizing violence itself: the giddy process of documentation, the visual evidence of corporeal shame, the keen ecstatic eye of the voyeur, the haunting of surveillance, the dissemination of the images, like pornography on the Internet, the speed of transmission an aphrodisiac in itself, "swapped from computer to computer throughout the 320th Battalion,"[69] perpetuating humiliation ad nauseam. Taken between 2 A.M. and 4 A.M., the digital photos project their anticipated audience not as a representational demographic but through the affective economies of speed, time, pace, circulation, transit, distribution, flows, and, of course, exchange. It is difficult to fathom that the thought of the photos being leaked—what does that mean in our digital age when viruses can surreptitiously send e-mails and hackers can break into web servers, not to mention the sheer speed at which multifarious transmission occurs—had not occurred to someone somewhere at some moment.

One could argue that what is exceptional is not the actual violence itself, but the interplay of technologies, circuits, and networks that enable the digital capture and circulation of these acts, the photographic qualities of which are reminiscent of vacation snapshots, mementos of a good time, victory at last, or even the trophy won at summer camp. Unlike images of the collateral, purportedly unavoidable deaths of war, these photos divulge an irrefutable intentionality. We have inescapable proof of what we know to be true not only in Iraq, Afghanistan, and Guantánamo Bay, but in U.S. detention centers and prisons (although visual evidence of U.S. prison abuse has hardly been absent either).[70] Thus these images not only represent these acts, and allude to the procedural vectors of ever expansive audiences, but also reproduce and multiply the power dynamics that made these acts possible in the first place. In a now infamous article, Susan Sontag argues, "The photographs are us." Comparing the images to the photographs of black lynching victims taken between 1880 and 1930 that depict "Americans grinning beneath the naked mutilated body of a black man or woman hanging behind them from a tree," Sontag argues that a shift has occurred in the utility of photos. Once collectable items for albums and display in frames at home, photos are now "less objects to be saved than messages to be disseminated, circulated."[71] In Hazel Carby's response to Sontag, pointedly titled "A Strange and Bitter Crop: The Spectacle of Torture," she charges Sontag with minimizing the role of the collective spectator violence of lynching and objects to Sontag's implied characterization of private viewing: "The photographs of these bodies were not designed merely for storage, but rather functioned as public documents," such as postcards and adverts. Disturbed by Sontag's recourse to a narrative of exceptionalism, one that hinges on the historical severing of slavery from contemporary modes of violence, Carby forcefully contends, "The importance of spectacles of abuse, the taking of photographs and videos, the preservation and the *circulation* of the visual image of the tortured/lynched body, the erotic sexual exploitation which produced pleasure in the torturers—all these practices are *continuities* in the history of American racism."[72]

Obviously, technology is one difference that has been a major catalyst in this debatable transition from trophy to propaganda: the digital camera, sexy and absorbing software to assist in manipulating and perfecting images, and Internet sites that serve as virtual photo albums seem ubiquitous. It is a transition from stillness to proliferation, from singularity to fertility, like ejecting dandelion spores into the wind. But more important, motility, speed, and performance function as primary erotic and addictive charges of modernity: clicking the "send" button marks the ultimate release of productivity and consumption; dissemination is the ultimate form of territorial coverage and conquest, yet one more layering of the sexual matrix. While the visages and corpses of American casualties in Iraq remain protected material—even the faces of deceased soldiers were considered unseemly in a television program commemorating them—Iraqi bodies are accessible to all, available for comment, ridicule, shaming, scrutiny. If we were to honor Žižek's invocation of the theatricality of Abu Ghraib, they would indeed qualify as what Cynthia Keppley Mahmood, writing about the display of tortured Sikh bodies in Sikh living rooms and *gurdwaras* (temples), calls "massacre art": "In their very gruesomeness, [they] assert themselves in a room; they are impossible to ignore, and intrude in conversation, meditation, and everyday activities. Their potency derives only in part from their blood; it also derives from their unwillingness to be masked, covered, or distorted."[73]

Abu Ghraib's massacre art disrupts the placid, Pleasantville-like aura of the American family room, the streaming images from the television set mesmerizing us into silence. They are so potent not only for their naked honesty, but also because they are the evidence of how much power we can actually, and stunningly, command over others. Since July 2003 reports compiled by Amnesty International, the Red Cross, and other humanitarian organizations, as well as the testimonies of hundreds of detainees and re-leased prisoners, have been easily ignored by the Bush administration and the general public.[74] But these kinds of "facts," note theorists of "postmod-ern warfare" such as Patrick Deer, matter little, or certainly less, in an era dominated by virtual realities.[75] The photos and their circulatory modalities double as meaning and information, as the representation of information, and the only information taken seriously and validated by corporate media sources. In *Regarding the Pain of Others*, Sontag somewhat mechanically states, "Something becomes real—to those who are elsewhere, following it as 'news'—by being photographed," and adds that "all photographs wait to be explained or falsified by their captions."[76] But as information, these photos defy any need for the elucidation of captions. The force of com-prehension occurs not via what these photographs *mean*, in their contextual and symbolic specificity, but through what these images *do*—do to us, to the Iraqi prisoners, to the U.S. guards, to our sentimentalizing and hopeful notions of humanity, justice, peace. In other words, their productive force of affect renders language impotent: by looking we experience all that we need to know.

As with the weaving of the pyramid into simulacra, it is clear that mimi-cry, and not contextual meaning or deep knowledge of cultural difference, is the guiding interpretative paradigm. Calling the torture an initiation of those subjected into the "obscene underside" of "American culture," Žižek avers, "Similar photos appear at regular intervals in the U.S. press after some scandal explodes at an Army base or high school campus, when such rituals went overboard."[77] Again, Žižek's limp analogizing effectively evacu-ates the political context of forced occupation and imperial expansion within which specificity and singularity must be retained. While the com-parison to fraternity house hazing (I assume Žižek means college campus rather than high school) and army pranks is not without merit—for cer-tainly proliferating modalities of violence need and feed off one another—there is an easy disregard of the forced, nonconsensual, systemic, repetitive, and intentional order of violence hardly attributable to "rituals" that have gone "overboard." We might also ask, in another essay perhaps, whether these acts of torture really reveal anything intrinsic or particular to "American culture" or whether they can instead be linked more broadly to war cultures, rape cultures, and states of occupation at large. Again, this slippery analysis is fodder for the conservative right: Rush Limbaugh sanctioned a similar statement by a caller on his radio show by responding:

> Exactly my point. This is no different than what happens at [Yale University's secret fraternity] the Skull and Bones initiation, and we're going to ruin people's lives over it, and we're going to hamper our military effort, and then we are going to really hammer them because they had a good time. . . . You know, these people are being fired at every day. I'm talking about people having a good time, these people. You ever heard of emotional release?[78]

Later he said, "This is something you can see onstage at Lincoln Center from an N.E.A. grant, maybe on 'Sex and the City.' "[79] The references to theatricality and staging draw together liberal and right-wing commentators, efface the power dynamics of occupation, war, and empire, and ultimately leave a distasteful sense of smugness, from Limbaugh in particular, at having neatly trivialized something into next to nothing.[80]

The Photographs Went Away

We now know more about Lindsey [sic] England and Charles Grainer [sic] (two of the accused military police) than we do about any of the people who were the prisoners in those pictures. We know very little of their own narratives, identities, or their perspective on the U.S. occupation. Given that, we have to remember that their own histories, genders, and sexualities are as complex as our own. The U.S. media has managed to once again make them subjects of a war that are marginal in their own story. And the question remains: for which culture would these acts of sexual assault, rape, and murder be less appalling?—Trishala Deb and Rafael Mutis, "Smoke and Mirrors"

Trishala Deb and Rafael Mutis accurately point out that the majority of what has been reconstructed about the events at Abu Ghraib has been through the voices of the perpetrators and not the victims.[81] Sontag was mistaken: the photographs did indeed "go away," evaporating into the ether along with Ronald Reagan's horrific presidential record, as if any self-reflexive recursive loop that might offer time for reflection disappears with exhausting speed. It is devastating, but hardly surprising, that the U.S. public's obsessive consumption of this story nevertheless did not result in any deep-seated or longer-term demand to know who the victims are, what they experienced and felt, and how their lives are today. The problems with the testimonial genre notwithstanding, fourteen victims' testimonies that were interpreted and transcribed in January 2004 are available in full in their original text versions on the *Washington Post* website in downloadable PDF files.[82]

These testimonials obviously deserve deeper scrutiny and analysis beyond the scope of this chapter, especially as more stories are revealed from the survivors of Abu Ghraib. For now, what emerges from most popular, institutional, feminist, and even variants of gay and queer discourses on homosexuality and its intersections with the violence at Abu Ghraib is the following, a list that schematizes either the suppositions or the inferences of U.S. hetero- and homosexual exceptionalism:

1. The sexual acts simulated are all specifically and only gay or homosexual sex acts.

2. Homosexuality is taboo in Islamic cultures, making such acts the worst forms of humiliation for Muslims to endure. This insinuates that these forms of torture would be easier for other, supposedly less homophobic populations to tolerate (a rationale that appears preferable to a more expansive notion of bodily torture as violating for all); this explanation works to completely discount the presence of gay-identified Muslims in Arab societies, what Joseph Massad terms the "Gay International," but also obscures those engaging in same-sex erotics even if not within the rubric of identity.[83]

3. American tolerance for homosexuality, an imperative fantasy for homonationalism, is elevated in relation to Islamic societies, as symptomatized by the unspecific, ahistorical, and generalized commentary on the taboo of homosexuality for Muslims.

4. The enactment of gay sex (consolidated around the act of sodomy) constitutes the worst form of torture, sexual or otherwise.

5. Iraqi prisoners, having endured the humiliation of gay sex, are subjects worthy of sympathy and pity, an affective, temporally confined, emotive response more readily available than a sustained political critique of the U.S. occupation in Afghanistan and Iraq.

6. The question of race and how it plays out in these scenarios is effaced via the fixation on sexual torture; gender likewise becomes effaced when the acts are said to originate from a homophobic military culture instead of a misogynist one.

7. Sexuality is isolated within the purview of the individual (and through specific parts and zones constructed as erogenous, erotic, and sexual within heteronormative cartographies of the body),[84] as opposed to situated as an integrated diagrammatic vector of power.

8. The language favoring gay sex acts over torture once again casts the shadows of perversity outside, onto sexual and racial others, rather than contextualizing the processes of normalizing bodily torture.

9. Technologies of representation work to occlude the lines of connectivity (affective and bodily, in terms of proximity and positionality) between captors and prisoners.

Despite the absence of public debate about sexuality and the war on terrorism, the "Abu Ghraib prisoner sexual torture/abuse scandal," as it is now termed, vividly reveals that sexuality constitutes a central and crucial component of the machinic assemblage that is American patriotism. The use of sexuality—in this case, to physically punish and humiliate—is not tangential, unusual, or reflective of an extreme case, especially given continuities between representational, legislative, and consumerist practices. But not all of the torture was labeled or understood as sexual, and thus the odd acts—threatening dogs, for example—need to retain their idiosyncrasy. Imposing nudity itself is not automatically and innately sexual; it must be made to signify erotics, to signify sex. The legal scholar Kathleen M. Franke cautions against "over-eroticizing" assaults that involve sexual or intimate body parts, noting the danger of then "under-eroticizing" other bodily subjugation tactics. Calling for "desexualization of sodomy, rape, and other assaults labeled sex crimes" in her interpretation of the Abner Louima case, Franke avers, "Is it the sexual/erotic nature of these practices that make them wrong? For the most part, I think not. . . . These incidents should be analyzed to uncover the way the sexual/erotic operates as a particularly efficient and dangerous conduit with which to exercise power. Thus, to say that the Louima assault was sexual is at once to say too much and not enough about it."[85] Thus, the terms "scandal," "sexual," and "abuse" need to be semiotically discharged. This does not mean that this treatment is not sexual, but following Foucault (as Franke does), technologies of sex create and regulate, rather than reflect, the sexual bodies they name. If we then amend Foucault's biopolitical frame of the "management of life" with Achille Mbembe's "necropolitics," in which systems of domination are more "anatomical, tactile, and sensorial,"[86] we can say that sexual*ized* assault is a normalized facet of prisoner life, and "the sexual" is always already inscribed in necropolitical power grids implicating corporeal conquest, colonial domination, and death.

State of exception discourses doubly foster claims to exceptionalism: the violence of the United States is an exceptional event, antithetical to Americanness, and thus by extension, U.S. subjects emerge as morally, culturally, and politically exceptional through the production of the victims as repressed, barbaric, closed, uncouth, even homophobic, grounding claims of sexual exceptionalism that hinge on the normativization of certain U.S. feminist and homosexual subjects. The Abu Ghraib scandal, rather than being cast as exceptional, needs to be contextualized within a range of practices and discourses (particularly those less damning than prisoner abuse) that lasso sexuality in the deployment of U.S. nationalism, patriotism, and, increasingly, empire. Despite the actions of those in charge of Abu Ghraib, perversity is still withheld for the body of the queer Muslim terrorist, insistently deferred to the outside. This outside is rapidly, with precision and intensity, congealing into a population of what Giorgio Agamben has called *homo sacer*, those who "may be killed without the commission of a homocide," as their lives do not register within the realm of legal status.[87] Žižek considers this space "between the two deaths"—dead in the eyes of history but still alive for the countdown—as the fate of the prisoners at Abu Ghraib, the ghost detainees.[88] As with the systemic failure of U.S. military operations at the prison, which was not the fault of a handful of individuals but rather due to the entire assemblage of necropolitics, sexuality is not the barometer of exception, a situation out of control, or an unimaginable reality. Rather, it constitutes a systemic, intrinsic, and pivotal module of power relations.

In *Lawrence v. Texas*, the Supreme Court performed a double move, creating a dramatic discursive moment: it both decriminalized consensual homosexual relations between adults, and, simultaneously, authorized a new regime of heightened regulation of homosexuality. —Nan Hunter, "Sexual Orientation and the Paradox of Heightened Scrutiny"

intimate control, infinite detention:

rereading the *lawrence* case

On June 26, 2003, consensual adult sodomy was decriminalized in the United States. While the ruling was understandably lauded by gay and lesbian civil rights activists, others were quick to caution against an easy acceptance of the terms of the decision. The legal scholar Nan Hunter, for example, argues that the *Lawrence and Garner v. Texas* decision (hereafter referred to as *Lawrence-Garner*) "performed a double move, creating a dramatic discursive moment." A generative project of liberalism, the purportedly liberating process of deregulation inaugurates yet again the multiplication of pools of knowledge—particularization, minutiae, what Hunter terms "heightened scrutiny"—of queer bodies.[1] This time, unlike sexology, psychiatry, and other fields embedded in the study of deviance, liberalism works through the positive register of incorporation (the productive effects of exclusion notwithstanding).

Paradoxically, the decriminalization of sodomy results in accentuated state regulation of sexuality rather than a decline in such patrolling,[2] commissioning many other actors to intensify other types of scrutiny, for example, to assess the suitability of homosexuals for adoption and parenting. Hunter locates this heightened scrutiny as part of the subterranean "examination of the social acceptability of those persons who are the objects of the government's interventions" specific to jurisprudence regarding sexuality. Highlighting the Foucauldian entanglement of freedom and regulation, Hunter argues that "deprived of criminal law as a tool, opponents of equality for lesbians and gay men are likely to concentrate increasingly on the strategy of containment." She delineates several areas where containment tactics might be most efficacious: disputes involving children, control over expressive space, otherwise known as the public sphere, and distinguishing the "respectability" of queer relationships that reinforce hierarchies of race, class, gender, and citizenship.[3]

These points regarding containment are well taken, but other forms of power focus less on state regulation and the scrutiny of actors and instead foreground floating mechanisms of continuous control, enacted through the proliferation of management devices and details, an implosion and explosion of information about sexual subjects that subtends the emancipatory ideals of the liberal subject, straddling the disciplinary apparatus of the state and the more diffuse registers of control societies. Disciplinary containment—discursive, ideological, and spatial—is still very much in operation as a panoptic power player even while new grains of information, indeed, information that was once only superfluous or seemingly superfluous to circuits of domination, feed the epistemological will-to-know of control societies: the dance between the "internalization of the gaze" and the "processes of administration, social sorting and simulation," the latter dubbed "superpanopticism."[4]

These tensions reflect an ongoing discussion about the uses of the panopticon as a surveillance model, whereby subjects are disciplined through regulations, and the "superpanopticon" of informational surveillance through which there is a regularization of population construction and the proliferation of "regularities." For Foucault, normalization of society entails tendencies from "technologies of drilling" that are enacted in various institutional sites of confinement (hospitals, prisons, schools, barracks) to populations as they are produced through what he calls "technologies of security"—insurance and reassurance—that work through the "regularization" of risk, profoundly different from regulation and the regulatory modes invested in disciplinary sites. In his later work, Foucault contends that biopolitics shifts or even overrides the emphasis on disciplining subjects to the regularization of populations, with a "normalizing society" as the object and objective of both.[5]

While regulatory power is maintained through the minimum amount of exertion to delineate internals and externals, "powers of exuberance" characterize the productive capacity of informational economies, fecund circuits that exponentially multiply through intersections, overlaps, matches, points of contact, coordinates, and contradictions. The focus is regenerative rather than retributive, producing more and more rather than mediating inclusion and exclusion. Thus, unlike power that banishes and excludes, or includes and organizes and manages, this power operates through calculation and intervention, characterized by tendencies and degrees, adjusted through tweaking and modulation rather than norming.[6] There is less emphasis on the outside or inside to regulate, less emphasis on "closed site[s] differentiated from . . . another closed site"; instead, closed sites give way to "frightful continual training . . . continual monitoring."[7] Detailing the trajectories of the move "from disciplining to biopolitical control," Patricia Clough argues that governance and representational politics, adapting to the "disorganization of nationally organized capital," transit into expansive modalities of "risk management, militarism, and policing"[8] that dislocate or slice through the imagined coherency of contained sites, identity categories (race, class, gender, sexuality, nation), and the body-as-organism: a tension between disciplinary normativization of subjects and their "behavioral expression of internalized social norms"[9] and the social control of pools of bodies both human and nonhuman. Thus, the "new regime of heightened regulation of homosexuality" that Hunter speaks of must be understood in conjunction with, not separate from, profiling, surveillance, and information technologies currently in use.[10]

In this chapter, I situate the *Lawrence-Garner* ruling in the context of an array of American exceptionalisms generated by counterterrorism ideologies that are deployed within and across transnational and global arenas. What does the overruling of the seventeen-year-old Supreme Court decision that upheld a state's right to criminalize sodomy signify in this deeply conservative, regressive political climate of U.S. imperial expansion? The decision was handed down on June 26, 2003, not even four months after the U.S. invasion of Iraq and less than two years after the passage of the USA PATRIOT Act of 2001 and George W. Bush's executive order on November 13, 2001. For Giorgio Agamben, these events represent the most egregious abuse of presidential power in the state of exception in U.S. history, demonstrating that "the state of exception appears as a threshold of indeterminancy between democracy and absolutism."[11] It is rather striking that sodomy has been decriminalized in the United States during a period when the Orientalist versions of sodomy and linked perversions resonate so deeply with the conscious and unconscious psychic registers of American nationalism (legal precedents and the composition of the U.S. Supreme Court notwithstanding). An accelerated frenzy stalks sodomy and its specters in the war on terror, with sensationalist reportage on pedophilia among so-called terrorist populations (such as Pashtun Afghanis), the Catholic Church sexual abuse and molestation scandals, "gay sex" used as torture at Abu Ghraib, and the ludicrous media spectacle of the Michael Jackson trial, among other recent examples.[12] Sodomy angst is palpable. Can we, as critical scholars, activists, and scholar-activists, afford to separate the legalization of sodomy from the politics of racism, empire, and war mongering? If we resisted the compartmentalization of publics and privates, the analogizing of sexuality and race, would this historic moment seem so jubilant?

I am also interested in fleshing out the convivial relations between distinct yet entangled forms of power, part and parcel of what can be named the "environmentality," rather than governmentality, of mutually reinforcing, rather than teleological or serial, habitations of discipline and control, regulations and regularities. Some questions pertinent to this analysis include the following: What is the force and effect of queer representational praxis and critique, much of it focused on the dynamics of the inclusion and exclusion of subjects of human rights—the queer liberal subject of *Lawrence-Garner*, the subject of rehabilitation, for example—and their silences and exclusions, voice and inclusion, in the face of power that refuses any singular locational demarcation? What is the combined impact of representational politics with affective politics? If there is an overriding of individual subject formation, what kinds of subjects are formed through population construction, the subjects of regenerative capacity? There is an oscillation in this chapter between sexuality as an incorporated object, instrument, target, and subject of control, and sexuality as a term in a self-other/ing dialectic predicated on subject formation.

Reading Sideways, against Analogies

Siobhan Somerville argues that the practice of looking at legal precedents, as opposed to cross-reading contemporaneously, privileges a teleological narrative whereby isolated fragments of the past are mobilized in the service of "naturalizing a progressive teleology of rights."[13] This narrative has detrimentally encouraged what Miranda Joseph terms an "analogic inclusion," which proffers connectivity in order to disguise an equivalence as an equal.[14] Analogies appear to compare objects when in actuality they compare relations, differentiating and isolating components (in this case, race as separate from sexuality) while assimilating this difference into a form of similarity. As Gayatri Chakravorty Spivak observes, each analogous component is internally reified while "excluding the fields of force that make them heterogenous, indeed discontinuous," if not antagonistic.[15] This analogizing of race and sexuality has a protracted history in gay liberationist tenets that eventually rendered sexuality a form of minoritization parallel to ethnicity and race.[16]

The foundational analogizing argument of gay and lesbian civil rights discourses proceeds as follows: gays and lesbians are the last recipients of civil rights that have already been bestowed on racial minorities. This lackadaisical approach does not only naïvely propagate "an optimistic reading of the history of civil rights in the twentieth-century United States," perpetuating a belief that the issues addressed by civil rights legislation for people of color have really been resolved (as evidenced by multiculturalism). It also relieves mainstream gays, lesbians, and queers from any accountability to antiracist agendas, produces whiteness as a queer norm (and straightness as a racial norm), and fosters anti-intersectional analyses that posit sexual identity as "like" or "parallel to" race. An example of this is found in the "miscegenation analogy" that situates the 1967 decriminalization of interracial heterosexual marriage as the precursor to the legalization of same-sex marriages, thus cleaving race from homosexuality and "enact[ing] a kind of amnesia about how U.S. legal discourse historically has produced narratives of homosexuality in relation to race."[17]

In some senses, this amnesia has pervaded the celebratory aftermath of the *Lawrence-Garner* decision. Franke, for instance, comments, "Gay rights activists and scholars have rejoiced. . . . Indeed, some have gone so far as to label the decision in *Lawrence v. Texas* 'our Brown.' "[18] With the exception of the work of Franke, Hunter, Somerville, Nayan Shah, and Kendall Thomas, most commentaries and scholarly expositions hail the decriminalization of sodomy strictly within the parameters of historical narratives of progressive inevitability, issuing huge sighs of relief following this rather stunning reversal of the 1986 *Bowers v. Hardwick* ruling, the case that upheld states' rights to criminalize sodomy.[19] Within this reading practice, the merriment has been tempered by queer theorists who, like Hunter, are quick to point out that the language of *Lawrence-Garner* prescribes the privatization of queer sex, rendering it hidden and submissive to the terrain of the domestic (subjected to insidious forms of surveillance), an affront to queer public sex cultures that sought to bring the private into the public.[20]

As Somerville predicts, the sole focus on sexual orientation roots out racial formation from sexuality, an example immediately found in the particulars of the case. The interracial pairing of Tyron Garner, a younger black man, and John Geddes Lawrence, an older white man, are not details re-marked upon in any court documents of the case. Nor was the general public specifically made aware of this fact until photographs of the two were published in the media *after* the decision.[21] My usage of *Lawrence-Garner*, instead of the citing practices of legal cases that typically use the first litigant's familial name, accentuates the invisibility of Tyron Garner's blackness. Indeed, the historical documentation, official record, and schol-arly exposition will ensure that this case goes down in history with the name of the white gay man involved.

Somerville demonstrates the interlinked histories of racial and sexual regulation in the two decades following World War II, noting that the 1952 Walter McCarren Immigration and Naturalization Act dropped the lan-guage of racial exclusion, shifting instead to a rhetoric of inclusion via the national origin quota system while adding new language spotlighting sex-ual outlaws, homosexuals, and adulterers.[22] This overlapped with the legal-ization of interracial marriage in 1967, coinciding with the "increasing vis-ibility and overt criminalization of homosexuality in U.S. laws." These historical "shifts in federal juridical constructions of homosexuality [that] coincide[d] with major changes in the legal discourse of race" imply that there was a "trading in" of racial integration for sexual regulation.[23] In actuality, the subtext of the regulation of sexual deviance was put into the service of policing racialized subjects.[24] Similarly, one could argue for a reversal of sorts: in our contemporary milieu, the growing visibility and "inclusion" of gay and lesbian subjects into the national legislative fold of the United States (not to mention market interpellation) appear to be at the expense of racialized subjects (signaled by the demise of critical multi-culturalism as a post–civil rights discourse and the escalation of racial profiling justified by the war on terror). Considering the contemporaneous consolidation of new racial populations, a racialization of religion, im-plicating Arabs, Muslims, and South Asians and those mistaken for them ("terrorist look-alikes"),[25] the impact of *Lawrence-Garner* must be examined in this intensely charged racial atmosphere, which repetitively defines the slippery contours of racial markings not only in relation to a dominant white American formation, but also among people of color themselves. For those who are positioned or position themselves as members of the popula-tion situated at the crossroads of *Lawrence-Garner* and of indefinite deten-tion—that is, doubly interpellated by racial *and* sexual othering such that they are inseparable—the political climate fosters an especially pernicious regulatory policing, the efficacy and brutality of which should not be underestimated. My intent here is not to capitulate to analogical modes of analysis but rather to flesh out the "identity effects" of such analogies within the juridical discourses for the subjects they overtly claim to protect and for those they covertly or overtly disavow.

And yet, the impact of *Lawrence-Garner* will be rendered most forcefully not only in terms of the sexual subjects it liberates in exchange for the racial subjects it imprisons—an approach that highlights the recognition of analogous rights-bearing subjects—but also by the spatial politics of surveillance, race, and racialization and the incorporative energy of control apparatuses. Forms of profiling (e.g., FBI scanning for radioactive materials in mosques and the homes and businesses of Muslims)[26] work through registers of inclusion—the inclusion of the homo sacer—not quite the othering of racial profiling, but a specific mode of othering that is both endemic to a claim of incorporation yet specific in its targeting: not a Hegelian self-othering dynamic, but othering within inclusion. These distinctions in operations of power reflect the connections between regulatory state power and diffuse control regimes.

When reading sequentially, to the exclusion of simultaneity, or reading vertically, rather than horizontally or "sideways," as Somerville advocates, the nation-state may rebind to itself, restricting transnational registers of which sexual and racial others are very much constitutive.[27] I am interested in peering sideways to cross-read *Lawrence-Garner* against seemingly unrelated and often disjunctively situated moments and their effects, tracing the limits of its juridical legality in the context of indefinite detention, affirmative action, gay marriage, and the May 2004 Abu Ghraib "sexual torture scandal." I begin with a brief sketch of the debates that are conventionally raised when reading *Lawrence-Garner* through *Bowers*. This exposition is by no means comprehensive, and certainly the decriminalization of sodomy in the United States is an event of tremendous import and impact. I trace the contours of discussion—the discursive outcomes—rather than the intricate details of the cases themselves. Next, I look at the actualization of an American national queer liberal subject before the law, emboldened not only by the legalization of her or his assigned sexual act, but also through the reracialization of sodomy elsewhere that allows for the sanitization of her or his intimate sexual being. This protected subject materializes with particular force during the aftermath of the Abu Ghraib scandal, an argument that I develop from my analysis of media and scholarly comment in chapter 2. Finally, I proffer a biopolitical reconceptualization of intimacy as an affective modality central to the regulatory and control operations of the

Lawrence-Garner ruling and the baggage attached to it. Through the evaluation of the spatiotemporal elements of the ongoing practices of indefinite detention—practices accruing cumulative spatial effects—in regard to Muslim families and communities in Brooklyn and Queens, I demonstrate that the distribution of intimacy is crucial to sexual-racial biopolitical management of life as well as necropolitical propagation of "pure" death.

Sodomy, Public and Private

It is a curious form of liberty that Justice Kennedy reaches for in *Lawrence.* "Liberty protects the person from unwarranted government intrusions into a dwelling or other private places," he writes. "Freedom extends beyond spatial bounds. Liberty presumes an autonomy of self that includes freedom of thought, belief, expression, and certain intimate conduct." Yet the liberty principle upon which the opinion rests is less expansive, rather geographized, and, in the end, domesticated. It is not the synonym of a robust liberal concept of freedom.—Katherine M. Franke, "The Domesticated Liberty of *Lawrence v. Texas*"

The U.S. Supreme Court case *Lawrence and Garner v. Texas* (2003) was spurred by the 1998 conviction of a white gay male and a black gay male prosecuted under the Texas "Homosexual Conduct" law, wherein sodomy is denigrated as "deviate sexual intercourse" between persons of the same gender. Responding to a false report of a "weapons disturbance" at a private residence, Texas police found John Geddes Lawrence and Tyron Garner engaged in anal sexual intercourse in Lawrence's apartment. As there was no record of this law used in Texas in the arrest for sodomy in a private home, one could surmise that the race of Garner and the sodomitic miscegenation were implicated in the false disturbance call and the arrest, a point to which I return later.[28] At the time of the *Lawrence-Garner* ruling, four states (Oklahoma, Missouri, Kansas, Texas) prohibited sodomy for homosexuals only, while nine states had laws criminalizing all sodomy regardless of gender configuration. Favoring the "broader privacy argument" over the "narrower equal-protection argument,"[29] the decision overturned the 1986 *Bowers* ruling, in effect decriminalizing consensual sodomy, both homosexual and heterosexual, on the federal level. In 1986, *Bowers* upheld a Georgia sodomy statute that was used to arrest, though ultimately not prosecute, Michael Hardwick for oral sex. As the details of the arrest and the case itself are extensively documented, I do not rehearse them here.[30] Key to my argument is that the language and framing of *Bowers* sutured, if not intensified, the relationship between homosexuality and sodomy. That is, in the *Bowers* proceedings, the Court deliberated these very questions: Are homosexuals allowed the right to consensual sodomy? Do privacy rights extend to homosexual sodomy?

The rhetorical force of these queries was efficient in the discursive circumscription of sodomy as the homosexual act par excellence. Implicitly relegating heterosexual sodomy as unfathomable, this demarcation of sodomy as the perverse homosexual act stages the difference between homosexual and heterosexual identities. As Janet Halley argues, this collapses sexual act into sexual identity; in other words, the sexual act defines one's sexual identity. It also produces sodomy as a metonym of homosexuality, a correspondence encouraged not only by conservative factions—"homophobes"—but also by "homophiles" and progressive factions.[31] The technical definition of sodomy as oral-genital or anal-genital sex (and in some definitions, fisting and oral-anal sex, although for the most part analingus appears to be unaccounted for)[32] challenges this stitching of sodomy to homosexuality. Halley notes the metonymic regulation not only of homosexual identity, which is stabilized, homogenized, and therefore fictionalized, but also of heterosexual identity, which must disavow the act of sodomy in order to normatively produce itself against homosexuality, specifically against gay male sexuality (androcentric, despite the use of sodomy laws for various rationales against lesbians).[33] Moreover, a number of "expansionist interpretations of *Hardwick*" in the postruling period led to a deeper entrenchment of sodomy (already linked to incest and adultery in the decision) as a "criminal, loathsome act" equated with "homosexual desire or identity."[34] Thus, as George Chauncey explains, these criminalizing expansionist interpretations were used to "justify everything from the exclusion of gays from the military to the removal of children from the homes of their lesbian mothers. Sodomy laws were an ideological cornerstone in the legal edifice of antigay discrimination."[35]

The *Lawrence-Garner* ruling shifted the terms of discussion from the preoccupation with the apparent singularity of the homosexual practice of sodomy in *Bowers* to the question of homosexual occupation of intimacy, within the domains of the domestic and the private, to ascertain "whether homosexuals possess the same liberty of intimacy in physical relationships as heterosexuals." The *Lawrence-Garner* opinion claimed to unequivocally denounce *Bowers*, finding that the framing of the issue was completely flawed: "The *Bowers* Court focused on whether states possess the power to regulate and prohibit sexual acts, the *Lawrence* Court focused on whether the states possess the power to regulate personal relationships."[36] Franke, however, points to the "palimpsestic presence of *Bowers* in the wake of *Lawrence*," reflected in the way "*Lawrence* both echoes and reinforces a pull toward domesticity in current gay and lesbian organizing," relying on a "remind[er to] the world that gay people, too, have families."[37] In brief, Franke's brilliant exposé of the sobering pitfalls of the *Lawrence-Garner* ruling catechizes "privatized liberty," declaring that "the liberty interest at stake is one that is tethered to the domestic private. Repeatedly, Justice Kennedy territorializes the right at stake as a liberty to engage in certain conduct in private." Protecting the liberty of homosexual sex in private, "closeted behind the closed doors of the bedroom," Franke argues, entails relapsing into an archaic legal notion of the private historically deployed within privacy rights litigation, disposing recent versions of privacy that are more abstract, less literal, and less territorial and that emphasize a "zone of personal autonomy and decisional privacy." A conversion from the vilified and repulsive "sodomitic outlaws" to the what Franke denotes as the civilized gay "domestinormative" is also performed, sanctioning homonormative relationships that mimic heteronormative domesticity while further ostracizing nonnormative sexual and kinship praxis of not only homosexuals, but heterosexuals as well.[38] Further, Franke implies that the relegation of decriminalized sodomy to the domestic private realm, which refuses to empower public performatives of sexual expression, is tantamount to recriminalizing sodomy and other forms of sexual incarnation outside of the immediacy of one's private home. What Nayan Shah notes as the "Supreme Court's focus on individual autonomy and privacy of homosexual conduct in the home" is exemplified in the following passage from the ruling: "When sexuality finds overt expression in intimate conduct with another person, the conduct can be but one element in a personal bond that is more enduring."[39] Franke ascertains that "Justice Kennedy takes it as given that the sex between John Lawrence and Tyron Garner took place within the context of a relationship."[40] The assumption of conjugal connectivity is paradigmatic of the domestinormative, making clear that turning tricks, sex for material gain, sex parties and clubs, and other queer acts exceed the protective bounds of the ruling.

After the 1970s' gay liberation cynosure on "right-to-privacy in public: a zone of immunity from state regulation, surveillance, and harassment" promoting "a right to publicize 'private' matters considered offensive to the phantom 'general public,'" *Lawrence-Garner* looks a tad like cleaning up the homeless and moving them out of view, a sanitizing of image and physical as well as psychic space.[41] Lisa Duggan notes that by the 1980s, antigay forces conceded to "the right to privacy," defining privacy as "a kind of confinement, a cordon sanitaire protecting 'public' sensibilities."[42] Western liberal feminists have typically understood the private as an axiomatic space of women's subjugation to men, the domestic dominion that lassos women to unpaid work in the home, reproductive expectations, heteronormative nuclearity, and vulnerability to domestic violence: the "patriarchal family home." Feminists of color, however, have berated Catherine MacKinnon and other feminist interpreters who consign the state to the public and disregard the vicissitudes of state racism that permeate the domestic private domains of women of color and immigrant women. That is, in liberalism, the private for women is theorized as a space outside of and untouched by (much-needed) state intervention, while the public is hailed "as a space of recourse and as a zone automatically lying outside an easily and singularly recognized 'home.' " Neither, argues Ananya Bhattacharjee, are useful or accurate paradigms for immigrant women, especially for those who are undocumented and for whom the state is inescapable even in the private, the presence of which most often transpires as state racism.[43]

The queer liberal interpretation of the relegation to privacy as a kind of confinement that is nevertheless a privileged void from state intervention (the fantasy that the *Lawrence-Garner* ruling fosters) illuminates the taken-for-granted access to privacy and raises many questions about the unacknowledged forms of privilege necessary to indulge such a reading. Who is able to occupy the private in the manner that *Lawrence-Garner* mandates? A claim to the right to privacy is not even on the radar screen for many sectors of society, unfathomable for whom being surveilled is a way of life. Discussing the "compulsory visibility of the welfare poor," John Gilliom reminds us that "the welfare administration demands that a client open her life to them in the form of income verification, computer matches and other tactics in what can only be called a full-scale surveillance assault."[44] If we are to examine just one other coordinate of disenfranchisement, such as homeless youth, we see that LGBT youth constitute 25 to 40 percent of the total homeless youth population, an indictment of private liberty at home if there ever was one.[45] The private is, therefore, offered as a gift of recognition to those invested in certain normative renditions of domesticity and as an antidote, with many strings attached, to those otherwise unable or unwilling to avoid public surveillance or who cannot make recourse to the private in any sustained manner.

More important, the private is a racialized and nationalized construct, insofar as it is granted not only to heterosexuals but to certain citizens and withheld from many others and from noncitizens. As Mary Pat Brady remarks, "Spatial analysis has not considered the degree to which constructions of race and sexuality further constitute and hold together the distinctions between public and private spheres, nor has it taken into account that the obverse operates as well, because spatial distinctions help to structure sexuality, race, and class."[46] The intertwined existence of race and sexuality mark the contours of private and public even as private-public boundaries disaggregate racialized sexualities and sexualized racializations. The private liberty of *Lawrence-Garner* is not merely normative in gender and kinship terms, it is also a form of racial and citizenship privilege. Franke's domestinormative gestures to homonormative subjects of class, racial, legal status, and gender privilege who have material access to it *against* the sexually nonnormative racialized subjects discursively and perhaps even literally barred from it. It also produces the very criterion by which the homonormative can be readily distinguished from nonnormative sexual, class, national, and raced subjects.

Without an intersectional analysis (and here, intersectionality as a heuristic may well be indispensable), the private is naturalized as a given refuge from state scrutiny. Franke's critique resonates most trenchantly with populations who identify primarily through a single-axis identity lens, who experience disenfranchisement and regulation mostly if not entirely through their sexual orientation. Those who already enjoy to some extent unmediated or taken-for-granted access to the public and zones of public space, whether it be cruising areas, sex clubs, restrooms, parks, rest stops, or other spots where queers rendezvous, or the prospect of seeing themselves reflected in popular media, are subjects whose queer visibilities are not compromised by racial profiling, undocumented status, or gender-queer phobia. *Lawrence-Garner* can offer protection only to those who inhabit the fantasy of, and can mark and traverse across, bounded notions of public and private. In her otherwise fantastic mediation of the conservative pulses of *Lawrence-Garner*, Franke appraises the homonormative subject envisioned by the ruling, but the like-minded subjects she presumes to be in her reading audience also inhabit a particular myopic queer identity from which race is cleaved: the queer liberal.

Franke, as well as Judith Butler, approach these regulatory regimes through the single-axis identity lens of sexuality, sexual activity, and their attendant kinship arrangements. Butler argues that the binary between heterosexuals and homosexuals has been displaced by an emphasis on illegitimate and legitimate partnerships, via the push for respectability though gay marriage, the private liberty of sodomy, and gay and lesbian civil rights.[47] There is no question that *Lawrence-Garner* does this: the parameter of legitimacy is neither expanded nor challenged; rather, its contours are reified and hardened despite its welcoming inauguration of formerly excluded subjects.[48] But Butler's is actually not a wholly accurate picture, for other hierarchies (class, gender, race, citizenship) are also resolidified in this formulation of legitimate and illegitimate lives, not to mention the untouched question: What does the ruling say, if anything at all, to women? to lesbians? Ruthann Robson writes that *Lawrence-Garner* "perpetuates the invisibility of lesbians and the myth that there is no history of persecution against lesbians."[49]

The precious haven of the private, always a relative, tenuous, and often impossible affair for people of color and immigrants, is even further spatially and temporally contained through the notion of intimacy. The "private liberty of intimacy" implies that sex happens only in the privacy of one's home, and the liberal ideal of home as sanctuary and as property that one owns is expressed repeatedly in the decision. There is as well a particular judgment of quality attached to the relationship and security attached to the home and the sex taking place within it. Evidence of such judgment surfaces in the commitment defined by normative frames of linearity and temporality, gay or civil marriage or domestic partnership, (joint) property ownership and financial entwinement. Conspicuous consumption, class privilege, or signs of class inhabitation or rehabilitation through upward mobility—the "market virility" that Nast speaks of[50]—join stability, longevity, and duration, affective modalities nostalgically invoked as lost attributes of postmodernism, to present a recognized, well-integrated, publicly valorized, and productive kinship formation: labor, nation, and simulated fertility—the productive citizen. Insofar as queer subjects should not or cannot reproduce the national population in conventional terms, productive here is understood as the capitalist capacity to adopt or to "rent wombs" within formations that not only mimic heterosexuality but also replicate the privileged racial norms (whiteness) of heteronormativity.[51] These are attributes of the ascendancy of whiteness that stand in deep contrast to the black welfare queen, the accused Muslim terrorist who must register with the INS or expatriate himself and his family, and the incarcerated black or Latino prisoner. Further, implicit in the notion of privacy favored by the *Lawrence-Garner* ruling as well as those critically commenting on it is an assumption that the gay subject automatically belongs to the American nation as a citizen. As Bhattacharjee writes, "The absence of

FIGURE 9. Daryl Cagle, *Sodomy Decision*, June 26, 2003. Reprinted with permission from PoliticalCartoons.com.

analysis of the nation-state in U.S. mainstream feminism leads to the un-critical and automatic assumption of a public whose subject, then, is a U.S. citizen."[52] I would add that the same goes for the U.S. citizen who assumes the right to the private, now gay or queer. The homonormative subject of *Lawrence-Garner*, as well as the queer liberal subject who should resist its interpellative normativity, are *both* U.S. citizens. The absence of a discussion about and analysis of the ramifications of the ruling in terms of citizenship and sexual citizenship means we do not ask the question: What kind of sexual citizen is the protected subject of *Lawrence-Garner*?

Understandably, Franke, in sheer frustration, demands answers to the following queries:

How has this become a community that privileges recognition so highly, and seems to have abandoned some of the more radical strategies and goals grounded in a politics that sought to destabilize dominant forms of sexuality and kinship, rather than seeking to be stabilized by them? Might there be something politically valuable in resisting that transformation of the gay political subject from pervert to domesticated couple?

. . . Why have the gaining of rights and the politics of recognition been substituted for earlier political goals in the gay community that were committed to making viable a range of sexual and kin affiliations other than those that are narrowly domestinormative?[53]

One disheartening answer, of course, does not focus on the collapse of radical queer kinship and sexual ideals that now appear to be assimilative (as Franke bemoans) but takes us instead to the interrelation between the ascendancy of heteronormativity and the ascendancy of whiteness. *Lawrence-Garner* partakes in U.S. exceptionalism through its contribution of national homonormative subjects. The case set off a flurry of attempted and realized gay marriages around the country not only, nor simply, because of normative desires in terms of coupling, kinship, reproduction, and procreation. More important, the push for these legislative affirmations is fueled by conscious and unconscious yearnings to reinstate the privileges of whiteness, in fact, white Americanness. The benefits of *Lawrence-Garner* and gay marriage initiatives disaggregate strata of racial privilege and racial disenfranchisement at the same time that legalization proffers a much coveted return to American citizenry that was lost with the taking on of a nonnormative sexual identity. Thus, the conservatization of sexual, gender, and kinship norms cannot be disaggregated from its nationalist, classist, and racist impulses, or from the liberal underpinnings of subject formation. The ascendancy of whiteness does not require heterosexuality as much as it requires heteronormativity, or its mimicry in the form of homonormativity or what Franke calls the domestinormative.

This f(r)actioning of homosexuality with white racial, capital, and citizenship privilege cleaves it away from other homosexual racial and class alliances it might otherwise encompass.[54] These dynamics are fueled by uninterrogated racial and citizenship privileges and unacknowledged racism, xenophobia, and nationalism in gay, lesbian, and queer communities and organizing, a special facet of the white liberal alibi that allows one to disaffiliate from even the remote possibility of the perpetration of such violence. At this historical juncture, homonormative and queer liberal desires for state recognition become indistinguishable from the racial and national exclusions upon which such affirmations float. Thus, the *Lawrence-Garner* ruling effectively produces homonational subjects in accordance with American nationalist ideals, finally conferring sexual citizenship, but along the most narrow of lines.

Furthermore, the enduring frame of the public-private binary is one often invoked to qualify the domestic as an interior enclosure, with the public equivalent to the state. A vast literature problematizing public-private divisions has developed, pointing to a range of discrepancies: public mechanisms that intrude on privacy, enactments of the private in public spheres, dissolution of the division altogether.[55] However irksome, it remains the guiding spatial paradigm of juridical discourse at large and sodomy regulation in particular, informed by assumptions that private and public zones still function as operative ideological and spatial distinctions by which people organize their lives.

If we foreground regulation and surveillance through *and* beyond their disciplinary strictures, however, we go beyond the clean delineation between who is watching and who is being watched. Otherwise termed by surveillance studies (never sucked into the quagmire of public-private debates) as networks of control that crisscross publics and privates, this approach renders the notions of discrete publics and privates implausible, incoherent, and obsolete.[56] Control networks spiral through those who look, see, hear, gather, collect, analyze, target, scan, digitize, tell, e-mail, and tabulate, mixed in with those who are seen, heard, told, gathered, collected, targeted, and so on, the doers and those having something done to them indistinguishable from each other, as one in the same body, on both sides concurrently or alternatively on no sides at all. Specific to a Deleuzian model of control societies is an emphasis on affective resonance, on how surveillance technologies activate, infect, vibrate, distribute, disseminate, disaggregate; in other words, how things feel, how sensations matter as much as if not more than how things appear, look, seem, are visible, or are cognitively known. Interrogating the heightened regulation of sexual-racial others entails not displacing but rather enhancing older models of discrete and finite space and time with spatiotemporal genres that are mobile and fluid.

In light of this theoretical shift, the notion of intimacy is a moralistically charged spatial form pivotally mobilized in the briefs supporting the decriminalization of sodomy. As an asset worth protecting, a crucible of affective economy, intimacy (along with fear, terror, security, hope) has incurred a redoubling of investiture since September 11, 2001—think of the fixation on close relationships, on renewed contact with persons from the past, on not acting out sexually.[57] In this insurial economy, intimacy is rearticulated beyond the domain of the private or elicited through negotiated public-private interplay. While Hunter argues that *Lawrence-Garner* "is important less for its explicit protection of a private sphere of intimate decision making than for its implicit unmasking of the interrelationship between sexuality and the state as a properly public sphere,"[58] it is not merely that intimacy continues to be monitored publicly even as it is deemed a properly private matter. Rather, intimacy circulates through a spatial exchange network whereby proximity, in/security, anxiety, quality, abstraction, particularity, porousness, opacity, and transparency, among other affective modalities, are produced through experiences of surveillance.

To allege a complete shift in privacy rights orientation, however, from land, property, self-autonomy, bodily integrity, liberty, and physical space to the tabulation of "bodies of data and information" underestimates the integrated system of racial profiling and surveillance through which the lucrative partnership of panopticism and superpanopticism cooperate.[59]

Black Is, Black Ain't

The silent issue in the Lawrence v. Texas case is race. While race was not on trial, it was certainly the elephant in the room. . . . The interracial component of Garner's and Lawrence's relationship disgusted some folks—black and white—just as much as them being gay. Many have speculated that the bogus call to the police about a burglary from a prying neighbor was . . . also motivated by racism.— Irene Monroe, "Justice Begins in the Bedroom"

I now turn to the silent interraciality floating upon the *Lawrence-Garner* case to demonstrate the "sneaking in through the backdoor" nature of racist and nationalist queer liberal imaginaries and the impossibility of fully understanding the impact of the ruling without examining its conservative pulses that cohabit gender and sexuality.[60] It is not incidental that the case involves an interracial pairing: a white man and an African American man. (Of note is their age difference: Lawrence, 55 at the time, and Garner, 31, which may or may not be peripheral to the details of this incident; I do not address that issue here.) While the 1967 *Loving v. Virginia* case legalizing interracial marriages is narratively overdetermined as the historical barometric precursor to gay marriage in the admittedly flawed genealogic praxis of precedent, it is rarely mentioned in relation to *Lawrence-Garner*, which, as the quotation from Monroe reminds us, could as easily be apprehended for its interracial as for its sexual implications.

It is also highly plausible that the outcome and the aftermath of the decision—the ruling itself, how it was framed, and the manner in which it has been received and interpreted—have also been influenced explicitly, but more often implicitly, by the apparition haunting this case. Likewise, the effect of the ruling cannot escape the racial implications of sanctioning the sexual privacy and intimacy of a gay African American man. This is one corporeality caught within the orbit of dramatic debate pathologizing African American men on the down low, the generally myopic responses of African American communities and mainstream gay communities to the rising HIV seroconversion rates among African American men,[61] the specter of homosexual sex between incarcerated (black) men, and the force with which a mutually exclusive binary between gay and black identities has been vigorously policed.

In *Black Is, Black Ain't*, an early exploration of the life forces of this binary, Marlon Riggs challenges the either/or logic that endlessly produces racialized subjects as heterosexual and gay subjects as white, cleaving race from queerness, leaving unruffled the homophobia in black communities and the racism in gay communities. But more significantly, this dynamic proliferates homophobia in gay communities, homophobia that disallows toleration of a different kind—that is, not white—of homosexuality; homophobia toward homosexuals who are incommensurate with dominant frames. Likewise, racism in African American communities parallels this discourse: gay men are not black, as such racism disavows blackness in its fullness. These subtler forms of ethnosexual discrimination flourish, unseen amid the fray of charges against black homophobia and queer racism. Moreover, the fixation on the certainty of greater homophobia in black communities, cultures, and attitudes serves the salivating conservative right well in diversifying its constituency via the antigay marriage agenda (also reinforcing that white America is always more tolerant of homosexuality, mirroring the dynamic of sexual trumping that dominated analyses of torture at Abu Ghraib). The minimization of black gay support in favor of imagery of black homophobia has a maximal economy of representation. As one commentator points out:

> Americans are much more likely to know that Colin Powell opposed allowing gays to serve openly in the military than to know that supporters of gay marriage include such prominent African-Americans as Coretta Scott King, Congressman John Lewis, former Surgeon General Jocelyn Elders, actress Whoopi Goldberg, Democratic presidential hopefuls Al Sharpton and Carol Moseley Braun, and the Rev. William Sinkford, president of the Unitarian Universalist denomination.[62]

So how must we address the symbolic economy of this interracial pair, and what is at stake in the silences of this economy? For one, the interracial pair forcefully jolts a recognition of the incongruent agendas of white gay constituencies and black gay organizing. As black gay activist Keith Boykin dryly remarks:

> For black gays and lesbians, life after *Lawrence* looks pretty much like life before *Lawrence*. While mainstream gay activists plot their next move, some black gay scholars . . . questioned the relevance of the gay agenda. The problem is not that black gays and lesbians disapprove of same-sex marriage or any other issue on the gay agenda. . . . Those issues seldom top the list of priorities for the black LGBT community. Many black gays and lesbians are just as concerned about AIDS, healthcare, affirmative action, racial profiling, and unemployment as they are about civil unions. The black LGBT folks I've talked to do not feel as empowered by the progress of recent months as their white counterparts do. . . . Blacks are rarely represented in the visible images of the LGBT community, and when we are represented we are often depicted negatively or unsympathetically.[63]

Boykin goes on to state that the May 11, 2003, hate-crime murder of the 15-year-old black lesbian Sakia Gunn in Newark, New Jersey, received almost no media attention, comparatively speaking, to that of Matthew Shephard in Wyoming in 1998. There were 507 media stories in the first two months for Shepard, compared to eleven for Gunn in the comparable time period.[64] But aside from emblematizing divergent worlds, interracial black-white gay male and lesbian unions are also propped up as a modality of gay, lesbian, and queer hybridization central to U.S. discourses of diversity and multiculturalism—think of *The L Word* and *Six Feet Under*—in addition to evidencing the dissipation or even the absence of white gay racism.

There are two points I want to stress here. First, sodomy is and always has been perceived as a "racialized act," and in the United States it has been adjudicated as such. By racialized act, I mean that the act itself is already read through the raciality of the actors even as it accords raciality to those actors. Nayan Shah's research on sodomy cases at the turn of the twentieth century suggests that "sexual identity is not the determining factor in prosecuting sodomy, but rather differentials of class, age and race as well as migrant sociability in public and private space . . . shape the policing that leads to sodomy and public morals arrests."[65] A routine form of surveillance in the central valley of California, "vagrancy sweeps" scoured for "Oriental Depravity" and "Hindu Sodomites," elements that "endangered the state as well as national masculinity." Antisodomy, vagrancy, and other public indecency laws were used to prosecute individuals in interracial pairings unevenly, through which "amoral foreigners" (external threats) and "natural degenerates" (internal threats: irretrievable American masculinities) became salient positions, though not ones of "categorical certainty."[66]

My second point is that the figure of an African American male as a protected American citizen—involved in same-sex sexual activity, no less—resonates within the tense history of black and immigrant community relations. Between so-called model minority immigrants and African American communities, this friction revolves around perceived and actual class differences that are then sublimated as cultural, religious, and ethnic differences.

The most recent manifestation of this fissuring occurred after September 11, 2001, when policing resources (in New York City to an extreme but also nationally) purportedly shifted from black neighborhoods, establishments, families, churches, and bodies to South Asian, Arab American, and Muslim temples, mosques and gurdwaras, stores, and religious and community associations. Such securitization measures have taxed the long-standing animosity between the two "groups" fueled by differential treatment and access to jobs and state resources based on citizenship privileges as well as racist hostility perpetuated by South Asians, for whom racism toward blacks and Latinos has long been a rite of passage into model minority citizenship. This rite of passage is complemented by disinterest in the economic disenfranchisement and the struggles against police brutality of African American communities. While provocative survey data amassed after the events of September 11 suggested that high percentages of African Americans supported terrorist profiling, Miles Parks Grier argues convincingly that the continuities between the "old" racial profiling of the war on drugs and the "new" profiling must be at the heart of any examination of state racism; not to do so simply expands the efficacy of current practices of profiling, partially because "advocacy groups [proceed] as if terror suspects shield blacks and Latinos from state racism," thus perpetuating racial divisions. Grier also points out the obvious but underacknowledged point that African Americans and Africans certainly comprise a part of the Muslim detainee population.[67]

Thus, the multicultural production is indebted to those who do not or cannot fully escape the markings of race. Add to this mix the ambivalent affirmative action ruling in Michigan in summer 2003.[68] On the one hand, the ethnic (model minority immigrant, native) is the proper, desired subject of affirmative action, a deposal of African American citizen-subjects that lends itself to the fragmentation of post–civil rights coalitions as well as to multiple subjects of blackness. (A recent survey suggested that elites from

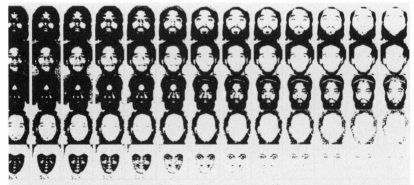

n' (Peter Brimelow, who also went for immigrants in "Alien Nation"), "super predators" and the "full moon" effect. Pete Hamil informed New York, "They were wearing Aborigam from a world of crack, welfare, girls, knives, and a condition as an indicator of whether the wig's are here to roll an honest living or blow up the world trade center. African-Americans complain to the police about who the deserve for Wilson called plan. Pataki told a homeowner." Elayne Cleaver's severe new restrictions evoke DHS "no fly' laws: "I'] I was not to go outside a seven mile area; specifically, I was not to cross the Bay Bridge. A] I was to keep my name out of the news play dead, or I would be sent back to prison." During the Washington DC sniper case, NRO Online editor Goldberg, made confident predictions of Al Qaeda cells. "This is part of the fall offensive, along with the attacks. American Gulf War vet African-Americans are 98% of the US Muslim population, and the fastest growing group among prison populations. Arabs by comparison are only 0% and South Asians 99.%, is an inverted pyramid.

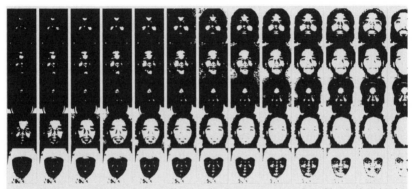

n Central Park "Wilding" entered the lexicon and we heard about "savage wolf packs," "beasts in the park" (Peter Brimelow, who also went for immigrants in "Alien Nation"), "super predators" and the "full moon" affect tion in coverage of Black Muslims today. A carefully constructed tender narrative looks for names, accents, and a condition as an indicator of whether the wig's are here to roll an honest living or blow up the world buildings. "America is a house on fire" "Freedom Now!" — or let it burn, let it burn. Praise the Lord and pass the ammunition." Elayne Cleaver's severe new restrictions evoke DHS "no fly" laws: "I] I was not to go outside a anything critical of the California Department of Corrections in any California prison. In short, I was to play dead, or I would be sent back to prison." During the Washington DC sniper case, NRO Online editor Go "That I will scream me as way too professional." The sniper was indeed Muslim, but inconveniently an African-American Gulf War vet. African-Americans are 98% of the US Muslim population, and the fastest growing

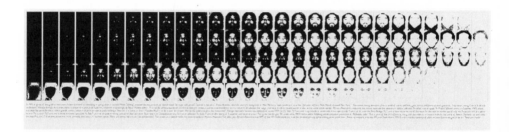

FIGURE 10. Visible Collective/Naeem Mohaiemen and Aimara Lin, *Driving While Black Becomes Flying While Brown*, 2006. Photocopy collage, ink on paper, 8 ft. x 2 ft. Originally installed at Yerba Buena Arts Center, San Francisco. Reprinted with permission from Naeem Mohaiemen.

" 'Wilding' infects the lexicon as we see 'savage wolf packs,' 'beasts in the park,' 'super predators' and the 'full moon effect' enveloping the Central Park jogger rape case. Pete Hamill whispers, 'they were coming downtown from a land with no fathers.' That hyper-racialized orphan beast is strangely absent from current terrophobia. Melanin supplemented by names, accents, and assimilation to understand if the wogs are here to roll an honest burrito or blow up the trade center. Our orphans don't fit because the deportation solution collapses. The sleeping ghosts no one wants to disturb are those of Robert Williams and Negros With Guns. 'America is a house on fire. Freedom Now! Or let it burn, let it burn. Praise the Lord and pass the ammunition!'—a Christian god in 1968, but still a volatile mix of righteous fury and black rage. Eldridge Cleaver's letter prefigures today's No Fly list: '1) I was not to go outside a seven mile area; specifically, I was not to cross the Bay Bridge. 2) I was to keep my name out of the news for the next six months; specifically, my face was not to appear on any TV screen. 3) I was not to make any more speeches. 4) And I was not to write anything critical of the California Department of Corrections or any California politician. In short, I was to play dead, or I would be sent back to prison.' Goldberg's confident thesis about the DC sniper's Al-Qaeda link suddenly under crisis—sniper turns out to be Muslim (good!) but also Black (not so good!) and Gulf War vet. (terrible!). The largest group of Muslims are Black (40%) followed by Deshis (24%) and Arabs (12%). An inverted pyramid of the sum of our national fears." (Artist's caption)

Africa are greater beneficiaries of affirmative action policies than African Americans.[69]) On the other hand, the citizenship struggles of immigrants of color are often understood to be of less interest to African Americans.

One message that Tyron Garner's black body *in conjunction with the white body of Lawrence* sends to the American citizenry is that certain homonormative subjects of color are amenable to the national body politic. This is not to suggest a different outcome of the case had a naturalized immigrant (or an immigrant with a green card or various work, student, or tourist visas, i.e., subject to deportation) been implicated. It is abundantly clear that the racialization of Garner needs to be assimilated into a celebratory narrative of multicultural queerness at best and thoroughly ignored, effaced, or annulled at worst. I am, however, placing the decision within a racial context that continues to scrutinize, ostracize, and penalize terrorist look-alikes through overt and insidious forms of Orientalist racial profiling while rehabilitating enfranchised ethnics through multiculturalization.

In this regard, the language in the *Lawrence-Garner* ruling is telling, explicitly mobilizing notions of western civilization by referencing European legislation. I quote from its text: "To the extent *Bowers* relied on values we share with a wider civilization, it should be noted that the reasoning and holding in *Bowers* have been rejected elsewhere." And, countering Chief Justice Burger's appeal to "the history of Western civilization" and to "Judaeo-Christian moral and ethical standards" by foregrounding its own modern western civilizational model, the majority Court summarizes "account[s] of other authorities pointing in an opposite direction."[70] In 1957, the British Parliament advocated the repeal of laws punishing homosexual conduct, detailed these recommendations in the 1963 Wolfenden Report of the Committee on Homosexual Offenses and Prostitution, and implemented the legislation in 1973. Also mobilized as a counternarrative about western civilization is a European Court of Human Rights ruling on a case in Ireland from 1981, five years prior to *Bowers*, *Dudgeon v. United Kingdom*:

> An adult male resident in Northern Ireland alleged he was a practicing homosexual who desired to engage in consensual homosexual conduct. The laws of Northern Ireland forbade him that right. He alleged that he had been questioned, his home had been searched, and he feared criminal prosecution. The court held that the laws proscribing the conduct were invalid under the European Convention on Human Rights. . . . Authoritative in all countries that are members of the Council of Europe (21 nations then, 45 nations now), the decision is at odds with the premise in *Bowers* that the claim put forward was insubstantial in our Western civilization.

And later:

> To the extent *Bowers* relied on values we share with a wider civilization, it should
> be noted that the reasoning and holding in *Bowers* have been rejected elsewhere.
> The European Court of Human Rights has followed not *Bowers* but its own
> decision in *Dudgeon* v. *United Kingdom*. . . . Other nations, too, have taken action
> consistent with an affirmation of the protected right of homosexual adults to en-
> gage in intimate, consensual conduct. . . . The right the petitioners seek in this case
> has been accepted as an integral part of human freedom in many other countries.
> There has been no showing that in this country the governmental interest in
> circumscribing personal choice is somehow more legitimate or urgent.[71]

Discourses of civilization have been the cornerstone of the obstinate
justification of the war on terror and the dichotomy of evil in relation to
good. They also submerge the visage of U.S. state-sponsored terrorism in
order to headline the "barbaric" forms of violence speciously immanent to
Islamic fundamentalism. The expediency of civilizational teleologies, regardless of their categorical utilization in the *Lawrence-Garner* case, causes
them to reverberate heavily through these Islamophobic polemics. David
Palumbo-Lui postulates:

> In our present incarnation of civilizational thinking, the dichotomy between
> national identity and international civilizational thinking has collapsed, the two
> positions intermingling and recombining into a potent ideological position, now
> mobilized by the events of September 11th. To the enemy within (ethnic and
> diasporic populations) is now added a viable enemy without. . . . The enemy will
> be civilizational: It will be Islam.

Samuel Huntington's thesis in *Clash of Civilizations* (of which Palumbo-Lui
does quite a nice deconstruction) situates multiculturalists (ethnic minorities) and "diasporics who retain allegiance to their homelands" as the
plague that entices the "double erosion of the national character." Within
this "inflammatory rhetoric of civilizations," diversity is tolerated only
insofar as multiculturalism is resided by "new immigrant, ethnic, and diasporic groups [that] agree to be politically inactive."[72] The annexing of a
black-white sodomy duo to civilization can be read in at least two ways: as
the ascendancy of whiteness achieved through the sexual and racial hybrid
couple, a token of tolerance and diversity that now invites homosexuals
despite or perhaps even because of national identity becoming more hegemonic than ever; or as a surrogate citizenship to black subjects who remain
economically disenfranchised to the extent of their exclusion from the

model minority ethnic, proffering sexual citizenship in the face of the failures of racial inclusion.

Queer Liberalism and Abu Ghraib

In May 2004, less than a year after the June 2003 *Lawrence and Garner v. Texas* ruling, the Abu Ghraib photos started hitting the newsstands and blaring from the Internet. One of the most curious facets of the response to the photos was the quick metonymic sealing of the torture to homosexuality. Largely cast as torture that simulated or forced "homosexual sex," "gay sex," and "homosexual acts," this association prompted a flurry of interviews with queer theorists, organizational press releases from LGBTIQ associations, and articles within the mainstream and the gay press. Remarkably, numerous spokespersons descanted knowledgably about "Muslim sexuality," proffering opinions without any apparent hesitation. Even more troubling, as I discuss in chapter 2, was the reason given for the exacting efficacy of the torture: the taboo, outlawed, banned status of homosexuality in Islam, Iraq, the Middle East, and any and all available referents, supplemented by an aversion to nudity, proclivity toward male-on-male contact, and sexual modesty with the rarely seen opposite sex.

A loose genealogical tracking—a trace not necessarily of the origin of this line of thinking but a portrait of its intense diffusion and echo—reveals that one of the endlessly quoted passages from Seymour Hersh's "Torture at Abu Ghraib," was the following information from Bernard Haykel, assistant professor of Middle Eastern studies at NYU.[73] In the piece that broke the story on April 30, he claimed, "Homosexual acts are against Islamic law and it is humiliating for men to be naked in front of other men." This line surfaced ad nauseam: it must have been among the most cited sound bites of the whole media spectacle.[74] Transposing a cultural explanatory frame onto economic and political contextualizations of the torture, this statement was uttered and reproduced without any ironic reference to the fact that sodomy (collapsed as homosexual sex) less than a year earlier had been illegal in several states in American law.

Homosexual acts are against Islamic law. I reiterate this sentence because I am so struck by this blatantly problematic evocation that nonetheless explicated for much of the American public, in one stroke, what was most vexing about Abu Ghraib, thereby easily gesturing to the fate the prisoners wrought on themselves. Conservative factions predictably ran with the homophobia track to blame Abu Ghraib on everything from gays in the military to western liberal sexual mores to gay pornography. By May 11, a posting titled "Abu Ghraib: The Root of the Problem," discussing a CIA gay pride meeting, was littered over hundreds of listservs.[75] Michael Savage, on his radio show *The Savage Nation*, called the abuse "typical homosexual behavior."[76] But the homosexual sex act line, notably, is sourced from a Middle Eastern expert, presumably intended as a progressive mobilization of a notion of radical cultural difference in order to, first, express vehement outrage and, second, counter Orientalist colonial fantasies of Muslim sexual deviance and corruption. What we have in its place, however, is an emergent neo-Orientalist (and purportedly less violent by liberal humanist standards) human rights frame resting upon the absoluteness of Muslim sexual repression.

On *The Charlie Rose Show* that aired on May 3, Hersh and Haykel were at it again, both highlighting the simulation of homosexual acts. Hersh claimed that the treatment of John Walker Lindh, stripped of his clothing and left for two or three days "naked, critical word, naked," foreshadowed tactics used as "the way to get to what they think an Arab is," claiming, "We're a society that runs on guilt. The Arab world, Islamic world runs on shame."[77] Professor Haykel reiterated the nudity and homosexual acts line, claiming that what "makes these crimes much worse" is that the perpetrators "were culturally extremely sensitive and . . . knew exactly what annoyed Arabs."[78] In other words, while conservative right-wing homophobes were invariably bent on producing this reading of the photos, it was actually progressive, scholarly forums that accepted, without hesitation or analysis, the cultural difference line of defense, reproducing it in the service of accentuating the humiliation of the Iraqi prisoners and the atrocity of the torture. Testimony by the guards as well as the prisoners elucidates that homosexual scenes were explicitly plotted and staged. That there was no distinction between what the theatrical torture scenes might have been intended to convey, and the Orientalist assumptions these exhibitions relied upon, rhetorically naturalizes "Arab" or "Muslim cultural difference."

What is most distressing about this naturalization is that homosexuality is used to mark the space of radical cultural difference. Cultural difference is embodied by Muslim homophobia and sexual repression as a distinct ontological reality that effectually deems irrelevant the discursive structures of such proclamations, eliding the regulatory mechanisms of modernity that produce the Orientalist fantasy of homosexuality as taboo. A deeply heterosexist (and racist and imperialist) reading of sodomy is mobilized in order to emphasize the extremity of violence, to provide what is understood, in essence, as a progressive, attentive, multicultural, postcolonial interpretation of cultural difference. We might point once again to the production of repression, the replay of the repressive hypothesis that Foucault so carefully deconstructs. As a crucial kernel in the regulatory mechanism endemic to queer and gay and lesbian liberal ideologies, its performative consequences materially engender the very repression it names.[79] This explanatory frame works to consolidate the exceptionalism of U.S. heterosexual norms, as any heterosexist reading of sodomy elsewhere would, as the "problem" reverts from the behavior of the guards to a subtle discourse of blame-the-victims for their homophobic and repressive sexual norms. This framing also works to consolidate the exceptionalism of U.S. homosexual norms, norms apparently working in the service, à la *Lawrence-Garner*, of intimacy rather than sodomy.

Furthermore, as I demonstrated in chapter 2, this uncritical blanket acceptance of sodomy as homosexual sex was enacted by all sorts of liberal, left, and progressive commentators, many of them from LGBTIQ communities. The metonymic fusing of sodomy to homosexuality, a fusing that the *Lawrence-Garner* ruling actively sought to *de*-fuse, exerted its spectacular force with the Orientalist readings of Abu Ghraib. That is to say, sodomy as homosexual sex is produced outside of the ever-narrowing parameters of legitimate homosexual American subjects; those protected by *Lawrence-Garner* are now exempt from this fusing. This legislation compels some homosexuals into the fold of American nationalism and into collusion with contemporary U.S. expansionism. The terrorist body retains a connection to sodomy that renders it incapable *and* unworthy of the kind of intimate homosexual sex possible for proper homosexual national subjects, a distinction that projects its effects externally but also to subjects within the boundaries of U.S. nationalism and citizenship.

The critical response to the Abu Ghraib publicity feast demonstrates that sodomy is still the homosexual act par excellence in the national imaginary. It also demonstrates, and this is no surprise, that the legal protection offered by the *Lawrence-Garner* ruling has yet to disrupt popular understandings of what sodomy is and who can do it. Most vividly overdetermined as oral-genital sex as opposed to its more common referent, anal-genital sex (though it is to this sex act that the pyramid formations were clearly indebted), sodomy must not only be disavowed with totality by heterosexuality in order to maintain its distance from homosexuality; it must be displaced from whiteness in order to retain its demonizing capacity to perversely racialize bodies. Of course, the arranging of two men in a tableau of oral-genital sex cannot escape the inference of homosexuality; the reliance on the notion of acts in this discourse, as in "homosexual acts," suggests that the act itself is always already racialized and homosexualized before the actors involved can even be located. The usage of other terminology such as oral sex and anal sex is completely foreclosed. Thus, in the highlighting of homosexual sex acts as somehow deeply and intrinsically relevant to the torture at Abu Ghraib, we see an insistent replay of the sexual logics that informed *Bowers*, which were at least legally overturned in the *Lawrence-Garner* decision. Thus, a pernicious version of U.S. sexual exceptionalism is enacted via the discursive tactics through which the identity categories of "homosexuality" and "Muslim sexuality" are relegated to mutually exclusive spaces.

My cross-reading suggests another instance of the perpetual splitting of race from sexuality in the race of the (nonnational or alien, presumptively sexually repressed, perverse, or both) terrorist and the sexuality of the (national, presumptively white, gender-normative, male) gay subject. Resonant with the effects of analogous or vertical thinking, the *Lawrence-Garner* ruling itself, which ideologically as well as textually refuses any reference to *inflections* of race, assumes whiteness as a queer norm, as does the critical response to the ruling. To verbalize the obvious, not all acts of sodomy are equivalent.

Indefinite or Infinite Detention?

The modalities of social identity (ethnicity, gender, occupation) previously available to express solidarity, dissent, or grief seemed incommensurate to the unruly materials of biopolitical life. Faced with the unappealing alternatives of resigned silence or contestatory refusal to play stereotypic terrorists in Hollywood action films, Ahmed revised his comedy routine. The available airport regulations provided sufficient basis for a monologue intent on addressing racial profiling, ambient post-9/11 anxieties provoked by ethnic others, and the hysterical will to administrative regulation. Ahmed recounts a recent attempt to board an airplane. When asked "Did you pack your bags yourself?" he answers in the affirmative and is immediately carried off by police authorities.—Diane Rubenstein, "Did You Pack Your Bags Yourself?"

Now I want to move us from the queer liberal subject of *Lawrence-Garner* to the darkened and queered monstrosities of terrorist populations being constructed through and against queer and homonormative rights-bearing subjects, from the regulation of subjects to the regularization of populations, and from the public-private binary to "networks of control." If we ponder the spatiotemporal reorganization implicit in the *Lawrence-Garner* ruling, what emerges is a reification of privacy realms, now relegated to the conjugal bedroom of everlasting love, or serial monogamy. This depoliticization of publics, in exchange for the consolation prize of protection in the private, emphasizes a particular liberal notion of intimacy that roots its dignity in the accoutrements of longevity, proximity, consistency, stability, and financial, social, and reproductive enmeshment and the normative telos of transit through marriage, birth, and death. Situating the ruling within the context of indefinite detention denotes greater constriction of privacy (beyond the well-documented limitations of privacy rights discourses) and acknowledges the manifold sectors and points of surveillance, control, and capture, a festering security state in the throes of its disciplinary frames being challenged and, according to some, gradually supplanted by those of control.

November 13, 2001: On that date a military order from George W. Bush authorized trial by "military conventions" and "indefinite detention" for detainees. The USA PATRIOT Act of October 26, 2001, is often decried as the most egregious post-9/11 state of exception legislation, as it "potentially exerts controls over white citizens that were formerly reserved for blacks and non-Americans."[80] In actuality, it nevertheless mandated the release of detainees within seven days of incarceration.[81] Agamben argues that the military order revokes the writ of habeas corpus and "radically erases any legal status of the individual, thus producing a legally unnamable and unclassifiable being."[82]

The state of exception is not only a legal structure that shifts decision making from the legislative to the executive wing, a paradoxical abnegation *of* the legal *by* the legal. It also antagonizes bodies; that is to say, it disaggregates and taxonomizes. States of exception make bodies legible or illegible, accorded the value of life or castaway as "human waste."[83] Zygmunt Bauman translates Agamben's theorization from Roman law of *homo sacer* (a life void of value, whose death neither warrants punishment nor serves sacrificially) for contemporary contexts: "In its present-day version the *homo sacer* is neither defined by any set of positive laws nor a carrier of human rights that precede legal rules."[84] Agamben adds that biopolitics is defined by "the power to decide the point at which life ceases to be politically relevant."[85] Detainees exemplify for Agamben and Bauman present-day *homines sacri*.[86] Their indefinite detention, the torture they are subjected to, and their murders are inconsequential; their deaths warrant no punishment, nor do they even have archetypal weight within the scope of normative liberal democracy, insofar as their lives cease to be "politically relevant." They are, in effect, exceptional entities. Judith Butler writes of detainees, "The language with which they are described in the U.S. . . . suggests that these individuals are exceptional, that they may not be individuals at all, that they must be constrained in order not to kill, that they are effectively reducible to a desire to kill, and that regular criminal and international codes cannot apply to beings such as these."[87]

While there has been much scholarly cogitation on the indeterminate legal status (or the disposal of legal status altogether) of detainees at Guantánamo Bay and those interred in the United States, little has been written, beyond activist of color missives and organizing tools (press releases, pamphlets, and policy documents) on the impact of indefinite detention on the detainees and those connected to them. This is not a pitch for nativist recourse to the voice of the people; rather, it is an observation regarding the incommensurate priorities of theoretical discourses excavating the contours of the subject and those mapping the spatiotemporal effects of population production.

In their December 2004 report, "Worlds Apart: How Deporting Immigrants after 9/11 Tore Families Apart and Shattered Communities," one of their many publications issued in the same vein, the American Civil Liberties Union centers testimonials of detainees and their families to underscore the impact of indefinite detention on immigrant communities. Stating that "their stories vary widely," the summary goes on to claim that "the stories of these men are similar in important ways. All came to the United States seeking a better life for themselves and their families." The report meticulously details the "hold until cleared" policy, which effectively inverts "innocent until proven guilty" to "guilty until proven innocent" for detainees who are often held despite an absence of any charges brought against them or of "credible evidence" of criminal activity; they are denied "access to counsel" and "release on bond" and held in solitary confinement, often shackled. The testimonial form works to great effect, describing detainees who were "awakened in the middle of the night by immigration officials," forcefully "dragged . . . out of their houses in the middle of the night in front of wives and children," unable to "contact their families with their whereabouts. . . . Their families, too, have been traumatized by what happened."[88]

The report (and like materials, of which there are many) exemplifies the

FIGURE 11. Visible Collective/Naeem Mohaiemen and Kristofer Dan-Bergman, *American Gothic* (*Casual, Fresh, American Style* Series), 2006. Translucent print installed in row house. Originally installed at Project Row House, Houston. Reprinted with permission from Naeem Mohaiemen.

quintessential use of personal testimony to incite outrage and dissidence. It is not my intent to dig into the multifarious debates regarding the precarious tactic of the testimonial, a genre that may well already be crystallized as racist, imperialist, and heteronormative in structure and form in addition to content.[89] For my purposes, this collection of tragic stories is notable for two reasons. First, the United States is nostalgically constructed as the homeland that is deeply missed, but despite their unrequited love for America, there is a clear indication that these formerly tolerated ethnic and racial minorities have betrayed the nation and thus are no longer welcome. Most of the testimonial narratives have explicit lines about the anguish of not being able to return home to the United States or subtle valorizations of American ways of being (from detainee Ansar Mahmood: "I love strawberry oatmeal with bananas!").[90] Imaging the United States as homeland and embracing the logic of return—a scorned lover heartbroken by the rejection of the motherland—also gestures to the beginning formation of another diaspora, a U.S. diaspora, a diaspora informed by deportation, expatriation, asylum seekers, and exile. (How can one miss the irony of asylum seekers seeking refuge in Canada from the United States?[91]) "Many have been deported to countries where they haven't lived for years, and where unemployment rates are high and salaries are low. Many have been harassed because of their connections to the U.S. or taunted for being deported."[92]

The report emphasizes that for many who have fled or were deported to the Middle East or South Asia, their U.S.-born children often do not speak local languages, are not schooled in local customs, and are not able or willing to readily acculturate. The ACLU manipulates affective responses to deportation and expatriation to convey the desirability of U.S. residence and the economic and cultural need to repatriate those deported. There is recognition of difference, yet it is subsumed under a homogeneous image of the detainee as a typical immigrant escaping his or her politically inhospitable, culturally backward, uninhabitable, and economically deprived country of origin. Despite damning its fascist deportation policies, the report nonetheless portrays the United States as a desirable land of opportunity for the very population exiled from its soil. If, as Bhattacharjee claims, "immigration laws have privatized the nation,"[93] for immigrants, the private is a spatialized configuration of the elusive and aspired to affects of national belonging. For the most part, these nationalist discourses are part of the ideological leanings of the ACLU, whose logo is the Statue of Liberty and whose ultimate goal is to make the U.S. legal system live up to its stated ideals in the Constitution. More discouraging is the parallel rhetoric mobilized by grassroots efforts to free the detainees.

Second, the ACLU report is notable for its presentation of detention. Indefinite detention creates new spatiotemporal registers not only in terms of racial, religious, diasporic, and national subjectivities, but also through its regulation of kinship formations. Post-9/11 detention praxis produces a rupturing of transnational heterosexual kinship formations, as Muslim men—brothers, husbands, fathers, uncles, grandfathers—are disappeared, vanishing from work, while going to pick up groceries, from their homes in the middle of the night.[94] Family members dependent on these male figures for a primary income or legal status were left to search for their whereabouts. Clearly, the intimate is a protected space of citizenship, unavailable to members of Muslim families whose separation merits no consideration. This is hardly a surprise, given that, as Bhattacharjee claims, "the sanctity of the family is selectively respected by the nation-state. . . . For immigrant homes, the state can hardly be accused of inaction—if anything, it is actively involved in determining the very existence of the family."[95]

The radical disregard and dismissal with which these family relations have been treated also destabilizes any inhabitation of heteronormativity for these populations. The consequences of detention and deportation challenge the stabilization of nuclear heterosexual and extended kinship intimacy of these families. Heteronormativity is out of reach, literally disallowed by the state, utterly untenable for these families, thus respatializing heterosexuality to the extent that it can no longer be, if it ever was, heteronormative. Yet these practices also reiterate and reinforce the heterosexual parameters of American citizenship, straining while simultaneously demanding nuclear heterosexual kinship ties, severely delimiting the visibility, and perhaps even foreclosing the possibility, of alternative household, partnering, and child-rearing alliances. If we examine the respatialization due to government practices of indefinite detention, there is both a perverse homosexual othering at work in the construction of the terrorist detainee and a vast widening of the gulf that fissures heterosexuality and heteronormativity. That is to say, these practices make heterosexuality a mandate while making heteronormativity impossible.

Heteronormativity is consolidated through the physical site of the family home, immune from upheaval, and a spatial array of concatenating entities: property, citizenship, privacy, and intimacy, laboring to widen the gulf between itself and heterosexuality. Considered nonnational and thus cast beyond the ambit of normativity, detention respatialization is a note-

FIGURE 12A. Karthik Pandian, *Happy Birthday Karthik Ramanan*, 2000. Mixed media with slides, slide projector, suitcase, wall painting, fabric, wood, sound. Installation, School of Visual Arts, New York City. This installation simulates the artist's childhood living room, with suitcase projecting snapshots from his third birthday party and blaring South Indian Tamil film music. Visitors to the installation could enter the living room (first choosing whether or not to take their shoes off) or peek at the reverse of the images projected on the screen through a peephole from the outside. Reprinted with the artist's permission.

FIGURE 12B. Karthik Pandian, *Happy Birthday Karthik Ramanan*, 2000. Installation, School of Visual Arts, New York City. Reprinted with the artist's permission.

worthy site for the production of nonnormative transnational sexual kinship arrangements, a production that is rendered against the stability, security, and cosmopolitan mobility of American multicultural heteronorms. As an anticosmopolitan formation—for despite its global dimensions, mobility is prohibitively contained—un-homed detainee family networks occupy the space of perverse heterosexuality, poorly lived and unworthy of state protection. (Mainstream immigration lawyers have noted with some interest that Muslim women are also taking this opportunity to escape violent domestic relations and situations. It is also the case, however, that women speaking on behalf of their disappeared husbands, sons, fathers, and brothers, have become highly competent organizers within antidetention activism.)[96] The hurdles blocking the way to heteronormativity are an important overture to the racialized differentiation between heteronormativity and heterosexuality; the ascendancy of whiteness and the ascendancy of heteronorms are biopolitical comrades.

It is perhaps both strategic and ironic that in the ACLU's and other activists' literature, the plea for repatriation is enunciated through normative heterosexual terms, reinscribing the western heterosexual family romance even as the testimonials themselves attest to the complete disregard by U.S. policy of the detainees' family networks.[97] The pitch to reinstate the possibility of habilitation to American family and community heteronormativity is reflective of several tendencies. First, it reflects and responds to a general liberal heteronormative nationalism that is unable to perceive or account for multiple and alternative family and community formations. Second, it speaks to the reliance on and compulsory reinforcement of nuclear heteronormativity in immigration law. Third, the repetition of this heteronorm by activist organizations reconsolidates and naturalizes notions of immigrant families and communities as singularly heterosexual, and thus by extension, ontologically unconducive to homosexuality and prone to homophobia. Fourth, it suggests that the antidetention movement is implicitly heterosexual and perhaps reinforces heteronormativity. Fifth, it foregrounds the overdetermined position of patriarchs and sidelines the experiences of women who are detained or affiliated with detainees.

The spatiotemporal implications of population production entail scrambled redistribution (akin to a tightening vise or a round of musical chairs) of job and residential stability and security; access to social services, immigration, asylum, unemployment, and welfare benefits; work, student, or visitor visas; the truncation of diasporic settlement, reproduction, and financial networks such as legitimate Muslim charities; and constraints on bodily safety and ease of mobility and movement. Immigrants and other people of color are subjected to scrutiny along a continuum of activities: consumption patterns; religious affiliations; financial transactions;[98] Internet and telephone communications; travel itineraries; infiltration and raiding of mosques and other religious and community sites and institutions; raiding of offices and private homes; the probing of household, religious, and business waste; mandatory registration, secret incarcerations, closed deportation hearings; vandalizing of mosques and gurdwaras, which include defecating, urinating on property, arson; the censoring of academic freedom and the denial of visa after visa to certain postcolonial academics and artists; and, as contiguous and complicitous with state racism, hate crimes targeting women in hijab and turbaned men (assaults tacitly sanctioned by the state and the citizenry that must be read for their revulsion toward nonnormative gender and sexual identities in addition to racial monstrosity).

The "militarization of urban space" is accomplished largely through clamping down on the routine circuits of diasporic connectivity: air travel, financial remittances to family back home, contributions to homeland charities, political organizations and foundations, communication networks.[99] It mandates a unilateral nationalism (especially in the case of Pakistan, and excepting the case of India), squeezing and jeopardizing the multinational sites and lines of flight that compose the crux of diasporic subjectivity. The list is endless, and these quality of life issues are always already under duress for immigrant populations. Sally Howell and Andrew Shryock report that even in "the capital of Arab America," Detroit—a city dominated by multicultural motifs of inclusion and dubbed an "immigrant success story," remarkable for the success of its Arab entrepreneurs—"the privilege of transnational identification, that is, the ability to sustain political and economic ties to sites of belonging and social reproduction that are not American and are not fully subject to U.S. sovereignty—has been . . . the first casualty of the War on Terror."[100] Basic "quotidian transactions"—sending cash wedding gifts to Iran, for example—become suspect, while business practices are monitored to "reward and punish Arab entrepreneurs and the diasporas they support," in other words, to allow those circuits that connect the U.S. to regimes it supports, while prohibiting others, impelling, to borrow from Mahmood Mamdani, a "Good Muslim, Bad Muslim" scenario.[101]

The INS Special Registration Program launched in June 2002, also known as the National Security Entry-Exit Registration System (NSEERS), required mandatory registration of males 14 and older from twenty-four predominantly Muslim countries (as well as North Korea).[102] The ACLU claims that mandatory registration propelled the mass exodus of Brooklyn's Pakistani population. "Little Pakistan," in the Midwood section of Brooklyn, which once housed "at least 100,000 Pakistanis," is now haunted by a quiet main drag, Coney Island Avenue, and the deportation or preemptive flight of anywhere from 15,000 to 45,000 dwellers.[103] (Some estimate that Pakistanis make up at least 40 percent of the detainee population; the Pakistani Embassy in Washington reported that 15,000 Pakistanis had left for Canada, Europe, and Pakistan by June 2003).[104] At least thirty businesses went belly-up in the three years between September 11 and the date of this report, and those that remain suffer from a 30 to 40 percent decline in patronage.[105] In Jackson Heights, a section of Queens known for its diverse migrant populations as well as the visible predominance of South Asian dhabhas, theaters, tailors, clothing stores, and restaurants, men were "disappeared" by the state. Martin Manalansan reports that, ironically, the containment of Middle Eastern and South Asian terrorist bodies is complemented by the proliferation of a vibrant gay scene, contradictory "disintegrating and fear-laden landscapes and an emergent and vibrant gay nightlife" propelling cycles of disappearance and emergence. Noting that the surveillance of street corners, loiterers, the homeless, and cruising spans across rather than localizes through racial categorization, Manalansan writes that "the reported evacuation of particular scenes and the alleged disappearance of groups coincided with other discourses around Jackson Heights as the new exotic gay mecca" characterizing long-term residential queer of color communities via the lingo of risk, adventure, danger, and consumption.[106]

Sunaina Maira writes of Muslim communities in the greater Boston area, "There is . . . a heightened sense of fear and vulnerability . . . particularly among working-class immigrants who cannot as easily afford legal counsel if they are harassed or detained. . . . It would not be too dramatic to say that many in these communities feel under siege." She argues that another by-product of the NSEERS program entails the manufacture of a population living in the shadows, a "subliminal and precarious world of individuals who cannot fully admit they exist."[107] The ephemera of control simulates homologous affects and intensities as detention: fear, anxiety, discomfort, disorientation, uncertainty, despair, anger, vertigo, nausea. (We can ponder the bountiful palimpsest: policing activist events and activists themselves, patrolling educational sectors and academic freedom of speech, the surge of video surveillance in public arenas.)[108] As Judith Butler wonders, "What kind of public culture is being created when a certain 'indefinite containment' takes place outside the prison walls, on the subway, in the airports, on the street, in the workplace?"[109] But the metaphor of containment is not quite right, for there is mass distribution of these "technologies of suspicion";[110] hence the sliding between *indefinite* and *infinite* detention. Silence, then, the silence of a discordant American citizenry, or the silence (relative to the historical and the geographical) of U.S. antiwar protests, or the silence of the academy, or the silence of people of color and immigrants, undocumented or not: these silences not only point to political apathy, defeatism, denial, or detachment, but also to the workings of control that surpass the walls of detention. Another symptom of societal control is that those who are not silent—global protests, alternative media, resistant strands of politics—are rarely heard, seen, or responded to by the state, in part because the apparatuses of control diffuse the state as the regulatory center of control.

The vacating of entire predominantly Muslim neighborhoods in Brooklyn, Queens, Detroit, Boston, and other cities suggests that the means of control bleed far beyond the disciplinary apparatus of the prison. That is, the affects of detention are mimicked in public spheres. Indeed, detention sites themselves have become sites of activism and protest, along with antiwar protests, and thus of expanded surveillance, while the administrative control tool of the "list" is an accomplice to forcible detention and deportation; in actuality, the list brings much better results than direct policing. The NSEERS program aggregates national, religious, ethnic, and racial identities from subjects to populations; that is, the "Muslim population" or the "terrorist look-alike" population is collected as a target (the targeting happening through the collecting) of these regulations as are those who fall outside these parameters or could perform as if outside these parameters.

Data Bodies

The security of biopolitics is precisely this challenge of managing a network of bodies, data, and their interlinkages—travel advisories, global health alerts, emergency-response protocols, selective quarantines, high-tech diagnostics, and the medical and economic assertion of newer and better prescription drugs. The problem of security for biopolitics is the problem of creating boundaries that are selectively permeable.—Eugene Thacker, *The Global Genome*

Dismayingly, the TIA [the Defense Department's Total Information Awareness] panel reverentially quotes Michel Foucault, one of the biggest academic frauds of the late twentieth century, for the proposition that "'modern society increasingly functions like a super Panopticon [prison watchtower] in which government constrains individual behavior by the threat of surveillance." One should hope that this is the first and last time that a Defense Department advisory board has invoked Foucault, since this French poseur, who presented Western culture as one big plot to suppress dissent, difference, and minority rights, has less than nothing to contribute to the national defense. Like Foucault, who never troubled himself with evidence, the Washington wise men offer no backup for their claim that government increasingly "constrains individual behavior by the threat of surveillance."—Heather MacDonald "What We Don't Know *Can* Hurt Us"

The "technological sublime" refers to the totalizing, overarching, and inflated power falsely accorded to surveillance, hyperbole that conveniently forgets that interactions between user and interface are often consensual, that security and information systems often fail in their objectives, and that control does not always espouse or shape value systems.[111] I turn now to a preliminary sketch of surveillance technologies to construct a perfunctory understanding of intimacy and security within control societies. I am not interested in appraising the relative intrusiveness or privacy-hindering effects of surveillance. More significant is that the *perception* of an all-encompassing, impenetrable, and infallible surveillance structure affectively breeds fear, terror, and insecurity.

The private within rights discourses is overwhelmingly a "flat discourse. It largely ignores the vertical dimension and tends to look across rather than to cut through the landscape."[112] Eyal Weizman, through what he terms "the politics of verticality," details the spatial reconceptualization of the shift from two-dimensional space—an expanse of horizontal and vertical coordinates, latitudinal and longitudinal positions, over here and over there, inside and out—to a three-dimensional space of volume, depth, and verticality.[113] Addressing the flatness of mapping and its inaccuracy or inadequacy, the politics of verticality oscillates from representational space to informational space, from epistemological comprehensions of space to ontological presences and experiences. The variances between "looking across" and "cutting through" drive transformations in corporeal phenomena of space, territory,

FIGURE 13A. Karthik Pandian, *SubText*, 2005. Installation, L train, New York City subway. Reprinted with the artist's permission.

FIGURE 13B. Karthik Pandian, *SubText*, 2005. Vinyl sticker (one of three hundred stickers printed). The sticker is a translation of the Metropolitan Transit Authority's "If you see something, say something" surveillance campaign into Arabic. Reprinted with the artist's permission.

and occupation. Weizman's point is that the penetrative force of surveillance is also vertical rather than only lateral, unaligned and punctuated by "kissing points" (a pleasant misnomer, lending a sweetness to it all) and other momentary contacts rather than invasion or gentrification. The politics of verticality transgresses a notion of panoptic surveillance enabled through the expanse of looking from above and beyond, able to witness the visibly aberrant body in question within the prescribed sites of deviance (for queers, especially gay men, this has conventionally meant cruising zones and gay neighborhoods) to thinking about networks of contact and control, of circuits that cut through.[114]

Networks of surveillance in this three-dimensional, vertical setup are not removed, abstract, or cohered, but viciously intimate: unlike the apartheid of separation, these "new and intricate frontiers" invented for domination demand intimacy, not just penetration but interpenetration, matrices of scalar layers that are discontinuous yet transversal.[115] They are discontinuous in that intimate proximities are orchestrated to produce the ephemera of nonconnection, of not-touching—not through a vacuum of distance or of severing or separation, but in the proactive, provocative swerve away from contact, the refusal of tactile knowing; the discontinuity is a deliberate rupturing, not simply a missing or a missed connection, but an intimate, brutal, *almost-but-no* kind of taunting. Intimacy in biopolitical terms is not bound to protection in the private or exposure in public. It mediates relations between transparency and opacity, waves of proximity, observation and invisibility, gazes, traces and profiles, electric and erotic charges, passing by and bypassing, tightness, looseness, comfort, orderliness and chaos, order and disarray, rubbing and brushing against. Control networks are systems of unleashed circuitry, exuberant, fertile, that taunt the boundaries of inside and outside and, more important, beginning and end.

Legislation after September 11, 2001, exacerbated an already occurring blurring of the dissimilarities between law enforcement and intelligence. The former is a reactive activity, the purpose of which is "to capture and prosecute criminals." Intelligence, on the other hand, is proactive, "collected for the prevention of, and warning about, national security threats," allowing for the "government mining of third-party private transactional data," easing barriers in obtaining "warrants for electronic surveillance," and permitting the "FBI to collect public information . . . and conduct surveillance in public places absent to a link to suspected criminal activity."[116] What we also see is a profound sway in the tenor of temporality: the realignment from reactive to preemptive is a conversion from past-tense subject formation to future-tense subject anticipation, from the rehabilitative subject whose violated rights can be redressed through social representation and legal recognition, to regenerative populations who are culled through anticipation.

Felix Stalder observes, "Our bodies are being shadowed by an increasingly comprehensive 'data body.' However, this shadow body does more than follow us. It does also precede us," lurking as an "informational doppelganger."[117] Systems such as the Department of Defense's Total Information Awareness enable mining "transactional data" to locate "patterns of terrorist activity."[118] Creating ratings of mobility risk naturally favors " 'low risk' frequent travelers" through "smart border" agreements. Such pacts include the Secure Electronic Network for Travelers' Rapid Inspection system (at the U.S.-Mexico border south of San Diego); the Free and Secure Trade program (easing truck congestion at border points for human as well as nonhuman entities); Nexus (at the U.S.-Canada border, as well as, in the future, the Ottawa and Montreal international airports); and the Immigration and Naturalization Service Passenger Accelerated Service System (in six U.S. airports, including Los Angeles International). A "trusted travelers" database allows selected individuals to bypass regular security lines.[119] The Transportation Security Agency's Computer Assisted Passenger Prescreening System II project is designed to "profile prospective airline passengers using commercial databases."[120] Identity recognition technologies involve biometric facial and iris recognition; hand geometry recognition; "electronic body scanner[s] that sees through clothing"; and the Human Identification at a Distance system that "identifies an individual's unique walking style and gestures."[121] A "virtual borders" program commissioned by the government and developed by Accenture aims to standardize the use of biometric data not only at U.S. ports of entry but prior to departure, at the point of origination. Visa applicants will be screened through fingerprinting and again upon departure from the origin country to the United States, the goal being to make "technology and information systems the first line of defense, and allow U.S. border inspectors to become the last line of defense." A description of the program is as follows: "Virtual borders of the United States would extend to the point of origination for visitors. The bulk of the security checks will be performed at the time of application for a visa to visit the United States."[122]

These "surveillant assemblages," invested in witnessing the mobility of human and nonhuman actors, as well as affectively undulating movement itself, create the sameness of population through democratization of monitoring at the same time they enable and solidify hierarchies—in other words, the circuit amid profiling and racial profiling.[123] Despite reports that terrorist circles are recruiting non-Arabs and non–South Asians who can pass and thus carry out attacks, racial profiling continues to be an important security measure.[124] Yet unlike an older "masculinism as protection" model of surveillance, whereby "patriarchal logic . . . gives to protective services a right to rule over those who count on their expertise at keeping watch and apprehending,"[125] in the move from the containment and normativization of the subject to the control of populations (here we must perpetually drag ourselves from the subject as an object of inquiry, if only for a moment), self-regulation becomes less an internalization of norms and more about constant monitoring of oneself and others, watching, waiting, listening, ordering, positioning, calculating.

One sees emerging through these practices not necessarily the crafting of the individual subject cohered through acquiescence to or internalization of norms but assemblages of "militarized bodies." As John Armitage explains, these comprise "an assortment of practices consisting of the conversion of civilian bodies to military use and the inculcation into such bodies of military principals."[126] Militarized bodies arise from both conventional nation-state militaries and their supra- and subnational counterparts (militias, paramilitary groups) and also through technologies that produce zones where "the 'redundant' population . . . rubs shoulders with the 'useful' and 'legitimate' rest."[127] In the context of civilians who have no direct links with conventionally defined military spaces, the force of mobilization takes on a different role. Going beyond meaning or interpretations of bodies in the military, militarization is produced through flows of information and series of activities, the everyday activities of civilians that participate in and contribute to the military complex. These vectors of militarization that permeate the everyday once again produce public spheres where many affects of detention cells are mimicked. Thus, militarization is not only heightened and intensified, not only expanded in expanse or range; in constellation fashion, it is disseminated precisely and insidiously, from bodies to entertainment to consumption. Militarized bodies are crafted through the dissemination and diffusion of control, rather than within concentrated and isolated patches of discipline or via overt methods of force. These networks of control are distributed and interactive, intent on mobilizing the populace: participation is therefore a patriotic mandate.

For exceptional militarized citizens, the sites of this diffusion are mediated through several figures of proper patriotic citizenship, all imbricated in each other: the informant-citizen cum vigilant spy (TIPS, Amber Alert, airline passengers demanding the removal of seemingly strange passengers, training New York City apartment building supers to spot suspicious subjects); the consumer-citizen (patriotic spending to boost the economy, self-taught financial investing as an aesthetic of security, tracking Internet usage, video and library book loans, financial transactions, and travel patterns, marketing information that may also be used to assess risk, microchips embedded in the body that act as identification and credit cards);[128] the simulated soldier (terrorist videogames, bombed-out dollhouses such as Forward Command Post, Hollywood war movie blockbusters, antiterrorist training camps for civilians, the Minute Men on the Mexico-U.S. border and other vigilantes); the compliant citizen (airport security measures, biometric technologies such as face and eye recognition, video surveillance, tracking devices in prescription drugs and Wal-Mart products); the prepared citizen (the security mom, duct tape, radiation tablets, metal detectors, bioterrorism defense kits, and other forms of emergency do-it-yourself readiness); the physically fit citizen-soldier (exercise, hygienic and dietary directives, bodybuilding cultures); the student-citizen (eligible for graduate fellowships in science, technology, and languages from the U.S. Department of Homeland Security); and the mentally prepared citizen-soldier (the proposed New Freedom Initiative, which would administer a standardized test for mental illness to all Americans, and the Bush administration's "No Child Left Behind" policy).

While the militarization of civilian bodies is contingent upon discourses of voluntary participation, corporeal containment presented in the guise of attuned multiculturalism and self-regulating "freedom" links terrorist and patriotic civilian bodies through the disbursement of technologies of militarization. Multicultural practices of detention mimic the intimate, sentimental, and subtle influences shaping the bodies that constitute the opposition to the terrorist: free patriot-citizen-soldiers, Armitage's militarized bodies. Coexisting with practices of torture, the crafting of corporeal affectivities is a central tenet in the accommodation and recognition of cultural difference. Forms of corporeal practice, more insidious and less overt than torture, groom the detained body. The detainee defies the distinction between life and death, bringing biopolitics and necropolitics into crisis. The detainee is not left to die, but mandated to live. It is crucial that he or she remain alive to impart his or her knowledge of terrorist secrets to the outsourced corporate counterterrorism interrogators. How is the detainee not only left for dead, as it were, but also primed for life, primed to live *through* his or her dying?

Incarcerated detainees at Guantánamo Bay undergo a full (intrusive) medical examination (for some, purportedly the first ever), are assessed for mental illness and depression, and gain an average of thirteen pounds within the first three months of arriving.[129] They are given individual copies of the Koran in Arabic and English (on which guards have been accused of urinating) and are able to pray five times a day next to arrows inscribed with the number of kilometers of distance between Camp X-Ray and Mecca. These bodies are not only being commanded to the restoration of the properly visible. (The name of the detention site, Camp X-Ray, suggests in itself a profound yearning for the transparency of these bodies, the capacity to see through them and render them known, taciturn, disembodied.) It is the reterritorialization of the body that must be performed through the ritual of cutting and shaving hair.

As a regulatory mechanism of population, the "detainee"—not legal or illegal, but *un*-legal—is a machination of ceremonial scrutiny and sheer domination,[130] disallowed from the rehabilitating forces pressed upon and adopted by others. Butler argues that detainees are subjected to "reduction . . . to animal status," while José Esteban Muñoz wonders if they are "border brujos. . . . haunting the public sphere."[131] Illegible as legal subjects, are these bodies illegible as well through normative identity registers, not human nor animal, but un-human? That is to say, we could ask, are these bodies queer? Do they have a race or a sex? How do we see, speak, interpret, feel the matter of these bodies? Butler fleetingly poses a similar query: "To what extent is there a racial and ethnic frame through which these imprisoned lives are viewed and judged such that they are deemed less than human, or as having departed from the recognizable human community?"[132] Or does the un-human work in part through denying or demanding the relinquishing of all identitarian markers? Are they illegible because they are un-human or un-human because they are illegible?

We can surmise two possibilities: that the moment of un-legality affirms the always already impossibility of the raced, sexed, gendered body; or that these impossibilities, the un-gendered, un-raced, un-sexed, un-nationed body, are the inaugural characteristics of the subject formation of *homo sacer*. In either case, the particulars of human materiality that is otherwise accorded as a right intrinsic to human intelligibility are disallowed. Identity is foundational to the control of population through state racism and the division of bodies; simultaneously, identity markers are stripped as the particulars—Afghani, Pakistani, Iraqi, Sunni, Shi'ite, Arab, Palestinian, African, and so on—are subsumed in the designation "terrorist detainees."

Populations, Race, and Sex

There is an overriding of a representational politics of recognizing individual subjects in terms of communities of belonging by a political economy of biopolitical control where human life is being deterritorialized into statistical populations that become the condition of possibility for the distribution of chances for life and death, health and morbidity, fertility and infertility, happiness and unhappiness, freedom and imprisonment.—Patricia Clough, "Future Matters"

The population is not only a political matter, but also a biological matter—and today, a genetic matter.—Eugene Thacker, *The Global Genome*

Patricia Clough describes this affective economy of information that aggregates and disaggregates populations: "ratings profiles, preference listings, risk statuses, that is, bodies of data and information (including human bodies as data and information)" enabling "a never-ending modulation of moods, capacities, affects, potentialities statistically assembled in genetic codes, identification numbers."[133] As Foucault writes in *"Society Must Be Defended,"* biopower, after the "anatomo-politics of the human body established in the course of the eighteenth century," is a "new technology of power [that] is not exactly society . . . nor is it the individual-as-body. It is a new body, a multiple body, a body with so many heads that, while they might not be infinite in number, cannot necessarily be counted: biopolitics deals with the population, with the population as political problem, as a problem that is at once scientific and political, as a biological problem and as power's problem." He cautions that this power "does not exclude disciplinary technology, but it does dovetail into it, integrate it, modify it to some extent, and above all, use it by sort of infiltrating it, embedding itself in existing disciplinary techniques."[134] This notion of population leaves the work of delineating who is in and who is out to disciplinary techniques; immanent to generating populations are mobile scales, layers, grades, and strata, ranked and reranked in terms of biopolitical regenerative capacity: everyone is accounted for and included, however minimally or brutally. In the biopolitical control of populations, no one is left out, though many are left behind.

As bodies with multiple heads, populations are of course not diametrically opposed or ontologically discrete; they intersect, counteract, interlock, and combine in places. Eugene Thacker writes that biopolitics both "universalizes and individualizes the population":

> Biopolitics accounts for "each and every" element of the population, the individual and the group, and the groups within the group (the poor, the unemployed, the resident alien, the chronically ill). In this gradated approach, populations can exist in a variety of contexts (defined by territory, economic/class groupings, ethnic groupings, gender-based divisions, or social factors)—all within a framework analyzing the fluxes of biological activity characteristic of the population . . . not just the individual subject, but a subject that can be defined in a variety of ways, marking out definitional boundaries of each grouping. As individuated subjects, some may form the homogenous core of a group, others may form its boundaries, its limit cases. The method of biopolitics is thus informatics, but a use of informatics in a way that reconfigures biology as an information resource. In biopolitics, the body is a database, and informatics is the search engine.[135]

In statistical terms, race and sex are experienced as a series of transactional informational flows captured or happened upon at chance moments that perceive and render bodies transparent or opaque, secure or insecure, risky or at risk, risk-enabled or risk-disabled, the living or the living dead.

Terrorist bodies as a "statistical population" coagulate through an imagined worldwide collectivity—the Muslim world—that perversely transcends national boundaries and is metaphorized through viral networks of contagion, infection, and the frustration generated by inaccessibility of sleeper cells that need no contact to reproduce themselves: rampant, uncontainable, spontaneous, and untraceable mimicry.[136] The body and its color—because color and its contextual habitation and deployment still matter—both undergird the progressive accumulation of this statistical population and at times override it. The population "Muslim terrorists" comes to light not only through the Orientalist metonymic linking of Muslim and terrorist within the economy of meaning and representation. This population is made up of those caught in the violent chaotic shuttling back and forth between the statistical informational ontologies deemed "Muslim" and those that begin to bleed into "terrorist." We can say that this process of informationally creating bodies goes far beyond forms of neo-Orientalizing or racialization of religious affiliation. "The Muslim," summarily dismissed from its place as one subject of multiculturalism, is an emergent, incipient Race, the Muslim Race. The ascendancy (rising up, evolutionary domi-

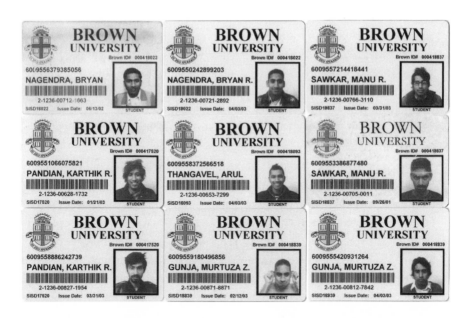

FIGURE 14. Karthik Pandian, *Brown University*, 2003. Nine Brown University–issued identification cards, arrangement variable. Relying on the (accurate) assumption that the card office would not be able to distinguish the South Asians before them from the pictures they had on file, the artist had five South Asian males get ID cards issued in each others' names. At the project's completion, everyone who participated had someone else's picture on their ID. Reprinted with the artist's permission.

nance) of whiteness is complemented and supplemented by the manufacture of Muslim as race.

Racialization has become a more diffuse process, not only informed by the biological body, what it looks like and what it can do, but also disassembled into the subhuman and the human-as-information. The dance between the profile that is racialized and the racial profile: a speedy (re)turn to genetic engineering technologies (stem cell research, cloning, sex selection, biological warfare, DNA manipulation, plastic surgery), informative bits and pieces encountered randomly or deliberately (the tapestry of the hand, the patterning of the iris, the motions of one's gait, the isolation of various traits and mannerisms of the body to discern trusted from untrusted: anybody can be untrustworthy until proven trustworthy, but not vice versa) interacting with the numbers and facts that matter (visa status, place of residence, country of origin, student activity, Social Security number, traveling risk status, criminal record, consumption habits, and any evidence of nonassimilative behavior). Data collection enables a mapping of race through aggregates and disaggregates that, as Thacker demonstrates, "becomes bifurcated along genotypic (genetic code), phenotypic (visible characteristics), and informatic (statistical) lines," while sex is removed from its associations to sex acts, sexuality, sexual orientation, and erotics and resigned to "genetic and informatic terms: *blood, sex, data.*"[137] The profile establishes the individual as imbricated in manifold populations (not community—the designation to a dehumanizing population instead of the communalism of community is significant).

The deterritorialization of communities of belonging, those communities laboring under the identity signs of race, sexuality, gender, ethnicity, and nationality to secure the status and recognition of the subject (and its voice, history, community, intersectional coordinates), instead scrambles statistical populations. The subject is divided up into subhuman particles of knowledge that nevertheless exceed the boundaries of the body, yet it is also multiply splayed through, across, and between intersecting and overlapping populations, departing from intersectional identity paradigms insofar as compartmentalization, or analyzing components whether separately or together, is untenable. In this deterritorialization, epistemological empiricisms of statistical population are misconstrued as ontological truths about the subject and his or her culture, identity, reality. Again, a version of culture trumps or disengages itself from the circuits of capital and the political economy that produces it. Identity politics, both a symptom of and a response to these networks of control, capitulates once again to chasing the space of retribution for the subject. Control masks itself, or masks its effects, within the endless drive to recoup the resistant subject. We must instead advocate that resistance give way to delinquency.[138]

Genealogical Grids

State, public, and personal worth of a family should be based on the intimate recognition that occurs between two people, on the choice to love and the love that circulates through this choice. No matter that one of the major distinguishing features of modern intimacy is an expectation of a blurring of choice and compulsion in the context of love, of a dynamic among self-risk and self-elaboration, personal transcendence, and the fall back onto the self. Indeed, love thematizes and indicates the affective site where choice and compulsion are blurred.—Elizabeth A. Povinelli, "Notes on Gridlock"

In Elizabeth Povinelli's brilliant exposition on the gridlock of intimacy and genealogy, she reminds us that "practices and relations that fall off the genealogical grid" are deemed illegible by or incommensurate with state offerings of recognition.[139] As an elaboration of the interior self, intimacy registers affective tendencies—intensity, turbulence, chemistry, attraction, repulsion, sonic waves—betwixt and between human bodies, thus ordering and fixing these bodies along the genealogical grid. As a legitimating technology, intimacy goes beyond establishing heteronormativity; it is the basis on which the self is judged to have value, merit, substance. Miranda Joseph notes that the turn to intimacy produced by the "shift of production from domestic to public spheres" endowed the family with the "compensatory role as the site of reprieve from public work."[140] What the fantasy of intimacy most forcefully affords and reflects is the capacity to disengage from the specific capitalist relations and political conditions that make the liberal notion of intimacy imaginable in the first place. Further, intimate love as love of or between persons is extended to love of country,[141] making the continuity between the domestinormative and the proper emotional orientation of the American citizenry quite clear. For Orientalized Muslim bodies, love is superseded by social structure—business, clan, tribe, totem, kinship—that lend themselves to polygamy, sex segregation, arranged marriage, marriage within (royal) families, and male-male sex stemming from the lack of intimate contact with women. That is to say, noble love is not operant, and thus intimacy is absent. This might be the only judgment where the Orient is accorded the space of the rational, but one that is deficient of soul, in contrast to the passionate compulsions of the west. But it is consistent with the valorization of liberal individualism, borne by an evolved subject, in contrast to the group mentality of those who are seen to cede all decision making to the collective.

Queer theory, Povinelli notes, makes one break between intimacy and genealogy visible; she cites the work of Michael Warner on "stranger intimacy," Candace Vogler on "depersonalized intimacy," and Lauren Berlant on "critical utopian intimacy" (we can also add Berlant's "intimate public sphere," where contentious public politics are sublimated into the private).[142] These accounts usefully unhook intimacy from the family, and from the centrality of sexuality to the family, challenging the boundaries of legitimate and illegitimate intimacy, diversifying and to some extent democratizing modalities of intimacy. Nevertheless, the focal point of sex and of corporeal experiences of sexuality and sensuality remains.

While these theorists vastly expand the purview of legitimate intimacy, deconstructing and interrogating the terms on which intimacy accords legibility to who touches or should not touch whom, the terrain of intimacy is reworked only insofar as new actors are accorded the right to it, not in terms of what intimacy actually is and *how* it is. Thinking about intimacy as a technology of legibility must go beyond Oedipalization, beyond sexually interactive bodies of subjects to the militarization of bodies and the multiple bodies of the population that Foucault speaks of. What of intimacy with machines, for example: intimacy with the gaze of the nonorganic machinic assemblages of technology such as biometric surveillance scanners? (What is reality television if not constant intimate relating with omnipotent surveillance equipment?) Or even intimacies with other species (recall Donna Haraway and her doggies),[143] surfaces, spirits, and other ethereal beings and preternatural presences beyond this world.

In reorienting our attention from public-private paradigms to the intimate, it seems almost ludicrous to inquire about the sector of the intimate for the suspected terrorist, the detainee, the exiled immigrant. Intimacy in its liberal fantasy form is historically the province of heteronormativity and now, as I have argued, homonormativity. Thus, heteronormativity and homonormativity are spatiotemporal sites that are bolstered, doubly so, through *Lawrence-Garner* and infinite detention. The *Lawrence-Garner* ruling's fictional private turf of American queer sex (Vice President Dick Cheney's daughter, Mary Cheney, and former New Jersey governor Jim "I am a gay American!" McGreevy can retreat with nobility to the protection of their private liberty) exists only in and through vast contradistinction to the completely infiltrated, no-longer-and-perhaps-never-was private confines of the accused immigrant-terrorist (among, let us not forget, other disenfranchised figures).[144]

Therefore, when mapping the budding regimes of heightened regulation of (homo)sexuality that Hunter avows, intimacy is not an object to be had or to be accorded or denied. Intimacy is a crucial part of an affective economy within surveillance systems that provoke, subsume, and muffle feelings and emotions but also sensations, hallucinations, palpitations, yearnings of security and insecurity. Further, the intimacy of the private radiates beyond an encircled physical site of disciplinary power to a form of cultural capital, a commodity circulating within power networks of control.

In control societies, surveillance imprints its presence far beyond an egregious intrusion of privacy or intimacy, as has been theorized in the case of panoptic disciplinary sites. To imply that only the privacy and intimacy of the bodies are violated through such intimate bodily practices of surveillance belies a liberal fantasy about bodily integrity, a projection of wholeness that many are not accorded, a privileged marker of liberal subjecthood as well as a marker of privileged liberal subjecthood. Experiences of intimacy are qualitatively altering due to the regularization of monitoring that Foucault speaks of. One could even argue that there is no inside of intimacy to violate, penetrate, or disturb from the outside, no depth that is safeguarded. The phantasmatic construction of this inside, this depth, or safeguarded interior intimacy is the prescriptive work of biopolitical control. That is not to say that surveillance is not violating, penetrating, disturbing, but instead that the perception of intrusion is diluted rather than concentrated, diffuse rather than focalized, multiple rather than singular. Gesturing to a biopolitical control view of contact, proximity, transparency, and corporeality entails a partial disengagement from the primacy of the self-other relay of subject formation to the regularization of quotidian affective modes of be/longing and recognition, tactility that congeals populations and distributes moments, brushings, looks, stares, and touches.

It would appear that I have traveled far afield from the *Lawrence-Garner* case with which I began this chapter. I believe this is symptomatic of an analysis that reveals connectivity in places where it is generally assumed none exists. In summary, and in an attempt to connect the dots of the road I have just traversed, *Lawrence-Garner* conveys most insistently that, in the context of the war on terror, in the deconstruction of analogic frames of race and sexuality, citizenship remains a critical yet undertheorized facet of sexual regulation in the United States. As regulation shifts objects instead of decreasing its reach or effects, the policing of sexuality will be displaced onto or fortified through a range of other surveillance mechanisms; the praxes associated with torture, infinite detention, and deportation are prime examples. Muslim (male) subjects are not only unable to perform or inhabit heterosexuality properly; they are also deemed unfit for an upright (national) homosexuality. As such, the *Lawrence-Garner* ruling can be thought of as a subsidiary tool in the quest of the ascendancy of whiteness. By *regularizing queerness*, it patrols the boundaries between queer subjects who are invited into life and queer populations who come into being through their perverse sexual-racial attributes and histories.

"the turban is not a hat":

queer diaspora and practices of profiling

"The turban is not a hat" became the slogan for an educational Sikh crusade, a central organizing refrain for numerous national Sikh advocacy
groups soon after September 11, 2001, who were reckoning with a surge of
reported assaults on turbaned men mistaken for Muslim terrorists.[1] The
first victim of these hate-crime murders was in fact a turbaned Sikh, 52-
year-old Balbir Singh Sodhi, who was shot five times in the back at a gas
station in Mesa, Arizona, on September 15, 2001.[2] His killer, Francisco Silva
Roque, proclaimed, "I'm an American. Arrest me and let those terrorists
run wild."[3] Sodhi subsequently became the poster child for a wronged Sikh
American citizenry, the symbolic and material evidence of the fact that
Sikhs were indeed most certainly not Muslims. At this time I was involved
with efforts at the Garden State Sikh Association (GSSA; a temple community in New Jersey that I have been a member of throughout my childhood
and some of my adult life) to protect its membership, especially turbaned
men facing various turban clawing and grabbing incidents, many of them
working at gas stations and in bodegas.[4] Our gurdwara community, as with
many across the United States and in Britain and France, went to exacting
pains to enact a performance of allegiance to the nation, one bolstered by
the display of heteronormative model minority ideals.

Along with the typical assimilative but self-preservationist tactics—
candlelight vigils, flags covering the temple, red-white-and-blue turbans,
and patriotic statements aligning themselves with the American citizenry
as victims—public relations firms were hired to manage the damage control
and "deal with this misunderstanding among the American public," while
an endless stream of lawyers went to Washington to meet with senators and
other public officials to expound upon Sikh commitment to American civic
life.[5] The cry of "mistaken identity" thus became central to Sikh lobbying
efforts. Organizations such as the Sikh Mediawatch and Resource Task
Force (SMART; a Sikh American civil rights advocacy group) have released
statements, talking points, and photos explaining the differences between

"those" turbans and Sikh turbans.[6] (The attacks themselves were becoming increasingly bizarre in their execution. Often the turban itself was the object of the assault, and the unraveling of hair signified a humiliating and intimate submission, hinting at homosocial undertones.)[7] Sikh communities were flooded with missives on how to navigate airport security and promote interfaith exchange, and also released many documents.[8] One such document is "The Turban Is Not a Hat," which instructed Sikhs dealing with airport security to insist that their turbans, if it was required that they be checked for weapons, be scanned with a sensor wand rather than being removed and sent through x-ray machines or forcibly unwrapped, both prevailing practices at the time. In hopes of avoiding inspection altogether, SMART directed Sikhs to claim that the turban could not be removed without its unraveling: "The turban is not a hat. It is a mandatory symbol of the Sikh religion. I cannot simply remove it; it must be unwrapped."[9] The widespread campaigns undertaken by liberal Sikh advocacy groups to educate "ignorant Americans" about Sikhs also responded to a series of offensive videogames (like *Hitman 2*) and cartoon strips (Carol Lay's "A Field Guide to Turbans" and "Randy bin Laden"), as well as demands that the turban be removed for driver's license and work-related photos and other administrative jobs and work-related procedures. Largely disregarding that there is a wide variation of turban styles, colors, material, sizes, and even uses *between* Sikhs from varying diasporic locations, class backgrounds, and even genders—for Sikh women may also don turbans, however rare—these efforts were driven by a desire to inhabit a proper Sikh American heteromasculinity, one at significant remove from the perverse sexualities ascribed to terrorist bodies.[10] Further, the hypothesis of mistaken identity as the main causal factor for post-9/11 hate crimes, along with the liberal push to educate an unknowing citizenry, relies on multiple premises: that the viewer (assumed to be white despite the proliferation of these attacks by people of color) is open to and willing to discern the visual differences between Sikh turbans and Muslim turbans; that the ideals of multiculturalism as promulgated by liberal education acknowledge that differences within difference matter; that violent backlash toward Sikhs is a displacement of hostility from the rightful object, the "real" Muslims. Thus these political tactics encouraged amnesia of the turban assaults that stretch back to the late 1800s, when the "tide of the turbans" came forth to the northwestern United States, and more recent spates such as that following the 1984 assassination of Indira Gandhi.[11] At the limit here, then, is the acknowledgment of the perverse masculinities

FIGURE 15. Illustration from the *Bellingham Morning Reveille*, 1909. Image text reads as follows: "This is the type of man driven from this city as the result of last night's demonstration by a mob of 500 men and boys." Courtesy of the Center for Pacific Northwest Studies, Western Washington University and *The Bellingham Herald*.

encrypted into Sikh bodies, specifically through the rescripting of these masculinities via an enactment of anti-Muslim sentiment. The disavowal of the perverse queernesses attached to Muslim terrorist bodies thus functions as a rite of initiation and assimilation into U.S. heteronormative citizenship.

Concurrently, I was also part of a group of activists loosely working together, many of whom were part of the South Asian Lesbian and Gay Association based in New York City. In the months following September 11, 2001, SALGA members across the tristate area reported numerous sexual, verbal, and physical assaults on queer South Asians who were mugged, beaten, and molested. We were struggling to articulate a relationship between queer bashing and what were narrowly defined as racist hate crimes, a connection that was being patently ignored by mainstream queer anti-violence organizations, such as the New York Anti-Violence Project, and only preliminarily approached by many Arab American, South Asian, and Muslim groups, some of which were admirably attempting to tackle issues about sexuality for the very first time. It certainly appeared to be the case that our queer South Asian communities were doubly vulnerable to these attacks, especially those more conspicuously marked by visible traits associated with gender nonnormativity, working-class and working-poor backgrounds, and immigrant bodies and speech. Some of those assaulted encountered very specific references to faggotry or other homophobic slurs. But by and large it was more obvious that the invocation of the word "terrorist" in these crimes always already betrayed an implicitly installed prerequisite of perverse sexuality, queerness, and gender nonnormativity beyond the pale of proper citizenship sexuality, both heteronormative and homonormative. We labored to produce materials and resources for the queer South Asian community that specifically addressed racist and homophobic crimes, recognizing that the queer perversity of terrorist bodies was being both *read from* their bodies as well as *endowed upon* their bodies; that is, queerness was both an identificatory modality producing individual bodies and a generalized rubric applied to populations. The interstices between the brown queer subject who is hailed as a terrorist and the terrorist who is always already pathologically queer surfaced as a complex activist scotoma that challenged the bounds of our work (a limitation that has everything to do with an understanding of queerness that is unable to address its often subterranean proclivities toward sexualities that are adamantly secular). Ironically, South Asian queer diasporic subjects were and continue to be under even greater duress to produce themselves as exceptional American subjects, not necessarily as heteronormative but as homonormative, even as the queernesses of these very bodies are simultaneously used to pathologize populations configured as terrorist. In response, a double movement has been enabled: an invitation into queer and homonormative folds of American patriotism to participate in and reproduce narratives of U.S. queer exceptionalism in contradistinction to perverse (Orientalist) *and* repressed (neo-Orientalist human rights discourse) sexualities of the East; or an investment in foregrounding and reclaiming the sexual perversities of the brown terrorist implicit in the queering of terrorist populations. In this latter move, however, there seemed to be a figure, or should I say an object, at the limit of this strategy: the turban, and the body that it sits upon. Its historical attachments to hypermasculinity, perverse heterosexuality (and at times pedophilia and homosexuality), and warrior militancy rendered these turbaned bodies neither within the bounds of respectable queer subjecthood nor worthy of a queer intervention that would stage a reclamation of sexual-racial perversity, suggesting that it is a body almost *too perverse to be read as queer,* a problematic that is specific to certain diasporic contexts and not generalizable to South Asia itself. As contagions

The Turban

that trouble the exceptionalisms of queer South Asian diasporas, male turbaned Sikh bodies are read as patriarchal by queer diasporic logics because they challenge the limits of queer diasporic identity that balks at the non-normativity of turbaned bodies (even as it avows the pathological and sexual-racial renderings of terrorist bodies). Many queer South Asians in New York during fall 2001 were working with South Asian community-based organizations, such as Desis Rising Up and Moving, the Asian American Legal Defense and Education Fund, Manavi (a help line for South Asian women), and the New York Taxi Workers Alliance. However, despite the best efforts of South Asian queer organizers and gurdwara community leaders, the two activist initiatives I have just sketched—even in light of the obvious commonalities of circumstance and concerns about racial profiling, surveillance, and security —did not and dare not converge.

On the one hand, a queer diasporic subject may contest the limits of the liberated subject of *Lawrence-Garner*, produced through privileges of class, whiteness, and gender normativity; on the other, this subject may be unable to respond to the turbaned Sikh victim and the related figure of the Muslim terrorist, both of whom are seen as conservatively heteronormative and antiqueer, yet in the perverse sexualities ascribed to them are almost too queer to rehabilitate. But where they converge is crucial: these subjects of resistance, to one degree or another, fail. Further, to a greater or lesser extent, both queer diasporic and GSSA's responses rely on the specular as the conduit for the transfer of correct information, the former through recourse to a queer visibility that forecloses the turbaned body as an object worthy of a queer intervention, and the latter through the privileging of "seeing" as a naturalized activity that can be easily disrupted in order to redress misrecognition and rearrange configurations of gender, sexuality, and race.

Queer Diasporas

Brian Keith Axel, in his ground-clearing essay, "The Diasporic Imaginary," poses two radical modifications to the study of diaspora as it has developed in anthropology, cultural studies, and interdisciplinary forums. Referencing his study of Sikh diasporas, he argues first that "rather than conceiving of the homeland as something that creates the diaspora, it may be more productive to consider the diaspora as something that creates the homeland." Axel is gesturing beyond the material locational pragmatics of the myth of return, the economic and symbolic importance of the nonresident Indian (NRI), Khalistan, and Hindutva nationalist movements funded by diasporic money, or the modalities of homeland that are recreated in the diaspora. The homeland, he proposes, "must be understood as an affective and temporal process rather than a place." But if not the fact of place, what impels a diasporic sensibility or collectivity? The "temporalizing and affective aspect of subjectification" involved in the creation of the homeland pulls "the homeland into relation with other kinds of images and processes . . . different bodies or corporeal images and historical formations of sexuality, gender and violence."[12]

Axel's formulation can be productively reworked to further query the habitus of nation and its geographic coordinates. The paradigm of queer diaspora retools the notion of diaspora to account for connectivity beyond or different from sharing a common ancestral homeland.[13] That is, to shift away from origin for a moment allows other forms of diasporic affiliative and cathartic entities—for Axel, primarily that of bodies—to show their affiliative powers. This is especially critical given that for Sikhs, "the homeland" (Khalistan) is a perpetual fantasy and not a current political fact; thus an experience of temporality is already commanded to futurity rather than only organized through tradition, a common past, an origin. Furthermore, an unsettling of the site of origin (i.e., nation) as one of the two binding terms of diaspora de facto wrenches ancestral progression out of the automatic purview of diaspora, allowing for queer narratives of kinship, belonging, and home. While Axel is primarily interested in *images* of the tortured Sikh male body, I would argue that a focus on affect reveals how actual bodies can be in multiple places and temporalities simultaneously, not (only) tethered through nostalgia or memory but folded and braided into intensifications. The sensation of place is thus one of manifold intensities cathected through distance. To extend Axel's formulation, the homeland is not represented only as a demographic, a geographical place, nor primarily through history, memory, or even trauma, but is cohered through sensation, vibrations, echoes, speed, feedback loops, recursive folds and feelings. Axel argues that the homeland is a spatial rather than a locational or place-based phenomenon, coalescing through corporealities, affectivities, and, I would add, multiple and contingent temporalities, as much as it is memory of place, networks (of travel, communication, and informational exchange), the myth of the imminent return to origin, and the progressive telos of origin to diaspora.

Queer diasporic theorizing has emphasized self-crafted kinship, erotic and affectionate networks or lines of affiliation, rather than filiation. David Eng's wonderfully generative writing on queer diaspora is instructive here:

Reconceptualizing diaspora not in conventional terms of ethnic dispersion, filiation, and biological traceability, but rather in terms of queerness, affiliation, and social contingency[,] "queer diaspora" emerges as a concept providing new methods of contesting traditional family and kinship structures—of reorganizing national and transnational communities based not on origin, filiation, and genetics but on destination, affiliation, and the assumption of a common set of social practices or political commitments.[14]

Foregrounding queer diasporic affiliations, bound through conscious adoption of alternative networking, may cohere and centralize a prediscursive agential queer subject proactively creating nonassimilatable diasporic circuits, rather than elucidate the ontological presences that constitute and are constitutive of queer diasporas. Shifting focus to affect also unsettles a longstanding preoccupation with queer diasporic representational practices. We move from What does this body mean? to What and who does this body affect? What does this body do? While the notion of contagion is slightly overdetermined in relation to unwanted and afflicted bodies, in this case I am suggesting not that specific bodies be read as contagions, but that all bodies can be thought of as contagious or mired in contagions: bodies infecting other bodies with sensation, vibration, irregularity, chaos, lines of flight that betray the expectation of loyalty, linearity, the demarcation of who's in and who's not. Contagions are autonomous, unregulated, their vicissitudes only peripherally anchored by knowable entities. They invoke the language of infection and transmission, forcing us to ask, How does one catch something whose trace is inchoate or barely discerned? Contagions conduct the effects of touch, smell, taste, hearing, and sight—the five primary senses (from the vantage of western science)—into shivers, sweat, blushes, heat, and pain, among many other sensations. Contagions thus complicate even the most complex articulations of affiliation; that is, contagion returns the process of affiliation to indeterminacy and contingency. These oppositions that subtend Eng's proposition—origin/destination, filiation/affiliation, genetics/sociopolitics—are thus defied by the unpredictability of contagions, whose unregulated forces have no designated a priori affinities nor opponents, coagulating instead through sympathies. Contagions add an important factor in this equation, for they bypass the question of what constitutes a viable affiliation. This question returns us to the opening activist scenario whereby Sikh gurdwara sectors and South Asian queer diasporics are seen as incommensurate affinities or affiliations.

It is this shift from origin to affectation, from South Asia as unifying homeland to contagions—the assemblage of the monster-terrorist-fag, for instance—that troubles queer diasporic exceptionalisms, but also impels their exponential fortification and proliferation. South Asian queer diasporic communities in the United States (as well as Britain) are disproportionately impacted by the production of terrorist corporealities, navigating the figures of the Muslim terrorist, the turbaned Sikh man so often mistaken for him, and the woman in hijab who must be rescued from them. These generative figures, always already sexually pathological, speak to the prolific fertilization and crosshatching of terrorist corporealities amid South Asian queer diasporas. As such, South Asian queer diasporas must contend not only with the stigmatization of their communities via these perverse terrorist bodies, but also with the forms of queerness-as-exceptionalism that are often offered in response to this stigmatization. As a regulatory construct, this queer exceptionalism may mimic forms of (U.S.) model minority exceptionalism,[15] positing queerness as an exemplary or liberatory site devoid of nationalist impulses, an exceptionalism that narrates queerness as emulating the highest transgressive potential of diaspora. But the tensions—and overlaps—between the now fetishized desi drag queen or even the hijra (think of the British and Broadway stage performances of *Bombay Dreams*) and the turbaned or otherwise Sikh- or Muslim-identified terrorist invariably temper this exceptionalism.

Since September 11, 2001, for example, many activists and community members from SALGA in New York have voiced sentiments similar to this one, expressed by a Pakistani Muslim queer man: "My sexuality has taken a back seat to my ethnicity."[16] This statement reveals some reentrenchment of organizational relations away from mainstream queers, a recomposition of the categories of race and nation, a rehashing of intersectionality as a viable identity framework, and the differential impact of surveillance optics. Furthermore, the war on terror demands a dual homonationalism, as allegiances to the nation-state of India are unwittingly or often deliberately rearticulated through allegiances to the United States. (This is reflective of the recent rise of an India-U.S. power couple.)[17] Forms of regulatory queerness that collude with and are rooted in the quest for queer diasporic representational purchase, operating in tandem with the historical narrative of South Asians as a model minority population in the United States, must contend with the contagions of differently queer terrorist bodies. We have again the attempted splitting off of the queer liberal subject—this time surfacing as the exceptional queer diasporic model minority subject, regulatory insofar as it must disavow neighboring contagions of populations, regulated insofar as it is both domesticated by and domesticating of spatially and temporally constricted amenable national populations, in this case, Indian and American—from attachments and associations to terrorist bodies.[18] The shift we can mark, then, is that these queer diasporic subjects are under duress, perhaps more so than any other population at this historical juncture, to naturalize or normativize their exceptional U.S.-ness or Americanness, not through a heteronormative mandate but through homonormativity, at the exact moment that queerness is a modality of nominalization that demarcates these very same bodies as terrorists.

As much queer diasporic theorizing seeks to enact the elaboration of a transgressive agential queer diasporic subject, I would like to offer an interpretation of affect that does not demand that the (agential) queer (diasporic?) subject be read in line with affective or emotional resonance, nor that the queer subject be produced through these resonances. I am not interested in reading the turbaned body as a queer body or queering the turbaned body. As a figure that deeply troubles the nation's security, the turbaned body can be most fruitfully rearticulated, not solely as a body encased in tradition and backwardness, attempting to endow itself with modernity, nor as a dissident queer body, but as an assemblage, a move I make to both expand the expectations and assumptions of queer reading practices (descriptive and prescriptive) and to unsettle the long-standing theorizations of heteronormative frames of reference for the nation and the female body as the primary or sole bearer of cultural honor and respect. My aim is to rethink turbaned terrorist bodies and terrorist populations in relation to and beyond the ocular, that is, as affective and affected entities that create fear but also feel the fear they create, an assemblage of contagions (again, this is distinct from the perverse body as contagious), sutured not through identity or identification but through the concatenation of disloyal and irreverent lines of flight—partial, transient, momentary, and magical. (In this sense I am departing from the currently emerging convention of queer theory on affect, or on queer affect, which I discuss in greater detail in the conclusion.) This rereading of turbaned bodies offers a critical counternarrative to both queer subjects that regulate the terms of queerness (in this case, hinting at the foreclosure of a queer diasporic turbaned Sikh, male or female, a subject that is distinct from the queernesses that have often been attributed to Sikh masculinities) and the pathological queernesses endowed upon terrorist populations that Sikh gurdwara communities seek to evade.

Crucially linked to this, the purported coherence and cohesion of the organic body is at stake here, as I suggest, first, that the intermixing of the organic with the inorganic turban needs to be theorized across an organic/inorganic divide, a machinic assemblage, and second, that informational and surveillance technologies of control both produce the body-as-information and also impact the organic body through an interface—again, organic and machinic technologies that interface to points of mutual dissolution. My reading thus elaborates the biopolitics of population that racializes and sexualizes bodies not entirely through their visual and affective qualities (as they are acquired historically and discursively) but rather through the data they assemble, what are otherwise known as "data bodies," bodies materialized through information and statistics. Here I proffer some speculations about the connections and divergences—the dance—between the profile and the racial profile, keeping in tension with each other the ocular, the affective, and the informational. What is the concept of race in profiling if we are not to privilege the visible, the knowable, the epistemological? Is the informational body, the data body that precedes and follows us racial, or racist, and if so, how is it articulated within profiling? This is of particular concern to me in part because the notion of "surveillance assemblages" that is currently emerging from the field of surveillance studies, while rightly depriviling the visual field in favor of affect and information, tends toward discounting and dismissing the visual and its capacity to interpellate subjects. This discounting is simply not politically viable given the shifts around formations of race and sex that are under way in response to a new visual category, the "terrorist look-alike" or those who "look like terrorists."

Turbans Becoming Strange Attractors

The turban is accruing the marks of a terrorist masculinity. The turbaned man—no longer merely the figure of a durable and misguided tradition, a community and familial patriarch, a resistant antiassimilationist stance—now inhabits the space and history of monstrosity, of that which can never become civilized. The turban is not only imbued with the nationalist, religious, and cultural symbolics of the Other; it both reveals and hides the terrorist, a constant sliding between that which can be disciplined and that which must be outlawed. Despite the taxonomies of the turban, its specific regional and locational genealogies, its placement in time and space, its singularity and its multiplicity, the turban-as-monolith profoundly troubles and disturbs American national imaginaries and their attendant notions of security.

The turban has faded in and out of U.S. historical consciousness.[19] In 1923, Bhagat Singh Thind, a turbaned Sikh man, petitioned the U.S. Su-

FIGURE 16. Bhagat Singh Thind, ca. 1918. Reprinted with permission from David Bhagat Thind.

preme Court to grant Indians citizenship status. Arguing that North Indians have a Caucasian Aryan ancestry similar to white Americans', Thind forced the issue of racial exclusion in relation to citizenship, despite ultimately losing his case. In the literatures of ethnic, South Asian, migration, and Asian American studies, the *Thind* case is hailed as a landmark ruling about the racial status of South Asians in the United States, but in the broad citational span of the case, little commentary has been offered on the specific markings of the (Sikh) bodies that were represented in this claim.[20] Nevertheless, the presence of the turban confirms a priori the properly religious Sikh man within essentializing Sikh historical scholarship. The language of the ruling itself speaks of the importance of "resemblance" between "cultivated citizens": "The term 'race' is one which, for the practical purposes of the statute, must be applied to a group of living persons now possessing in common the requisite characteristics, not to groups of persons who are supposed to be or really are descended from some remote, common ancestor, but who, whether they both resemble him to a greater or less extent, have, at any rate, ceased altogether to resemble one another. It may be true

FIGURE 17. Sikh men on the ss *Minnesota*. Photograph by Asahel Curtis, 1913. Reprinted with permission from the Washington State Historical Society.

that the blond Scandinavian and the brown Hindu have a common ancestor in *the dim reaches of antiquity*, but the average *man knows* perfectly well that there are unmistakable and profound differences between them today" (emphasis mine).[21] By invoking the everyday experience of race over the scientific and anthropological evidence presented by Thind, the decision confirms the anxiety regarding dominant imagery of brown turbaned "Hindoo" laborers at that time.[22] The ruling is thus symptomatic not only of the demand for phenotypical resemblance, but also for *resonance* of visceral properties of the body. It is not only that the blond Scandinavian cannot see himself in the brown Hindu, and vice versa. Rather, the bodies inhabit different tactile and affective economies, insofar as touch, texture, sensation, and turban-as-appendage render the impossibility of resonance, of appearing to feel the same. There is a refusal to allow the simultaneous inhabiting of tactile economies that cut through and across these representational divides.[23]

Thus, the pressure to naturalize the aspirant citizen is reflected in the erasure of nomenclature and the psychic de-turbaning (as castration?) that

FIGURE 18. Unknown artist, *A New Problem for Uncle Sam*. Originally published in *San Francisco Call*, August 13, 1910.

promotes a representational but not ontological assessment of the historical impact of the *Thind* case (though the ruling might suppress turbaned embodiments, it never completely forgets them). As a form of unveiling, deturbaning functions to allow the true nature of the Hindoo to emerge and be recognized; bodily practices involving hair, beard, turban, and the cultural body are under duress to conform. Furthermore, the claim of Aryan ancestry links into a foundational belief system of Hindu nationalism, which centrally asserts the truth of this connection; Hindu racial, cultural, and civilizational purity and superiority vis-à-vis Muslims, as well as the Hindutva state of India, are also complicit with the production of Sikh and Muslim terrorist corporealities.[24]

Mistaken as Hindu in the early twentieth century and now mistaken as Muslim, middle-class Sikhs, conservative and progressive factions alike, have embraced the hypothesis of mistaken identity as the main causal factor for post-9/11 hate crimes, thus paralleling the official response of the Bush Administration.[25] Since September 11, 2001, Sikh men wearing turbans, mistaken for kin of Osama bin Laden, have been disproportionately affected by backlash racist hate crimes. Let us ponder for a moment the span of violence: verbal harassment (being called "bin Laden," "son of bin Laden," "Osama"), especially on the phone and while driving; tailgating; hate mail; defecating and urinating on Sikh gurdwaras, Islamic mosques, and Hindu temples, leading in some cases to arson; blocking the entrance of a Sikh temple in Sacramento with a tractor and truck and jumping into the sacred holy water at the temple; throwing bricks, gasoline bombs, garbage, and other projectiles into homes of Sikhs and Arabs and slashing car tires; death threats and bomb threats; fatal shootings of taxi drivers, the majority of whom have been turbaned Sikhs; verbal and physical harassment of primary and secondary school children, as well as foreign students on college campuses; and attacks with baseball bats, paintball guns, lit cigarettes, and pigs' blood.[26] This enumeration is provided to detail the prolific creativity engendered within these attacks in order to situate the importance of the turban not as an entity that merely represents any given meanings in these instances, but rather as a vector of information, a point of contact, a transfer and conduit of turbulence.

The deturbaning undertaken by massive numbers of Sikh men was one manifestation of the demanded domestication of Americanness, where removal functions as a reorientation into masculine patriotic identity. More important, deturbaning, along with hate crime statistics, underscores the costs of an association with terrorist bodies. Assaults of turbaned men continue to escalate, attributed in part to a "resurgence of backlash" since the beginning of the war in Iraq; the Sikh Coalition estimates that in 2003 there was a 90 percent increase in bias incidents since 2002, and that a vast majority of crimes go unreported because of language barriers and unfamiliarity with hate-crime legislation.[27] The nature of these assaults has also become more sophisticated and more complex. Recent attacks (in the United States but also globally) involve not only verbal commands to deturban—"Hey you fucking terrorist, take that turban off!"—but also the grabbing, unraveling, or knocking and pulling off of the head covering. It is not for nothing that in one hate crime incident after another, turbans are clawed at viciously and unshorn hair is pulled, occasionally even cut off. The intimacy of such violence, in this case conventionally defined in terms of liberal autonomy and privacy, cannot be overstated. Indeed, it is often the actual turban itself, an embodiment of metaphysical substance, that is the desired object of violence, suggesting that it is understood as much more than an appendage. Within Sikh community contexts, de-throning someone's turban is the paramount insult to the wearer, the most humiliating form of disrespect, the sheer force of which is usually unknown to hate crime

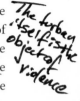

The turban itself is the object of violence

perpetrators. The attack functions as a double emasculation: the felling is an offense to the (usually) male representative of the community, and the shearing of hair entails submission by and to normative patriotic masculinities. Yet the colliding of discourses of normative patriotic enforcement—"Take that turban off, you fucking terrorist"—and community shame is noteworthy, suggesting that even without any understanding of the turban's contextual significance, its magnitude is somehow comprehended.

As substitute embodiments for an elusive Osama bin Laden, Sikhs are a sanctioned hate crime target for what Muneer Ahmad has called "a socially appropriate emotion [expressed] in socially inappropriate ways."[28] No longer remarkable, these hate crimes have become normalized within a refashioned racial landscape.[29] But more significant, they have become immanent to the counterterrorism objectives of the state, operating as an extended arm of the nation, encouraging the surveillance and strike capacities of the patriotic populous.[30] The duality at work here—the centrality of multiculturalism and diversity to the discourse of citizenship coupled with the surveillance, domestication, quarantine, and containment of the corporealities that attempt to approximate these democratic ideals—enables the emergence of liberal multiculturalism not only as a consumptive project and as a process of inclusion, incorporation, normalization, and assimilation, but more perniciously as a form of governmentality.[31] Writing in December 2003 during the peak of France's debates on banning religious head coverings, Timur Yuskaev and Matt Weiner claim:

> In the aftermath of Sept. 11 the American model of a secular state that is tolerant of religious difference has worked remarkably well, though not perfectly. The public's anxiety over the Muslim "enemy within" was higher than ever. *Yet not a single official asked Muslims to become invisible and remove their headscarves.* The official policy was to protect the freedom to be visibly Muslim. Had the government acted otherwise, it would have sided with the ignorant bullies who harassed and physically attacked so many Muslims, Arabs and Sikhs. (emphasis mine)

This exalting of the United States in contrast to France is sorely ironic, for the function of the state in retaining the visibility of religious difference is hardly benevolent. Rather, the state depends on that isolated difference, the oh so celebrated difference (of food, clothing, literature, art, tourism, film) that allows for the watching and the assaulting of these different bodies, of "those whose difference is hard to stomach."[32] No official request is necessitated: the dual imposition of discourses of citizenship for Sikhs—normalization and expulsion—is not merely realized in the form of cultural or discursive negotiations. The state works doubly to promulgate anti-Sikh rhetoric on the one hand, while welcoming Sikhs as a protected population under hate crime legislation on the other.[33]

Turbans, in their symbolic weight, are the masculine counterparts to veils, and in their usage irrevocably link Sikhs and Muslims, signifying honor, dignity, purity, virginity, chastity; a *sardar* removes his turban as an offering of his word, a commitment to a promise. My intent here is not to draw any simple analogy or equivalence between the practices, but rather to highlight the ways they converge (and diverge in western queer, feminist, and national imaginaries). Similar to the way veils have generated Orientalist fantasies of female submission, emerged as nodal fixation, been established as a standard topic of discussion in women's studies curriculum, and become an easy marker of an other (Muslim/Arab/Islamic) femininity—one of the most potent self/othering mechanisms in the history of western feminisms— turbans are emerging as a signal of an "other masculinity." Within these heteronormative frames, the turbaned man is the warrior leader of the community, the violent patriarch, and at the same time, the long-haired, feminized sissy, a figure of failed masculinity in contrast to (white) hegemonic masculinities. Like the burqa, the hijab, and the headscarf, turbans mark gender (though women, usually converted white American Sikhs, do don turbans), religion, and region, as well as signal, to the untrained eye, the most pernicious components of oppressive patriarchal backward cultures and traditions, those that have failed at modernity. Turbans have become strange attractors, centripetal forces to which the eye is instantly drawn. As with veils, the turban is multiple. Sizes, shapes, and colors designate gender, caste, religiosity, militancy, marital status, and age. Assembled through a taxonomy of regional and religious differences (Sikh, Muslim, Middle Eastern, South Asian, Northern Indian, Sunni, Shi'ite), turbans mark not only difference within U.S. discourses of banal multiculturalism, but also racial and sexual differences among South Asian, Middle Eastern, and Arab communities. Indeed, they are vehemently used *within* communities to demarcate insider versus outsider, devout believer versus religious fake. Yet turbans acquire a bizarre singular momentum, the sheer might of multiplicity collapsed into one stagnant pool of meaning. Like veiling, turbaning generates anxiety in the observer, the sense of inaccessibility, of something being out of place and out of time, of incomprehensibility.

Unlike veiling, however, turbans have not preoccupied western feminist scholarship and organizations concerned with missionary liberationist practices; in this sense, turbans do reiterate a masculinist centrality of cultural and religious norms, and as such have not been the target of social protests seeking to liberate those deemed to be subjugated. This is a crucial distinction, one that informs contemporary debates about head coverings in several parts of the world (France and Britain for instance).[34] While veiling, not turbaning, in migrant communities has been the primary source of disquiet in France, where such practices are most visible, turbans have been the central focus of debate in Britain. This is partially fallout from the history of incorporation of Sikhs into the British colonial military in India, a disciplining that established Sikhs as warriors but also as colluding with British imperial occupation and as figures of guilt and treason to the anticolonial movement. However, as a form of cultural continuity and the maintenance of tradition, the plight of male turban wearers problematizes decades of feminist inquiry that locates women as the bearers and transmitters of authentic culture.[35] Thus, my concentration on turban profiling, which displaces the conversation about racist backlash against hijabed women, or violence against women generally, is nonetheless committed to an unearthing of the often obscured issues of gender and sexuality in relation to masculinity and effeminization. The turban is a contested icon imbued with the possibilities of remasculinization and nationalism. That is to say, attending to the vulnerability of male turbaned bodies also opens up the possibility of their very restoration, their rephallicization and recentering within patriarchal nationalisms, a restoration that this chapter reluctantly courts (perhaps fed by its major shortcoming, the absence of specific discussion on turbaned women).

Turbans are also loaded with the weight of victimology, an overdetermined discourse about the trauma and suffering of turbaned Sikh men, the fetish of injury. This victimology, which predates September 11, 2001, is often entangled in discourses about racism and racist encounters, in part narrated through relations with the white gaze, thus reestablishing the ascendancy of whiteness. What Ahmed terms "injury as identity,"[36] this exceptional narrative of victimhood—the claim that Sikh men encounter more racism than Sikh women, for example, conveniently effacing gender inequities between Sikh men and women—is complemented by a reclaiming of the turban as a form of religious and multicultural excellence. This example foregrounds once again the heterosexual mandates of national belonging, a circuitry implicating homonational subjects, model minority heterosexuality, and perversely queered populations. This circuit casts immigrant communities and communities of color as "more homophobic"— solidifying them, ironically, as simplistically heterosexual (mindlessly, carelessly reproducing) or heteronormative in an uncosmopolitan, regressive manner (unable or unwilling to participate in the nuclear familial individuation of market capitalism that promotes child raising and kinship as consumption projects)—thus opening up greater liberatory possibilities for white queer liberal and homonormative subjects and foreclosing, in an enactment of "interested denial,"[37] queer of color subjects. Further, regulatory queerness (liberal, homonormative, or even diasporic) denotes queer turbaned Sikhs (male or female) as improbable, if not impossible, subjects.

Ocular and Affective

Judith Butler, in her examination of the Rodney King case, has written, "The visual field is not neutral to the question of race; it is itself a racial formation, an episteme, hegemonic and forceful." The field of the visible is a racially contested terrain. "Seeing" is not an act of direct perception, but "the racial production of the visible, the workings of racial constraints on what it means to 'see.'" Therefore, the act of seeing is simultaneously an act of reading, a specific interpretation of the visual. But this reading passes itself off as a seeing, a natural activity, hiding the "contestable construal" of what is seen. This racist organization and disposition of the visible also works to define what qualifies as visual evidence; thus the ocular distinctions between various turbans—the visual evidence of their differences— can be rendered meaningless in advance: "For when the visual is fully schematized by racism, the 'visual evidence' to which one refers will always and only refute the conclusions based upon it; for it is possible within this racist episteme that no black person can seek recourse to the visible as the sure ground of evidence." What Butler terms "inverted projections of white paranoia"—in this case, extended to a nationalist paranoia—posits the recipient of the violence, the object of violence, as the subject of violence, the threat of impending violence that was justifiably curtailed.[38] In the way that the visual field situates the black male body as always already the site of violence and a source of danger to whites and model minorities, the turbaned Sikh is always already circumscribed as a dangerous terrorist lookalike or aspirant terrorist. The principal place of the anticipatory future tense secures the necessity of the preemptive strike: the infantilized attacker, in need of protection, locates the about-to-be-attacked body as the site and source of danger, and, convinced of the desire for the turbaned individual to become a terrorist, defends against the imminent conversion through the attack. This narrative coheres the attacker as a patriotic vigilante and obscures the reading of the attacker's violence in favor of locating the attackee's probable, always about to occur violence. Butler claims that this completes the circuit of white paranoia, whereby attackers initiate "the projection of their own aggression, and the subsequent regarding of that projection as an external threat." This can be thought of as "the reversal and displacement of dangerous intention" such that the attackee comes to represent "the origin, the intention, and the object of the selfsame brutality. . . . He is the beginning and the end of violence."[39]

Butler's account, while attentive to the materialization of the violent black body, does not elucidate how the black body, beyond its discursive baggage, comes to be feared as such. There is as well a reliance on the very act of seeing that Butler problematizes; while she is critical of the relationship between seeing and what then counts as visual evidence, she nonetheless centralizes the visible black body whose difference is seen rather than *felt*, whose episteme cannot escape the chain of signs of danger qualified as the beginning, the end, the origin, intention, and object. To augment Butler, I turn to Sara Ahmed's exploration of hate and fear: "Hate does not reside in a given subject or object. Hate is economic; it circulates between signifiers in relationships of difference and displacement." In this challenge to the localization of fear in a body, the materialization of the feared body occurs through a visual racial regime as well as the impossibility of the containment of feared bodies. The anxiety of this impossibility of containment subtends the relegation of fear to a distinct object, producing the falsity of a feared object. Further, it is precisely the nonresidence of emotions, their circulation between bodies, that binds subjects together, creating pools of suspicious bodies. Riffing on Fanon, as does Butler, Ahmed focuses not on the black body that will assault, but the one that passes by:

> The black man becomes even more threatening if he passes by. . . . The economy of fear works to contain the bodies of others, a containment whose "success" relies on its failure, as it must keep open the very grounds of fear. In this sense, fear works as an affective economy, despite how it seems directed toward an object. . . . It is this lack of residence that allows fear to slide across signs, and between bodies. This sliding becomes stuck only temporarily, in the very attachment of a sign to a body, whereby a sign sticks to a body by constituting it as the object of fear, a constitution taken on by the body, encircling it with a fear that becomes its own.

This is a different claim to an anticipatory, preemptive temporality: the real danger, as it were, is not that he will attack, but that he will pass by, the imminent attack unknown in terms of when, where, how, or if. Passing, or passing by, raises the possibility that the difference is imperceptible: the injury is endlessly deferred to the future. The object that once appeared to contain the fear, and was thus containable, instead contaminates and multiplies into many bodies through a sliding that works metonymically to ooze and seep these bodies into one another, "construct[ing] a relation of resemblance between the figures: what makes them alike may be their 'unlikeness' from 'us.'" Stickiness implies that the temporary reprieve granted through passing by is muted by residual remnants and echoes of older bodies that rub off, leaving traces of nearly getting off clean: "The word *terrorist* sticks to some bodies as it reopens past histories of naming, just as it slides into other words."[40] Both Butler and Ahmed ground their analyses in signification: for Butler the visible black body is a priori signified as threatening, while for Ahmed emotions circulate between bodies and thus signs stick, however momentarily. Unmoored emotion such as fear slides amid bodies, getting stuck on them: Is it the fear that is sticky, or the bodies that are already somehow signified as sticky, or both? But there are two distinct temporalities of anticipation and preemption at work here. Butler foregrounds the dangerous subject in need of rehabilitation, a temporality of preemption where the black body, already known as scary, must be beaten before he is able to beat first. The subject is created, known, and confirmed as the body is beaten. In Ahmed's frame, some subjects are known, but others are anticipated: the circuit of passing by–sliding-sticking entails that sliding emotions must invariably stick to bodies, giving other bodies their (new or accentuated) sign. Subjects can be anticipated but never known for certain; the contagious body that passes by (if we are even sure of the danger of this body) infects other bodies. The preemptive force is not focused on one body, in this case the black man or the turbaned terrorist; rather, stickiness can draw into question almost anyone in this affective economy of fear: pools of bodies, populations. The difference between Butler and Ahmed can be qualified as the difference between a defensive position (I am ready to attack to preempt your attack) and a defended position (I am preempting altogether the *conditions of possibility* for your attack, much less the attack). In other words, the defended position or posturing attempts to preempt the necessity of a defensive position. What is being preempted is not the danger of the known subject but the danger of not-knowing.

Ahmed's move from residence to circulation can lead to a fruitful understanding of the forces of population construction, their control necessitated

FIGURE 19. Vinanti Sarkar, cover image for the film *Mistaken Identity: Sikhs in America*, 2003. Reprinted with the artist's permission.

not by knowing who they are but by the impossibility of fully knowing, as this circulation "work[s] to differentiate some others from other others, a differentiation that is never 'over' as it awaits for others who have not yet arrived." Sliding works to create likenesses—relations of feared objects to each other—among differences that, despite such variance, appear to be distinctly different from the "us" at stake. The fact that fear does not reside in a body, but could be materialized in any body within a particular profile range, allows for the figure of the terrorist to retain its potent historical significatory ambiguity while it also enables the fear to "stick" to bodies that "could be" terrorists.[41] Ahmed's focus on *resemblance* allows emotions to slide to and between bodies, impelling stickiness of signs and creating the relations of resemblance of feared objects to each other. Thus, the affective economy of fear that Ahmed lays out is a democratization of sorts: it does not rely solely on internal and external positionings (black man, white cop); instead, it modulates differentials of fear of populations that are caught within, rounded up, sutured as well as defected from these resemblances. The scenario is never finalized.

In the context of mistaken identity, passing functions doubly as a modality where the distinctions between turbans may be incomprehensible—the Sikh passes for terrorist or the terrorist passes for Sikh—and where the Sikh must pass for American, and in that sense, may pass by, as it were. The proof offered in any performative of loyalty is betrayed by the demand to articulate oneself as American, this demand acting precisely as the evidence that the subject is neither constituted nor understood as American. The turban is thus a "sticky" signifier, operating as a fetish object of fear, and the ontological becoming of the turbaned Sikh is intricately tied into the temporal logic of preempting his futurity, a deferred death, a becoming that is sutured through its failure, its decay. It is fear, then, as it materializes the turban, rather than the turban itself, that creates the chasm between subject and objects and mediates the conviviality among objects; these boundaries do not exist and then produce fear, but rather fear produces these boundaries. As Ahmed has argued, "The other is only read as fearsome *through* a mis-recognition" (emphasis mine), not despite it.[42] Visibility is an inadequate rubric because of an old liberal predicament—visibility invites surveillance—but also because regimes of affect and tactility conduct vital information beyond the visual. The move from visibility to affect takes us from a frame of misrecognition, contingent upon the visual to discern the mistake (I thought you were one of them), to the notion of resemblance, a broader affective frame where the reason for the alikeness may be vague or repressed (You remind me of one of them): from "looks like" to "seems like." As distinct from the "looks like," relegated to the optical restrictions of visibility, the "seems like" is mired in loaded tactile economies, an affective space that pushes the "seems like" toward "feels like" and even, to explain the conviction of radical difference, "feels like nothing I could ever feel like" or "nothing I have ever felt before." The "mistaken for" itself is not a mistake, insofar as it is the very point. The claim to have made a mistake functions as an alibi, a foil, for the prominence of resemblance, indicating either that the Sikh is a fine replacement (one other is as good as another other) or a substitution (the Other is undifferentiated and needs to remain so); both reflect the circulatory economy of fear proffered by Ahmed: feared bodies are contagious.

The widespread campaigns undertaken by liberal Sikh advocacy groups to educate "ignorant Americans" about Sikhs, focusing both on who Sikhs are (not terrorists but peace-loving good Americans, model minority immigrants, our turbans look like *this*) and who they are not (Muslims, terrorists, our turbans do not look like *that*), while important, do not address the

I am not a terrorist. I am an American.
I am not a "Towelhead." I am a Sikh.
My turban and beard symbolize my religion.

Is every white man a member of the KKK?
Is every man with a turban a terrorist?

STOP THE HATE.

FIGURE 20.
Flier created by Harneet Pasricha, 2001.
Reprinted with the artist's permission.

affective economies that conflate resemblance into misrecognition.[43] Flooding the media and Internet with "positive images" of Sikhs uses a representational fix for an ontological dilemma, where what one "knows" about "the turban" is still trapped in an epistemological ocular economy, and where one assumes the differences within and among difference actually matter.[44]

In Ahmed's usage, "affect," however usefully deployed, remains within the realm of signification. Signification, narrative, and epistemological coherence—known or unknown—is what subtends and mediates the stickiness, or slipperiness, of objects. For Ahmed and Butler, fear is still produced predominantly, if not exclusively, by signs. As Butler's incisive commentary on the Rodney King trial lays bare, the visual is saturated by a racial schema that is built upon layers of racial knowings and displaced unknowings of the fearsome and violent black male body. But there is little sense of how the black male body comes to be feared as such. Similarly, in Ahmed's schema, we might query: How do bodies become sticky in the first place? "History" is Ahmed's answer. Must bodies already be signified as something sticky in order to become even stickier? Is stickiness only a product of signification, of epistemic formation rather than ontological properties? The assumption that drives Ahmed's analysis of affect is a form of narrativized discursive knowing that ironically functions as a prediscursive necessity for "stickiness" to have any force at all. (That is, the body is already known discursively as a body to fear; its signification is a prediscursive necessity for an argument that claims that the attachment of signs to bodies is the primary way they come to be feared.) How did stickiness come to be? It is not quite clear. We learn only how it feels to feel fear, never how it feels to be feared. (Butler and Ahmed rely on acts of reading to contest epistemological truths; that is, the logic of visibility is challenged through the logic of visibility by pointing out the instability of visual evidence, rather than moving aside the visual, however momentarily, as the primary epistemological terrain of racial knowledge. Similarly, the logic of signification is contested through pointing out the instability of signs.)

Brian Massumi, whose work in *Parables for the Virtual* is critical fodder for my project, insists upon ties to affective processes that mediate cognitive and epistemic knowing. The body's "visceral sensibility" precedes sense perception: "It anticipates the translation of the sight or sound or touch perception into something recognizable associated with an identifiable object." So the lungs spasm even before the senses cognate the presence of a shadow in a "dark street at night in a dangerous part of town." The "dangerous part of town" and the shadow are then the identifiable objects for which epistemic force is confirmed only after, or, more accurately, as affective response has taken place.[45] What we have, then, between Butler, Ahmed, and Massumi, are differentials of bodily participation: Butler reading meaning on the epidermis of the black body; Ahmed locating chains of signs between bodies, in this case those already prone to stickiness around the figure of the terrorist; and Massumi foregrounding the body that knows before it cognates, an antedating body, distinct from the preemption of anticipatory temporality. However, despite his attentiveness to the matter of bodies, for Massumi, in his perhaps unintentional reproduction of the generic body of science, race seems also to be relegated to the cultural, the discursive. Foregrounding "phenotypical encounters in public spaces," Arun Saldanha offers a different notion of stickiness from Ahmed's through the "figure of *viscosity*":

> Neither perfectly fluid nor solid, the viscous invokes surface tension and resistance to perturbation and mixing. Viscosity means that the physical characteristics of a substance explain its unique movements. There are local and temporary thickenings of interacting bodies, which then collectively become sticky, capable of capturing more bodies like them. . . . Under certain circumstances, the collectivity dissolves, the constituent bodies flowing freely again. The world is an immense mass of viscosities, becoming thicker here, and thinner there.[46]

Unlike Butler's rendition of phenotype, which exists within discursive signification, and Ahmed's stickiness, which also only has force through signs,

FIGURE 21. Vishavjit Singh, *The Scream*, 2006. Originally published at www.SikhToons.com. Reprinted with the artist's permission.

Saldanha is interested in the matter of phenotype and how phenotype matters.[47] Saldanha argues that "bodies gradually [become] sticky and [cluster] into aggregates" because of how "certain bodies *stick* to certain spaces, how they are chained by hunger, cold, darkness, mud, poverty, crimes, glances full of envy and anxiety." If one agrees that "race is devious in inventing new ways of chaining bodies," this chaining or linking occurs not only through the force of historically blighted signifiers that metonymically link and bleed into each other, as Ahmed suggests. They also occur through the encounter of smell, sweat, flushes of heat, dilation of pupils, the impulses bodies pick up from each other, the contagions of which we know little, the sense of being touched without having been physically touched, of having seen without having physically seen, "what immanent connections [bodies] forge with things and places, how they work, travel, fight, write, love . . . become viscous, slow down, get into certain habits, into certain collectivities, like city, social stratum, or racial formation."[48] Saldanha privileges the encounter of phenotypical difference itself: not only bound to visual representation or historical signification of phenotypical difference, but phenotype experienced outside of or beyond the visual, through the haptic where the visual induces the sensation of touch. Presumably, the experience of phenotypical difference is where the representational weight (of blackness, for instance) might actually rupture and defuse rather than endlessly reify.

Turban Modernities

It starts my identity and ends my identity. It kills a part of you to take it off.—*Targeting the Turban: Sikh Americans after September 11*, directed by Valerie Kaur Brar

Is it not a strange thing to be so marked by an object which is limited in temporal terms, requires recreating on a daily basis and outside of the body of the wearer is simply three to five meters of cotton cloth, dyed in various shades?—Virinder S. Kalra, "Locating the Sikh *Pagh*"

In the inaugural issue of *Sikh Formations: Religion, Culture, Theory*, the first journal devoted to fostering a critical Sikh cultural studies that diverges from anthropological, sociological, theological, and area studies approaches to Sikhs and Sikhism, a meditation on turbans (known as *paghs* or *paghardis*) is proffered by the British South Asian scholar Virinder Kalra. Arguing that the advent of Sikh modernity is contingent upon the turban being perceived as just another article of clothing, Kalra states that the turban is, after all, merely a piece of cloth. An inability to grasp this simplicity renders Sikhs "in some halfway house between tradition and modernity" because of the policing norm of a "non-turbaned head" as well as the turban's enduring signification and fierce ties to tradition, eternally "deferred from the time of the present," a tradition-modernity binary that is in effect produced as a religious-secular dichotomy. Asking if "the *pagh* can become . . . just an accepted dress of a modern person" through a "rapprochement with the modern, a secular removal," or even become a "fashion accessory" through redemptive consumer markets that now advocate a pliable modernity through the combination of jeans and turbans, such as in Turkey, Kalra avers, "Something more is at stake than just the question of six yards of cloth. The question that is posed is ultimately whether a Sikh modernity is at all possible." Kalra rightly points to British colonial incorporation of turbaned Sikhs (a masculinity narrated against an effeminate Hindu masculinity) into military units, made possible through the oscillation of the turban as "a mark of discipline and obedience" and also as a trace of savagery and wildness, double significations delicately bound up in each other.[49] British colonialism is therefore complicit with the fusing of the turban in the late nineteenth century with an emergent Sikh identity, one that is ironically mocked and vilified in contemporary Britain.[50]

While the terms of this debate are of great importance, I want to turn from this predicament momentarily. Thinking turbans through assemblages allows us to exit this question of temporality that doggedly binds all cultural forms navigating the yesterday of tradition with the futurity of the modern, to instead inspire anew other temporal and spatial possibilities. For one, there is the fact of the daily ritual as it is repeated morning after morning, of selecting, tying, binding, pinning, folding, winding what might seem to be endless (certainly copious) amounts of cloth, altering on a rhythmic basis the color and form and the context in which it is wrapped. The daily temporal frame therefore is actually operating differently in its relation to limits. The repetition is key; it enables not only the repetition of the familiar and time-worn but also the becoming of something open to the future, the repetition with a difference. Each turban is unique; repetition is never the same. Each turban is tenuously held together, as the rigidity of coarse fabric fades through the day. Repetition is also open to huge variation over lifetimes as turbans are adopted, discarded, worn one day but not the next, used for special occasions, and used with unshorn as well as shorn hair. Thus the temporal life of turbans should not be defined primarily by longevity but rather by repetition, pacing, fluctuation, and lines of flight that always hold open the chance of a disruption of the exact terms of mimesis.

Reading turbans as appendages and prostheses postulates the turban as an extension of the body, usually considered a phallic extension or an extension of the phallus, or the body as an extension of the turban, taking for granted the body as whole, that it corresponds exactly with the body-as-organism. This notion of this discrete organic body persists even in Massumi's thinking. He presumes the discreteness of an organic body in relation to a "thing":

> What is a perceiving body apart from the sum of its perceivings, actual and possible? What is a perceived thing apart from the sum of its being-perceiveds, actual and potential? Separately, each is no action, no analysis, no anticipation, no thing, no body. The thing *is* its being-perceiveds. A body *is* its perceivings. "Body" and "thing" and, by extension, "body" and "object" exist only as implicated in each other. . . . Body and thing are extensions of each other. They are mutual implications: co-thoughts of two-headed perception. That two-headed perception is the world.

Extensions. The thing, the object, can be considered *prostheses* of the body—provided that it is remembered that the body is equally a prosthesis of the thing.[51]

While there is a mutual relation here between body and thing, that mutual relation is contingent upon the clear and finite separation of the two entities. Further, the thing is assumed to be nonorganic, without any force of its own, and only a thing of relevance insofar as it is a sum of its total being-perceived: how the body perceives the thing is the thing itself. The body is apparently not a thing at all. The body perceives and the thing is perceived; the possibility of an inversion is not entertained. But what if the thing perceives? Or if the body and thing perceive together, one-headed rather than two-headed perception? Or more pointedly, what if the enactment of this relation of perceiving to being-perceived then changes altogether this separation of perception? That is, what if perceiving and being perceived can no longer be separate processes, nor processes that act as extensions of each other? This would be one difference (among many) between appendage and assemblage: thinking of the turbaned man as a man with an appendage and thinking of the turbaned man as an assemblage that cuts through such easy delineations between body and thing, an assemblage that fuses, but also scrambles into chaotic combinations, turban into body, cloth into hair, skin, oil, pores, destabilizing the presumed organicity of the body. On assemblages, Deleuze and Guattari write:

> On a first, horizontal, axis, an assemblage comprises two segments, one of content, the other of expression. On the one hand it is a *machinic assemblage* of bodies, of actions and passions, an intermingling of bodies reacting to one another; on the other hand it is a *collective assemblage of enunciation*, of acts and statements, of incorporeal transformations attributed to bodies. Then on a vertical axis, the assemblage has both *territorial sides*, or reterritorialized sides, which stabilize it, and *cutting edges of deterritorialization*, which carry it away.[52]

Even if the turban is indeed witnessed as an appendage that is the total of its being-perceiveds, it is often represented by the wearer as part of his or her body, not as an appendage or thing that has properties and qualities separate from the body. The horizontal axis of "actions and passions" *between* bodies reveals the "phenotypical encounters" that Saldanha writes of, but also implodes bodies from *within*, shooting through and past bodily boundaries. Accomplice to this is the representation of the turban as "part of the body."

The turban is thus always in the state of becoming, the becoming of a turbaned body, the turban becoming part of the body. In all its multiple singularities it has become a perverse fetish object—a point of fixation (one that is most certainly reproduced in this text)—a kind of centripetal force, a strange attractor through which the density of anxiety accrues and accumulates. For the wearer, the rituals and sensations attached to these parts of the body—the smells during the weekly starching of the linens, the stretching of yards of coarse fabric to induce softening, the wrapping and pinning of the turban into place—are experiences in the midst of becoming qualitatively different from before. Reworking Michael Taussig's notion of "tactile knowing,"[53] May Joseph eloquently asserts, "For cultures whose forms of social knowledge have been fragmented and mutated by multiple experiences of conquest and cultural contact . . . tactile practices are difficult to read and contain multiple meanings. Such exchanges are frequently informal events intrinsic to everyday life through which cultural knowledge gets cited, transmitted or re-appropriated. The senses acquire texture." As that which "immerses the senses beyond the structuring logic of vision and dislodges memory as the fascia of history," tactile knowledges install normativizing traces of danger, fear, and melancholia into the bodies of racialized terrorist look-alikes.[54] (Deleuze and Guattari warn against use of the term "tactile," stating that it forces a divide between seeing and touching, preferring instead the term "haptic" as one that "invites the assumption that the eye itself may fulfill this nonoptical function [of touching]."[55] However, I believe Joseph is using the term congruently.) Tactile economies reassert ontological rather than epistemological knowing, and highlight touch, texture, sensation, smell, feeling, and affect over what is assumed to be legible through the visible. Even within the study of the "human sensorium," as Rey Chow points out, seeing and hearing have been the privileged rubrics of analysis, "dictating the representational issues being discussed."[56] (Thus any perceived dichotomy between affect and representation is manufactured, obscuring the question of *which* sensorial functions are centralized in representational practices and analyses.)

In the case of turbaned Sikh men, the notion of racist backlash also invokes the temporal confinement of "the return of the repressed," a scapegoating mechanism insinuating that previously submerged, and thus disciplined and conquered, racial hatred reemerges during state and capitalist resource crises. Recall, however, that for Foucault, racism is not linked to scarcity theory, nor is it an ideological project driven by notions of difference or contempt between races, a displacement of hostility, or the produc-

*Racism is
about the destruction
of the enemy race*

tion of the Other in order to consolidate the Self, but rather about the
destruction of "the enemy race." Racism is thus endemic to the production
of populations and the shifting and fuzzy demarcations between biopolitics
and necropolitics, as well as multifarious ambiguous spaces we could call
spaces of the deferral or deflection of death. As Foucault writes in *"Society
Must be Defended,"* "What in fact is racism? It is primarily a way of introduc-
ing a break into the domain of life that is under power's control: the break
between what must live and what must die." The separating out of groups
into populations or those that exist within populations is, Foucault writes,
"the first function of racism: to fragment, to create caesuras within the
biological continuum."[57] Instead of body and event, a body that has suffered
a traumatic event, we have Massumi's "body-as-event" and the trauma of
the hate crime rescripted as "intensification": "The best word for a complicating immediacy of self relation is intensity."[58] Following Joseph again,
memory (of trauma) is dislodged as the primary arbiter of remembering
(and forgetting). This is a reading that can potentially be mobilized politically to address victim narratives of racism toward turbaned men that
discount Sikh women's experiences of racism. The three domains of "intensification" relevant for Sikhs—partition, Operation Bluestar and the pogroms following Indira Gandhi's assassination in 1984, and the terrorist
acts of 2001—actually articulate bias attacks not as singular traumatic
events or phenomena, but as an ongoing, nonlinear process of collecting
and discharging intensities.[59]

Furthermore, turban wearers, usually male, bear the burden of safeguard-
ing and transmitting culture and of symbolizing the purity of nation typically ascribed to women. But this does not automatically or only feminize
turbaned men. And here we are pressed to rethink race, sexuality, and gender
as concatenations, unstable assemblages of revolving and devolving energies, rather than intersectional coordinates. The fusion of hair, oil, dirt,
sweat, cloth, skin, the organic melding into the nonorganic, renders a turban, not as part of a queer body nor as a queer part of the body, but as an
otherwise foreign object acculturated into a body's intimacies between
organic and nonorganic matter, blurring the distinction between them,
blurring insides and outsides, speaking to the fields of force—nonorganic
entities having force—in relation to and melded into the organic, the body
and turban folding in on themselves, quite literally, as folds press against
other folds, folds of cloth and skin. On the body folding in on itself, Massumi
writes, "A knitting of the brows or pursing of the lips is a self-referential
action. Its sensation is a turning in on itself of the body's activity, so that the

action is not extended toward an object but knots at its point of emergence: rises and subsides into its own incipiency, in the same movement."[60]

It is this assemblage of visuality, affect, feminized position, and bodily disruption of organic-nonorganic divides, the not-fully-organic not-fully-nonorganic body, which accounts for the queer figuration of the turban in the calculation of a hate crime. And this line of analysis does not even approach theological considerations of turbans, their significance, and affective realms of the divine, the spiritual, the ethereal that inhabit turbans and that turbans inhabit. Additionally, according to religious tenets, practicing and baptized Sikhs do not cut, shave, or pluck the hair on any part of their body, and body modification (piercings, tattoos) is prohibited. The turban thus theologically signifies not a modification to an otherwise pure, intact body, but is rather part of a body that is left unmodified.

The curious undermining of the distinction between organic and nonorganic entities that I am interested in affirming in turbaned bodies resonates with other bodies of our war times: the (female) suicide bomber, the burqa'ed figure (female? male passing for female?), the monstrous terrorist-fag, the activist crushed by a bulldozer in Palestine, the Iraqi civilians brutally tortured by American soldiers in Abu Ghraib, the oddly charismatic (sexy, even?) Osama bin Laden. The becomings of these bodies, many blurring the distinctions between machinic and organic, have disruptive and eruptive capacities.

Trapped by precisely these poles—tradition versus modernity—this placement enables a disavowal of turbaned sexualities by queer diasporic subjects seeking to approximate cosmopolitan status, as well as queer diasporic subjects seeking to embrace the illegitimate and perverse sexualities ascribed to terrorist bodies (again, the turban is almost *too* perverse). Further, it continues the preoccupation of Sikh communities with positive representation, even if in the United States the turbaned Sikh can perform, especially in middle-class communities, allegiance to modern American citizenship through religious faith and conviction, resembling a commitment to Christian fundamentalism, rather than predominantly a secular identity that views the turban as simply a form of dress. The overdetermined reliance on narratives of visibility by all of these discourses—queer, Sikh respectability, and the state regulation of visible difference—both privileges an epistemological knowing over an ontological becoming and foregrounds a process of panoptic racial profiling, disregarding other contemporary uses of profiling.

Racial and Informational Profiles

In a 2006 *New Yorker* article that contrasts the profiling of pit bulls as dangerous, vicious, and constitutionally violent dogs to the profiling of terrorists, drug smugglers, and other mobile, detectable criminals, Malcolm Gladwell describes the New York City Police Department policy against racial profiling as it was instituted by Raymond Kelly, New York City's police commissioner. A list of forty-two suspicious traits was replaced with a list of six "broad criteria": "Is there something suspicious about their physical appearance? Are they nervous? Is there specific intelligence targeting this person? Does the drug-sniffing dog raise an alarm? Is there something amiss in their paperwork or explanations? Has contraband been found that implicates this person?"[61]

This is a shift from "unstable generalizations" (race, ethnicity, gender, as well as what people do: arrived late at night, arrived early, arrived in the afternoon; first to deplane, last to deplane, deplaned in the middle) to "stable generalizations": how people seem. A patrolling of affect changes the terms of "what kind of person" would be a terrorist or smuggler, recognizing that the terrorist (terrorist is brown versus terrorist is unrecognizable) could look like anyone and *do* just like everyone else, but might *seem* something else. ("After Kelly's reforms, the number of searches conducted by the Customs Service dropped by about seventy-five percent, but the number of actual seizures improved by twenty-five percent.")[62] But in this revised frame, the ocular, affective, and informational are not separate power grids or spheres of control; rather, they work in concert—not synthetically, but as interfacing matrices.

On contemporary profiling practices and their historical antecedents, Horace Campbell writes, "The racial profiling and targeting of suspected terrorists in the United States brings the ideas and organization of yesterday's racial oppression in line with new technologies and the contemporary eugenics movement." Thus profiling is the extended modern, biotech version of eugenics (fugitive slave laws, sterilization laws and practices, Tuskegee experiments), while it also is extended by biotechnology, genetic engineering (cloning, stem cell research), viruses such as AIDS and ebola (if not engineered in the lab as biological warfare experiments, the political responses to the AIDS pandemic certainly suggest killing via neglect).[63] The profile, as a type of composite, also works, as Deleuze maintains, as a mechanism of information collection and analysis that tabulates marketing information, demographics, consumer habits, computer usage (cookies), public policy data, airplane passenger alerts, and public intellectual and political activist blacklists.[64]

And now to return to the turbaned body. So if the turban is not a hat, in the way skullcaps and hijabs are deemed to be religious headcovers, what is it? "This ain't no rag, it's a flag," begins a song by the country musician Charlie Daniels, written in October 2001. "And we don't wear it on our heads."[65] As discussed in the opening of this chapter, Sikh advocacy groups received complaints that turbaned men were being asked to remove and unravel their turbans at airport security checkpoints to check for weapons; alternatives recommended by Sikh advocacy groups included using x-ray technology (sensor wand, x-ray machine) to scan the turbans. This scenario—how to monitor the turban and the body to which it is attached—reflects the joint operations of ocular, affective, and informational profiling. The turbaned body is not only available for disciplining, not only meant to enable internalization of the sense of being watched. On the effects of this internalization, Butler remarks, "It's a kind of patrolling the phantasmatic Arab, on the streets and in the cities of the U.S. It strikes me as a way of defining who is American, the ones who are on alert, watching, and the ones who are not, the ones who are watched, monitored."[66] But this again is a singular model of discipline: there are fixed locations, positions, distinctions between those who are watched and those who are not, those who watch. Of a biopolitical model of control, Deleuze writes, "Control is short-term and rapidly shifting, but at the same time continuous and unbounded, whereas discipline was long-term, infinite, and discontinuous."[67] Insofar as racial profiling of the panopticon works to discipline the patriot, the informational profile works to accuse in advance of subject formation. The panopticon serves to isolate, centralize, and detain; the profile disperses control through circuits catching multiple interpenetrating sites of anxiety. As strategies of surveillance, the panopticon and the profile work simultaneously to produce the terrorist and the patriot in one body, the turbaned body. The panoptic and the profile work together, not synthetically (that is, I am not arguing here for a notion of synthesis of these differing technologies), but through interlocking layers of vulnerability that are produced and distributed in their wake.

The intimacy of the turban unwrapping and the intimacy of surveillance technology that x-rays the turban are bifurcated thus: the first produces the violated subject of regulation, the penetration of the sacred private, similar to the queer liberal subject of *Lawrence-Garner*, that hinges on a liberal fantasy of bodily integrity, a projection of wholeness. We can say that part

FIGURE 22. Vicky Singh, *Are You?*, 2003.
Originally published at www.SikhToons.com.
Reprinted with permission from Vishavjit Singh.

of the panoptic policing embedded in this submissive ritual of sorts is indebted to regimes of regulatory heteronormativity *as well as* regulatory homonormativity and even regulatory queerness; the turbaned body appears not amenable to any of these frames, yet rehabilitation is nevertheless attempted. The second, the turban departing on the conveyor belt, toppled, slightly askew as it maneuvers entry into the x-ray apparatus, or the sensor wand that scans the fabric and folds, is part and parcel of affective population control that rewrites bodies and their intimacies as it surveils them, the perception of intrusion diffuse rather than penetrative or focalized, multiple rather than singular. In either scenario, there remains the moment-to-moment shifting assemblages of turbaned, de-turbaned, and re-turbaned bodies. We have multiple bodies here: the "body of excess" that is constitutive of any reading that foregrounds the racial and sexual excesses of the visual, representational body (here, the gender of the turbaned body is given substance); the affective body (shifting from turbaned man or turbaned woman to turbaned assemblage), whose transformations and transformative potentiality lies in its *contagions*, its energetic transmissions, that is, its affective capacity to affect;[68] the data or informational body cohered through digitalized bits. The body is both *seen* and *seen through*. The visual is expanded through a certain kind of transparency, not only by looking at the body, but by looking through it. The x-raying of the turban is a surveillance event that does not dismantle or disaggregate the coherent body bit by bit; rather, it is a rematerialization of the body, a splaying of the body across multiple registers that adumbrates the terms of intimacy, intensity, and interiority. Joining biometric procedures that capture the iris of the eye, the geometry of the hand, the gait of the walk, these digitizing informational and surveillance technologies of control both produce a data body or the body-as-information and also impact and transform the contours of the organic body through an interface of organic and nonorganic machinic technologies that tempt the mutual dissolution of their boundaries.

In this economy of sight, to be able to "see" the terrorist is not contingent upon the surveying of the entire body; rather, the securitization that aims to make something visible to ensure its capture relies on an assemblage of subindividual capacities. These technologies of "attention that suspend certain assumptions in order to make others," Massumi states, "perturb to make perceptible."[69] Race and sex are reread not only through the regulatory (i.e., resistant) queer subject, but through the regularizing of this rematerialization of the body. Pivotal here is the notion of capacity, in other words the ability to thrive within and propagate the biopolitics of life by projecting potential as futurity, one indication of which is performed through the very submission to these technologies of surveillance that generate these data. Following Rey Chow's statement that biopolitics is implicitly about the ascendancy of whiteness, the terms of whiteness cannot remain solely in the realm of racial identification or phenotype but extend out to the capacity for capacity: that is, the capacity to give life, sustain life, promote life—the registers of fertility, health, environmental sustainability, and the capacity to risk. Race and sex are thus not disposed of as analytic categories, but supplemented by their redefinition as the capacity to regenerate, identity categories working with the kinds of statistical racisms that sees some populations as worthy of life and others as decaying, as destined for death. Optimizing the body entails oscillation between the subject of rehabilitation, an already cohered subject that can and must be represented, and populations of regeneration, forward-looking, regenerative bodies that appear to have the capacity for capacity.

Thus it is not necessary to eliminate the turbaned man (as is implied in the French ban on head coverings) nor to sequester him—quite the contrary. Turbans function in multiple power sites of perpetual monitoring linked together to stimulate a continuous circuitry and regime of control, interconnected pathways of surveillance and discipline. The turban exists not as a closed site of differentiation, but among proliferating vectors of capture: at airport security, while driving or in a vehicle, in a detention cell, in a driver's license photo that disallows "hats," in a police force that bans the wearing of turbans because of the official uniform hat, in a terrorist videogame, through rapidly disseminated and repetitive Internet and media imagery. The mistake itself (making the mistake) of mistaken identity must be available in multiple tactile economies, whether through the cut and paste of Photoshop, the simulacra of videogames,[70] the imprint of the

FIGURE 23. Billboard of the World Sikh Syndicate near exit 15 of I-78 E in Pennsylvania. Photograph by Lucas Gravely, 2006. Reprinted with the artist's permission.

replayed image of Sher Singh—not solely in terms of a representational space (positive versus negative images) but also in terms of speed, pace, repetition, and informational flows. What is at stake here is the repetition and relay of the ubiquitous images, not their symbolic or representational meaning.

Invariably this analysis participates in the very fixating on or fetishizing of turbaned bodies that it seeks to disrupt, and again this is an enterprise pivotal to the coagulation of Sikh diasporas. I would also argue, however, that my reading suggests the applicability of this analysis to all sorts of other bodies to destabilize the taken-for-granted assumption that the discursive body, however socially constructed it may be, is always already presumed to be a wholly discrete, intact, and fully-abled organic body. It would be a mistake, and the most damning interpretation of this work, to transpose this reading onto the most obvious bodies that lend themselves to a discourse of cultural alterity (burqa'ed or veiled bodies, disabled or dismembered bodies, diseased bodies). While the frame I proffer may still privilege bodies that are engaged with technology, assemblages that are in some sense machined together, all bodies are to some extent machined; in this case the turban is not remarkable at all. We return, albeit obliquely, to the nexus of Sikh modernity that Kalra proposes, one that calls for a neutralizing of the difference of turbans, ironically through the commodification of their purported alterity. But instead of being tagged as sporting just another fashion accessory, turbaned bodies join all other bodies in destabilizing the boundaries between organic and nonorganic entities and forces. For LGBTIQ communities, it is this type of reading that can enable a rethinking of violence against queers and attendant strategies to combat hate crimes. It also encourages Sikh masculinities that transcend or refute a victim status, but without recourse to a muscular nationalism. Ultimately, queer and gurdwara organizing may open up creative political conjunctures that are not bound through identity politics but gel instead, in a manner however transitory and contingent, through the politics of affect.

For having lost its power to interpellate subjects as raced subjects, the raced image can no longer broker processes of identity formation and struggles for social recognition, and in effect, remains in force solely as an instrument of social techniques for identification and exclusion. The result is a profound paradox of our contemporary moment: the very subjects targeted by these racist techniques can only misrecognize themselves in the images that—precisely for this reason—manage all the more effectively to exert their violence upon them.—Mark Hansen, "Digitizing the Racialized Body, or, The Politics of Universal Address"

The more resistive (that is, on the outside) X is imagined to be, the more unavoidably it is to lose its specificity (that is, become appropriated) in the larger framework of the systematic production of differences, while the circumstances that make this framework possible (that is, that enable it to unfold and progress as a permanently self-regulating interiority) remain unchallenged. This is, I believe, one reason why so many new projects of articulating alternative identities, cultures, and group formations often seem so similar in the end. Whether what is in question is a particular ethnic work or the identity of an ethnic person, what has become predictable—literally, already spoken—is precisely the compulsive invocation of difference with interchangeable terms such as "ambivalence," "multiplicity," "hybridity," "heterogeneity," "disruptiveness," "resistance," and the like; and no matter how new an object of study may appear to be, it is bound to lose its novelty once the process of temporal differencing is set into motion.—Rey Chow, *The Age of the World Target*

conclusion:

queer times, terrorist assemblages

These are queer times indeed, temporal assemblages hooked into an array of enduring modernist paradigms (civilizing teleologies, Orientalisms, xenophobia, militarization, border anxieties) and postmodernist eruptions (suicide bombers, biometric surveillance strategies, emergent corporealities, counterterrorism in overdrive). With its emphases on bodies, desires, pleasures, tactility, rhythms, echoes, textures, deaths, morbidity, torture, pain, sensation, and punishment, our necropolitical present-future deems it imperative to rearticulate what queer theory and studies of sexuality have to say about the metatheories and the realpolitik of empire, often understood, as Joan Scott observes, as "the real business of politics."[1] Queer times require even queerer modalities of thought, analysis, creativity, and expression in order to elaborate upon nationalist, patriotic, and terrorist formations and their imbricated forms of racialized perverse sexualities and gender dysphorias.

Throughout this book I allude to queer praxes of futurity that insistently disentangle the relations between representation and affect, and propose queerness as not an identity nor an anti-identity, but an assemblage that is spatially and temporally contingent. The limitations of intersectional identitarian models emerge progressively—however queer they may be—as I work through the concepts of affect, tactility, and ontology. While dismantling the representational mandates of visibility identity politics that feed narratives of sexual exceptionalism, affective analyses can approach queernesses that are unknown or not cogently knowable, that are in the midst of becoming, that do not immediately and visibly signal themselves as insurgent, oppositional, or transcendent. This shift forces us to ask not only what terrorist corporealities mean or signify, but more insistently, what do they do? In this conclusion, I review these tensions between affect and representation, identity and assemblage, posing the problematics of nationalist and terrorist formations as central challenges to transnational queer cultural and feminist studies.

I propose the assemblage as a pertinent political and theoretical frame within societies of control. I rearticulate terrorist bodies, in particular the suicide bomber, as an assemblage that resists queerness-as-sexual-identity (or anti-identity)—in other words, intersectional and identitarian paradigms—in favor of spatial, temporal, and corporeal convergences, implosions, and rearrangements. Queerness as an assemblage moves away from excavation work, deprivileges a binary opposition between queer and not-queer subjects, and, instead of retaining queerness exclusively as dissenting, resistant, and alternative (all of which queerness importantly is and does), it underscores contingency and complicity with dominant formations. This foregrounding of assemblage enables attention to ontology in tandem with epistemology, affect in conjunction with representational economies, within which bodies interpenetrate, swirl together, and transmit affects and effects to each other.

It also aids in circumventing the fatigued "temporal differencing" of resistant identity paradigms of the Other that Chow problematizes. Invariably, Chow argues, poststructuralist self-referentiality produces alternating temporalities of "non-coincidence." Mystification exoticizes the Other through a referential inward-turning "temporality as self-deconstruction" that refuses continuity between self and other, producing difference as a complete disjuncture that cannot exist within the same temporal planes as the Self. Concomitantly, futurization occurs where "temporality as allochronism" produces the Other as the "perpetual promise" that is realizable, but only with a lag time, not in the present.[2] Both Hansen and Chow hint at the ends of identity. Chow suggests that attending to the specificity of others has ironically become a universalizing project, whereas Hansen implies that othering itself is no longer driven by the Hegelian self-other process of interpellation. While the language of "misrecognition" problematically harks to an older Marxian model of false consciousness, Hansen avers that taking up the position of the Other only capitulates to state and capitalist modes of domination and surveillance.

Affect, Race, and Sex

Representational analyses, identity politics, and the focus on rights-bearing subjects are currently being complemented with thinking on affect and on population formation that recognizes those who are living not only through their relation to subjecthood, but are coming under control as part of one or many populations, not individuals, but "dividuals."[3] Norma Alarcón intimated as much in her brilliant 1990 essay "The Theoretical Subject(s) of *This Bridge Called My Back* and Anglo-American Feminism." In this essay she asks, "Do we have to make a subject of the whole world?" suggesting that the modern subject is exhausted, or rather that we have exhausted the modern subject.[4] We have multiplied it to accommodate all sorts of differences (i.e., a politics of inclusion), intersected it with every variable of identity imaginable, split it to account for the unknown realms of the subconscious, infused it with greater individual rights (the rights-bearing subject). Foucault's own provocations include the claim that sexuality is *an intersection*, rather than an interpellative identity, of the body and the population. We can read both of these pronouncements as attempts to highlight what Rey Chow calls "categorical miscegenation": that race and sex are for the most part not only indistinguishable and undifferentiable from each other, but are a series of temporal and spatial contingencies that retain a stubborn aversion to being read.[5] While Foucault's formation hails the feminist heuristic of "intersectionality," unlike intersectional theorizing which foregrounds separate analytics of identity that perform the holistic subjects' inseparableness, the entities that intersect are the body (not the subject, let us remember) and population. My own reliance upon and calls to intersectional approaches notwithstanding, the limitations of feminist and queer (and queer of color) theories of intersectionality are indebted in one sense to the taken-for-granted presence of the subject and its permutations of content and form, rather than an investigation of the predominance of subjecthood itself. Thus, despite the anti-identitarian critique that queer theory launches (i.e., queerness is an approach, not an identity or wedded to identity), the queer subject, a subject that is against identity, transgressive rather than (gay or lesbian) liberatory, nevertheless surfaces as an object in need of excavation, elaboration, or specularization.

The "affective turn" in recent poststructuralist scholarship indicates, I believe, that no matter how intersectional our models of subjectivity, no matter how attuned to locational politics of space, place, and scale, these formulations may still limit us if they presume the automatic primacy and singularity of the disciplinary subject and its identitarian interpellation.[6] Patricia Clough has recently anointed this resurgence of interest in affect in poststructuralist inquiry the "affective turn," marked by the spheres of technoscience criticism (Massumi, Hardt, Hardt and Negri, Clough, Parisi, De Landa) and queer theory on emotions and tactile knowings (Muñoz, Ahmed, Sedgwick, Cvetkovich).[7] While reflective of the effects of poststructuralist exhaustion with representational analyses—in both Spivakian

[handwritten marginal notes:] Intersubjectivity is limited by its presupposition of subjectivity. The subject—even of the Anti-identitarian subject

senses of portrait (*Darstellung*) and proxy (*Vertreten*)[8]—an interesting split genealogy is emerging in these efforts. There are those writers who deploy affect as a particular reflection of or attachment to "structures of being" or feeling (per Raymond Williams; that is, a state prior to interpellation) that otherwise remains unarticulatable. In many cases affect in these works is situated in a continuum or becomes interchangeable with emotion, feeling, expressive sentiment ("gay shame" is one such overdetermined fixation). The other genealogy we can point to is situated within a Deleuzian frame, whereby affect is a physiological and biological phenomenon, signaling why bodily matter matters, what escapes or remains outside of the discursively structured and thus commodity forms of emotion, of feeling. Brian Massumi, for example, posits affect as what escapes our attention, as what haunts the representational realm rather than merely infusing it with emotive presence. He regards affect in terms of ontological emergence that is released from cognition, codified emotion being the evidence of the escaped excess that is affect. On the autonomy of affect he writes, "Affect is synesthetic, implying a participation of the senses in each other: the measure of a living thing's potential interactions is its ability to transform the effects of one sensory mode into those of another. . . . If there were no escape, no excess or remainder, no fade-out to infinity, the universe would be without potential, pure entropy, death. Actually existing, structured things live in and through that which escapes them. Their autonomy is the autonomy of affect."[9]

This somewhat circuitous debate about the relationship of affect to representation still leaves both trajectories mired in the original problematic: if theorizations of affect are currently being employed to supplement or counter representational analyses, then whether affect is "mistakenly" (as the technoscience theorists might claim) hailed in the representational form of emotion or instead in the excess of emotion as it is represented (whereby the project becomes to represent the intrinsic unrepresentability of affect), it is nonetheless caught in the logic it seeks to challenge. The collective project, since all we can really enact is a representational schema of affect, is what we are now developing: an epistemology of ontology and affect.

But the question remains: Why affect at all, why affect now, and, for my purposes here, why affect and queer theory? What is a queer affect? Is this queer work on affect signaling a desire to delineate something that can be named and isolated as queer affect? Or is it the case that there is something queer about affect, that affect is queer unto itself, always already a defiance of identity registers, amenable to queer critique? And is there something specific about our contemporary political moment that makes the turn to affect that much more urgent, more efficacious, more pertinent, that is, both a product of and response to necropolitical, anatomical, sensorial forms of domination and oppression? What do we make of the economic circuits that have already fully invested in affect—risk management, for example—and our collusion with these capitalist endeavors through our production of theories of affect?

One partial answer to these questions is indicated, I would suggest, in what the supposed "mistake" of grounding affect in a symbolic economy symptomatically reveals. For despite what these crudely mapped genealogies might have in common—desires to move beyond representational critiques of poststructuralism and an interest in a "post-Foucauldian" critique beyond the disciplinary subject—another major point of divergence entails the import of communities of belonging. Perhaps what these slippages between emotion, feeling, and affect are performing in queer critique are continuing efforts to elaborate different and alternative modalities of belonging, connectivity, and intimacy, a response, in fact, to paradigms that have privileged the deterritorialization of control societies to such an extent that identitarian frames appear no longer relevant in the face of the decentralization of interpellated subjects. In his piece "Feeling Brown," for example, José Esteban Muñoz parses official "national affect" and "ethnic affect," stating, "The affect of Latinos/as is often off. One can even argue that it is off-white." Describing communal affect as the ties that bind utopian community, Muñoz invokes affect as always already within signification, within narrative, functioning as a form of critical resistance to dominant modes of being and becoming.[10]

Another salient tension between Muñoz and Massumi is reflected in the distinction between regarding specific affects and emotion as elements generated by, owned by, and attached to subjects and the communities they represent (racial melancholia, feeling brown or off-white), and the place of biological bodies in relation to affective processes. As Amit Rai has recently argued, foregrounding the body as a creative site of indeterminacy promotes "affective confusion" that allows for new affects, and thus new politics, to emerge.[11] The body in question, Elizabeth Wilson contends, would not necessarily or only be "the social, cultural, experiential or psychic object that touches on the biological realm only lightly, discreetly, hygienically." Arguing against a self-evident or automatic disjunction between the material and the cultural body, Wilson writes, "Despite an avowed interest in the body, there is a persistent distaste for biological detail" because, in fact, "the idea of *biological* construction [has] been rendered either unintelligible or naïve." She continues: "The biological body is coded in these routinized projects as the untheorized body, the mechanical, tangible, artless body"—in other words, a body to be overwritten by an overlay of cultural construction.[12] Understandably, sexuality studies and queer theory, as paradigmatic cultural studies knowledge formations, historically have had ambivalent and vexed relationships to science studies and biological discourses in general.[13] (Emergent work on "queer disability" seeks to revitalize the study of biological matter, emphasizing how bodies move, meet, commingle, and mesh with technology, architecture, and objects.)[14] As Arun Saldanha points out, however, debates about race and racism are stalled through a rather peculiar conundrum: having argued against biological renditions of scientific racism through discourse, culture, and social constructivism, much poststructuralist thought has left waylaid questions of the biological matter of the body—for example, phenotype as it might affectively operate beyond the signification of color. With especial fervor directed at Paul Gilroy's *Against Race*, Saldanha argues for an "ontology of the materiality of race" that is not solely predicated upon epistemological renditions of the materiality of bodies; "there is simply too much at stake to continue brushing aside the biological as 'discursive practice.'" Rejecting a Hegelian self-other dialectic through a rereading of Elizabeth Grosz on "a thousand tiny sexes," he suggests that phenotype be thought as assemblages of "a thousand tiny races": "Every time phenotype makes another machinic connection, there is a stutter. Every time bodies are further entrenched in segregation, however brutal, there needs to be an affective investment of sorts. This is the ruptural moment in which to intervene. Race should not be eliminated, but *proliferated*, its many energies directed at multiplying racial differences so as to render them joyfully cacophonic."[15]

This book is a labor of passion that, in its wholehearted embracing of representational analysis and critique, inveighs against its limitations as the text unfolds, effectively undoing the book as it was written, as it is read. I would argue that the contradictions and discrepancies rife in this endeavor—creative mistakes, perhaps—are not to be reconciled or synthesized but held together in tension. They are less a sign of wavering intellectual commitments than symptoms of the political impossibility to *be on one side or the other*. I do not claim to properly situate what Wilson calls a "phenomenology-scientism conjunction," but I do posit the problematic of the material body in relation to affect in order to highlight that "to separate affect from . . . biological, cybernetic, and neurological tenets is to miss the point."[16] This is not to discount constructivism as a social force, but to pose anew the conundrum of the relationships of the biological to the discursive, the organic to the nonorganic. Defining "abstract sex," Luciana Parisi writes, "In the age of cybernetics, sex is no longer a private act practiced between the walls of the bedroom. In particular, human sex no longer seems to involve the set of social and cultural codes that used to characterize sexual identity and reproductive coupling." She argues that assemblages of sex coagulate on the planes of technology, virtuality, cloning, information transmission, genetics, cybernetics, a "blurring of the boundary between artificial and natural sex," an interfacing of biology and technology that is "the assemblage of the forces of reproduction with those of technical machines." Crucially, these assemblages of sex work through material, psychic, energetic, technological, aesthetic, and geographic substrates and planes that "[do] not aim to reiterate the identity of sexual difference and femininity in the disciplinary formation."[17] While Saldanha and Parisi are still indebted to the categories of "race" and "sex" to name their assemblages, or, perhaps more accurately, to name the function of their assemblages (respectively, to undermine discourses of racial identity, and to undermine discourses of sexual difference), Patricia Clough elucidates assemblages that do not reiterate such distinctions:

> Race, ethnicity, sexuality, gender, and class are to be treated politically as elements of a machinic assemblage, matters of a desiring production that does not reduce to an individual's desire, but rather points to the direct links between microintensities and various territories—human bodies, cities, institutions, ideologies, and technologies. In this sense, race, class, sexuality, ethnicity, and gender are not simply matters of subject identity . . . they are rethought in terms of the connections and disconnections on a plane of consistency, the interlacing of given materialities of the human body and cultural inscriptions, given over, however, to the speeds of deterritorialization and reterritorialization, to the vulnerabilities of exposure, under- and overexposure to media event-ness, such that politics involve the when, where, or how of acknowledging, elaborating, resisting, or refusing the visible and invisible markings and effects of desiring production.[18]

A polemic call, then, to refuse "reproductive futurism," the term coined by Lee Edelman to describe contemporary fixation on the precious child and all its potential, also misses the mark.[19] By assuming that reproduction is at the center of futurity and the platform against which future-negating queer politics should be oriented, Edelman, despite his call for an end to futurity, an end that locates itself outside reproduction and normative kinship and the hegemony of child-adulating culture, ironically recenters the very child-privileging, future-oriented politics he seeks to refuse. Instead, we must encourage genealogies of sexuality that suspend, for a moment, the rubrics of desire, pleasure, erotics, and identity that typically subtend "sex acts," yet simultaneously avoid collapsing sexuality into a thin biopolitical frame of reproduction, hetero or homo. For if race and sex are to be increasingly thought outside the parameters of identity—Clough, Parisi, and Saldanha exhort—as assemblages, as *events*, what is at stake in terms of biopolitical capacity is therefore not the ability to *reproduce*, but the capacity to *regenerate*, the terms of which are found in all sorts of registers beyond heteronormative reproduction. The child is just one such figure in a spectrum of statistical chances that suggest health, vitality, capacity, fertility, "market virility," and so on. For queer politics, the challenge is not so much to refuse a future through the repudiation of reproductive futurity, what Edelman hails as the reclamation and embracing of "No Future" that he claims is always already attached to gay bodies,[20] but to understand how the biopolitics of regenerative capacity already demarcate racialized and sexualized statistical population aggregates as those in decay, destined for no future, based not upon whether they can or cannot reproduce children but on what capacities they can and cannot regenerate and what kinds of assemblages they compel, repel, spur, deflate.

Intersectionality and Assemblage

There is no entity, no identity, no queer subject or subject to queer, rather queerness coming forth at us from all directions, screaming its defiance, suggesting a move from intersectionality to assemblage, an affective conglomeration that recognizes other contingencies of belonging (melding, fusing, viscosity, bouncing) that might not fall so easily into what is sometimes denoted as reactive community formations—identity politics—by control theorists. The assemblage, as a series of dispersed but mutually implicated and messy networks, draws together enunciation and dissolution, causality and effect, organic and nonorganic forces. For Deleuze and Guattari, assemblages are collections of multiplicities:

> There is no unity to serve as a pivot in the object, or to divide in the subject. There is not even the unity to abort in the object, or "return" in the subject. A multiplicity has neither subject nor object, only determinations, magnitudes, and dimensions that cannot increase in number without the multiplicity changing in nature (the laws of combination therefore increase as the multiplicity

grows). . . . An assemblage is precisely this increase in the dimensions of a multiplicity that necessarily changes in nature as it expands its connections. There are no points or positions. . . . There are only lines.[21]

As opposed to an intersectional model of identity, which presumes that components—race, class, gender, sexuality, nation, age, religion—are separable analytics and can thus be disassembled, an assemblage is more attuned to interwoven forces that merge and dissipate time, space, and body against linearity, coherency, and permanency.[22] Intersectionality demands the knowing, naming, and thus stabilizing of identity across space and time, relying on the logic of equivalence and analogy between various axes of identity and generating narratives of progress that deny the fictive and performative aspects of identification: you become an identity, yes, but also timelessness works to consolidate the fiction of a seamless stable identity in every space. Furthermore, the study of intersectional identities often involves taking imbricated identities apart one by one to see how they influence each other, a process that betrays the founding impulse of intersectionality, that identities cannot so easily be cleaved. We can think of intersectionality as a hermeneutic of *positionality* that seeks to account for locality, specificity, placement, junctions. As a tool of diversity management and a mantra of liberal multiculturalism, intersectionality colludes with the disciplinary apparatus of the state—census, demography, racial profiling, surveillance—in that "difference" is encased within a structural container that simply wishes the messiness of identity into a formulaic grid, producing analogies in its wake and engendering what Massumi names "gridlock": a "box[ing] into its site on the culture map." He elaborates:

> The idea of positionality begins by subtracting movement from the picture. This catches the body in cultural freeze-frame. The point of explanatory departure is a pin-pointing, a zero point of stasis. When positioning of any kind comes a determining first, movement comes a problematic second. . . . Of course, a body occupying one position on the grid might succeed in making a move to occupy another position. . . . But this doesn't change the fact that what defines the body is not the movement itself, only its beginnings and endpoints. . . . There is "displacement," but no transformation; it is as if the body simply leaps from one definition to the next. . . . "The space of the crossing, the gaps between positions on the grid, falls into a theoretical no-man's land."[23]

Many feminists, new social movement theorists, critical race theorists, and queer studies scholars have argued that social change can occur only through the precise accountability to and for position/ing. But identity is unearthed by Massumi as the complexity of process sacrificed for the "surety" of product. In the stillness of position, bodies actually lose their capacity for movement, for flow, for (social) change. Highlighting the "paradoxes of passage and position," Massumi makes the case for identity appearing as such only in retrospect: a "retrospective ordering" that can only be "working backwards from the movement's end." Again from Massumi: "Gender, race and sexual orientation also emerge and back-form their reality. . . . Grids happen. So social and cultural determinations feed back into the process from which they arose. Indeterminacy and determination, change and freeze-framing, go together."[24]

For example, intervening in the circuitous debates in "lesbian studies" regarding the preoccupation of the invisibility of lesbian sexuality in representational formats, Annamarie Jagose discourages attempts to restore integrity to a lesbian figure by countering its derivative status through the representational tactics of excavation, restoration, and visibility. For Jagose, the "prioritizing [of] sequence over visibility" is not a substitution of tropes. Rather, sequence informs the very logic that drives desires for visibility, both chronological (lesbian as second order to the first orders of heterosexuality, vis-à-vis sexuality, and male homosexuality, vis-à-vis gender) and retrospective (lesbian as anachronistic and belated, linked to the "reparative project of constructing lesbian history"). Instead, she argues, it is the regulatory and "self-licensing logic of sexual sequence" itself that produces hierarchies of intelligibility for *all* sexualities and thus must be interrogated, rather than restoring the lesbian to proper representational visibility, a tactic which merely reiterates the centrality of sexual sequencing rather than deconstructing its frame, reifying the politics of recognition, retribution, and rehabilitation rather than transforming their utility. An embracing of derivative status reveals, Jagose claims, that "categories of sexual registration themselves, not lesbianism particularly, are always secondary, always back formations, always belated." The "certified specification of lesbian difference" is thus a tautological endeavor whereby "problem and solution, cause and effect repeatedly assume each other's form."[25]

"Grids happen." As such, intersectional identities and assemblages must remain as interlocutors in tension, for if we follow Massumi's line of thinking, intersectional identities are the byproducts of attempts to still and quell the perpetual motion of assemblages, to capture and reduce them, to harness their threatening mobility. Endless becomings surface on our radar screens when, drawing on philosopher Henri Bergson, Massumi tells us,

"Position no longer comes first, with movement a problematic second. It is secondary to movement and derived from it. It is retro movement, movement residue. The problem is no longer to explain how there can be change given positioning. The problem is to explain the wonder that there can be stasis given the primacy of process."[26]

Linked to this is what Massumi calls "ontogenetic difference" or "ontogenetic priority," a concept that rescripts temporality exterior to the sheer administrative units that are mobilized to capture the otherwise unruly processes of a body:

> To say that passage and indeterminancy "come first" or "are primary" is more a statement of ontological priority than the assertion of a time sequence. They have ontological privilege in the sense that they constitute the field of emergence, while positionings are what emerge. The trick is to express that priority in a way that respects the inseparability and contemporaneousness of the disjunct dimensions: their ontogenetic difference.

And later: "The field of emergence is not pre-social. It is open-endedly social. . . . One of the things that the dimension of change is ontogenetically 'prior to' is thus the very distinction between individual and the collective, as well as any given model of their interaction. That interaction is precisely what takes form." The given models of interaction would be these bifurcated distinctions between the body and the social (its signification) such that the distinctions disappear. Massumi's move from ontology (being, becoming) to ontogenesis is also relevant to how he discusses affect and cognition and the processes of the body: "Feedback and feed forward, or recursivity, in addition to converting distance into intensity, folds the dimensions of time into each other. The field of emergence of experience has to be thought of as a space-time continuum, as an ontogenetic dimension prior to the separating-out of space and time. Linear time, like position-gridded space, would be emergent qualities of the event of the world's self-relating."[27]

This ontogenetic dimension that is "prior" but not "pre" claims its priorness not through temporality but through its ontological status as that which produces fields of emergence; the prior and the emergence are nevertheless "contemporaneous." "Ontological priority" is a temporality and a spatialization that has yet to be imagined, a property more than a boundedness by space and time. The ontogenetic dimension that articulates or occupies multiple temporalities of vectors and planes is also that which enables an emergent bifurcation of time and space.

Identity is one effect of affect, a capture that proposes what one is by masking its retrospective ordering and thus its ontogenetic dimension—what one was—through the guise of an illusory futurity: what one is and will continue to be. However, this is anything but a relay between stasis and flux; position is but one derivative of systems in constant motion, lined with erratic trajectories and unruly projectiles. If the ontogenetic dimensions of affect render affect as prior to representation—prior to race, class, gender, sex, nation, even as these categories might be the most pertinent mapping of or reference back to affect itself—how might identity-as-retrospective-ordering amplify rather than inhibit praxes of political organizing? If we transfer our energy, our turbulence, our momentum from the defense of the integrity of identity and submit instead to this affective ideation of identity, what kinds of political strategies, of "politics of the open end,"[28] might we unabashedly stumble upon? Rather than rehashing the pros and cons of identity politics, can we think instead of affective politics?

Displacing queerness as an identity or modality that is visibly, audibly, legibly, or tangibly evident—the seemingly queer body in a "cultural freeze-frame" of sorts—assemblages allow us to attune to movements, intensities, emotions, energies, affectivities, and textures as they inhabit events, spatiality, and corporealities. Intersectionality privileges naming, visuality, epistemology, representation, and meaning, while assemblage underscores feeling, tactility, ontology, affect, and information. Further, in the sway from disciplinary societies (where the panoptic "functioned primarily in terms of positions, fixed points, and identities") to control societies, the diagram of control, Michael Hardt writes, is "oriented toward mobility and anonymity. . . . The flexible and mobile performances of contingent identities, and thus its assemblages or institutions are elaborated primarily through repetition and the production of simulacra."[29] Assemblages are thus crucial conceptual tools that allow us to acknowledge and comprehend power beyond disciplinary regulatory models, where "particles, and not parts, recombine, where forces, and not categories, clash."[30]

Most important, given the heightened death machine aspect of nationalism in our contemporary political terrain—a heightened sensorial and anatomical domination indispensable to Mbembe's necropolitics—assemblages work against narratives of U.S. exceptionalism that secure empire, challenging the fixity of racial and sexual taxonomies that inform practices of state surveillance and control and befuddling the "us versus them" of the war on terror. (On a more cynical note, the recent work of Eyal Weizman on the use of the philosophy of Gilles Deleuze, Félix Guattari, and Guy Debord by the Israeli Defense Forces demonstrates that we cannot afford to ignore concepts such as war machines and machinic assemblages, as they are already heavily cultivated as instructive tactics in military strategy.)[31] For while intersectionality and its underpinnings—an unrelenting epistemological will to truth—presupposes identity and thus disavows futurity, or, perhaps more accurately, prematurely anticipates and thus fixes a permanence to forever, assemblage, in its debt to ontology and its espousal of what cannot be known, seen, or heard, or has yet to be known, seen, or heard, allows for becoming beyond or without being.[32]

Terrorist Assemblages

The fact that we approach suicide bombing with such trepidation, in contrast to how we approach the violence of colonial domination . . . indicates the symbolic violence that shapes our understanding of what constitutes ethically and politically illegitimate violence.— Ghassan Hage, " 'Comes a Time We Are All Enthusiasm' "

Ghassan Hage wonders "why it is that suicide bombing cannot be talked about without being condemned first," noting that without an unequivocal condemnation, one is a "morally suspicious person" because "only unqualified condemnation will do." He asserts, "There is a clear political risk in trying to explain suicide bombings."[33] With such risks in mind, my desire here is to momentarily suspend this dilemma by combining an analysis of these representational stakes with a reading of the forces of affect, of the body, of matter. In pondering the modalities of this kind of terrorist, one notes a pastiche of oddities: a body machined together through metal and flesh, an assemblage of the organic and the inorganic; a death not of the Self nor of the Other, but both simultaneously, and, perhaps more accurately, a death scene that obliterates the Hegelian self/other dialectic altogether. Self-annihilation is the ultimate form of resistance, and ironically, it acts as self-preservation, the preservation of symbolic self enabled through the "highest cultural capital" of martyrdom, a giving of life to the future of political struggles—not at all a sign of "disinterest in living a meaningful life." As Hage notes, in this limited but nonetheless trenchant economy of meaning, suicide bombers are "a sign of life" emanating from the violent conditions of life's impossibility, the "impossibility of making a life."[34] This body forces a reconciliation of opposites through their inevitable collapse— a perverse habitation of contradiction.

Achille Mbembe's devastating and brilliant meditation on necropolitics notes that the historical basis of sovereignty that is reliant upon a notion of (western) political rationality begs for a more accurate framing: that of life and death, the subjugation of life to the power of death. Mbembe attends not only to the representational but also to the informational productivity of the (Palestinian) suicide bomber. Pointing to the becomings of a suicide bomber, a corporeal experiential of "ballistics," he asks, "What place is given to life, death, and the human body (especially the wounded or slain body)?" Assemblage here points to the inability to clearly delineate a temporal, spatial, energetic, or molecular distinction between a discrete biological body and technology; the entities, particles, and elements come together, flow, break apart, interface, skim off each other, are never stable, but are defined through their continual interface, not as objects meeting but as multiplicities emerging from interactions. The dynamite strapped onto the body of a suicide bomber is not merely an appendage or prosthetic; the intimacy of weapon with body reorients the assumed spatial integrity (coherence and concreteness) and individuality of the body that is the mandate of intersectional identities: instead we have the body-weapon. The ontology of the body renders it a newly becoming body:

> The candidate for martyrdom transforms his or her body into a mask that hides the soon-to-be-detonated weapon. Unlike the tank or the missile that is clearly visible, the weapon carried in the shape of the body is invisible. Thus concealed, it forms part of the body. It is so intimately part of the body that at the time of its detonation it annihilates the body of its bearer, who carries with it the bodies of others when it does not reduce them to pieces. The body does not simply conceal a weapon. The body is transformed into a weapon, not in a metaphorical sense but in a truly ballistic sense.[35]

Temporal narratives of progression are upturned as death and becoming fuse into one: as one's body dies, one's body becomes the mask, the weapon, the suicide bomber. Not only does the ballistic body come into being without the aid of visual cues marking its transformation, it also "carries with it the bodies of others." Its own penetrative energy sends shards of metal and torn flesh spinning off into the ether. The body-weapon does not play as metaphor, nor in the realm of meaning and epistemology, but forces us ontologically anew to ask: What kinds of information does the ballistic body impart? These bodies, being in the midst of becoming, blur the insides and the outsides, infecting transformation through sensation, echoing knowledge via reverberation and vibration. The echo is a queer temporality—in the

I have no longer where I start nor where I end ...

The body weapon

The weapon forms part of the body

Deleuzism the realist of becoming

relay of affective information between and amid beings, the sequence of reflection, repetition, resound, and return (but with a difference, as in mimicry)—and brings forth waves of the future breaking into the present. Gayatri Spivak, prescient in drawing our attention to the multivalent textuality of suicide in "Can the Subaltern Speak," reminds us in her latest ruminations that suicide terrorism is a modality of expression and communication for the subaltern (there is the radiation of heat, the stench of burning flesh, the impact of metal upon structures and the ground, the splattering of blood, body parts, skin):

> Suicidal resistance is a message inscribed on the body when no other means will get through. It is both execution and mourning, for both self and other. For you die with me for the same cause, no matter which side you are on. Because no matter who you are, there are no designated killees in suicide bombing. No matter what side you are on, because I cannot talk to you, you won't respond to me, with the implication that there is no dishonor in such shared and innocent death.[36]

We have the proposal that there are no sides, and that the sides are forever shifting, crumpling, and multiplying, disappearing and reappearing, unable to satisfactorily delineate between here and there. The spatial collapse of sides is due to the queer temporal interruption of the suicide bomber, projectiles spewing every which way. As a queer assemblage— distinct from the queering of an entity or identity—race and sexuality are denaturalized through the impermanence, the transience of the suicide bomber, the fleeting identity replayed backward through its dissolution. This dissolution of self into other/s and other/s into self not only effaces the absolute mark of self and other/s in the war on terror, but produces a systemic challenge to the entire order of Manichaean rationality that organizes the rubric of good versus evil. Delivering "a message inscribed on the body when no other means will get through," suicide bombers do not transcend or claim the rational nor accept the demarcation of the irrational. Rather, they foreground the flawed temporal, spatial, and ontological presumptions upon which such distinctions flourish. Organic and inorganic, flesh and machine, these wind up as important as (and perhaps as threatening) if not more so than the symbolism of the bomber and his or her defense or condemnation.

Figure 24 is the November/December 2004 cover of a magazine called *Jest: Humor for the Irreverent*, distributed for free in Brooklyn (see also jest .com) and published by a group of counterculture artists and writers. Here

FIGURE 24. *Jest Magazine*, cover image, November/December 2004.

we have the full force of the mistaken identity conundrum: the distinctive silhouette, indeed the profile, harking to the visible by literally blacking it out, of the turbaned Amritdhari Sikh male (i.e., turban and unshorn beard that signals baptized Sikhs), rendered (mistakenly?) as a (Muslim) suicide bomber, replete with dynamite through the vibrant pulsations of an iPod ad. Fully modern, animated through technologies of sound and explosives, this body does not operate solely or even primarily on the level of metaphor. Once again, to borrow from Mbembe, it is truly a ballistic body. Contagion, infection, and transmission reign, not meaning.

The body of Mbembe's suicide bomber is still, however, a male one, and in that universalized masculinity, ontologically pure regardless of location, history, and context. Whereas for Mbembe, sexuality—as the dissolution of bodily boundaries—is elaborated through the erotic ballistic event of death, for female suicide bombers, sexuality is still announced in advance: the petite manicured hands, mystical beauty ("beauty mixed with violence"), and features of her face and body are commented upon in a manner not requisite for male suicide bombers; the political import of the female suicide bomber's actions are gendered out or into delusions about her purported irrational emotional and mental distress.[37] Female suicide bombers disrupt the prosaic proposition that terrorism is bred directly of patriarchy and that women are intrinsically peace-manifesting. This rationale is reinscribed, however, when observers proclaim that women cast out of or shunned by traditional compositions of gender and sexuality (often accused of being lesbians) are most likely to be predisposed toward violence. Insofar as female suicide bombers are mentored within masculinist organizations, Spivak notes, "the female suicide bomber, thus persuaded, does not make a gendered point . . . there is no recoding of the gendered struggle."[38] These discursive identity markers reflect the enduring capacities of intersectionality—we cannot leave it completely behind—but also its limitations: we are once again stuck within a resistance-complicity binary circuit.[39] Assemblage is possible not through the identity markers that encapsulate this body, but through the temporal and spatial reorderings that the body iterates as it is machined together and as it explodes. The assemblage is momentary, fleeting even, and gives way to normative identity markers even in the midst of its newly becoming state.

Queer Futurity

Power can be invisible, it can be fantastic, it can be dull and routine. It can be obvious, it can reach you by the baton of the police, it can speak the language of your thoughts and desires. It can feel like remote control, it can exhilarate like liberation, it can travel through time, and it can drown you in the present. It is dense and superficial, it can cause you bodily injury, and it can harm you without seeming ever to touch you. It is systemic and it is particularistic and it is often both at the same time. It causes dreams to live and dreams to die.—
Avery Gordon, *Ghostly Matters*

Mbembe and Spivak each articulate, unintentionally, how queerness is constitutive of the suicide bomber and the tortured body: de-linked from sexual identity to signal instead temporal, spatial, and corporeal schisms, queerness is a prerequisite for the body to function symbolically, pedagogically, and affectively as it does. The dispersion of the boundaries of bodies forces a completely chaotic challenge to normative conventions of gender, sexuality, and race, disobeying normative conventions of "appropriate" bodily practices and the sanctity of the able body. Here, then, is a possible rereading of these terrorist bodies, typically understood as culturally, ethnically, and religiously nationalist, fundamentalist, patriarchal, and often even homophobic, as assemblages. The political import of this queer rereading should not be underestimated: in the upheaval of the "with us or against us" rhetoric of the war on terror, a queer praxis of assemblage allows for a scrambling of sides that is illegible to state practices of surveillance, control, banishment, and extermination.

These nonexceptional, terrorist bodies are nonheteronormative, if we consider nation and citizenship to be implicit in the privilege of heteronormativity, as we should. Following Cathy Cohen, who argues that heteronormativity is as much about (white) racial and (middle- to upper-) class privilege as it is about sexual identities, identifications, and acts,[40] the (American imperialist) nation also figures as an important axis of psychic and material identification, repeatedly casting these bodies into the spotlight of sexual perversity. In attending to affective processes, ones that foreground normativizing and resistant bodily practices beyond sex, gender, and sexual object choice, queerness is expanded as a field, a vector, a terrain, one that must consistently, not sporadically, account for nationalism and race within its purview, as well as insistently disentangle the relations between queer representation and queer affectivity. What does this rereading and rearticulation do to Cohen's already expansive notion of queer coalitional politics? What types of affiliative networks could be imagined and spawned if we embrace the already queer mechanics and assemblages—threats to nation, to race, to sanctioned bodily practices—of terrorist bodies?

Terrorist assemblages not only counter sexual exceptionalisms by reclaiming contagion—the nonexceptional—within the gaze of national security. In the commingling of queer monstrosity and queer modernity, they also creatively, powerfully, and unexpectedly scramble the terrain of the political within organizing and intellectual projects, weakening the tenuous collusion of the disciplinary subject and the population for control. We cannot know assemblages in advance, thus taunting the temporal suffocation plaguing identity politics to which Chow draws our attention. Displacing visibility politics as a primary concern of queer social movements, assemblages demonstrate the import of theorizing the queer affective economies that impact and engrave but also announce, trail, and emblazon queer bodies: suicide bombers, the turbaned Sikh man, the monster-terrorist-fag, the tortured Muslim body, the burqa'ed woman, the South Asian diasporic drag queen, to name a few. These terrorist assemblages, a cacophony of informational flows, energetic intensities, bodies, and practices that undermine coherent identity and even queer anti-identity narratives, bypass entirely the Foucauldian "act to identity" continuum that informs much global LGBTIQ organizing, a continuum that privileges the pole of identity as the evolved form of western modernity.[41] Yet reclaiming the nonexceptional is only partially the point, for assemblages allow for complicities of privilege and the production of new normativities even as they cannot anticipate spaces and moments of resistance, resistance that is not primarily characterized by oppositional stances, but includes frictional forces, discomfiting encounters, and spurts of unsynchronized delinquency (the jamming of technological and informational infrastructures such as underground hacker subterfuge, viruses, mobile models of crowd gathering at antiwar protests). These unknowable terrorist assemblages are not casual bystanders or parasites; the nation assimilates the effusive discomfort of the unknowability of these bodies, thus affectively producing new normativities and exceptionalisms through the cataloguing of unknowables. Opening up to the fantastical wonders of futurity, therefore, is the most powerful of political and critical strategies, whether it is through assemblage or to something as yet unknown, perhaps even forever unknowable.

acknowledgments

The work of this book has been, to borrow from Jacques Derrida (who borrowed from Freud), the work of mourning.

My younger brother, Sandeep, died suddenly on February 20, 2003 while in India with his partner and his son, who had just celebrated his first birthday. Three weeks later, to the day, the United States invaded Iraq. I went to work that morning and discovered that I had completely and utterly forgotten about the impending war. I was shocked to realize that, floundering in my own shock, it is possible to disintegrate into such a small place that one can forget these things. I relate these circumstances because I believe it is important to understand where a book comes from and why it shows up in the way it does. Most of the time this commitment can be met without such explicit detail, hinted at within the interstices of what is stated and what is felt, what is written in order to navigate what must remain unsaid. In *The Work of Mourning* Derrida points out that it is an obscenity to speak of the dead in any type of instrumental manner. Yet, he also notes, it is a betrayal to not speak of them at all, a travesty not to share one's sadness.

It is in between these two scenes of death that this book emanates. Simultaneously confronted with the devastation of a personal death so proximate and intimate and the political deaths of those at a distance, I began writing. From the vantage of a Spivakian "textuality of an event," these two scenes of death, seemingly disjunctive, revealed themselves to be delicately intertwined. I emphasize *delicately* because their obvious differences of scale, magnitude, and import leave them incomparable—they should never stand side by side—the death of a privileged young Sikh physician whose funeral was attended by four hundred people, and the thousands of faceless, nameless deaths shoved under the term "collateral damage" whose bodies, if lucky, were cremated en masse. The singularity of each death defies scalar ordering. One death can completely upturn the landscape of those left behind, while the senseless killing of thousands can remain the most unspectacular and normalized of occurrences, rationalized for the sake of securing just one life. Often numbers matter not, or matter only in the context of ratios, as the valuation of life, or of death, is uneven and incalculable.

Scale does not reflect normative ordering but is actually a modality that produces normative ordering, a grid of ascending and descending power vectors, assignments of priority, impact, and force. Because of this, the task of giving thanks is precarious at best. Sometimes, a simple look from a student, a word in a condolence note from a bare acquaintance, an unanticipated touch from a stranger, sustained me for untold days or weeks. The progressive scale, then, of the "acknowledgment genre" attempts to manage a far more haphazard experience of liminal yet intense connectivities. It is also the case that these particular acknowledgments extend past the usual intellectual and personal debts to include those who committed, in big ways and small, to traveling together with me through the work of mourning

I thank my wonderful colleagues at Rutgers University in the Women's and Gender Studies Department as well as the Department of Geography, in particular Nancy Hewitt, Louisa Schein, Ed Cohen, and Judith Gerson. I could not have asked for a more wonderful department chair than Joanna Regulska. Working alongside Carlos Decena and Ethel Brooks has enriched my intellectual and personal life tremendously. Several graduate seminars at Rutgers shaped the tenor of this project, and I thank the students who so generously indulged my preoccupations. Two fellowships at the Institute for Research on Women gave me writing time and necessary feedback on drafts, and in particular allowed me to interface with awesome colleagues at Rutgers who compose a wonderful cadre of intellectual and political companions: Edlie Wong, Sonali Perera, Nicole Fleetwood, and Julie Livingston. And to our wonderful administrative staff, Joanne Givand and Margaret Pado, their work in our department is truly indispensable.

To those who offered assistance, feedback, and incisive critique on various parts of this book or pieces of this work published earlier in article form, I am deeply indebted: Inderpal Grewal, Gillian Harkins, Erica Rand, Eithne Luibheid, Sharad Chari, Amit Rai, Katherine Sugg, Dereka Rushbrook, Patricia Clough, Jennifer Terry, Jackie Orr, Laurie Prendergast, Barbara Balliet, Lisa Duggan, Anna Marie Smith, David Eng, Virinder Kalra, Louisa Schein, Negar Mottahedeh, David Serlin, Ara Wilson, and Nayan Shah. Carlos Decena was also generous enough to read the final draft in its entirety at the very last minute. I also thank wonderfully rigorous, engaged audiences at Cornell University, New York University, the CUNY Graduate Center, Syracuse University, Old Dominion University, the University of Washington, Lancaster University (especially Anne Marie Fortier and Adi

Kuntsman), Manchester University (Nicole Vitellone, Lisa Adkins, Virinder Kalra, and Rajinder Dudrah were fantastic hosts), Utrecht University, the University of Pennsylvania, the University of California at Berkeley, Wesleyan University, Mt. Holyoke College, and the University of California at Irvine, for inviting me to present longer versions of chapters and articles. I also thank the *Social Text* collective for support, encouragement, and intellectual community over the past three years. Ken Wissoker's steadfast belief in this project was indispensable. I am also deeply grateful to two anonymous reviewers who were wildly enthusiastic about the project. I do also want to thank Eric Zinner, José Esteban Muñoz, and Ann Pellegrini at New York University Press for their interest in the manuscript; I hope there will be an opportunity to work with them in the future. I am also deeply grateful to the artists who gave permission to reproduce their work, including Poulomi Desai, Karthik Pandian, Naeem Mohaiemen and the Visible Collective, Vishavjit Singh, and Richard Serra.

To those who were not necessarily involved in this project but were mentors during my graduate years at UC Berkeley and the research and writing of my dissertation, I thank Patricia Penn Hilden, Trinh Minh-ha, Michael Omi, Aiwha Ong, Laura Perez, Sau-Ling Wong, Minoo Moallem, Geeta Patel, Kath Weston, Angela Davis, and Kris Peterson. Inderpal Grewal has been a special mentor and friend, sharing with me an interest in the politics of Sikh identity and community as it plays out in the academy and in organizing venues. Marisa Belausteguigoitia's companionship in graduate school was indispensable and her home in Mexico City is a refuge of solace. Caren Kaplan epitomizes the ideal feminist mentor and treated me as a colleague from the moment I arrived. Norma Alarcón, my brilliant and passionate dissertation advisor, taught me the most about the political risks of disrupting hegemonic knowledge formations. To my friends in the Bay Area, some of whom are no longer there, I thank you for the pleasures of communal living: Priya Jagganathan, Anand Pandian, Mona Shah, Musa Ahmed, Neeru Paharia, Everlyn Hunter, Surveen Singh, Madhury Anji, Harleen Kahlon, Sangeeta Chowdhry, Stephen Julien, and Tania Hammidi; all the folks in Trikone, especially Dipti Ghosh; and everyone at Narika who challenged all of my theoretical leanings with the pragmatics of community outreach and nonprofit organizing, especially Chic Dabby, Amisha Patel, and Naheed Sheikh.

I have been incredibly fortunate to spend two summers working intensively with my research assistant, Ariella Rotramel. Along with her sharp political eye I thank her profusely for her ministering to me in big ways and small and for taking such good care of my dog, Mozilla. I also am indebted to Julie Rajan for several years of steady research assistance, as well as Kelly Coogan, Una Chung, and Soniya Munshi for stepping in at crucial moments. The bibliography, the index, as well as the selection and procurement of many of the visuals, are indebted to Andrew Mazzaschi's meticulous care and brilliance; I am grateful for his diligence and willingness to suffer, with good humor, my very last round of deadlines. Soniya Munshi and Janhavi Pakrashi continue to work with me on a video project that interfaces with this book. Their political, aesthetic, and community visions have endlessly inspired me. In New York City I enjoyed the benefits of the early millenium South Asian Lesbian and Gay Association days with Atif Toor, Aamir Khandawala, Ashu Rai, Javid Syed, Vidur Kapur, Trishala Deb, Svati Shah, Priyabishnu Ghosh, Sangeeta Sibal, Rohini Suri, and Ishu Bhutani. Other local companions I would like to acknowledge include Catherine Zimmer, David Kazanjian, David Breeden, Carol Joyce, Sally Rappeport, and Ron Lavine. Prithika Balakrishnan brings much needed levity to every day.

Patricia Clough has become a beloved mentor, colleague, and most importantly, friend. Her intellectual breadth saturates these pages. Amit Rai unflinchingly wrote with me when I could not do it alone; his darkness is his fierce refusal to pretend, and I admire this in him deeply. Katherine Sugg repeatedly sought out my pain with the care and attention that only devoted friends can enact. And to Rebecca Coleman, who took my grief as her own and loved my family as her own, who witnessed every minute and tended to me in every way imaginable, I am humbly and forever indebted.

My mother, Surinder K. Puar, and my father, Mohindar S. Puar, continue to amaze me daily with their ethical commitments to community, family, education, prolific gardening, and the integrity with which they carry their wounds. Despite the complexities my life and my work present for them, their support of me seems only to grow and deepen. My sister, Kimpreet, traversed the sibling transition from three to two with such honesty and truthfulness; I will always admire the freedom she has to let herself go there, along with her quick wit and her sharp intellect. I also send love to Kirpal Singh, my brother's son, whose unfailing toddler energy sustained us through many difficult months.

My greatest challenge over the past three and a half years has been to accept the bittersweet spiritual gifts that Sandeep's death has bestowed upon me. This book, along with the big apple he conjured one morning, is one of those gifts. Written through deep reverence for magic, for mysticism.

Aware of his hauntings, his laughter, the times his ephemeral devotion would surface when I was struggling in front of my computer. Openings to conversations sustained ethereally, through temporalities and presences only experienced through the surrendering of one's heart to heartbreak. Since we had no choice but to say goodbye to you, Sandeep, I wouldn't have missed this ride for the world.

September 2006

notes

preface

1. The complete list of cities in which protests took place is New York, Washington, Provincetown, San Diego, San Francisco, Fort Lauderdale, Sioux Falls, Seattle, Chicago, Tulsa, Salt Lake City, Toronto, Vancouver, Dublin, Mexico City, Bogotá, Milan, Warsaw, Amsterdam, The Hague, London, Stockholm, Marseille, Moscow, Brussels, Vienna, and Gloucester; Ireland, "Global Protests." Duncan Osborne reports that approximately fifty people gathered on July 19 outside of Iran's Mission to the United Nations in New York, and another fifty people attended a panel discussion on "gays in Iran" at the Lesbian, Gay, Bisexual and Transgender Community Center in New York, an event sponsored by IGLHRC. The Commission was originally the sponsor of the vigil at Iran's Mission to the UN, but pulled out five days before the event, opting for the panel discussion instead; Duncan Osborne, "Mashad Hangings Anniversary." Also, in "Washington, Rob Anderson led a protest at Dupont Circle. In San Francisco, Michael Petrelis assembled speakers at Harvey Milk Plaza. In Provincetown, Andrew Sulliven led a quiet vigil outside Town Hall. In Toronto, Arsham Parsi, Human Rights Secretary of the Persian Gay and Lesbian Organization (PGLO), spoke at a commemorative gathering. In Iran, PGLO members lit candles privately." Rosendall, "No Excuses for Iran."

2. A more extensive list of endorsements includes Andy Humm and Ann Northrop of Gay USA cable TV news, Walter Armstrong of *POZ* magazine, Sandy Rapp (a lesbian feminist singer-writer), Rosario Dawson, Doric Wilson, Martin Duberman, Church Ladies for Choice, Allen Roskoff (presdent of Jim Owles Liberal Democratic Club), the Stonewall Democratic Club, the Metropolitan Community Church of New York, Darren Rosenblum (associate professor at Pace Law School), Larry Kramer, John Berendt (author of *Midnight in the Garden of Good and Evil*), Lawrence D. Mass (cofounder of Gay Men's Health Crisis), Arnie Kantrowitz (professor emeritus at the College of Staten Island, CUNY), Sean Strub (founder of *POZ* magazine), Kenneth Sherill (professor at Hunter College, CUNY), the International Lesbian and Gay Association, the Center for Culture and Leisure, Tupilak (the association of lesbian and gay cultural workers in the Nordic area), the Nordic Homo Council, Nordic Rainbow Humanists, the website GayRussia.ru, the Austrian gay group Homosexuelle Initiative Wien, *Independent Gay News* of Fort Lauderdale, *Seattle Gay News*, the Campaign for Peace and Democracy, the Italian organization ARCIGAY, the Irish organization BeLonG to Youth, the Mexican magazine *Enkidu*, and the Columbian organization Colombia Diversa; Ireland, "Global Protests," The MAHA quotation comes from a statement released by the editors; see MAHA, "A Message from Iran."

3. Ireland, "Global Protests."

4. See Tatchell, "Iran—10 Arabs Face Execution." Tatchell claims the executions are part of the "ethnic cleansing of Ahwazi Arabs in south-west Iran" that are also motivated by homophobia. Long, "Debating Iran." See Sullivan's post "Islamists versus Gays."

5. Richard Kim, "Witness to an Execution."

6. See Human Rights Campaign Foundation, "Secretary Rice." See two HRW documents regarding the Dutch moratorium on gay Iranian deportations. The first is a press release, the second, a letter to Minister Verdonk penned by Scott Long: Human Rights Watch (HRW), "Dutch Officials"; Long, "HRW Letter." Richard Kim, "Witness to an Execution."

7. Alam, "Gay Media's Failure."

8. Ettelbrick, open letter.

9. I use the terms "gay" and "lesbian" in conjunction with "queer" to demarcate important differences in positionality, yet I also want to suggest that some queers are implicated in homonormative spaces and practices. I feel that the notion of queerness as an identity resistant to gay formations, while historically salient, is less evident in the contemporary political climate in the United States. In the rest of the text I use "gay" as shorthand to include lesbians; I use the term "homosexual" when it is an appropriate differentiation of subject positioning from heterosexual; and I use the acronym LGBTIQ (lesbian, gay, bisexual, transgender, intersex, queer) to signal organizing, activist, and other collective contexts; this acronym, however, does not include two-spirit identity, among other formations. While I adhere to these contextual usages within rotating contexts, I note the inadequacy of all of these terms, because they are both excessive and simultaneously too specific. The attempt to mediate this tension is precisely symptomatic of the problem.

I would like to thank Patricia Ticineto Clough for crucial and timely conversations regarding the frame of this project, which is indebted to her thinking on contemporary social theory.

10. Chow, *The Protestant Ethnic*, 11.

11. See Al-Fatiha, "Al-Fatiha."

12. For a sampling of these authors' work, see the following edited collections: Puar, "Queer Tourism"; Nast, "Queer Patriarchies"; Cruz-Malave and Manalansan, *Queer Globalizations*; Puar et al., "Sexuality and Space"; Eng, Halberstam, and Muñoz, "What's Queer about Queer Studies Now?"; Cantú and Luibhéid, *Queer Migrations*; Patton and Sanchez-Eppler, *Queer Diasporas*. Also see the following monographs: Luibhéid, *Entry Denied*; Rodriguez, *Queer Latinidad*; Ferguson, *Aberrations in Black*; Manalansan, *Global Divas*; Gopinath, *Impossible Desires*; Brady, *Extinct Lands*; Barnard, *Queer Race*; Fiol-Matta, *A Queer Mother*.

13. Chow, *The Age of the World Target*, 39.

14. Mbembe, *On the Postcolony*, 16, 4, 8–9.

15. Bill Brown writes of rupture and September 11, "The event has already attained an autonomous periodizing force. In the United States, people speak of life before and after 9/11." Continuing, he claims, "Postmodernity would thus seem to have found an appropriate historical breach. . . . And yet this rupture seems to signal something other than the postmodernity we too comfortably imagined; it is as though the

hyperreal has dried up in the sands of what Slavoj Žižek has named the 'desert of the real' "; "The Dark Wood," 735, citing Žižek, *Welcome to the Desert*.

16. The multitude of statements that circulated on the Internet immediately after the attacks, many denouncing war, were an important genre and marker of public debate and increasingly the only one available for dissent. These were released from postcolonial theorists and public intellectuals such as Arundhati Roy, "The Algebra of Infinite Justice"; Edward Said, "Islam and the West"; and Susan Sontag, "Talk of the Town." Statements from Suheir Hammad, Ayesha Khan, Medica Mondiale, Barbara Lee, Minoo Moallem, Madeleine Bunting, and Sunera Thobani are available in Amrita Basu et al, "Creating an Archive." "Creating an Archive" also contains post–September 11 statements from the Revolutionary Association of Women in Afghanistan, Women Living under Muslim Laws, Women in Black, Coalition of 100 Black Women, and the statement "Transnational Feminist Practices against War," by Paola Bacchetta, Tina Campt, Inderpal Grewal, Caren Kaplan, Minoo Moallem, and Jennifer Terry. Other statements were released by the Black Radical Congress, "Terror Attacks"; Section for the Study of Islam, "Statement"; and a coalition of forty-eight organizations including Amnesty International USA, Bahá'ís of the United States, Food for the Hungry, Human Rights Watch, Immigration and Refugee Services of America, Sikh Dharma International, Sikh Mediawatch and Resource Task Force, Students for a Free Tibet, U.S. Committee for Refugees, Unitarian Universalists Association of Congregations, and World Organization against Torture USA, "Statement of Principles." See also the text of Judith Butler's December 2001 CLAGS Kessler lecture: "Global Violence, Sexual Politics."

17. Göle, "Close Encounters."

18. Ibid.

19. Kazanjian, *The Colonizing Trick*, 27. See Benjamin, "Theses on the Philosophy of History."

20. Sedgwick, *Touching Feeling*, 131.

21. See Spivak, *The Postcolonial Critic*, 46, 95–112.

22. Sacks, "Speed," 63.

23. A. Gordon, *Ghostly Matters*, 7, 8.

24. Ibid., 8.

25. Sacks, "Speed," 62, 63–64, 60, 63.

26. Freeman, "Time Binds," 58, 63.

27. De Landa, *Intensive Science*, 106–7.

28. Sacks, "Speed," 65–66.

29. Muñoz, *Disidentifications*, 108.

30. CNN, "Bauer Compares." The phrase "domestic terrorists" comes from the Concerned Women of America. See the National Gay and Lesbian Task Force's press release, " 'Anti-Gay Groups.' "

31. See U.S. Department of State, Bureau of International Information Programs, USINFO, "Response to Terrorism." For a detailed analysis of this website, see Puar and Rai, "The Remaking of a Model Minority."

32. Spivak, "Terror," 81.

introduction

1. Kaplan cites Krauthammer, as quoted in Eakin, "Ideas and Trends."

2. Most discussions of "Don't Ask, Don't Tell" do not discuss the racialization of sexual subjects in the military or mention race as a determining factor in the policing of nonnormative sexualities. When mentioned, it is often analogized in relation to sexuality as an earlier and successful diversification of the military. See, for example, Belkin, and Embser-Herbert, "A Modest Proposal." For an assessment of the place of people of color in the military, see Fears, "Draft Bill Stirs Debate." Fears writes that

> 38 percent of the military's 1.1 million enlistees are ethnic minorities, while they make up only 29 percent of the general population. In the largest branch, the Army, the percentage of minorities approaches half of all enlistees, at 45 percent. African Americans alone account for nearly 30 percent of Army enlistees, according to Defense Department statistics compiled in 2000. Latinos represent nine percent of the Army and 12 percent of the population. Black women comprise nearly half the Army's enlisted women. . . . The percentage of minorities enlisted in the armed services far exceeds the percentage of minorities in post-secondary education colleges and universities, according to the National Center for Education Statistics.

3. Agamben, *The State of Exception.*

4. Derrida, *Specters of Marx.*

5. S. Ahmed, "Affective Economies."

6. Gregory Jay points out that while the United States may have "exceptional power" to efficaciously deploy its forms of nationalism globally, it is "*not* exceptional in narrating the nation as originating in a special physical and cultural landscape that purportedly gives rise to a 'homogenous' people united in their special relation to truth, beauty, goodness, and God"; "White Out," 782.

7. For overviews, see Kammen, "The Problem of American Exceptionalism"; Rauchway, "More Means Different"; Zinn, "The Power and the Glory."

8. Mohanty, "Under Western Eyes."

9. Grewal, *Transnational America,* 150.

10. The construction of Islam as a threat to women has been reinforced through the work of Muslim authors such as Irshad Manji. See her "America's Wild West," for example. Manji has found an admirer in the gay conservative Andrew Sullivan. His review of her unimaginatively titled *The Trouble with Islam* commends her for "do-[ing] what so many of us have longed to see done: assail fundamentalist Islam itself for tolerating such evil in its midst. And from within"; "Decent Exposure." For a contrasting analysis, see Dahir, "Proud of 'Intolerance.'"

11. Brown, "A Coalition of Hope," 66; Miller, "An Open Letter."

12. Smeal, "Special Message." For further discussion of the problematic relationship between the Feminist Majority Foundation, RAWA, and Afghan women, see Hirshkind and Mahmood, "Feminism."

13. Also acting that evening in "The Vagina Monologues" were Queen Latifah, Glenn Close, Jane Fonda, Marisa Tomei, Rosie Perez, and Claire Danes. Feminist Majority Foundation, "Eve Ensler's Tribute."

14. Reporting on ambivalent feminist responses to the events of September 11, 2001, and the war on terror include Bunting, "Women and War"; Lerner, "What Women Want"; Marks, "In This War"; J. Goldstein, "John Wayne and GI Jane." For an example of pro-war feminism, see Stolba, "Feminists Go to War."

    Those feminists and feminist analyses that countered or questioned support for the war include Abu-Lughod, "Do Muslim Women Really Need Saving?"; Thobani, "War Frenzy"; N. Joseph, "9-11, from a Different Perspective"; Henry, "Trouble and Strife"; Douglas, "NWSA Looks at September 11"; Hyndman, "Beyond Either/Or." With a slightly different tone, in "State of Emergency," Catherine A. MacKinnon questions how the events of September 11 are used to promote a war on terror, while simultaneously taking on the events of that day as a metaphor for violence against women.

15. Cornell, "The New Political Infamy," 314–15. As the most indicative example of this spectacle, the Bush administration used Laura Bush to showcase the purportedly feminist concerns of the United States; see Bumiller, "First Lady to Speak."

16. Spivak, "Globalicities," 89.

17. Merom, "Israel's National Security," 414, 413.

18. A. Kaplan, "Violent Belongings," 3.

19. Losurdo, "Preemptive War," 365.

20. A. Kaplan, "Violent Belongings," 5–6. Kaplan cites Hassner, "The United States."

21. In the United States, Agamben argues, the dialectical relationship between the authority of the president and that of Congress form the cornerstone of state of exception discourses in the Constitution (*The State of Exception*, 19). This dialectic is textually marked by two sets of conflicting dictates: one, the writ of habeas corpus, can be suspended in cases of rebellion or invasion, but it is unclear to whom this authority is accorded; two, while the power to declare war and fund the military is the domain of Congress, the president holds the title of commander in chief of the army and navy, granting the president overwhelming sovereign power (20). The president's authority is most fruitfully maximized in times of war, making the thought of "endless war" rather appealing while also encouraging the attachment of metaphors of war to sometimes contentious domestic policies (the war on poverty, the war on drugs; 21).

22. Ibid., 23.

23. Agamben, *Homo Sacer*, 37.

24. Adam, "The Defense of Marriage Act."

25. For a succinct overview of these debates, see Kammen, "The Problem of American Exceptionalism." A summary of Edward Said's critiques of American exceptionalism can be found in Rowe's "Edward Said and American Studies."

26. Irshad Manji's viewpoints are especially egregious in this regard. Manji exalts the United States as the leader of civilizational tolerance and the land of opportunity, placing the "success" of Muslim integration in contrast to the "failures" of Muslim assimilation in Europe as the result of American cultural values, erasing all economic considerations. This section's discussion of queer secularism is indebted to conversations with Jinthana Haritaworn, Adi Kuntsman, Catherine Sameh, Bahia Munem, and Ethel Brooks.

27. Desai and Sekhon, *Red Threads*, 44.

28. Dahir, "Gay Imam." Dahir reports that his interviewee, "Mohammed," "says he sometimes feels as much at odds with the gay community about being Muslim as he does with the Muslim community about being gay, particularly since the terrorist attacks of September 11." Significant is the article's discussion on the conjoining of queer black Muslim and queer Arab Muslim interests given the stubborn and tenacious discourses of rampant homophobia in both black and Muslim cultures and communities. Dahir provides a reading of the relationship between Islam and homosexuality as complex rather than incommensurable. A case in point is the discussion of Mohammed's need to not identify as gay while studying Islam, while he simultaneously explains his understanding of Islam as "no more or less homophobic than any other religion."

29. Dahir, "Queer and Muslim," 93; Quinn, "Gay Muslims." Quinn states, "While Western societies offer a range of spiritual alternatives for gay Christians, Jews and others who seek to maintain some form of religious faith, Islam has traditionally closed the door to even the notion of homosexuality." This ahistorical statement (when did Western societies begin to "offer a range of spiritual alternatives for gay Christians, Jews and others"?) is not tied to any sources. It denies past and continuing homophobic practices in the name of Christianity and Judaism as well as the existence of practicing queer Muslims.

30. Massad, "Re-Orienting Desire," 363.

31. For an example of male homosociality = homosexuality, see C. S. Smith, "Kandahar Journal." Also see Anderson, "Letter from Afghanistan"; Bradley, "Saudi Gays"; Reynolds, "Kandahar's Lightly Veiled Homosexual Habits," and Stephen, "Startled Marines." Another interpretation is that homosexuality is always already understood as possible within certain homosocial spaces; thus the misreading resides not in equating homosociality with homosexuality, but in the assumption of homosociality functioning as a cover for homosexuality in the first place. For a discussion of the multiple relationships between Islamic law, Muslim nations and cultures, and female same-sex sexuality, see Ali, "Special Focus." On the Western media's problematic reporting on Pashtun male sexuality, see Skier, "Western Lenses." Skier argues that "British and American news media accounts . . . offered an incomplete, problematic and sensationalist characterization of this mode of same-sex relationality," and cites articles such as the October 5, 2001, *Times of London* feature "Repressed Homosexuality?" and the Associated Press's reference to Afghanistan as "Babylon with burqas, Sodom and Gomorrah with sand." In the LGBTIQ media, Skier identifies PlanetOut as going "out of its way to embrace same-sex sexuality in Afghanistan," while "LGNY [New York's Lesbian and Gay newspaper] makes a point to distance gay and lesbian sexual identities from this mode of relationality." Using different approaches, Skier argues, both news outlets work toward "the same goal of promoting Euro-American gay and lesbian identity" (17). For articles cited by Skier, see Griffin, "The Taleban"; Knickmeyer, "Vice Creeps Back."

32. Reporting on queer Muslims includes Gay.com UK, "Gay Muslims"; Bull, "Gay, Muslim, and Scared"; R. Smith, "More Acceptance." An earlier piece is Goldman, "Gay Muslims." Queer Muslim self-representations include Faisal Alam, "Remem-

bering September 11th"; and Frameline, "I Exist." Along with Al-Fatiha, there is Queer Jihad, "Queer Jihad." "Queer Jihad is the queer Muslim struggle for acceptance: first, the struggle to accept ourselves as being exactly the way Allah has created us to be; and secondly, the struggle for understanding among Muslims in general," according to their website; "About Queer Jihad."

33. Sharma, "Manufacturing Dissent." For discussion of Sharma's film, see Hays, "Act of Faith." Also see Hartley Film Foundation, "In the Name of Allah"; and In the Name of Allah, "In the Name of Allah."

34. Dahir, "Queer and Muslim," 91.

35. R. Smith, "More Acceptance."

36. No Pride In Occupation, "No Pride in Occupation."

37. Sheffer and Weiss, "Violence Erupts."

38. Bacchetta, "Rescaling Transnational 'Queerdom.'"

39. See Mustikhan, "Group Fights." The description of Palestinian queer persecution includes the statement "Reports of Nazi-style treatment of openly gay Palestinians are common." Linking Palestinians to Nazis in this manner seems inappropriate; first, as it is unclear what "Nazi-style" means and its relevance to the topic, and second, that it works to position Palestinians as analogous to the most infamous murderers of Jews, rendering the Israeli-Palestinian conflict a continuation of the Shoah.

40. For details on Palestinian Queer Activism, see ASWAT—Palestinian Gay Women, "Parade to the Wall"; and Morcos, "Queering Palestinian Solidarity Activism." WorldPride 2006 was held August 6–12. Conservative Christian, Jewish, and Muslim groups protested the event, and Jerusalem officials also opposed it, especially the mayor, Uri Lupolianski. See Freedman, "'Jerusalem Will Be No More Holy'"; Buchanan, "Broad Opposition." One such protest reportedly took the form of leaflets, distributed in Orthodox neighborhoods, which offered a monetary reward to anyone who "killed a sodomist"; DiGiacomo, "Hate Leaflets." The Hezbollah-Israel war occurring during the week of WorldPride was blamed for drastically reduced attendance (from an expected several thousand to several hundred). The war was also faulted for the cancellation of the parade scheduled for August 10: city police denied the necessary permit, citing an inability to guarantee the safety of the participants due to a lack of manpower caused by the war; Wilcox, "WorldPride Denied Parade Permit." This comes after WorldPride in Jerusalem was canceled in 2005 due to Israel's withdrawal from Gaza. Jerusalem Open House, the host organization for WorldPride 2006, held a demonstration at a gate separating Jerusalem from Bethlehem in order to "let [Palestinian Jerusalem Open House members, barred from attending any WorldPride events] know we haven't forgotten them," according to one Jerusalem Open House member; Zeesil, "Jerusalem WorldPride." The ubiquitous Michael Luongo, for his part, claims that the protest on the 10th (held as a replacement for the parade) was "hijacked" by "anti-war activists"; "WorldPride."

41. OutRage! "Press Photos." For commentary on the problematics of OutRage!'s approach, see Morcos, "Queering Palestinian Solidarity Activism."

42. Massad, "Re-Orienting Desire"; Fanon, *A Dying Colonialism*.

43. While being quite adept at finding cases of homophobic Muslim clergy, OutRage! fails to publicize or discuss British Muslim clerics' condemnations of homophobia.

See Gay.com UK, "U.K. Faith Leaders Unite." OutRage! appears to overly focus on Muslim homophobia in light of actualized violence carried out by English white supremacists. For example, white supremacists bombed a gay pub, the Admiral Duncan, in 1999. Two earlier bombings, possibly by the same perpetrators, targeted English Bangladeshi and Afro-Caribbean communities; NewsPlanet Staff, "Breaking News." Instead of focusing on grassroots coalition building, OutRage! publicly criticized Home Minister Jack Straw's meeting with members of the gay and lesbian advocacy group Stonewall, calling it "divisive" because the organization was not included; NewsPlanet Staff, "London Gay Bar Bombed."

44. Tatchell, "The New Dark Ages." Peter Tatchell is Britain's one-man gay human rights organization and solicits funds for the Peter Tatchell Human Rights Fund. His website, http://www.petertatchell.net, has a list of his "Gay and Human Rights Campaign" and the full text of "Peter Tatchell's Human Rights Report 2004." His self-referential narcissism (most blatantly found in the "Photos of Peter Tatchell" section) that dominates the site suggests that Tatchell, who claims his "direct action" campaigns are more effective that Amnesty International's work, imagines himself to be a singular liberator and missionary in a sea of ineffectual human rights organizations. Notably, it appears that Tatchell has moved on from OutRage!, as the site no longer exists. His activities can be found at "Peter Tatchell Human Rights Fund" and "Peter Tatchell: Gay and Human Rights Campaigns."

45. Tatchell, "The Rise of Islamic Fundamentalism." As a precursor to this press release, Tatchell wrote an article entitled "Islamic Fundamentalism in Britain." He takes this opportunity to warn that "Islamic homophobia in Britain is not limited to the Asian and Arab communities" but that the "black militant Nation of Islam" is another threat to queers. Another example of the perception of the threat that Muslim men pose to homosexuals can be found in coverage of efforts to combat hate crimes against the Dutch LGBTQ community, in which "men of possible Moroccan descent" are the only group mentioned as perpetrators of homophobic hate crimes. See PlanetOut Network, "Amsterdam Police." Discussions of Muslim homophobia in Europe are frequently tied to the failure of Muslim immigrants to assimilate or, in the words of the above article, "integrate." In these formulations, homophobic violence by Arabs/Muslims/foreigners is automatically tied to their religion, while Western integration offers a tolerant culture in which LGBTQs would have no fear of violence.

46. Livingstone et al., "The Fight against Oppression and Islamophobia."

47. OutRage!, "Muslim Cleric Says."

48. OutRage!, "Press Photos."

49. BBC News, "Obituary: Pim Fortuyn"; *New York Times*, "A Million Votes."

50. Yoshi Furuhashi, "A 'Clash of Civilizations.'"

51. S. Roy, "Can Gay Marriage Protect Europe."

52. This phenomenon is not limited to queer politics, as noted by Scroggins in "The Dutch-Muslim Culture War": "In what appears to be a Europe-wide pattern, some feminists are aligning themselves with the anti-immigrant right against their former multiculturalist allies on the left. Joining them in this exodus to the right are gay activists, who blame Muslim immigrants for the rising number of attacks on gay couples" (22).

53. OutRage!, "Terrorist Danger." The press release opens with a quote from the Out-Rage! leader Peter Tatchell: "Gay venues could be bombed by Islamic terrorists. All gay bars and clubs should introduce bag and body searches. Muslim fundamentalists have a violent hatred of lesbians and gay men. They believe we should be killed. Our community could be their next target. This is no time for complacency." Tatchell employs scare tactics that have become an all too familiar part of the war on terror, calling on gays to defend themselves against the Muslim threat. The warning is particularly interesting as it was posted on the same day that the United States convicted Eric Rudolph of the February 1997 bombing of the Otherside Lounge, a gay bar in Atlanta, Georgia, along with the bombings of two abortion clinics and at the 1996 Atlanta Olympic Games. Rudolph's conviction does not seem to have provoked a similar response to that of OutRage! among U.S. LGBT organizations. Instead of calling for a response to violent hatred of the queer community that is presumably based in American Christian conservatism, the article reports that a spokesman for the Human Rights Campaign (Jay Smith Brown), when asked if religious conservatives were in any way responsible for Rudolph's violence, replied, "We need to foster a dialogue of honesty and understanding and not a dialogue of hate and vitriol. Both sides of the debate should be responsible to bringing the other to a place of positive dialogue." See Curtis, "Gay Bar Bomber Eric Rudolph."

54. See Lunsing, "Islam versus Homosexuality."

55. S. Ahmed, *The Cultural Politics of Emotion*, 151, 152.

56. Mahmood, *Politics of Piety*, 9.

57. C. J. Cohen, "Punks, Bulldaggers."

58. Chow, *The Protestant Ethnic*, 3, 2–3.

59. Koshy, "Morphing Race into Ethnicity," 154, 156.

60. Ibid., 181, 155–56, 186.

61. Foucault, "*Society Must Be Defended*," 255.

62. Koshy, "Morphing Race into Ethnicity," 193.

63. S. Ahmed, *The Cultural Politics of Emotion*, 130–31; Bauman, *Wasted Lives*, 104.

64. Nast, "Queer Patriarchies," 878.

65. D'Emilio, "Capitalism and Gay Identity," 100–113.

66. Pellegrini, "Commodity Capitalism," 137.

67. Koshy, "Morphing Race into Ethnicity," 155–56.

68. Duggan, excerpt from *The End of Marriage*.

69. Duggan, "Holy Matrimony!," 16. This privatization is reflected in the explicit promotion of marriage in Bill Clinton's 1996 welfare reform provisions and extended by Bush's $1.5 billion package "to be used to hire counselors and offer classes in marital harmony." Women thus are dependent on men for economic support while tending to other dependents: children as well as elderly and disabled family members. These married couple households then absolve the state of responsibility for the welfare of single-parent households, while unpaid women become responsible for numerous defunct social services (child care, disability, home nursing), in essence privatizing welfare services.

70. Duggan, "Holy Matrimony!," 16.

71. Duggan, excerpt from *The End of Marriage*; see also Audre Lorde Project, *Communities*

at a Crossroads. The research conducted by the Audre Lorde Project examines the relationship between the heterosexualization of immigrant families through family reunification policies and welfare reform. For a sustained analysis of this research, see Reddy, "Asian Diasporas, Neoliberalism, and Family."

72. For discussions of George W. Bush's attempts at gaining African American support through his opposition to same-sex marriage, see Carnes, "Wooing the Faithful"; and Knippenberg, "The Long and Winding Road."

73. Nast, "Queer Patriarchies," 881.

74. Nast, "Prologue," 839. Nast's use of the term "patriarchy" is slightly odd, as it has been heavily problematized by U.S. Third World feminists of color and poststructuralist feminists seeking to destabilize its universalizing assumptions.

75. Duggan, "The New Homonormativity," 178–94.

76. Nast argues that the historical capital accumulation of white male privilege enables an assumed virility for white gay men "by differentially profitable engagement in market-based investments and transactions vis-à-vis women and persons of color and, in some cases, heterosexually identified elite white men." While this ability to consume is often hailed as the result of "the general lack of dependents," Nast notes that biological reproduction can be enacted through the purchase of wombs and transnational adoption. "Crudely put, paternity is acquired through the (re)assumption of breadwinner status and paternal authority"; "Queer Patriarchies," 878, 879–80.

77. Eng, "Transnational Adoption," 1, 6, 7, 3, 7.

78. Chow, *The Protestant Ethnic*, 14. In another critique of queer liberalism, Paola Bacchetta problematizes dominant configurations of "transnational queerdom" that privilege the activities of consumer queers (queer tourism), queer scholars, ("anthroqueer studies," for example), and activist queers (those involved in global NGO work and who are "national subjects who speak in transnational forums"); "Rescaling Transnational 'Queerdom,'" 951.

79. On the self-proclaimed political left, for example, Michael Moore's *Fahrenheit 911* is replete with "shades of Islamophobia" only faintly audible amid his roaring polemic against the (G. W.) Bush administration; Chari, "F 9/11," 908. Another example is the gay playwright Tony Kushner's critically acclaimed *Homebody/Kabul*, written before September 11, 2001, and staged in New York City and San Francisco shortly thereafter, deemed by Patrick Corcoran an example of "Orientalism with a liberal face." See Corcoran, "Ego Tourism." See also Minwalla, "Tony Kushner's *Homebody/Kabul.*"

   For some sectors, the renewed vigor of a political left is thus incumbent upon the reproduction of racial divides between whites and people of color, who disavow, for these very reasons, interpellation by a fabricated left. Less mainstream forums have used race not only as a critical intervention into white antiwar spaces, but also as a primary organizing structure meant to superintend localities such as neighborhoods, communities, church-based affiliations, and educational forums. Yet many of these efforts tend to understand their constituencies as singularly heterosexual. See Bloom et al., "An Open Letter." The letter begins, "Dear Sisters and Brothers."

80. Chow, *The Protestant Ethnic*, 11.

81. Butler, "Sexual Inversions," 85.

82. Foucault, *"Society Must Be Defended,"* 244.

83. Butler, "Sexual Inversions," 81–98.

84. In tracing the tenor of contemporary biopolitics in an age of terror, I am informed by the recent theoretical work of postcolonial and transnational scholars, including that of Inderpal Grewal (the convergences of biopolitics and geopolitics in neoliberalism), Michael Hardt and Antonio Negri (biopolitical production), Patricia Clough (biopolitical affect economies), Gilles Deleuze (biopolitical control societies), and Achille Mbembe (biopolitics and necropolitics): Grewal, *Transnational America*; Hardt and Negri, *Empire*; Deleuze, *Negotiations*; Deleuze and Guattari, *A Thousand Plateaus*; Clough, "The Affective Turn"; Mbembe, "Necropolitics." For my point of departure I am borrowing in part from a question posed by Eugene Thacker, who asks, "How do we understand Foucault's concept of biopolitics after Foucault? How has the concept of biopolitics been transformed in the current context?"; *The Global Genome*, 22. But I am also following the lead of a March 2006 conference hosted by Patricia Clough at the CUNY Graduate Center in New York City titled "Beyond Biopolitics."

85. Mbembe, "Necropolitics," 12.

86. Chow, *The Protestant Ethnic*, 9.

87. Foucault, *"Society Must Be Defended,"* 247, 248.

88. Mbembe, "Necropolitics," 40.

89. Foucault, *"Society Must Be Defended,"* 243, 249, 257.

90. Chow, *The Protestant Ethnic*, 6–7.

91. For a cogent analysis of Foucault's genealogical tracing of the analytics of race and sex, and the implications of their intersections, see McWhorter, "Sex, Race, and Biopower."

92. For examples of postcolonial scholarship that is attentive to sexuality beyond reproductive heterosexuality, see Hayes, *Queer Nations*; McClintock, *Imperial Leather*; the collection *Postcolonial, Queer* edited by Hawley; the collection *Postcolonial and Queer Theories*, edited by Hawley; the collection *Queering India*, edited by Vanita; Patel, "Homely Housewives Run Amok"; Arondekar, "Without a Trace" and "Border/Line Sex"; Najmabadi, *Women with Mustaches*.

93. See Stoler, *Race and the Education of Desire*. Stoler's work is groundbreaking in its discussion of biopolitics and colonialism, particularly in regard to the use of colonies as practice sites for what Foucault identifies as biopower in Europe. See page 129, footnote 93 for Stoler's comment on the centrality of heterosexuality to her argument, the "evil" of homosexuality as a racializing discourse, and the dearth of archival sources that might enable a deeper reading of nonnormative sexual figures such as the "perverse adult."

94. Butler, "Sexual Inversions," 82.

95. Mbembe, "Necropolitics," 11–40.

1. the sexuality of terrorism

An earlier version of this chapter was previously published under the title "Mapping U.S. Homonormativities," *Gender, Place, and Culture: A Journal of Feminist Geography* 13. 1 (February 2006): 67–88.

1. See Halbfinger, "Veteran Battles Charge," for reporting on Saxby Chambliss's television advertisement that accused the triple amputee Vietnam veteran incumbent Max Cleland of being unpatriotic through the usage of images of Osama Bin Laden and Saddam Hussein. On Hussein, see Driscoll, "Reverse Postcoloniality," 71.

2. LeCarré, "A War We Cannot Win." For further tracking of media discussions of bin Laden's supposed effeminacy, see Collar, "Responding to Sexual Stereotypes."

3. Volpp, "The Citizen and the Terrorist," 1576.

4. Puar and Rai, "Monster, Terrorist, Fag."

5. Duggan, "The New Homonormativity," 179.

6. Gregory, *The Colonial Present*, 17.

7. Judy Kuriansky quoted in Richard, "War and Sex," 4.

8. Falwell's and Robertson's comments were so inflammatory that Congressman Barney Frank's criticism was echoed by President George W. Bush, as well as the conservative talking heads Rush Limbaugh and Arianna Huffington; D. Allen, "Falwell from Grace."

9. On negotiations for compensation for gay and lesbian partners of people killed in the events of September 11, 2001, see Gay Today and Lambda Legal Defense Fund, "Government Keeps Door Open," which states that "Lambda Legal Defense and Education Fund has welcomed as 'encouraging' new federal regulations that open the door to compensation for surviving partners of lesbians and gay men killed in the September 11 attacks, but expressed disappointment that those partners were not explicitly recognized as spouses are." Also see Associated Press, "Gay Partners." In response to the marginalization of gay and lesbian surviving partners, the two major gay and lesbian Democratic and Republic groups, the National Stonewall Democrats and the Log Cabin Republicans, issued a joint letter demanding that gay and lesbian partners receive equal compensation. Rich Tafel was quoted as stating, "The issue of supporting all the families who were devastated by these attacks on America is so important that there should be no divisions between us. . . . We are a united community in support of our families in need, speaking with one voice in this joint action today"; Musbach, "Gay Politicos Unite."

   While some responses to difficulties in obtaining federal compensation kept rather closely to the details of ways in which gay and lesbian surviving partners faced an increasingly complex application process (Quittner, "New Hurdles"), other writers chose different ways of expressing their frustrations. John Aravosis's "9/11 Fund to Discriminate against Gays" sets up his discussion of barriers to gay and lesbian partner compensation through a discussion of Mark Bingham's heroics on September 11, 2001. Despite the fact that Bingham did not leave behind a partner, Aravosis claims that through the declaration by the head of the September 11th Victim Compensation Fund, Kenneth Feinberg, state laws on gay and lesbian partnership recognition would be used to decide who received compensation: "Mark Bingham (in addition to other gay heroes of September 11) is now officially being declared a lesser kind of hero because he was gay." Aravosis moves from claiming Bingham's patriotism as the rationale for granting gay and lesbian partners compensation to an attack on undocumented migrants and their partners. He declares, "Even illegal aliens, who aren't American citizens and who are in the U.S. in violation of federal law, will receive benefits. Feinberg even says that the Attorney General has promised that if undocumented aliens come forward, they won't be kicked out of the country, and their employers won't be penalized." While being distressed at the lesser valuing of gay and lesbian relationships compared to those of heterosexuals, Aravosis uses xenophobic logic to push his argument as one in which gays and lesbians are further devalued when (presumably heterosexual) undocumented migrants are not threatened with deportation when they seek to be compensated for the loss of their loved ones. Finally, in a homonationalist vein, Aravosis frames the homophobic policy of Feinberg in terms of patriotic gay Americans and their survivors versus "Mohammad Atta and his band of thieves."

Notably, New York governor Pataki on October 17, 2002, decided to extend the granting of equal benefits to gay and lesbian partners of victims of the events of September 11, 2001, to all gay and lesbian surviving partners of homicide victims. This extension was received as a sign of growing mainstream acceptance of homosexuals by the representatives from LGBTQ rights organizations such as Empire State Pride and the NYC Gay and Lesbian Anti-Violence Project; Empire State Pride Agenda, "NY State Crime Victims Board."

Gay and lesbian partnerships generally faced more obstacles as a result of the U.S. response to the events of September 11, as reported by Drinkwater, "Bi-national Couples." According to Drinkwater:

> In the aftermath of the terrorist attacks on Sept. 11, the situation for gay and lesbian Americans in relationships with non-resident foreign nationals has quickly changed from bad to nightmarish. . . . Gay and lesbian U.S. citizens, unlike their straight counterparts, have no legal right to sponsor foreign partners for U.S. residency or visas—a situation that in the best of times has forced gay couples to live apart or have the non-resident partner remain illegally in the country. Under the mounting pressure of a recession and the post-attack overhaul of U.S. immigration laws, the few legal loopholes bi-national same-sex couples managed to find—including the availability of H-1B work visas—may quickly be tightened.

10. See Dotinga, "Despite Emergency." Dotinga quotes Deborah Verkouw, spokeswoman for the Blood Centers of the Pacific, which serve the San Francisco Bay Area: "People feel helpless when buildings are blown up, and they want to help." This patriotic framing continued in another form as the *Village Voice* columnist Michael Musto, after writing about the continued ban, received "nasty e-mails saying: 'Now's not the time to quibble about gay rights. Now is when we have to concentrate on fighting the 'war,' " as reported by Wockner, "The Wockner Wire."

11. For a particularly outstanding example of this type of narrative, see Gorton, "Gay Rights." His essay describes that after September 11, "A new national mood, steeped in old-fashioned patriotism, surged everywhere, including in GLBT neighborhoods,

where American flags replaced rainbow flags on display. The new patriotism has shown itself to be remarkably inclusive, not only of gays and lesbians, but also of Muslim-Americans: the early spike in the number of hate crimes against Americans of Middle-Eastern origin has tapered off" (16). Additionally, Gorton states, "The Taliban's theocratic rulers have mostly occupied themselves with debating questions as to whether the proper punishment for homosexuality should be live burial or being dropped from a tall building. (The U.S. bombing campaigns have already relieved them of this quandary!)" (17). Contrary to Gorton's description of this "new" and yet "old-fashioned patriotism," some people did not share these sentiments. Douglas Sadownick in a coauthored manifesto, "War Fever and Gay Resistance," that appears in the same issue of *Gay and Lesbian Review* states, "I have been feeling just as outraged by the flag waving as by the 'cowardly' acts of terrorists" (26). Sadownick, Chris Kilbourne, and Wendell Jones collectively ask, "Where are the queer voices protesting the chauvinistic spiral of American national grieving, patriotic war-mongering, and pious slogans that know little dissent or actual reason following the September 11 terrorist attacks? And why is it so many gay people are buying into the false choice presented by the mass media to take sides in this extraordinary polarization between the 'good, freedom-loving victims' and the 'evil, cowardly terrorists'?" (26).

12. Reporting on gay and lesbian heroism included Mubarak Dahir's gay press article and cover story, both titled "Our Heroes." On media coverage of gays and lesbians in regard to the events of September 11, see the Gay and Lesbian Alliance against Defamation, "Heroes and Victims of 9-11-01."

13. For coverage of discussions on "Don't Ask, Don't Tell" and the possible suspension of the ban after the events of September 11, see Busbach, "Military Readies to Suspend Gay Discharges"; and Bull, "'Don't Ask, Don't Tell' Goes to War."

14. On fired linguists, see Johnson, "Military Gay Linguist Firings Escalate"; Cyphers, "Discharged Gay Linguist Speaks"; Schindler, "Gay Linguist Discharges Continue"; and Feingold, "Statement on the Discharge of Gay Linguists." Patrick Letellier's "Poll: Overwhelming Support for Gays in the Military" quotes John Aravosis: "Apparently, the Bush administration thinks the war on terror should take second place to the war on homosexuals" in a response to the firings.

Another explanation for the decline in military discharges is that fewer members may actually be revealing their sexual orientation, which in the past has resulted in 80 percent of discharges (the other 20 percent being those who are caught in compromising sexual situations or are being investigated for misconduct). There is also the possibility that fewer people are being dismissed even when they do reveal this information. See Nieves and Tyson, "Fewer Gays Being Discharged." The reported decline in discharges was contradicted a month later by Dan Kerman's report, "Military Gay Discharges Spiked in 2001." Kerman cites a Servicemembers Legal Defense Network report, "Conduct Unbecoming," that found a significant increase in discharges by the Pentagon and connected the discharges with a rise in antigay harassment. Military handling of gay and lesbian military servicemembers continued to be disjointed, as the experience of Roy Hill, a three-year navy medic, demonstrates. According to Tom Musbach, the navy refused to discharge Hill after he came out to his superiors in June 2001 and felt unsafe in the "anti-gay climate" where he was stationed; "Navy Refuses to Discharge Gay Member."

15. A question posed to LGBTQ organizers in New York City shortly after September 11 was why "New York City's lesbian, gay, bisexual and transgender community remained mostly silent and invisible and did not publicly, and collectively, react to the events"; TheGully.com, "Why Queers Were Silent." Calling the silence on political issues a "queer black hole," Ana Simo stated, "The message sent was that being queer is a highly specialized existential state. One that is suspended during emergencies"; "Civic Life and Death." The director of the New York Lesbian, Gay, Bisexual, Transgender Community Center, Richard Burns, challenged the characterization of silence, listing a string of emergency and logistical, but not political, responses: sending medical providers to the hospitals, setting up a water station, providing crisis counseling. At the Lesbian Gay Bisexual Transgender Community Center (New York) vigil and gathering on October 1, 2001, cosponsored by over eighty groups, there was not one mention by Kate Clinton (or other speakers) of the pending invasion of Afghanistan, nor of the growing list of hate crime victims; Clinton, " 'In Memoriam.' " Andres Duque, the coordinator of Mano a Mano (a coalition of New York Latino LGBTQ organizations), stated, "People of color queer organizing does not react to LGBT issues, specifically, but reacts to wider social issues. We've learned to avoid speaking about how the LGBT movement is feeling because we have taught ourselves to talk about general issues. . . . Also, some people were waiting to see the ramifications of things and how things reacted. We [the LGBT community] are so segmented that it's difficult to get a statement that is powerful and acceptable." He also noted that queer people of color had regrouped at several previously planned meetings on racial justice; TheGully.com, "Why Queers Were Silent."

16. In "Butching Up for Victory," Richard Goldstein notes a similar dynamic taking hold in the presidential elections, particularly with Howard Dean, about whom he asks, "Can a Democrat be an alpha male?" (13).

17. Clancy Nolan's article "Patriotic Pride" serves both as a description and an example of the upsurge in pride march patriotism. Nolan quotes the North Carolina Gay Pride parade organizer Keith Hayes: "At this moment, the parade needs to express national feelings, not just gay feelings. . . . We need to sound this national note." According to Nolan, "The march will begin with the National Anthem, and you may see as many American flags as rainbows and pink triangles." Nolan does remark that "there is inescapable irony in patriotic images leading a parade that began as criticism of America's stance on gay-rights issues. . . . Paula Austin, director of the North Carolina Lambda Youth Network . . . is concerned with, in her words, 'the push to mainstream and assimilate, led by some queer organizations that are primarily white and middle-class.' " While Nolan is sympathetic to Austin's concerns, the article ends with a dichotomous reading of the situation: "You can't help but wonder what's sacrificed in compromising a celebration of diversity and a demand for recognition in order to stand with mainstream America."

18. This line of argument can be traced back to the 1991 Gulf War. Hugh Coyle writes, "For a period during the war itself, I wondered why I didn't feel more concerned about the increasing threat of terrorism. . . . International terrorism didn't bother me

much because as a gay man, I'm growing accustomed to living in a terrorist state right here at home. Our community has had its meeting places stoned, bombed, and burned; our gay brothers and lesbian sisters have been targeted for brutal beatings; verbal harassment in the form of anti-gay slurs and slogans is on the rise in America once again"; "Terrorism Nothing New to Us." Additionally, articles such as Bill Ghent's "Tragedy Changed Gay Climate" suggest that responses to September 11 have included unexpected kindness on the part of Republicans and "traditionally conservative relief organizations." Ghent does qualify his description by replaying ideas of what areas of the United States are more gay-friendly than others: "Certainly, not all gay-rights successes after September 11 can be attributed to America's heightened sense of community. And more-liberal areas of the country have been quicker than, say, Virginia to reach out to gay survivors."

19. Dahir, "Stop Using Gay 'Liberation' as a War Guise." Dahir hammers at several hypocritical stances being adopted by those LGBTIQ people in favor of the war as well as informing the political rhetoric of conversion. Noting that the "forces that are supposedly emancipating our downtrodden GLBT brethren are themselves hyper-homophobic," he asks, "How can anyone seriously argue that the United States military is an instrument for GLBT liberation?" As ludicrous as the question appears, according to Dahir "gay hawks" have pointed out the oppression of homosexuality by regimes in Syria and Iraq while conveniently forgetting those in Saudi Arabia and Egypt. Claiming that the lives of gays and lesbians in Iraq will change very little regardless of the ousting of Hussein, Dahir writes, "The final and perhaps most personally infuriating aspect of the hypocrisy around the argument that we are invading foreign countries in the interest of freeing gay people is the way we treat gay Arabs and gay Muslims here in the United States." A similar narrative around the ongoing invasion and occupation of Afghanistan has been produced in the mainstream gay press. For example, see Chibbaro, "New Afghan Rulers."

20. The NGLTF and the Human Rights Campaign Fund were criticized for their lack of response after September 11 to the erosion of civil liberties and the "crusade abroad" and for their lack of presence at initial national antiwar protests in Washington, D.C., in fall 2001 by the Radical Women and Freedom Socialist Party, although in the same publication they declare, "Screw the USA Patriot Act! Our homeland is the *world*!"; "We're Here." Critiques about NGLTF's response to the wars in Afghanistan and Iraq continued in 2002 and 2003. Faisal Alam of Al-Fatiha, in response to the proposed NGLTF press conference "to address the pending war against Iraq" and other issues at its annual Creating Change conference, stated, "We urge NGLTF and other justice-seeking LGBT organizations to take a firm and vocal stance against the war, while standing firm in its commitment to social justice"; Al-Fatiha, "Queer Rights Leaders." Confusion about whether or not the NGLTF had joined the Win Without War coalition circulated in early 2003, after the publication of David Mariner's article "NLGTF Not a Win Without War Coalition Member." Mariner states that while the NGLTF claimed that they had joined the coalition, "Lynn Erskine, a staff member with Win Without War, said NGLTF is not a coalition member. . . . NGLTF has never approached Win Without War about joining the coalition." In response, the NGLTF issued a statement, "Response to Recent False Allegations Re-

garding NGLTF's Position against the War," stating that it had "made its position against the war and in support of the coalition statement eminently clear," and arguing that not only was it misrepresented in Mariner's article, but Win Without War had not responded effectively to NGLTF's "good faith actions to advise the Win Without War coalition founders that it desired to join the coalition. . . . On January 30th, the newly-hired staff member of the Win Without War coalition advised NGLTF that a formal process exists for 'officially' joining the coalition and she assured NGLTF that she anticipated no problems with NGLTF being approved as an 'official' member of the coalition," and that tenemos.net "advised the NGLTF Media Manager . . . that the deadline for response was Friday, January 31st. Yet tenemos.net posted its story on Thursday, January 30th, without giving NGLTF an opportunity to comment." Finally, David Mariner sent out an e-mail responding to the NGLTF press release, saying, "While the NGLTF communications person Sherri Lunn has yet to call me back or respond to my e-mails, they went ahead and sent out a press release today. I feel kinda bummed about this. . . . And here is the truth in this particular matter: They said they were a member of the coalition. They are not a member of the coalition. I'm very glad they contacted the coalition today to join, and I hope they will take a more active role in opposing the war in Iraq"; "NGLTF Response to Temenos Article."

An article by the historian and activist Michael Bronski, "Gay Goes Mainstream," published in January 2006 in the *Boston Phoenix*, declares that a new wave of queer activism is actually returning to the gay movement's foundational origins of multi-issue, broad-based politics of social change. Noting that "many pockets of the organized queer community are taking policy stands on the potential war," Bronski compares this to the silence of queer organizers during the 1991 Gulf War. At that time, the National Gay and Lesbian Task Force, the only national gay group to issue a statement against the war, expressed concern about gays and lesbians in the armed forces and the reduction of spending on the AIDS crisis. The Task Force was the target of much criticism and scorn for commenting on a national debate that was not a "gay issue." It should be noted that in 1991 Urvashi Vaid was the director of NGLTF's policy institute. Commenting on the current antiwar stance of NGLTF, the Metropolitan Community Church, the Lavender Green Caucus, and the Chicago Anti-Bashing Network, Bronski claims that the act of taking "positions on a matter of public policy that is not 'gay'" overturns three decades of "gay-issue" organizing.

Due to the same rationale that has been used to shunt to the side issues of queer sexuality in feminist and antiracism organizing (in other words, the proclamation that the antiwar effort is diluting energy from other, more important concerns), major national LGBT organizations have been reluctant to address the war. In an article titled "Capital Letters: Highlighting the Q in Iraq," Hastings Wyman argues, "For gay groups such as HRC, NGLTF, and others to take a position on a major issue that affects gay people no differently from the rest of society ultimately divides our community, dilutes our resources, and risks undermining our standing with the public."

21. Garry, "GLAAD Statement." On the initial response to the photo by groups such as Gay and Lesbian Alliance against Defamation (GLAAD) and Servicemembers Legal

Defense Network (SLDN), which resulted in the Associated Press asking its clients to remove the photo from their work, see Dotinga, "Navy Photo Shows Antigay Slur on Bomb." The uncritical and symptomatic use of the term "hijack" in academic queer theory forums is also commented on by Hiram Perez, who writes of the University of Michigan's March 2003 Gay Shame conference, which had been described by disgruntled participants as having been "hijacked by identitarian politics" by those critical of the white gay male dominance and racial politics of the conference: "The phrase . . . condensed for me the political dynamics of establishmentarian queer theory. In the era of the 'war on terrorism' and the USA Patriot Act, the word *hijacked* invokes the rhetoric of national belonging—and not belonging. The restriction of brown bodies from queer theory's institutional spaces shares ideological underpinnings with the expulsion of brown bodies from the nation-state"; "You Can Have My Brown Body," 174. U.S. Navy Rear Admiral S. R. Pietropaoli also wrote a letter to the Human Rights Campaign (which seems to not have issued a public response to the photograph, instead making a phone call to the navy), stating, "Clearly the photograph in question failed to meet our standards"; Brooke, "Clear Violation."

22. On drops in AIDS funding, see Siu, "Sept. 11 Aftermath." On the threat that the war in Iraq posed to AIDS funding, see Riley, "How War Imperils the Fight against AIDS." For a framing of battling HIV/AIDS in the language of "national security," see Musbach, "Group Warns Bush."

23. Metropolitan Community Churches, "A Call for Peaceful Resolution."

24. See Al-Fatiha's press releases, "LGBTQ Muslims Condemn Terrorist Attack" and "LGBTQ Muslims Express Concerns."

25. The Audre Lorde Project and the LGBT unit of the American Friends Service Committee jointly released "An Open Letter to Lesbian Gay Bisexual Two-Spirit and Transgender People of Color Communities Opposing War." Since its release in January 2003, hundreds of organizations and individuals across the country have signed the statement, which claims that the war on terrorism is a queer issue because of increased violence, reinstitutionalization of racial profiling, deprioritization of human needs and social programs, the increasing militarization of the Immigation and Naturalization Service, and attacks on civil and human rights.

On May 15, 2003, Queers for Peace and Justice initiated a "Call to Action—for Lesbian, Gay, Bi, Two-Spirit, Trans and Intersex and Queer Activists to 'Come Out against the War at home and abroad' at LGBT Pride Events across the country"; "LGBT Call to Action." According to Shawn Luby of the North Carolina Lambda Youth Network, as quoted by United for a Fair Economy's Autumn Leonard et al., "September 11th has actually made it pretty clear that our organization [a progressive multi-issue queer group] is not involved in the same communities as the white Gay and Lesbian communities. . . . It has strengthened [our] connections with low-income organizations and other social justice groups led by folks of color"; "Organizing after September 11." For media coverage, see Gerber, "Activists Mobilize."

26. I explore these issues of organizational affiliation at length in a forthcoming video on progressive South Asian organizing in New York City titled *India Shining*.

27. Khan, "Who Pays the Price of War?," 15, 16. Other sources for Khan's analysis are her interview with Michael Bronski: "Surina Khan, A Pakistani Advocate" and

"Bombing Afghanistan." For further information on the Cairo 52, see the Al-Fatiha press release, "Al-Fatiha Calls for a Second Day of Action"; Asher, "War Concerns"; Johnson, "Group" and "Frank Attacks Bush's Silence"; and Bendersky, "'Cairo 52' Trial Ends." Bendersky includes the following: "Also in question is the membership of Sherif Farhat, the lead defendant in the case, in the Islamic terrorist group Jihad. . . . Farhat's lawyer argues that his client could not be both a member of Jihad and be gay, since homosexuality is shunned in Islam. M. Faisal Alam, of the gay muslim group Al-Fatiha, called the 'insinuation' that Farhat is a member of the Islamic Jihad 'an excuse to justify the trial, especially in light of the new 'war on terrorism.'"

28. Ahmad, "Homeland Insecurity," 108.

29. New York's Anti-Violence Project (AVP), Lambda, and the Empire State Pride Agenda focused solely on same-sex surviving partner benefits. For coverage on New York's struggles over partnership benefits, see Humm, "The Rights of Same-Sex Partners." The definition of acts of hate-crime violence by the NY AVP included the victims of the World Trade Center, but not racial backlash attacks against South Asians, Arab Americans, and Muslims, a significant percentage of which have been LGBTQ folks. As such the NY AVP played into dominant national sentiment and opinion regarding hate crimes post-9/11, particularly as these crimes received almost no media attention. In general, community-based people of color organizations have borne the responsibility of offering support and services to victims of hate crimes. While organizations such as DRUM (for working-class South Asians in Queens and Brooklyn) and Manavi (dealing with violence against South Asian women and based in New Jersey) set up help-lines almost immediately and did extra outreach to South Asian and Muslim LGBTQ folks, just recently the Asian American Legal and Defense Education Fund set up a special help-line for LGBTQ victims of hate crimes, differentiating these from their regular help-line and addressing their queer Asian constituency. The NY AVP did not address its people of color constituency by reaching out to queer people of color who experienced backlash violence. These organizing rubrics not only reiterated the general racism of mainstreamed LGBTQ communities and organizations, they also provided openings for queer people of color to forge new links, work with progressive and mainstream organizations built through racial, ethnic, and religious identities, and foster deeper connections with South Asian and Muslim organizations that perhaps did not have any sexuality-specific outreach or programming.

Antigay hate crimes continue to be an issue in the post-9/11 era despite mainstream optimism about America's tolerance for queers. According to Becky Lee's article "The Wars We Are Still Fighting" in the Audre Lorde Project spring 2004 *ColorLife!* publication, the *Anti-Lesbian, Gay, Bisexual and Transgender Violence in 2002: A Report of the National Coalition of Anti-Violence Programs* demonstrated that

> there was a substantial increase from the previous year in the number of reported incidents of violence against LGBT People of Color. Reported violence against LGBT Arab or Middle Eastern identified people increased 26%; violence against Latino/a LGBT identified people increased 24%; and there was a 244% increase in violence against LGBT people identifying as "Other" if they did not identify with the racial and

ethnic groups listed on the coalition's intake sheet. The report affirms, "Further exploration of the identity of those identifying as 'Other,' indicates that a significant number of them belong to South Asian, African and other communities. . . . They also tended to represent communities especially impacted by attention, bias and law enforcement scrutiny since September 11, 2001."

The National Coalition of Anti-Violence Programs's report is available on their website. The increase of violence is corroborated by other sources, including Lisotta, "Los Angeles Reports Rise in Hate Crimes."

30. Bingham is profiled in numerous media articles; for example, see Barrett, "This is Mark Bingham," an article which highlights Bingham's interest in rugby. Barrett quotes Todd Sarner: " 'I keep having this image from watching Mark play rugby a couple of years ago,' he adds. 'His team had just kicked the ball, and there were probably 15 people between Mark and the guy who caught it. And I just remember Mark doing something I've seen him do a thousand times—duck down his head and go through the crowd fearlessly, like he wasn't even there, and tackle that guy.' " According to Barrett's article, Bingham "supported John McCain's 2000 presidential bid, for instance despite the Arizona senator's stand on gay issues—he opposes hate-crimes legislation and the Employment Non-Discrimination Act." McCain spoke at Bingham's funeral: " 'I know he (Bingham) was a good son and friend, a good rugby player, a good American and an extraordinary human being,' the senator said. 'He supported me, and his support now ranks among the greatest honors of my life. I wish I had known before Sept. 11 just how great an honor his trust in me was. I wish I could have thanked him for it more profusely than time and circumstances allowed' "; Musbach, "Sen. McCain Pays Tribute." Almost a year after Bingham's death San Francisco honored him by renaming a Castro gymnasium, as reported by Bendersky, "San Francisco Honors Mark Bingham." Bendersky's article concludes with a borrowed quote: " 'He was such an athletic, gung-ho guy,' Alice Hoglan, Bingham's mother, told the San Francisco Chronicle in August. 'I think it was those things that helped him and other passengers gain control of the plane.' "

31. Puar and Rai, "Monster, Terrorist, Fag"; Weinstein, "Gay Press Says: 'God Bless GLBT America.' " Weinstein discusses not only the "obsession to try and figure out how many were queer" of those who died in the events of September 11, but the willingness to take on the "slogan 'United We Stand' " by "the gay press mimicking the mainstream press." For an example of homonormative press, see Paul Varnell's "Why Gays Should Support the Iraq War." Varnell suggests that the impending war will happen "probably before the end of March, to avoid military operations during Iraq's hot summer," a point that is interesting in itself as U.S. military personel have now been in Iraq during the summer for three years. Varnell critiques antiwar LGBTQ arguments related to "Don't Ask, Don't Tell" and reduced funding for people living with AIDS: "These are strained arguments, the kind people make up after they have already decided what side they are on." He concludes with the statement:

To the extent gay progressives vocally oppose the war in order to ensure heterosexual progressive support for gay equality, that sounds like exactly as good a reason for all the rest of us to vocally support the war—to show moderate and conservative Americans that gays share many of their fundamental values and have the general interests of the country at heart. After all, the underlying benefit of the Iraqi war will be the pressure on neighboring Arab states to moderate and modernize, reducing their tendency to tolerate, support, or generate fundamentalist terrorism.

Varnell's argument relies on the idea of shared American values that apparently could encourage moderate and conservative Americans to stop being homophobic, in contrast to a generalized rabidly homophobic and fundamentalist Arab world. It should be noted that *Gay City News* published Varnell's piece along with a lead article titled "An Emerging Debate about War," which discusses a variety of perspectives, a "Community Groups Rally against War" call to action originated by the Audre Lorde Project and the American Friends Service Committee, and John Riley's "How War Imperils the Fight against AIDS." Two examples of progressive responses to the events of September 11 and the war on terror are Zupan and Peters, "Anti-War Protest"; and the special edition of the *Center for Lesbian and Gay Studies (CLAGS) Newsletter*, 11.3 (fall 2001), featuring articles such as "Insisting on Inquiry" by Alisa Solomon; "Beyond Blood" by Lisa Duggan; "Queer Feelings" by Ann Cvetkovich; and "The Value of Silence" by David Eng.

32. See Alexander, "Not Just (Any)*Body*"; Peterson, "Sexing Political Identities"; and Berlant and Warner, "Sex in Public." For a discussion of how queerness is produced for and through the nation-state, see Puar, "Transnational Configurations."

33. Gibson-Graham, *The End of Capitalism*, 127, 121 n. 2, 125.

34. As a counterexample: the politics of penetration in Mbembe's "Necropolitics" are profoundly phallic, but also undeniably queer, in that they do not reiterate or invert the binaried gendered rape script of globalization that Gibson-Graham are unable to dissolve. In Africa, the sovereignty of the postcolonial state is superseded by "war machines": militias and rebel movements. Regular state-run armies are replaced by private armies and security firms, whereby manpower is purchased and sold as needed and identity is evacuated of any signification or meaning; "enclave economies" dictate monetary flows. There are no sides. There are spaces of concentration and circulation, spaces of diffusion, and definitely acts and moments of penetration. But unlike the activo-passivo model, the penetration of capital comes in layers and clusters and from many chaotic trajectories.

35. Phelan, *Sexual Strangers*, 4–5.

36. I am referring primarily to Frantz Fanon's *Black Skins, White Masks*.

37. Peterson, "Sexing Political Identities," 52.

38. Alexander, "Erotic Autonomy," 65, citing Hart, *Fatal Women*, 8.

39. Foucault, *The History of Sexuality*, 45–46.

40. The White House's *National Strategy for Combating Terrorism* begins:

> Americans know that terrorism did not begin on September 11, 2001. Regrettably, its history is long and all too familiar. The first major terrorist attack on New York City's financial district, for instance, did not occur on September 11, or even with the 1993 truck bombing of the World Trade Center. It occurred September 16, 1920, when anarchists exploded a horse cart filled with dynamite near the intersections of Wall and Broad Streets, taking 40 lives and wounding about 300 others. Starting with the

assassination of President William McKinley in 1901 and continuing with the bombings of the U.S. embassies in Tanzania and Kenya in 1998 and the USS Cole in Yemen in 2000, American history in the 20th century was punctuated by terrorism. (5)

41. The Osama bin Laden expert Judith Miller describes the cell network operation:

   With a group as disparate and as decentralized as these networks . . . you can be listening and monitoring one cell and one group of the network, one part of the network that seems to be very active and seems to be preparing something, and that could actually be disinformation or a cover for another part of the network that is not being monitored. One of the hallmarks of Osama bin Laden is that he picks and chooses from the enormous range of militant groups that are affiliated with him. And if he thinks the Americans are watching, say, a cell in Italy, as we were this past year, he doesn't use or rely on a cell in Italy. He'll call on a Malaysian cell or a cell operating in Canada. ("Hunting bin Laden")

42. Butler, "Explanation and Exoneration," 179.
43. Said, "The Essential Terrorist," 158.
44. Bacchetta et al., "Transnational Feminist Practices," 305.
45. Kevin Toolis writes, "Terrorism studies are the new, new thing and graduate programs are springing up like intifada across the western world"; "Rise of the Terrorist Professors," 26.
46. Hudson, *The Sociology and Psychology of Terrorism*, 14–20.
47. Ibid., 26, 31–32. Subsequent notes to this source cited in text.
48. M. Crenshaw, "The Causes of Terrorism," 390.
49. Morgan, *The Demon Lover*, 63–65. This text also surfaces as a prominent feature in many post-9/11 women's and gender studies syllabi on war and terrorism. The class statistic has been qualified: while most terrorist leaders are well-educated and from economically secure backgrounds, many terrorist organizational recruits are the opposite: poor, un- or underemployed, and with nominal education.
50. Post, "Rewarding Fire with Fire?," 103–15, quoted in Hudson, *The Sociology and Psychology of Terrorism*, 2.
51. Toolis describes some of the early foundational moments of counterterrorism studies, originating mostly in Israel, including two seminal international antiterrorist conferences organized by Binyamin Netanyahu, brother of Johnathan Netanyahu, who was killed in the Israeli army's operation to rescue hostages in the 1976 Entebbe hijacking. See "Rise of the Terrorist Professors," 27.
52. Ibid., 26.
53. Morgan, *The Demon Lover*, 16, 139.
54. Tiger, "Rogue Males," 8. Also see Tiger's interview, "Is Manliness Really Back in Favor?"
55. Massad, "Re-Orienting Desire," 361–85. On the Orientalist literary traditions of European male travelers to North Africa, see Boone, "Vacation Cruises." See also the special issue of *Middle East Report*: Toensing, "Sexuality, Suppression, and the State."
56. Tiger, "Rogue Males," 8.
57. Another example of searching for a cultural pathology that can erase politics in

discussions of the motivations of bin Laden and Mohammed Atta is deMause, "The Childhood Origins of Terrorism." See also Borneman, "Genital Anxiety," on Mohammad Atta's obsession with his genitals. Also see C. Allen, "Return of the Guy."

58. Eisenstein, "Feminisms in the Aftermath of September 11," 86, 93.

59. Petchesky, "Phantom Towers."

60. Kimmel, "Gender, Class, and Terrorism," B11–B12. A good example of American homophobia is reflected in discussions that John Walker Lindh's father's queerness could have contributed to his becoming the "American Taliban." See LaBarbera, "Columnist."Additionally, Roche et al.'s *Time* article "The Making of John Walker Lindh," mentions that when Lindh returned from Yemen, "life at home, he soon discovered, had undergone a dramatic change. In late 1998 Frank [Lindh's father] said he was gay and moved out" (51). The next page features a discussion of Lindh's friendship with Khizar Hayat. Interestingly, after stating, "Hayat, who has a wife and four children, says he had sex with Lindh," and quoting Hayat's discussion of "liking" and "loving" Lindh, the authors interject that Hayat "has a good though not colloquial command of English" (52). It appears that the authors would prefer that Hayat describe his relationship to Lindh in more detail, an agenda that becomes more clear as they write that Lindh's teacher, Mufti Iltimas Khan, "does not discuss the nature of his relationship with Lindh, though he seems happy to talk about the young man. 'Everyone who saw him wanted to talk to him and look at him and to look at his lovely face. A very lovely face he had, John Walker.' " While the mufti does not define his relationship, the authors' quote about appreciating Lindh conversationally and in appearance works to tie his relationship with his teacher to that of his friend, both perverse interactions outside the bounds of the monogamous heterosexual family. Indeed, the authors state, "Lindh's lawyers deny that their client engaged in homosexual relationships," taking up words to describe Lindh's interactions with Hayat that Hayat seemingly does not have the knowledge of English to use (52). That Hayat could or prefers to think of his interactions with Lindh in terms of "liking" or "loving" is unallowable within the article's framing.

61. Kimmel, "Gender, Class, and Terrorism," B12.

62. Massad, "Re-Orienting Desire," 372.

63. Ehrenreich, "A Mystery of Misogyny."

64. Lila Abu-Lughod, for example, argues that the veil is a form of "portable seclusion" that symbolizes the importance of women's work in the home; "Do Muslim Women Really Need Saving?" For a discussion on the spectacle of gender and veiling, see Berger, "The Newly Veiled Woman."

65. Mahmood, *Politics of Piety*, 8.

66. Ehrenreich, "A Mystery of Misogyny."

67. Stern, "Holy Avengers."

68. Baudrillard, "The Mind of Terrorism."

69. Speaking to material realms, Nilüfer Göle offers this parallel: "The attack was an attack from within. The terrorists themselves were a product of the modern world, using modern arms, attacking modern targets. Islam was not turning against some kind of external, colonial, or occupant force of modernity. In an ironical sense, Islam was never so close to Modernity"; "Close Encounters."

70. Jakobsen, "Can Homosexuals End Western Civilization," 56, 60.

71. In 2001, Community Marketing claimed that 88 percent of the market are college graduates (as compared to a national average of 29 percent), and that an average of 54 percent took an international vacation in the prior year (45 percent in 1999), significantly higher than a national average of 9 percent. Furthermore, the growth in international travel is expected to continue to rise; visits to domestic locations are anticipated to decrease and trips to the Caribbean and East Asia will increase the most. The greatest increases are projected to be, in order, to South Africa (304 percent increase), New Zealand (262), Finland (212), Australia (211), Brazil (172), and the South Pacific Islands (165) (Community Marketing, "'A Place for Us' 2001," 15). Community Marketing reinforces its conclusions about the "Recession-Resistant" gay and lesbian market by stating, "Gay travelers, who hold over three times as many passports as their mainstream counterparts, think nothing extraordinary of going to London for a weekend of theatre, or to a party for a week in Sydney" (10).

72. Roth, "Welcoming Remarks."

73. It should be noted that 80 percent of those surveyed are men and that the demographic information represents those who attend gay and lesbian travel expos and/ or read gay magazines such as *Curve* and *The Advocate*: "It doesn't represent the whole community, but it does represent where you want your marketing dollars to go"; ibid.

74. The industry in general is uninterested in the consumption practices of queers of color, queer women, and working-class queers, and is altogether unconcerned with the productive roles of people of color, working-class queers, and immigrants employed in tourism service sectors. Furthermore, as the market has expanded globally, which locations are chosen as the latest "hot spots" and the advertising formats in which they are represented and marketed often reiterate neocolonial discourses of both travel and sexuality. In the conceptualization of a global market, both expulsion and normalization are at work, as third world locations are disciplined in narratives of exotic primitive pansexuality while more and more European, North American, and Australian cities are rounded into the modern gay urban framework. As such, gay and lesbian travel guides and the International Gay and Lesbian Expos can be read as mappings of the relationships among globalization, nationalisms, and sexuality, and as the visages of trackable sexuality, legible for global capital.

   There has been no response to gender profiling at airports. According to Riki Wilchins:

   > It occurs when a person is singled out solely because they are perceived as not conforming to gender norms. And if you are one of the millions of travelers who happen to be a little butch, a little femme, transgendered, or otherwise visibly queer, then there's a good chance it will happen to you. . . . Reports of gender profiling have flowed into GenderPAC since September 11, when airlines appropriately increased their focus on security. With the new focus came a shift in power in favor of security personnel—including the phobic few with a dislike for anyone who crosses gender lines. What we're seeing is a pattern of travelers being singled out for invasive treatment simply because they don't meet someone's ideal of a "real man" or a "real

woman." This prejudice falls disproportionately on travelers who are gay, lesbian, bisexual, transgendered, or queer. ("Airport Insecurity," 136)

75. Chasin, *Selling Out*, 101, 108–9.

76. For example, at the World Tourism Organization's 14th general assembly and the Millennium Conference of Tourism Leaders in October 2001 held in Osaka, Japan, the message was "Terrorism is the direct enemy of tourism": "Indian Prime Minister Vajpayee noted that terrorism is the foe of tourism. He said, 'Whereas terrorism feeds on intolerance and arrogance, tourism breeds tolerance and empathy. Terrorism seeks to erect walls of hatred between faiths and communities. Tourism breaks such barriers. Terrorism detests pluralism, whereas tourism celebrates it. Terrorism has no respect for human life. Tourism pays tribute to all that is beautiful in nature and in human life'"; Sakhuja, "Terrorism and Tourism."

77. Wilson, Executive Director's Report. For a discussion of the travel industry's economic downturn, see *Economist*, "A Business in Search of Customers."

78. For example, Michael T. Luongo discusses his visit to Afghanistan: "Most Americans have shunned international travel since 9/11, but for me the tragedy instilled a sense of camaraderie with war-torn areas. I felt that New York had become a war-torn city myself, so visiting another didn't seem daunting to me"; "Eroticism among Kabul's Warriors."

79. Ide, editorial.

80. Thompson, "Message from the IGLTA President."

81. Badgett, "Beyond Biased Samples." For an overview of gay and lesbian readership of mainstream and gay presses that are often the source of survey information, see also Fejes and Lennon, "Defining the Lesbian/Gay Community?"

82. Hardisty and Gluckman, "The Hoax," 209.

83. Chasin, *Selling Out*, 117.

84. This section is a significantly extended reading of an earlier version by Puar and Rai, "The Remaking of a Model Minority."

85. Driscoll, "Reverse Postcoloniality," 72.

86. Halberstam, *In a Queer Time and Place*, 37.

87. For a study of the "still agrarian South" that exemplifies a "regionalist critique of an urban-focused American gay and lesbian history," see Howard, "The Talk of the Country," 150. Also see Howard, *Men Like That*.

88. See also episode 612, where Saddam Hussein is building WMD in heaven, after having a homosexual relationship in hell with Satan, the Prince of Darkness, a storyline begun in the fourth season with episodes 410 and 411. "A Ladder to Heaven," *South Park*; "Do the Handicapped Go to Hell?," *South Park*, July 19, 2000, episode 410, written and directed by Trey Parker, Comedy Central; "Probably," *South Park*, July 26, 2000, episode 411, written and directed by Trey Parker, Comedy Central.

89. A. Roy, "The Algebra of Infinite Justice," 1.

90. Bersani, "Is the Rectum a Grave?"

91. Butler, "Sexual Inversions," 83.

92. Fanon, *A Dying Colonialism*, 57.

93. Afary and Anderson, *Foucault and the Iranian Revolution*, 138.

94. Foucault, *The History of Sexuality*, 57–58.

95. Ibid., 58.

96. Afary and Anderson, *Foucault and the Iranian Revolution*, 141–42. In their study of Foucault's thinking on Muslim sexualities, the authors trace his travels to Tunisia (as a visiting professor of philosophy in 1966–68) and his participation in "French tourist culture [that] shared similar assumptions about the openness of Arab and Middle Eastern culture on homosexuality" (141), as well as his 1978 visits to Iran, noting that many who came into contact with him thought him "naïve" (141) and were "baffled by [his] ignorance" (143). "In his admiration for the Mediterranean/Muslim world, Foucault avoided addressing the sexism and homophobia of these cultures" (141). The authors also argue that "Foucault's Orientalism extended itself" (139) to the ancient Greco-Roman world; the last two volumes of *The History of Sexuality* detailing ancient Greek homosexuality are also evidence, state the authors, that "Foucault may have been looking for parallels to contemporary sexual practices in the Middle East and North Africa" (139). In tandem with his "scattered remarks on gender and male sexuality in the Muslim world . . . he saw a continuity between ancient Greek homosexuality and male homosexuality in contemporary North African and Middle Eastern societies" (139).

97. Said, *Orientalism*, 167.

98. Ibid., 190, 167, 58.

99. Mbembe, "Necropolitics," 39.

100. Agamben, *State of Exception*.

101. Scheer, "Homophobia and Apple Pie."

2. abu ghraib

Previous versions of this chapter have been published elsewhere: "On Torture: Abu Ghraib," *Radical History Review*, no. 93 (fall 2005): 13–38; and "Abu Ghraib: Arguing against Exceptionalism," *Feminist Studies* 30.2 (summer 2004): 522–34.

1. Shanker and Steinberg, "Bush Voices 'Disgust.' "

2. Rachel Corrie was killed on March 16, 2003, when she was run over by an Israeli bulldozer that was razing homes in the Gaza Strip.

3. Bush administration memoranda photocopies are available at "Primary Sources: The Torture Debate." See also Danner, *Torture and Truth*. Danner's book collects a range of documents on U.S. torture practices, from Bush administration memoranda on the treatment of detainees and torture/"interrogation practices" to prisoner depositions and the Red Cross report. It concludes with the Taguba report, which was submitted in early March 2004 and was the basis of Seymour Hersh's breaking the Abu Ghraib story; the Schlesinger report, an "investigation of the investigations"; and the Fay/Jones report, which included an interview "notably with Lieutenant General Ricardo Sanchez, the commander of Iraq" (277–78). The Taguba report acknowledged that there were credible reports of

> breaking chemical lights and pouring the phosphoric liquid on detainees . . . threatening detainees with a charged 9mm pistol . . . pouring cold water on naked detainees . . . beating detainees with a broom handle and a chair . . . threatening male detainees

with rape . . . allowing a military police guard to stitch the wound of a detainee who was injured after being slammed against the wall in his cell . . . sodomizing a detainee with a chemical light and perhaps a broom stick . . . using military working dogs to frighten and intimidate detainees with threats of attack, and in one instance actually biting the detainee. (293)

The Schlessinger report states, "Abuses of varying severity occurred at differing locations under differing circumstances and context. They were widespread and, though inflicted on only a small percentage of those detained, they were both serious in number and in effect" (331). This statement is followed by a disavowal of any promulgation of abuse on the part of "senior officials or military authorities," but does argue that "there is both institutional and personal responsibility at higher levels" (331). The report also includes tables on the interrogation policies in Guantánamo, Afghanistan, and Iraq as well as techniques used in Guantánamo (392–93). The Fay/Jones report includes charts of "Allegations of Abuse Incidents, the Nature of Reported Abuse, and Associated Personnel" (532–44). The charts list the categories "Nudity/Humiliation, Assault, Sexual Assault, Use of Dogs, The 'Hole,' and Other."

A much larger collection of documents is Greenberg and Dratel, *The Torture Papers*. The authors introduce the text by stating, "The memos and reports in this volume document the systematic attempt of the U.S. government to authorize the way for torture techniques and coercive interrogation practices, forbidden under international law, with the concurrent express intent of evading liability in the aftermath of any discovery of these practices and policies." It includes major sections of memoranda and reports, as well as appendixes on torture-related laws and conventions and legal cases relevant to the incidences of torture. Both books have stylized cover art of the hooded detainees: *Torture and Truth* has the person in the infamous "Vietnam," and *The Torture Papers* has a person draped over what appears to be a fence.

4. Friedman, "Restoring Our Honor." OpenDemocracy.net offers a series of articles on the Arab response to the Abu Ghraib tortures, including: Khouri, "Abu Ghraib in the Arab Mirror"; Kazmi, "Shame"; and Ghoussoub, "Abu Ghraib: I Do Not Know Where to Look for Hope." The articles offer perspectives on the meaning of these acts, the U.S. war on terror, and the publicity, all of which are effaced in analyses such as Friedman's. Khouri's article discusses "how the events appear to ordinary Arab citizens. For them, the horrors inflicted in the prison are not primarily about the abuse of Iraqi prisoners by American soldiers. They are, rather, about autocratic power structures that have controlled, humiliated, and ultimately dehumanised Arab citizens for most of the past century of modern statehood—whether those powers were European colonial administrations, indigenous Arab elites, occupying Israeli forces, or the current Anglo-American managers of Iraq." The Pakistani American Kazmi comments, "Last week I read a letter from a mother who felt sorry for the young soldiers who were thrown into a war they didn't understand and were inadequately trained to handle the situation surrounding them. I would like to ask this mother: exactly how much training does a 21-year old require before he or she realizes that it is not alright to tie a leash around a man's neck and drag him like a

dog, or strip men naked and pile them on top of each other like animals then pose for photographs mocking them?" Ghoussoub, a European Arab, states, "The family of a woman soldier shown abusing prisoners have released a picture of her holding tenderly a young Iraqi child. It is meant to show that she is a loving person who cares for the Iraqis. She was told to obey orders, declare her family. Another familiar story! You may love children, be sweet and caring but the rules of war are special and they turn you into something particularly ugly. The secrecy of occupying armies turns soldiers into little gods shaping and coercing peoples' bodies." Clearly, none of these authors read the Abu Ghraib tortures as any less than part of a larger story about how Arabs have experienced colonialism and war, and how these acts demonstrate a disregard for the humanity of those held in Abu Ghraib that cannot be isolated to just those who carried out these specific acts.

5. Perry, "A Pastoral Statement."
6. Cushman, "A Conversation with Veena Das."
7. Maran, *Torture*, 82, citing Trinquier, *Modern Warfare*, xv.
8. Rejali, *Torture and Modernity*, 15.
9. Hersh, "The Gray Zone," 42, emphasis mine. Hersh's reporting on Abu Ghraib is notably tied to his earlier work. According to Frank Rich, "It was in November 1969 that a little-known reporter, Seymour Hersh, broke the story of the 1968 massacre at My Lai, the horrific scoop that has now found its match 35 years later in Mr. Hersh's *New Yorker* revelation"; "The War's Lost Weekend."
10. See Said, *Orientalism*, 308–9, 311, 312, 349; Furuhashi, "Orientalist Torture."
11. The Center for Constitutional Rights has filed a lawsuit against private firms participating in the "torture conspiracy." See Center for Constitutional Rights, "CCR Files Lawsuit." Trishala Deb and Rafael Mutis elaborate on the implications of outsourcing torture:

> CACI is a corporation that generates over $930 million in profit a year, 65% of its budget coming from government contracts. The question remains how these private contractors are accountable to U.S. and international laws, not to mention the international public. Given the restrictions on access to information about the functioning of the war machine since the establishment of the Patriot Act and Department of Homeland Security, we have even less access to information and accountability regarding some of the most important and dangerous aspects of this permanent war. The relevance of this information is that it exposes one of the most insidious sides to this story—the cycle of government expenditures on private contractors as enforcement agents in this war, and profits made by U.S. corporations which are awarded those contracts. In this way the prison industrial complex is at once exposed and expanded, not only were severe crimes against humanity committed but at least one corporation has profited from those crimes. For those corporations who are being paid to provide interrogators and intelligence, war crimes are not a consideration, just a consequence. ("Smoke and Mirrors," 5)

According to the *Financial Times* correspondent Peter Spiegel, no private contractors have been prosecuted for Abu Ghraib prisoner abuse despite evidence that they were involved; "No Contractors Facing Abu Ghraib Abuse Charges."

12. Emram Qureshi, "Misreading *The Arab Mind.*"
13. Žižek points out that it is not the known knowns, the known unknowns, nor the unknown knowns that matter most here, but the unconscious, the knowledge that doesn't know itself; "What Rumsfeld Doesn't Know."
14. The full text of the Taguba report can be found on numerous websites, for instance, NBC News, "U.S. Army Report."
15. Al Jazeera, "Israeli Interrogator." During February and March 2002, over two thousand Muslims were killed and tens of thousands more were displaced from their homes in rioting by Hindus; the police were complicit with this violence, and the Hindu nationalist Bharat Janata Party (BJP) is accused of premeditated orchestration of the pogroms. In regard to Muslim masculinity, the International Initiative for Justice writes in *Threatened Existence*:

> Muslim men, in the Hindu Right discourse, are not seen as "men" at all: they are either "oversexed" to the extent of being bestial (they can satisfy four wives!) or they are effeminate and not masculine enough to satisfy their women. . . . [The Muslim man is] a symbol of the "sexual superiority" the emasculated Hindu man must recover by raping and defiling Muslim women. . . . There have been calls to Hindu men to join gyms and develop muscular bodies to counter the "animal" attraction of the over-sexualized Muslim man. Of course, when Hindu men commit rape and assault their actions are not seen as bestial or animal-like but are considered signs of valour. Simultaneously, there is an attempt to show that Muslim men are not real men, but rather homosexuals or *hijras* (eunuchs)—considered synonymous and undesirable and are therefore unable to satisfy their women. As a VHP [Vishva Hindu Parishad] leaflet called *Jihad* (holy war) boasts:
>> We have untied the penises which were tied till now
>> Without castor oil in the arse we have made them cry
>> Those who call religious war, violence, are all fuckers
>> We have widened the tight vaginas of the bibis (women) . . .
>> Wake up Hindus there are still Miyas (Muslims men) left alive around you
>> Learn from Panvad village where their mother was fucked
>> She was fucked standing while she kept shouting
>> She enjoyed the uncircumcised penis. (29–30)

16. Horne, *A Savage War*, 197–98.
17. Danny Kaplan, *Brothers and Others*, 193, 193–94, 194.
18. Axel, "The Diasporic Imaginary," 420.
19. Judith Butler notes this process in the viewing of the Rodney King videotapes, where the "racist episteme of seeing" produces the object being beaten—the subjugated black male body—as imminently dangerous and threatening. See "Endangered/Endangering."
20. Mayer, "Q&A."
21. Priest and Stephens, "Secret World of U.S. Interrogation." See also Brody, "What about the Other Secret U.S. Prisons?"
22. Said, *Orientalism*, 167.
23. Hersh, "Torture at Abu Ghraib," May 10, 2004, 44.

24. Cogswell, "Torture and America."
25. Ehrenreich, "Prison Abuse."
26. Crea, "Gay Sex."
27. Eisenstein, "Sexual Humiliation."
28. Ehrenreich, "Prison Abuse."
29. Moore, "Gay Sexuality."
30. "Most Americans believe the abuses were isolated instances, not common occurrences. They believe the perpetrators were acting on their own, not following orders. And by an overwhelming margin, the public sees the abuses as a violation of military policy, rogue crimes, not a policy. As a result, most Americans blame the soldiers who carried out the abuses and the officers supervising them, not Secretary Rumsfeld or President Bush"; Schneider, reporting for *Insight*. Interestingly, media coverage such as Dao et al., "Abuse Charges," centralized the heterosexual families of the Abu Ghraib perpetrators. For example, the images on page 20 of the article include the following captions: "Staff Sgt. Ivan Frederick, one of the American soldiers who are expected to face courts-martial in the abuse of prisoners at Abu Ghraib, is shown with Iraqi police officers in a photograph that he sent his family"; "Sergeant Fredericks, Martha, joined by her daughters, spoke to television journalist by phone Tuesday"; "Pfc. Lynndie R. England, who flashed a thumbs-up sign for the Abu Ghraib photos, relaxing at her parents' home last year." The heterosexual family is idealized: England comfortably smiling in her parents' kitchen, families receiving photos of their loved ones in Iraq. Abu Ghraib is a tragedy for these families, as Martha Fredericks seems distraught as she stands, arms crossed, on the phone, while her one daughter slouches on the couch with her hand supporting her head, and her other daughter leans over to the couch, perched on a chair, resting her head in her hands. All three women have blank or saddened expressions, contrasting sharply with the smiles of Ivan Frederick and England in the photos above and below them.
31. Eisenstein, "Sexual Humiliation."
32. Cushman, "A Conversation with Veena Das."
33. In her interview, Das says:

    > A very good example of this is the idea that a woman gets higher status in society by being the hero's mother; or there are other examples in which a woman's honor may depend on the son's or husband's valiant performance in the world. There is a very subtle exchange of maleness and femaleness in these kinds of formations. So that, yes, you can get forms of sociality where violence is an exclusively male form of sociality from which women might be excluded or other forms of sociality in which she is incorporated within male forms of violence. (Ibid.)

34. Shrader and Shogren, "Officials Clash"; Al-Fatiha Foundation, "Al-Fatiha Condemns Sexual Humiliation." Al-Fatiha's founder and director Faisal Alam opines, "As queer Muslims, we must condemn in the most forceful terms, the blatant acts of homophobia and sexual torture displayed by the U.S. military. These symbolic acts of abuse represent the worst form of torture."
35. Stout, "Rumsfeld Offers Apology."
36. Fuoco and Lash, "A Long Way."

37. Crea, "Gay Sex," 38. Sullivan, "Daily Dish."

39. Chow, *The Protestant Ethnic*, 107.

40. Moore, "Gay Sexuality."

41. Foucault, *The History of Sexuality*, 6.

42. S. Ahmed, "Affective Economies," 134.

43. Crea, "Gay Sex." Osborne, "Pentagon Uses Gay Sex as Tool." See also OutRage!, press release.

44. Osborne, "Pentagon Uses Gay Sex as Tool."

45. Ibid.

46. Dahir, "Gay Sex and Prison Torture."

47. Jacques et al., "Fighting for Freedom."

48. Letellier, "Egyptians Decry 'Gay' Abuse."

49. Moore, "Gay Sexuality."

50. Amnesty International, "USA: Pattern of Brutality and Cruelty."

51. Rubin, "Thinking Sex," 11.

52. Deb and Mutis, "Smoke and Mirrors," 5. For a similarly politically astute analysis, see S. P. Shah and Young, "A 'Morning After Prescription.' "

53. Harding, "The Other Prisoners."

54. Axel, "The Diasporic Imaginary," 414. Axel is quoting Mamood, *Fighting for Faith*, 40.

55. Bourke, "Torture as Pornography."

56. S. Ahmed, *The Cultural Politics of Emotion*, 123, 131.

57. Zernike et al., "Accused Soldier."

58. Al Jazeera, "Hersh."

59. Rejali, "A Long-Standing Trick." Also see Hilton, "Torture." Hilton's article provides an overview of U.S. practices, support, and tolerance of torture beginning in the 1970s up through the current war on terror. Her article is notable for its mapping of American practices that lead to her concluding point: "The pattern is too widespread, the official response to the disclosures too muted to allow for any doubt that the sanction for torture comes from a high level of policy."

60. Although neither mentions the flag-as-hood, for more on Hieronymus Bang, see Salter, review of *"I'm Gonna Kill the President"*; Goldberg, "Is This Play Illegal?"

61. The San Francisco gallery showcasing Colwell's work was closed in May 2004 after the owner, Lori Haigh, received death threats and was physically assaulted. See Ryan Kim, "Attacked for Art."

62. Rejali, "A Long-Standing Trick."

63. Sontag, "Regarding the Torture of Others," 42.

64. Rejali, "A Long-Standing Trick." Additionally, the Prison Litigation Reform Act of 1996 delimits what are deemed to be frivolous lawsuits, ensuring that prisoners must demonstrate signs of physical injury prior to claims of mental or emotional injury.

65. Žižek, "What Rumsfeld Doesn't Know," 32.

66. Neumayr, "The Abu Ghraib Collection."

67. R. Goldstein, "Stuff Happens!"

68. Deleuze and Guattari, *A Thousand Plateaus*, 492.

69. Hersh, "Chain of Command," 39.

70. For instance, Human Rights Watch reports, "In Maricopa County, Arizona, a sheriff

who dresses male jail inmates in pink underwear introduced live 'jail cam' broadcasts on the internet in 2000. Three cameras covered the holding and searching cells of the jail, including shots of strip searches, inmates bound in 'restraint chairs,' and even, for a while, unobstructed views of women using the toilet. The broadcasts ended up being copied onto web porn sites"; Fellner, "Prisoner Abuse." See also Herbert, "America's Abu Ghraibs"; and Bernstein, "2 Men Charge Abuse," among many other reports.

71. Sontag, "Regarding the Torture of Others," 27.

72. Carby, "A Strange and Bitter Crop."

73. Mamood, *Fighting for Faith*, 189, quoted in Axel, "The Diasporic Imaginary," 414.

74. See Amnesty International, "USA Amnesty International's Supplementary Briefing": "Evidence continues to emerge of widespread torture and other cruel, inhuman or degrading treatment of detainees held in U.S. custody in Afghanistan, Guantánamo Bay, Cuba, Iraq and other locations. While the government continues to assert that abuses resulted for the most part from the actions of a few 'aberrant' soldiers and lack of oversight, there is clear evidence that much of the ill-treatment has stemmed directly from officially santioned procedures and policies, including interrogation techniques approved by Secretary of Defense Rumsfeld for use in Guantánamo and later exported to Iraq." Also visit Human Rights First, "End Torture Now." for updated coverage on U.S. military torture.

75. Deer, "Iraq and Postcoloniality."

76. Sontag, *Regarding the Pain of Others*, 10.

77. Žižek, "What Rumsfeld Doesn't Know."

78. Rush Limbaugh quoted in Sontag, "Regarding the Torture of Others," 28–29.

79. Limbaugh, posting. See a transcription of Limbaugh's comments at Media Matters for America, "Limbaugh on Torture of Iraqis."

80. The Abu Ghraib abuse scandal has prompted the production of a play, *Guardians*. See Charles Isherwood's review, "Shades of Abu Ghraib." Isherwood summarizes the plot:

> In London, a coldblooded tabloid journalist, his reptilian eyes on the prize of a column at a more respectable newspaper, *The Guardian*, finds an unexpected opportunity to further his career by manufacturing photographs supposedly depicting British soldiers abusing an Iraqi prisoner. His story is intercut with the confessional monologue of a young United States Army soldier from West Virginia who, in her role as a guard at a prison for insurgents in Iraq, becomes a scapegoat in a scandal involving photographs of actual abuse. . . . The story of the United States Army grunt, identified in the text as American Girl, is clearly based on the case of Lynndie England, also from West Virginia, who was convicted of misconduct for her role in the prisoner-abuse scandal at Abu Ghraib. And Fleet Street was indeed rocked, in 2004, by a fabricated photograph similar to the one described here that appeared in The Daily Mirror, the only one of London's tabloids to oppose the Iraq war. The paper's editor was forced to resign when the hoax was revealed.

81. For a summary of the nine convictions through September 2005, see the Associated Press, "A Look at Convictions." The most recent conviction related to the abuses at

Abu Ghraib was that of Sgt. Michael J. Smith, an army dog handler. See Schmitt and Zernike, "Iraq Abuse Trial," for reporting on the continued refusal to hold higher ranked military officials responsible for torture at Abu Ghraib. They report:

> Among all the abuse cases that have reached military courts, the trial of the dog handler, Sgt. Michael J. Smith, had appeared to hold the greatest potential to assign accountability to high-ranking military and perhaps even civilian officials in Washington. Some military experts had thought the trial might finally explore the origins of the harsh interrogation techniques that were used at Abu Ghraib; at the Bagram detention center in Afghanistan; and at other sites where abuses occurred. Sergeant Smith, who was convicted Tuesday for abusing detainees in Iraq with his black Belgian shepherd, had said he was merely following interrogation procedures approved by the chief intelligence officer at Abu Ghraib, Col. Thomas M. Pappas. In turn, Colonel Pappas had said he had been following guidance from Maj. Gen. Geoffrey D. Miller, commander of the military prison at Guantanamo Bay, Cuba, who in September 2003 visited Iraq to discuss ways to "set the conditions" for enhancing prison interrogations, as well as from superiors in Baghdad. General Miller had been dispatched to Guantanamo Bay by Defense Secretary Donald H. Rumsfeld and the Joint Chiefs of Staff to improve the interrogation procedures and the quality of intelligence at the compound in Cuba. But in Sergeant Smith's trial, General Miller was never called to testify. . . . Several generals and colonels have received career-ending reprimands and have been stripped of their commands, but there is no indication that other senior-level officers and civilian officials will ever be held accountable for the detainee abuses that took place in Iraq and Afghanistan.

Sgt. Santos A. Cardona, another dog handler, began his trial on May 23, 2006, and his attorney, Harvey Volzer, "said he would seek to have Mr. Rumsfeld, Gen. John P. Abizaid, the commander of American forces in the Mideast, and General Sanchez all testify at Sergeant Cardona's trial." The *Journal Star* (Peoria, Ill.) editorial "The Aftermath of the Abu Ghraib Abuse" serves as an example of how the convictions of some of those involved in the torturing of prisoners at Abu Ghraib have been used to reassert the belief that the war in Iraq and "American values" are compatable. The editorial states, "Though these were not isolated instances—230 enlisted officers and soldiers have been punished for abusing detainees in Iraq and Afghanistan—there was little evidence it was ordered by senior officers," at once acknowledging that torturing prisoners is not an exceptional practice by U.S. military personnel and disavowing any implications for higher level officials or the U.S. military (or prison industrial complex) as a whole. It concludes, "As outrageous as the Abu Ghraib incident was, how it was handled said some important things about America. First, there will be accountability for unacceptable behavior, even in a war zone. Second, the rule of law will prevail, no matter the consequences. Third, once inappropriate behavior is discovered, there will be full and fair investigation and subsequent public disclosure. Many a nation would not have owned up to such mistakes. Even in such an embarrassing episode, that says something positive about America." This call for national pride in response to the scandal at Abu Ghraib rings false not only in terms of the limited scope of prosecution and drawn-out arguments about what constitutes "torture," but also in light of accounts that rapes of women and young prisoners were included in photographs taken at Abu Ghraib. So far there has been no public prosecution of anyone specifically on charges related to sexual assault.

82. *Washington Post*, "Sworn Statements": "These documents are the official English translations of previously sworn statements by detainees at the Abu Ghraib prison in Iraq. Some of the names have been withheld from these statements by washington-post.com because they are alleged victims of sexual assault."
83. Massad, "Re-Orienting Desire," 373.
84. See Foucault, *The History of Sexuality*; Butler, *Gender Trouble*.
85. Franke, "Putting Sex to Work," 1161.
86. Mbembe, "Necropolitics," 34.
87. See Agamben, *Homo Sacer*, 159.
88. Žižek, "What Rumsfeld Doesn't Know."

3. intimate control, infinite detention

1. Hunter, "Sexual Orientation," 1528, 1529.
2. Ibid., 1534.
3. Ibid., 1529, 1542.
4. Simon, "The Return of Panopticism." Simon writes, "The icon for superpanopticism is neither the eye nor the camera but the database or even better *the form*: the marketing survey, the census form, application forms, medical forms, etc." (16).
5. Foucault, "*Society Must Be Defended*," 249, 252–53.
6. Massumi, untitled paper presented at "Beyond Biopolitics."
7. Deleuze, *Negotiations*, 174–75:

    We're definitely moving towards control societies that are no longer exactly disciplinary. Foucault's often taken as the theorist of disciplinary societies and of their principal technology, confinement (not just in hospitals and prisons, but in schools, factories, and barracks). But he was actually one of the first to say that we're moving away from disciplinary societies, we've already left them behind. We're moving toward control societies that no longer operate by confining people but through continuous control and instant communication. . . . One can envision education becoming less and less a closed site differentiated from the workplace as another closed site, but both disappearing and giving way to frightful continual training, to continual monitoring.

    On Foucault and surveillance, also see Simon, "The Return of Panopticism"; and Wood, "Editorial."
8. Clough, "Future Matters," 4, 14.
9. Ibid., 14.
10. Hunter, "Sexual Orientation," 1528.
11. Agamben, *The State of Exception*, 3–4.
12. For a well-developed discussion of the Western media's problematic reporting on Pashtun male sexuality, see Skier, "Western Lenses." See *The Boston Globe*'s "Spotlight Investigation," a website that includes "global coverage . . . divided into nine categories" and an archive of coverage beginning January 2002. One meeting of the

war on terror and the Michael Jackson child molestation scandal occurred in spring 2005 with the Internet circulation of a doctored photo of two presumably Iraqi boys holding a sign that reads in a computer font, "Still safer here than at Michael Jackson's!" and a white American soldier, all three smiling and giving the thumbs up. See the image at ThreeSources.com, "From Iraq." Thanks to Andrew Mazzaschi for drawing my attention to this and other related images.

13. Somerville, "Queer *Loving*," 335. Also see Somerville, *Queering the Color Line*.

14. Miranda Joseph, *Against the Romance of Community*, 149.

15. Spivak, "Scattered Speculations," 156. Also see Foucault, *The Order of Things*, 21.

16. See Jagose, *Queer Theory*, 59–63; and Seidman, "Identity and Politics." Seidman details a long history of the shift from liberationist to recognition politics (as the shift to an ethnic identity model).

17. Somerville, "Queer *Loving*," 335, 336.

18. Franke, "The Domesticated Liberty," 1399.

19. See Chauncey, " 'What Gay Studies Taught the Court' "; as well as SodomyLaws.org's listing and links to commentary on *Lawrence-Garner v. Texas*, "*Lawrence & Garner v. State of Texas*."

20. See Califia, *Public Sex*; and Warner, *The Trouble with Normal*.

21. Somerville, "Queer *Loving*," 346.

22. Somerville, "Sexual Aliens."

23. Somerville, "Queer *Loving*," 337.

24. Somerville, "Sexual Aliens," 83.

25. Volpp, "The Citizen and the Terrorist."

26. The breaking story on radiation monitoring was David E. Kaplan, "Exclusive." For other coverage, including responses by Muslim organizations, see Margasak, "FBI Monitors Radiation Levels"; Wald, "Widespread Radioactivity Monitoring"; United Press International, "U.S. Muslims Protest"; and Council on American-Islam Relations, "Muslims Meet with FBI."

27. See Sonia Katyal's useful reading of the case in relation to the globalization of gay civil and human rights frames, "Sexuality and Sovereignty." Katyal argues that the logic of containment foundational to the sexual sovereignty implicit in the *Lawrence* decision does not easily traverse varied cultural, national, and regional contexts.

28. Somerville, "Queer *Loving*," 346.

29. Richard Kim, "Sodomy for Some,"

30. SodomyLaws.org offers links to press coverage as well as amicus briefs filed on behalf of the plaintiffs, Lawrence and Garner, at "*Lawrence & Garner v. State of Texas*."

31. Halley, "Reasoning about Sodomy."

32. According to the *Oxford English Dictionary*, sodomy is "an unnatural form of sexual intercourse, esp. that of one male with another." As defined by *The People's Law Dictionary*:

> Sodomy is anal copulation by a man inserting his penis in the anus either of another man or a woman. If accomplished by force, without consent or with someone incapable of consent, sodomy is a felony in all states in the same way that rape is. Homosex-

ual (male to male) sodomy between consenting adults has also been found to be a felony but increasingly is either decriminalized or seldom prosecuted. Sodomy with a consenting adult female is virtually never prosecuted, even in those states in which it remains in the books as a criminal offense. However, there have been a few cases, including one in Indiana, in which a now-estranged wife insisted that a husband be charged with sodomy for sexual acts while they were living together. Traditionally, sodomy was called "a crime against nature." Sodomy does not include oral copulation or sexual acts with animals (bestiality)."

George Painter's legal history of sodomy in the United States, "The Sensibilities of Our Forefathers," details the shift toward prosecution of oral-genital sex at the turn of the twentieth century. Painter's discussion, however, does not mention analingus, leaving it questionable as to whether or not analingus had a history similar to oral-genital activities.

33. Halley, "Reasoning about Sodomy."
34. Katyal, "Exporting Identity," 106–7.
35. Chauncey, "'What Gay Studies Taught the Court,'" 509.
36. D. Gordon, "Moralism," 4, 4–5.
37. Franke, "The Domesticated Liberty," 1401, 1400; Ruskola, "Gay Rights versus Queer Theory," 241.
38. Franke, "The Domesticated Liberty," 1403, 1416, 1404, 1417.
39. N. Shah, "Policing Privacy," 276; *Lawrence v. Texas* 123 S. Ct. 2472, 2478 (2003), quoted in Franke, "The Domesticated Liberty," 1408.
40. Franke, "The Domesticated Liberty," 1407.
41. Duggan, "The New Homonormativity," 181. This also colluded with the continuing disavowal of gay liberationist goals; along with taking sex public, they wanted to dismantle marriage, end capitalism, and end imperialist militarism. Some references to gay liberationist texts make these goals explicit, such as Third World Gay Revolution (New York City)'s "What We Want."
42. Duggan, "The New Homonormativity," 181. The "sex wars" were also emblematic of the drive to privatize nonprocreative sex (and divided feminist camps) by controlling of the sites of production and consumption of pornography. See Gayle Rubin's postscript to "Thinking Sex," 41–44.
43. Bhattacharjee, "The Public/Private Mirage," 312, 320.
44. Gilliom, "Resisting Surveillance," 78.
45. The New York City Association of Homeless and Street-Involved Youth Organizations, "State of the City's Homeless Youth"; Earls, "Stressors in the Lives of GLBTQ Youth"; Ryan and Futterman, *Lesbian and Gay Youth*, 25.
46. Brady, *Extinct Lands*, 87.
47. Butler, "Is Kinship Always Already Heterosexual?," 18.
48. See Rubin, "Thinking Sex," 13. *Lawrence-Garner* can be read as signaling homonormative movement inward from the "outer limits" into the "charmed circle" of "Good, Normal, Natural, Blessed Sexuality."
49. Robson, "The Missing Word," 399. See also National Center for Lesbian Rights "National Center for Lesbian Rights Hails Supreme Court Decision."

50. Nast, "Queer Patriarchies," 878.
51. Anonymous, "Renting Wombs"; Human Rights Campaign Foundation, "Florida's Gay Adoption Ban." Three states currently have legislation that either explicitly or in effect denies homosexuals or same-sex couples the right to adopt. Florida has a law that explicitly prohibits adoption by gay and lesbian individuals and same-sex couples. Mississippi prohibits same-sex couples from adoption and second-parent adoption. Utah forbids adoption by any unmarried cohabiting couple, and as a result discriminates against all same-sex couples. Human Rights Campaign Foundation, "Second-Parent/Stepparent Adoption Laws." Eight states and the District of Columbia allow second-parent adoption or second-parent adoption by same-sex couples, while fifteen states allow second-parent adoption or second-parent adoption by same-sex couples in some jurisdictions. Four states (Colorado, Nebraska, Ohio, and Wisconsin) have a court ruling that does not allow second-parent adoption or second-parent adoption by same-sex couples.
52. Bhattacharjee, "The Public/Private Mirage," 317.
53. Franke, "The Domesticated Liberty," 1418–19.
54. Koshy, "Morphing Race into Ethnicity."
55. See Berlant and Warner, "Sex in Public."
56. For an overview of the burgeoning field of surveillance studies, see Lyon, "Editorial."
57. Defert, " 'Popular Life' and Insurance Technology," 214.
58. Hunter, "Sexual Orientation," 1535.
59. On geodemographic systems of profiling and the narrative devices they cannot eschew, see Curry, "The Profiler's Question."
60. The title of this section is taken from *Black Is . . . Black Ain't: A Personal Journey through Black Identity*.
61. C. J. Cohen, *The Boundaries of Blackness*.
62. Price, "Black Supporters."
63. Boykin, "Life after Lawrence-Garner."
64. Kim Pearson, cited in ibid.
65. N. Shah, "Policing Privacy," 277. See also N. Shah, "Perversity."
66. N. Shah, "Between 'Oriental Depravity' and 'Natural Degenerates,' " 714, 720, 705, 719–20.
67. Grier, "Having Their Cake." On figure 10, see disappearedinamerica.org: "Visible Collective/Naeem Mohaiemen work on projects that look at hyphenated identities and national security panic. The majority of detainees in recent paranoia times are from the invisible underclass—shadow citizens who drive taxis, deliver food, clean tables, and sell fruit, coffee, and newspapers. The only time we 'see' them is when we glance at the license in the taxi partition, or the vendor ID card. When detained, they cease to exist in the consciousness. The impulse to create an insider-outsider dynamic with 'loyalty' overtones has a long pedigree: WWI incarceration of German-Americans; 1919 detention of immigrants in Anarchist bomb scare; WWII internment of Japanese-Americans; execution of the Rosenbergs; HUAC 'red scare'; infiltration of Deacons For Defense and Black Panthers; and the rise of the Minutemen."
68. See Arensen, "The Supreme Court."
69. See Rimer and Arensen, "Top Colleges Take More Blacks."

70. *Lawrence v. Texas* 2003 U.S. LEXIS 5013, 524, 521 (2003).

71. Ibid., 522, 524. See European Court of Human Rights, *Dudgeon v. The United Kingdom*.

72. Palumbo-Lui, "Multiculturalism Now," 122, 118–22, 121, 126, 122.

73. Hersh, "Torture at Abu Ghraib," May 10, 2004. "Torture at Abu Ghraib" was posted to *The New Yorker*'s website over a week earlier than it was released in print. See www.newyorker.com.

74. Hersh's article was circulated extensively and could be located on antiwar and/or anti-Islamophobic websites in July 2005, more than a year later: Hersh, "The U.S.A.'s Abu Ghraib Torture Scandal," http://www.uslaboragainstwar.org; "Torture at Abu Ghraib," http://www.notinourname.net; "Torture at Abu Ghraib," http://www.november.org; "Torture at Abu Ghraib," http://www.globalpolicy.org.

    For examples of other uses of Haykel's verbiage, see Qidwai, "Abu-Ghrayb." This example is particularly interesting as the Independent Centre for Strategic Studies and Analysis (ICSSA) describes its goals thus: "At the ICSSA we believe there is a need to change the ways in which vested interest is forcing the policy makers and general public to perceive Muslims as 'the other,' who need to be civilized, liberated and de-mocratized in the image of the world mastering demo-gods in Washington. . . . The ICSSA promotes interaction with general public in the West and works at mutual listening for the simple reason to provide them with the real picture of the Muslim world other than what they have been subjected to through the 'mainstream' media distortion of the reality"; Independent Centre for Strategic Studies and Analysis, "About Us." See also Kennedy (a contributing writer to the *Boston Phoenix*), "Media Log."

75. MilitaryArticles.com, "Abu Ghraib."

76. Savage is quoted in Dave Gilson's "America's Laziest Fascist."

77. Hersh, "Implications of Photographs."

78. Haykel, "Implications of Photographs."

79. According to Joseph Massad, for example, the "Gay International and its activities are largely responsible for the intensity of this repressive campaign" directly referencing the Cairo 52 case ("Re-Orienting Desire," 383). Also see Massad on "always already homosexualized populations": "In contradistinction to the liberatory claims made by the Gay International in relation to what it posits as an always already homosexualized population, I argue that it is the discourse of the Gay International that both produces homosexuals, as well as gays and lesbians, where they do not exist, and represses same-sex desires and practices that refuse to be assimilated into its sexual epistemology" (363).

80. Kalra et al., *Diaspora and Hybridity*, 129.

81. Many community-based organizations that have tirelessly labored against the exploitations of the prison industrial complex, immigration and welfare regulations, and police brutality against people of color angrily pointed out after 9/11 that the Act and the subsequent military order hardly signaled an "erosion" of previously safe and sound civil liberties. Instead, the provisions of both, whose antecedents can be traced to the repressive Counter-Intelligence Program practices beginning in the 1950s, are digested as a vicious intensification of the conditions of possibility of the status quo; in other words, more of the same. Two community-based organizations that articulated a continuity between their pre- and post-9/11 agendas are DRUM

(Desis Rising Up and Moving), a nonprofit immigrant advocacy group, and the Audre Lorde Project, Inc., a nonprofit LGBT community organizing project for queers (and queer immigrants) of color; see Desis Rising Up and Moving, "About DRUM"; Audre Lorde Project, Inc., "About the Project."

82. Agamben, *The State of Exception*, 3.

83. Bauman, *Wasted Lives*, 13.

84. Ibid., 32.

85. Agamben, *Homo Sacer*, 142.

86. Slavoj Žižek characterizes the fate of the detainees as being "between two deaths"; "Between Two Deaths."

87. Butler, *Precarious Life*, 78.

88. American Civil Liberties Union, *Worlds Apart*, 1, 1–2, 3, 2.

89. For discussions of testimonial and human rights, see Schaffer and Smith, "Personal Effects"; and Rodriguez, *Queer Latinidad*. Further examples of heteronormative framings by liberals and progressives include American Immigration Lawyers Association, "The 107th Congress," in which a discussion of the USA PATRIOT Act explains that it does "preserve immigration benefits for the families of victims of the terrorist attacks and others impacted by the attack"; however, it "includes several troubling provisions. It includes language that will allow for the detention and deportation of people engaging in innocent associational activity and Constitutionally protected speech, and it permits the indefinite detention of immigrants and non-citizens who are not terrorists"; Human Rights Watch, "The United States' 'Disappeared,'" describes in the opening to its executive summary how a man's two sons, ages 7 and 9, were "picked up" as a complementary technique to waterboarding torture; Human Rights Watch, "United States: Locked Away," highlights detainees' lack of communication with their families; Ghani and Ganesh, *How Do You See the Disappeared?*, opens with the text from a *New York Times* report about the jailing and impending deportation of a man and how it has been experienced by his wife and daughter; and Amnesty International, "United States of America: Amnesty International's Concerns," again emphasizes the lack of access to family, wives particularly, of detainees. In contrast, articles published in *SAMAR: South Asian Magazine for Action and Reflection* are able to produce critiques of detentions and deportations without falling back on notions of heteronormative family. See South Asians against Police Brutality and Racism, "Not in Our Name"; and Vimalassery, "Passports and Pink Slips."

90. American Civil Liberties Union, *Worlds Apart*, 5.

91. On immigration to Canada, see Kobayashi and Ray, "Placing American Emigration to Canada in Context."

92. American Civil Liberties Union, *Worlds Apart*, 2.

93. Bhattacharjee, "The Public/Private Mirage," 317.

94. Visible Collective, *Disappeared in America*.

95. Bhattacharjee, "The Public/Private Mirage," 316.

96. Jeanette Gabriel, conversation with author, Rutgers University, New Brunswick, N.J., March 2005. Gabriel is a civil rights organizer. See details about Uzma Naheed in Dow, "The New Secret War."

97. There are numerous examples of heteronormativity being reinscribed in activist

work, ranging from the Visible Collective, *Disappeared in America*, to the American Civil Liberties Union, *Worlds Apart*, to the films *Brothers and Others*, *Rising Up: The Alams*, and *Lest We Forget*, to *Under Attack: Arab, Muslim and South Asian Communities Since September 11th*, a documentary audio CD.

98. See Jacinto, "Muslim Blacklisting?"; S. Roy, "Banks Allegedly Blacklisting Muslims"; and Russ, "Leave Home without It."

99. Graham, "Postmortem City," 185.

100. Howell and Shryock, "Cracking Down on Diaspora," 443, 445.

101. Ibid., 451; Mamdani, *Good Muslim, Bad Muslim*.

102. For background on special registration, see U.S. Department of State, Bureau of International Information Programs, USINFO, "National Security Entry-Exit Registration System"; and U.S. Department of Homeland Security, U.S. Immigration and Customs Enforcement, "Changes to National Security Entry/Exit Registration System." Call-in dates also have been grouped by country, presumably in order of perceived threat posed by nationals. See Brandeis University, International Students and Scholars Office, "National Security Entry-Exit Registration System." For a discussion of the effects of special registration and similar post-9/11 policies, see the American Immigration Law Foundation, "Targets of Suspicion." For a critique of the special registration policy, see Jachimowicz and McKay, " 'Special Registration' Program." See also the summary of the New York Advisory Committee's May 21, 2003, community forum in New York City: New York Advisory Committee, "Panel Summaries." For coverage of the mass arrest of mainly Iranian noncitizens, see Talvi, "Round Up," 3.

103. American Civil Liberties Union, *Worlds Apart*, 10.

104. Iyer, "A Community on the Front Lines," 43, 47, citing *Dawn*, "35pc of Deported from U.S. Are Pakistanis," and Powell, "An Exodus." Also see Rimer, "Pakistanis Unperturbed by U.S. Raid On Residence." The title of the article is misleading, in particular in light of quotes from Asif Kazi, a city accountant from Chester, Pennsylvania. As reported by Rimer, " 'I'm still in trauma,' he said. 'I cannot sleep properly. I cannot eat. You are worried of the fear of the unknown. What's going to happen tomorrow?' " " 'They broke the door,' he said. 'They kept her [Palwasha Kazi, Kazi's spouse] sitting at gunpoint, in the dining room on a chair. That's the standard procedure. I am not complaining.' " Asif Kazi's statements demonstrate the limited range of responses to being suspected of terrorism following the events of September 11. He can describe the experience, but he cannot fault anyone for suspecting him or his spouse of terrorism. The article ends with the following quote from Asif Kazi: "If, God forbid, I've done something wrong, hang me in the middle of the road. If not, leave me alone."

105. American Civil Liberties Union, *Worlds Apart*, 11.

106. Manalansan, "Race, Violence," 148, 147–48.

107. Maira, "Youth Culture," 220–21.

108. See Reilly, "Warning!"; and American Civil Liberties Union, "Surveillance."

109. Butler, *Precarious Life*, 77.

110. For a discussion of the distribution of trust through these technologies, see N. D. Campbell, "Technologies of Suspicion."

111. Maxwell, "Surveillance," 9; Mosco, *The Digital Sublime*, 22–24; Lianos, "Social Control after Foucault."
112. Weizman, "Maps of Israeli Settlements" in "The Politics of Verticality."
113. I am extrapolating upon Weizman's theorization of verticality from his work on the spatial control of the Occupied Territories of Palestine. See introduction to "The Politics of Verticality."
114. For a sample of formative, as well as representative, pieces on sexuality and space in the discipline of geography, see Myslik, "Renegotiating the Social/Sexual Identities of Places"; Binnie, "Trading Places"; Knopp, "Sexuality and Urban Space"; Rothenberg, " 'And She Told Two Friends' "; Valentine, "(Re)Negotiating the 'Heterosexual Street.' "
115. Weizman, introduction to "The Politics of Verticality."
116. De Rosa, "Privacy in an Age of Terror," 30–31, 33.
117. Stalder, "Opinion"; C. Parenti, *The Soft Cage*, 4.
118. De Rosa, "Privacy in an Age of Terror," 34.
119. Andreas, "Redrawing the Line," 97–98.
120. De Rosa, "Privacy in an Age of Terror," 34.
121. Andreas, "Redrawing the Line," 97.
122. Nathan Root, "Accenture Faces Daunting Task."
123. Hier, "Probing the Surveillant Assemblage."
124. Examples of discussions of non-Arab recruitment include the Suburban Emergency Management Project, "SEMP Biot #128"; and Kirkland, "Analysis."
125. Young, "Feminist Reactions," 224, 229.
126. Armitage, "Militarized Bodies," 1–2.
127. Bauman, *Wasted Lives*, 71.
128. Maxwell, "Surveillance."
129. For descriptions of the experiences of detainees at Camp X-Ray, see Human Rights Watch, *Guantanamo*.
130. The counterparts to terrorist bodies, patriot bodies, are also instructed, through numerous self-help bioterrorism books, in hygiene, nutrition, and exercise, all in the name of stress reduction and preparation for a bioterrorist attack. In particular, see chapter 2, "Safe at Home: A Family Survival Guide," in *When Every Moment Counts* by Bill Frist, billed as a book from the Senate's only doctor (thus conferring the status and authority of scientific governmentality).
131. Butler, *Precarious Life*, 78; Muñoz, "A Forum on Theatre and Tragedy," 123.
132. Butler, *Precarious Life*, 57.
133. Clough, "Future Matters," 14–15.
134. Foucault, "*Society Must Be Defended*," 243, 245, 242.
135. Thacker, *The Global Genome*, 25.
136. Maxwell, "Surveillance," 9.
137. Thacker, *The Global Genome*, 142, 141.
138. Deleuze, *Negotiations*, 175.
139. Povinelli, "Notes on Gridlock," 227.
140. Miranda Joseph, *Against the Romance of Community*, 164–65.
141. Povinelli, "Notes on Gridlock," 228.

142. Ibid., 234, citing Vogler, "Sex and Talk," Warner, "Publics and Counter Publics," and Berlant, "Intimacy." See also Berlant, *The Queen of America Goes to Washington City*.

143. Haraway, *The Companion Species Manifesto*.

144. For initial coverage of McGreevey's now infamous declaration "I'm a gay American," see CNN, "New Jersey Governor Quits." A more critical approach to the McGreevey scandal was written by Michael Musto, "Alien vs. Predator." On Mary Cheney, see R. Cohen, "The Mary Cheney Flap," in which he discusses the usage of Mary Cheney's homosexuality by both the Kerry and the Bush-Cheney campaigns during the 2004 presidential campaign. A different approach to Mary Cheney can be found at www.dearmary.com, a site devoted to pushing her to halt the antigay agenda of the Bush-Cheney administration: DontAmend.com and The Equality Campaign, Inc.

4. "the turban is not a hat"

1. One of the most enduring images from the media jamboree of September 11, aside from the determined charging and ramming of planes and the perverse magnificence of the cascading towers, was that of a turbaned Sikh man being briskly hauled off an Amtrak train at gunpoint by multitudes of police. Sher Singh was the first suspect arrested after 9/11, and the first casualty of a doctrine of civil liberties already compromised by racist and xenophobic logics. As Sher Singh describes it, on September 13, while on the train in Providence, Rhode Island, he was raided by policemen with "huge guns screaming profanity at me" (as depicted in *Targeting the Turban: Sikh Americans after September 11*, a documentary directed by Valerie Kaur Brar). His guilt was established by the mere coincidence of his travel itinerary and, of course, because he looked like a terrorist. His turban, complemented by a profuse moustache and lengthy beard, played a pivotal role in validating his guilt. The media disseminated this image of Sher Singh compulsively and without regard to his Sikh identity, criminalizing the turbaned Sikh male body tout court and reactivating an older genealogical trail of the terrorist Sikh. For a tracking of hate crimes against people presumed to be Muslim after the events of September 11, including a state-by-state list of hate crimes that occurred during the week after, see Jannah.org, "Muslim Victims of Terrorist Attacks."

   Sikhs also experience religious discrimination based on the wearing of *kirpans*, regardless of their gender. See Suan, "Suspension for Ceremonial Knives"; and the Sikh Coalition, "Coalition Continues to Defend Sikh's Rights to Practice Their Faith."

2. At the time, however, his death was not news; no photos of this turbaned Sikh man circulated on the television or in national print media; the *New York Times* reported his death on page A17 without comment. He remained largely faceless, and only due to the efforts of community-based organizations were the details of his death dispersed. His turban, of course, rendered him largely unimportant as a victim of post-9/11 racial backlash. Sodhi's brother, Lakwinder, publicly stated, "My brother was killed because of his turban and beard." When asked by reporters "What are you feeling about Americans?," Lakwinder Sodhi angrily responded, "Why are you asking me that? We are Americans also." Sodhi's killing prompted a phone call from

Indian Prime Minster Atal Bihari Vajpayee to G. W. Bush to "ensure the safety of Sikhs living in the U.S."; CNN.com, "Hate Crimes." Investigative reporting details the movement of white supremecist groups into the Valley, the area where Sodhi was shot, a year prior to his death. Hate crimes in this region continue to escalate. Less than a year later, on August 4, 2002, Sukhpal Singh, another brother of Balbir Singh Sodhi, and a turbaned taxi driver in San Francisco, was also shot and killed while on the job; Hanashiro, "Hate Crimes." Few know of the double deaths of these brothers. By the time of the second incident, hate crimes against turbaned Sikh men, the misrecognized/mistaken terrorist, had been neutralized and absorbed into the media sensationalism surrounding 9/11. For the responses of advocacy groups, see Sikh Mediawatch and Resource Task Force, "Multi-Jurisdiction Meeting"; and C. Leonard et al., "Sikhs Voice Outrage."

3. Scott Thomsen, "Arizona Man." Roque also stated, "I'm a patriot. . . . I'm a damn American all the way," according to Goodstein and Lewin, "Victims of Mistaken Identity." In 2003, Roque was found guilty of murdering Sodhi and received the death penalty. He was also found guilty on charges of drive-by shooting, attempted first-degree murder, and endangerment and received an additional thirty-six years. In response to the judge asking if he had any comment, Roque stated, "Just that I'm sorry that all this happened"; Associated Press, "Man Sentenced to Death."

4. The GSSA of Bridgewater, New Jersey, produced a series of public materials after the events of September 11. On September 14, 2001, they issued a press release that condemned the attacks and Osama bin Laden. In response to media coverage of bin Laden and the Taliban, they argued, "What is unfortunate is that the images of the likely perpetrators have made suspects and victims of Sikh communities. . . . In the days following the attack, anti-Arab, anti-Muslim, and anti-Sikh sentiments have steadily grown." They call for "the media, public advocates and politicians . . . to be careful and accurate about the distinctions between various religious, national, and ethnic affiliations that are implicated in rhetoric about who is responsible for the bombings." The press release was followed by fliers, including one titled "Our Fellow Americans and President Bush need our support to win the war against terrorism," an informational flier stating "SIKHS ARE FROM INDIA and have NO relation at all to OSAMA BIN LADEN or the TALIBAN," and a final flier that states "Sikhs are not Muslims." Despite the general opposition to hate crimes, GSSA materials clearly are invested in distancing Sikhs from Muslims and presenting them as deeply patriotic. The materials do not push for an analysis that acknowledges that one cannot assume a person's political allegiances based on characteristics such as religion, national, and ethnic identities. See Garden State Sikh Association, "Press Release"; "Our Fellow Americans and President Bush"; "Post–September 11th Flier"; "Flier: Sikhs Are Not Muslims."

5. The Sikh Mediawatch and Resource Task Force (SMART) responded with a press release, "Sikh Americans Denounce the Terrorist Attack, Ask Americans to Unite." Sikhs held vigils to mourn 9/11 in conjunction with the pogroms of 1984; United Sikhs in Service of America held a candlelight vigil in memory of the 1984 pogroms and September 11 on Saturday, December 8, 2001, in Madison Square Park; Sikh Coalition, "Please Participate." On uniting with Americans under the rubric of "vic-

tims of terrorist attacks," see *Times of India*, "Sporadic Violence"; Sikh Coalition, "Please Participate"; Singh, "Are Kashmiri Sikhs Next," and "35 Sikhs Murdered." Another tactic was the support of Sikh runners in the New York Marathon in 2003; Newindpress, "Sher-e-Punjab Sponsors 92-Year-Old Sikh."

Initially the Indian government responded to violence against Sikhs by using the phrase "mistaken identity"; Parasuram, "Indian Embassy Condemns Attacks." While much of this "damage control" colludes with Hindu nationalist agendas to discredit Muslims and Pakistan, Prime Minister Vajpayee was actually reprimanded by Sikh groups for both suggesting that women wear bindis in order to pass as Hindu and also for asking the U.S. government to protect Sikhs against hate crimes while not mentioning the need to protect Muslim Americans. See Sikh Mediawatch and Resource Task Force, Sikh-Sewa (N.Y.), Sikh Youth Federation of North America, United Sikhs in Service of America, Sikh Heresy Regulation Board, Sikh Network, Sikh Sisterhood, and Columbia University Sikhs, "Americans of Sikhs [*sic*] Extraction."

Reporting on U.S. hate crimes against Sikhs and community responses appeared in Indian as well as U.S.-based Indian papers, including Ashfaque Swapan, "South Asian Reporters"; IndiaExpress Bureau, "U.S. Sikhs' Initiative"; Associated Press, "Sikh Shot At"; Indo-Asian News Service, "White Hate Groups." See the press release from SikhNet, Sikh American Association, Sikh Coalition, Sikh Council on Religion and Education, Sikh Mediawatch and Resource Taskforce, and The Sikh Communications Council, "Sikhs Respond." The organizations authoring the press release state, "As Sikhs and as Americans, we are deeply distressed about the comments that Representative Saxby Chambliss made November 19th to a group of law enforcement officers in Valdosta, Georgia. He alluded to 'turning the Sheriff loose to arrest every Muslim that crosses the state line.' We in America look to our elected officials for responsible leadership and guidance." The Sikh Council on Religion and Education describes itself in the following manner: "Founded in 1998, the Sikh Council on Religion and Education (SCORE), based in Washington, serves as a think tank and represents Sikhs in various forums and venues. Its leadership has been invited repeatedly to the White House, Congress and by various non-governmental organizations to present the Sikh perspective from its inception and most recently, since the September 11th tragedy. The Sikh Council fosters understanding through education and interfaith relations, promoting the concept of community and working to secure a just society for all"; "About Us." The Sikh Coalition issued a "Resolution on Hate Crimes against Sikh-Americans: Congressional Briefing Package," on September 28, 2001.

See SikhNet, "Sikh Representatives Meet U.S. Congressional Leaders." On December 11, three months to the day after the September 11 tragedy, Sikh leadership from across the United States and Canada gathered under the dome of the U.S. Capitol Building for the first annual "One Nation United Memorial Program" sponsored by the Washington-based Sikh Council on Religion and Education; attending were members of Congress, government officials, and top leadership from commerce, labor, and the interfaith communities. This was the first event of its kind for the Sikh community to host in Washington. Senator Hillary Rodham Clinton stated, "We will always remember the sacrifices that were made by the Sikh Community in the wake of the terrible terrorist attacks of Sept. 11. No community suffered greater loss as a reaction to the terrible losses" of September 11. Leaders of Muslim, Arab, and Sikh communities met with Attorney General John Ashcroft on October 16, 2001, to voice their concerns about hate crimes; Frieden, "Ashcroft Meets with Muslim, Arab Leaders."

6. See Sanders, "Understanding Turbans"; and Pradhan, "The Mourning After." About SMART: "SMART was founded in 1996 to promote the fair and accurate portrayal of Sikh Americans and the Sikh religion in American media and society. The Sikh Mediawatch and Resource Task Force (SMART) is a nonprofit, nonpartisan membership based organization. Its mission is to combat bigotry and prejudice, protect the rights and religious freedoms of Sikh Americans, and provide resources that empower the Sikh American community." Sikh Mediawatch and Resources Taskforce, "SMART Calls for Action," http://www.saldef.org/.

7. See Mahabir and Vadarevu, "A Cultural Torment."

8. For a summary of the work of the Sikh American Alliance, a collaboration between SCORE, the Sikh Coalition, the Sikh Communications Council, and SMART, see Pradhan, "The Mourning After." Pradhan reports that the "Decreasing Hate by Increasing Awareness" campaign had a three-pronged plan: improving community relations (participating in prayers, vigils, relief efforts, and interfaith dinners), producing public relations materials for the media (press releases, educational videos), and creating stronger liaisons with government officials (meeting with the Departments of Transportation and Justice, inviting politicians to commemorative events).

9. See SikhNet's "Attack on America"; Sikh Mediawatch and Resource Taskforce, "SMART Initiates Airport Educational Campaign," and "SMART Encourages Community Members to Educate." Stating that many cases of "turban-removal have occurred at small or mid-size airports," such as Raleigh-Durham, Albany, and Phoenix, but also at larger airports such as JFK, SMART urges Sikhs to initiate educational forums for security personnel and airline employees about turbans and Sikhism and has developed presentations and other resources for this purpose. See also SikhNet, "Federal Aviation Administration." The Federal Aviation Administration (FAA) issued a set of directives detailing methods for conducting airport security based upon information presented by the Sikh Coalition and other Sikh organizations (SCORE, Sikh Communications, SMART, and USSA) "about the racial profiling that has caused turban-wearing Sikh-Americans to be denied air transportation while being publicly humiliated and embarrassed." "This kind of treatment to loyal Americans makes many feel humiliated, naked in public, victimized and most important, unwelcome in the country that many of us were born in," said Harpreet Singh, director of Community Relations of the Sikh Coalition. "It is especially upsetting since terrorists take great pains to wear typical American clothing in order to not stand out. We are grateful that the FAA has taken such a firm stand against this type of racial profiling as it is against everything America and Americans stand for." See also U.S. Department of Transportation, Federal Aviation Administration, "Guidance for Screeners"; Sikh Coalition, *Sikhs*, and "Your Rights and Avenues of Action"; Sikh Mediawatch and Resource Task Force, "Airport Security"; SikhWomen.com, "U.S. Department of Transporation"; Shenon and Toner, "Immigrant Arrests."

10. Distancing from Osama bin Laden and all else that threatens to tarnish the model minority image involves recourse to middle-class professionalism, benign multicultural patriotism, and heteronormativity. In this regard Gayatri Gopinath writes, "The Bollywood boom . . . incorporates South Asians into the U.S. national imaginary as pure spectacle to be safely consumed while keeping intact their essential alienness and difference; such incorporation holds safely at bay those marginalized noncitizens who function under the sign of terrorist and 'enemy within.'"; "Bollywood Spectacles," 162. It is worth mentioning the class and religious particulars of this stratification: the contemporary tensions between the Bollywood version of South Asian diaspora (the model minority gone global, as in the figure of the nonresident Indian) and the Sikh/Muslim terrorist version (underpinned by representations of working-class populations: taxi drivers, gas station workers, Indo-Caribbean immigrants) are emblematic of a new articulation of an older dynamic: the increasing polarization of model minority diasporic populations and discourses from those who may complicate or contaminate such discourses. Through this polarization we see increasing public and political paranoia regarding Sikhs, Pakistanis, Bangladeshis, and Muslim Indians paralleled by amplified forms of U.S. exceptionalism and escalating conservationism of the model minorities able to enact these exceptionalisms. Sikhs and Muslims, hypervisible because of the hijab and the turban, test the ambivalence of model minority ideologies and signal their unflattering excess.

11. In the early 1900s, the term "rag heads" was already being used in the northwestern United States to refer to turbaned men, mainly Sikhs. In 1907, hundreds of white workers rioted in Bellingham, Washington, "stormed makeshift Indian residences, stoned Indian workers, and successfully orchestrated the non-involvement of local police"; Shukla, *India Abroad*, 33–34. Some Sikhs evicted from Bellingham settled in Everett, Washington, where they were subsequently driven out in another riot; Hess, "The Forgotten Asian Americans," 109–10. On the violence in Everett and Billingham, also see Takaki, *Strangers from a Different Shore*, 297. The online exhibit *Echoes of Freedom* contains an image of a January 28, 1910, *New York Times* article, "Hindus Driven Out: Citizens at Marysville, Cal. Attack Them—British Consul Informed," briefly describing an attack on seventy "Hindus," which drove them out of Marysville; Library, University of California, Berkeley, *Echoes of Freedom*. See also Street, *Beasts of the Field*, 481–89, for an account of tensions between Punjabi and Japanese laborers.

On tensions between Hindu and Sikh communities in Canada after Indira Gandhi's assassination in 1984 and the downing of Air-India flight 182 in 1985, see Douglas Martin, "As Indian's Ranks in Canada Grow." On the reaction against Sikhs in the United States after the Air-India explosion, see Howe, "Sikh Leaders in U.S.," which quotes Jagjit Singh Mangat, president of the Sikh Cultural Society: "We have been dubbed as terrorists." On backlash after the Iran Hostage Crisis in 1979, see Chhibber, "Sikh Lives," which quotes Surinder Singh of Atlanta: "I had cut my hair, but kept my beard after the Iran hostage situation when I was heckled everywhere."

12. Axel, "The Diasporic Imaginary," 426.

13. Ibid.

14. Eng, "Transnational Adoption," 4. For other scholars theorizing queer diaspora, see Gopinath, *Impossible Desires*; Lee, "Toward a Queer Korean American Diasporic History"; Manalansan, *Global Divas*; Fortier, "Making Home"; Eng and Hom, "Q and A"; Sánchez-Eppler and Patton, "Introduction."

15. See Susan Koshy's work on the history of South Asian American exceptionalism, such as "Morphing Race into Ethnicity."

16. Atif Toor, interview by author, New York City, July 2004. Toor has been a SALGA organizer since 1990.

17. As the "India Shining" project launches the normative upper-cast Hindu Northern Indian subject as an economic, cultural, and cosmopolitan player on the global scene, national Indian queerness, a liability at home in relation to Hindutva politics, is a form of cultural capital, however tenuous, in the global consumer market and human rights and NGO arenas. That is, Hindu Indian queerness, as an identity paradigm indebted to modernity, works in the service of consolidating normative Indian modernity, in both the homeland and its diasporas. This is especially true, for example, with Indo-Caribbean populations, who historically and contemporarily function as "disavowed modernity"; see Niranjana, *Mobilizing India*. If Indo-Caribbean populations in the United States (predominantly New York and Miami) are already marginalized by dominant South Asian model minority prototypes, South Asian queer diasporic formations that leave their own Hindu-centric dynamics and representations uninterrogated may in fact enhance these dominant forms instead of being excluded from them, as is usually assumed.

18. Interviews with current and former SALGA members reveal that Islamophobia and anti-Muslim sentiment is and has been alive in the South Asian Gay and Lesbian Association's membership. We now have right-wing BJP supporters who refuse to march in the India Day parade or the gay pride parade if signs condemning communal violence, specifically of the genocide of Muslims in Gujarat, are present.

19. In the early 1900s turbaned Punjabi Sikhs constituted the majority of the first immigrants from India to arrive in numbers in the United States, working primarily on railroads and farms and in lumber mills in California, Oregon, and Washington. While initial press on these newly arrived laborers described them as Sikhs, they were rapidly assimilated into the lexicon of U.S. immigration racial categorization, despite a burgeoning separatist Sikh identity emerging in India at this time (this is documented in *Roots in the Sand*). Renamed "Hindoo," a term meaning "from Hindustan," Sikhs were simultaneously transfigured into the representative Indian majority, Hindus, as well as abnegated precisely through the difference from Hindus they sought to embody. Turbans, specifically Sikh turbans, proactively and intentionally mark a distinction from Hindus, who do not wear turbans (exceptions are events such as weddings). During partition, turbans were a primary factor in distinguishing Hindu from Sikh from Muslim.

20. Ronald Takaki's chapter "Tide of Turbans" in *Strangers from a Different Shore* speaks generally of turbans: "Yards upon yards of cotton, calico, or silk were swathed about their heads, forming turbans, cone-shaped or round like a mushroom button, with waves or points directly in the middle of their foreheads." Writing that Indians represented the specter of the new Yellow Peril, Takaki quotes Herman Sceffauer, a

writer for *Forum* magazine: "This time the chimera is not the saturnine, almond-eyed mask, the shaven head, the snaky pig-tail of the multitudinous Chinese, nor the close-cropped bullet-heads of the suave and smiling Japanese, but a face of finer features, rising, turbaned out of the Pacific and bringing a new and anxious question." See Takaki, *Strangers from a Different Shore*, 63, 296–97.

21. *United States v. Bhagat Singh Thind*, 1923 U.S. LEXIS 2544, 617.

22. The *Thind* case must also be read within the context of a number of immigration rulings at the time, including the Asiatic Barred Zone (created by the Immigration Act of 1917), a number of other citizenship petitions by Asians (including *Takao Ozawa v. United States*, ruled in 1922 and brought by a Japanese man; *In re Mohan Singh* in 1919; *In re Sadar Bhagwab Singh* in 1917; *In re Akhay Kumar Mozumdar* in 1913; and *United States v. Ali* in 1925), and the decline of the revolutionary Gadhr movement that sought to overthrow British colonialism in India. Further, as Nayan Shah's research on the policing and prosecution of sodomy indicates, there were growing anxieties attached to the masculinities and sexualities of Asian migrants, specifically "Hindu sodomites," who were often seen to be preying on white youth. Shah's research on the court cases of Arjun Singh, Jamil Singh, Rola Singh, and Keshn Singh reviews the descriptions that police gave of the apparently sexual positions in which these men were discovered, without mention of turbans; it is unclear if that signals their absence or if they were so prominent as to be a given attribute. See N. Shah, "Between 'Oriental Depravity' and 'Natural Degenerates.'"

23. We can read the *Thind* case, then, as an instance where the ocular-specular is hailed, but the recourse to "resemblance" is really about common sense, instinct, or "something everybody knows."

24. Finally, the slippage from Sikh to Hindu, while initially appearing semantic, is actually the foreshadowing of post-1965 model minority discourses and how and who those discourses exclude and include. That is to say, among South Asian populations, the normative Hindu has come to personify the idealization of the model minority construct. While this can correctly be ascribed to structural factors such as economics, immigration patterns, and the consolidation of bourgeois immigrant family models, the undertheorized variable is simply that Sikhs and Muslims *look and feel* different. This point was driven home during the Gulf War in 1991 but most recently and vigorously in a post-9/11 racial climate of scapegoating. A special irony is the global celebration of Desi-ness, not only through the skyrocketing popularity of Bollywood film, but also in fashion, food, lifestyle, and the lauding of India's technological-industrial presence (though increasing vexed by resistance to job outsourcing). These issues form the composite framing of *India Shining*. Complemented by the consolidation of the Hindu right in India and its burgeoning business and political relationships with the United States (and less overtly, Israel), the Bollywood film industry often represents Sikh characters as infantilized, idiotic, comic relief or as pathologically violent and hypermasculine, despite the prominence of Punjabi Bhangra music. The erotic charge of the turban is also a focal point of Bollywood films such as *Ghadhar*, whose most sensual and sexually suggestive scene is the languorous wrapping of the turban on the protagonist's head by his wife. *Mission Kashmir* is one example of a Bollywood treatment of the emasculated Sikh: a lone

Sikh soldier is afraid to jump off a platform that rests atop planted explosives for fear of setting them off. Eventually, he urinates on himself while other non-Sikh Indian soldiers assist him in jumping. Amit Rai has argued that, in *Mission Kashmir*, the Islamic terrorist is "an infection moving through the body politic"; "Patriotism." Adult Sikh characters frequently are depicted with the *patka*, a garment for underneath the turban, which is typically worn by boys until they reach adulthood. The movie *The Legend of Bhagat Singh* has also been criticized for ignoring Singh's apparent reembrace of Sikhism in the later years of his life.

Sikh turbans function as an ambivalent signifier of inclusion and expulsion, marking both the incorporation of Sikhs into the Indian nation and the violence inflicted upon them through this incorporation. There is a complex history that ties Sikh communities to the discourse of terrorism. As is well known, the Indian state throughout much of the 1980s was involved in a massive ideological labor as well as bloody police repression that sought to mark off Sikh groups in Punjab and in the diaspora as in fact terrorist and to contain the movement for Khalistan (a separatist Punjab). This history positions Sikh identity in an ambivalent relationship to the current war on terrorism: on the one hand, Sikhs in India and in the diaspora, especially gurdwara communities, face severe repercussions from the USA PATRIOT Act; on the other hand, their self-positioning as victims of both state-sponsored terrorism (for example, of the 1984 riots in New Delhi) and, as American patriots, victims of the "Islamic" terrorism of 9/11 simultaneously invokes a double nationalism: Sikh and American nationalisms. *OMB Watch* claims, "The 'USA PATRIOT Act' (PL 107-56) could pose big problems for nonprofits, especially those that advocate changes in U.S. foreign policy or provide social services to individuals that become targets of government investigations. The central problem is a vague, overbroad definition of a new crime, 'domestic terrorism.' In addition, greatly expanded search and surveillance powers can be invoked under a lowered threshold, requiring only that investigators assert that information sought is relevant to a foreign intelligence investigation"; *OMB Watch*, "Anti-Terrorism Bill."

For praise of the USA PATRIOT Act by Sikh organizations, see the Sikh Coalition's press release, "Measure Supporting Sikh Americans." This press release was also posted to the discussion board of www.sikhnet.com by the site's creator, Gurumuskuk Singh Khalsa. Khalsa augments the press release, writing, "Congratulations! As a result of your efforts the House and Senate Resolutions were included in the Patriot Act, approved in the House and Senate, and signed into law by the President of the United States!" The press release reads, in part: "S.Con.Res.74 and H.Res.255 condemn crimes against Sikh Americans in the wake of the September 11th terrorist attacks and state acts of violence against Sikh Americans are to be prevented and prosecuted. . . . 'This law represents a significant milestone for Sikh Americans as it addresses the unique nature of the issues faced by Sikhs in the aftermath of September 11th, and calls for protection of our civil liberties, along with those of all Americans,' said Gurpreet Singh Dhillon, Advisory Board member of the Sikh American Association." (About the Sikh Coalition: "The Sikh Coalition was started as an effort to educate the greater North American community on Sikhs and Sikhism, the coalition seeks to safeguard the rights of all citizens as well as to promote the Sikh identity and communicates the collective interests of Sikhs to the community at large. The coalition serves as a resource for all organizations and individuals as well as a point of contact to Sikh people.")

25. An exception was the Alliance of South Asians Taking Action: "As South Asians, we stand in solidarity with communities of color, including Middle Eastern/West Asian communities (Afghanis, Arabs, Arab-Americans, Iraqis, and Iranians), rather than trying to distance ourselves from them in order to secure safety. We also recognize that many South Asians are Muslim, and deserve to be free from prejudice and discrimination as Muslims"; "Press Release."

26. KRAC.com, "Man Accused." The perpetrator, John Lucas, turned himself in, stating that he committed these acts out of "senseless patriotism" after Sikhs did not lower the flag at the gurdwara. "I didn't understand it was a religious flag. I thought it was a village flag. I didn't understand why it couldn't be lowered for those who died." The news report includes the following description of his activities: "Investigators said that Lucas, in an act of defiance, also jumped into a pond of holy water at the temple—water transported all the way from India." See also Human Rights Watch, "Stop Hate Crimes Now."

27. See Kong, "Arabs, Muslims,"; Healy, "3 Indians Attacked"; Menchaca, "Sikh Community Outraged"; IndiaExpress Bureau, "U.S. Sikhs' Initiative." In response to the shooting of a truck driver, Avtar Singh, who survived his attack, the Anti-Defamation League offered a reward for information on his attackers; Associated Press, "Sikhs Coping"; Anti-Defamation League, "ADL Offers Reward." See Sikh Coalition, "Press Packet." Hate violence continued a year after September 11, 2001. See Associated Press, "Anti-Arab Incidents."

28. Ahmad, "Homeland Insecurity," 108.

29. Other early incidents included the fatal shooting of Adel Karas in San Gabriel; Associated Press, "FBI to Investigate." In St. Petersburg, Florida, a hijab'ed woman driving home had her car beaten with baseball bats; a mosque in Ohio was rammed into by a car; a 66-year-old turbaned Sikh man was beaten by four youths with a baseball bat outside a Sikh gurdwara in Queens, New York; Bishnoi, "Hate Crimes Rise." A Pakistani storeowner was killed in Dallas, Texas; IslamOnline and News Agencies, "Pakistani Grocer Shot Dead in Texas." Additional reporting includes CNN, "Hate Crimes"; Mangat, "Hate Crimes"; Bradford, "Re: Hate Crimes"; Nanda, "Sikhs Become Targets"; Purewal, "Threats, Snide Remarks"; and Naim, "SABA" (includes "Important Message to All NetIP North American Officers and Members"). For a collection of reported hate crimes that occurred in the first month after September 11, 2001, see Hamad, "Appendix." Actions described include throwing bags of blood at an immigration office and law office in San Francisco; attempting to run a Muslim woman off the road in St. Petersburg, Florida; attacking, robbing, and cutting the penis of an Indian man in Fort Wayne, Indiana; leaving a mutilated squirrel and a note in a mailbox in Minneapolis; beating a woman on her way to prayer in Memphis; and numerous fire bombings. This list is clearly not exhaustive, and activities range from various forms of verbal harassment and physical violence aimed at people and places assumed to be connected to Muslims and/or Arabs, as well as loss of employment and racial profiling.

30. As a logical amplification of the Terrorism Information and Prevention System, for example, hate crimes work on behalf of the nation-state by sanctioning a policing mechanism that the liberal multicultural state itself cannot openly propagate. It thus works to the benefit of the state to condemn racial hate crimes on the one hand while instituting growing measures for racial profiling on the other. Pleading for tolerance, President George W. Bush visited Arab American mosques and Muslim and Sikh community forums (in part to shore up U.S. alliances with conservative Arab regimes) during the same week that he initiated passage of the Anti-Terrorism Act, now known as the USA PATRIOT Act; Milbank and Wax, "Bush Visits Mosque." His opponent in the 2004 presidential campaign, Senator John Kerry, publicly linked Sikhs to terrorism. Kerry apologized under pressure from U.S. Sikh groups; see United News of India, "U.S. Senator Kerry Apologizes." Richard A. Gephardt released a statement that stuck to a message against violence and referenced the "shameful mistake of putting Japanese-Americans in internment camps where they were stripped of their rights, their dignity, their possessions" during World War II; "Gephardt Statement."

31. The U.S. National Visa Registry for the Green Card Lottery Scheme, for example, requires a photo of the applicant, who must not be wearing a hat or head covering. A British resident, Harjit Singh, had his application returned to him because in his picture he was, of course, wearing his turban. The National Visa Registry wrote, "NO covering on/around the head is permitted (in the ones you sent, you were wearing a hat, which is NOT permitted)." The new photo requirements, which also state that the applicant may not be wearing a "religious covering on the face," were purportedly authorized by the U.S. State Department in August 2001, one month before the 9/11 attacks. Harjit Singh explains it thus to the Registry: "As is the crown to sovereign, so is a turban to a Sikh. . . . For a Sikh the turban is the frontier of faith and unbelief. It is deemed to give the Sikh dignity, consecration, and majestic humility." The Registry responded to Singh's explanation of the religious significance of the turban by again requesting a photo without the turban, stating, "There are many here who do understand the difference, not only between the two faiths, but between those of any faith who advocate the use of violence, and those who do not. . . . Please do not think the requirement is related to the incident of September 11th." In Alabama, a post-9/11 policy which stated that no head coverings of any kind could be worn when taking a driver's license photo, thus prohibiting hijabs, turbans, and nun habits, was repealed in February 2004, after a campaign by the American Civil Liberties Union in conjunction with local Sikhs; Rawls, "Riley Administration." A similar problem was faced by Chitratan Singh when he attempted to get a driver's license; Sikh American Legal Defense and Education Fund, "Alabama Discriminatory Driver's License Policy Overturned."

    Struggles over whether or not turbans (and to some extent, at least in terms of reporting, head coverings) are appropriate work wear included those serving in the military and police. See Jewett, "Army Rules"; Sikh Coalition, "Allow Turbaned Sikhs to Serve"; Gardiner, "Sikh Wants End to Turban Ban"; Purnick, "Transit Rules?"; and Pete Donohue, "TA Edict."

32. Yuskaev and Weiner, "Secular and Religious Rights."

33. For example, the U.S. Department of State Bureau of Public Affairs released an educational video accompanied by curriculum materials, titled *Terrorism: A War without Borders*; fifteen thousand copies were distributed to middle and high schools throughout the country. In this first effort by the State Department to disseminate information about terrorism to students, Sikhs are categorically called terrorists— Sikh terrorists (there is no naming of right-wing Christian or Muslim terrorism)— and the 1984 occupation of the Golden Temple (Darbar Sahib) in Amritsar, India, is portrayed as a siege by Sikh terrorists. As with the other terrorist acts highlighted, including the Oklahoma City Bombing and 1997 Hamas suicide bombing, the complexities of the 1984 incident and the Khalistan movement are smoothed over and Indian state terrorism unmentioned. However, the video highlights the delicate balance for diasporic Sikhs who must inhabit a split identity: terrorist in India, patriot in America. Sikh advocacy groups failed to convince the State Department to revise the video, but more significant, in their responses they were unable to portray the conundrum of this liminal, straddled position. See also Kaur and The Sikh Sentinel, "State Department Tells School Children Sikhs Are Terrorists"; and Ek Ong Kaar Kaur Khalsa, "Re: State Department Tells School Children."

34. A lingering query that underscores this difference: Why is the turban exempt, for now, from the French ban on religious head coverings, intended for Islamic headscarves, Jewish yarmulkes, and large Christian crosses? While Sikhs have been arbitrarily asked to remove turbans, for example, when Jagmohan Singh was asked to take off his turban in order to enter a Paris government building in January 2004, French Education Minister Luc Ferry stated that turbans would be allowed provided they are "invisible." This has been interpreted by French Sikhs to mean that Sikhs would be allowed to wear a hairnet as a substitute, thus effectively invisibilizing the turban; R. Z. Ahmed, "Sikh Forced to Take Off Turban." Shortly prior to this comment, Ferry stated that the veil is "a militant sign that calls for militant countersigns," whereas the turban, if allowed to remain "discreet," would not be a problem; Sciolino, "Next Target."

35. From Frantz Fanon's "Algeria Unveiled" (which names women as the lynchpin of the nation), to the "Women's Question" foregrounded in Indian anticolonial and decolonizing movements (Partha Chatterjee argues that women uphold the inner domestic space of spirituality, culture, tradition, and home; men are the outward faces of modernity), women's bodies have been liminal demarcations of inside and outside, tradition and modernity, in terms of physicality (clothing, hair, veiling, modesty, rituals), behavior (chastity, heterosexual conformity, reproduction), and symbolism (myths, "mother tongue," territory/land). Cultural nationalism in these feminist accounts is reliant on a heterosexual matrix of sex (biology) and gender (subjectivity) and desire (sexuality): male is masculine and desires female, female is feminine and desires male (Butler); all that deviates is pathological. In the case of Sikhs, although women are expected to keep their hair unshorn, men embody the most visible vehicles of cultural adherence or betrayal. See Fanon, *A Dying Colonialism*; Chatterjee, "The Nationalist Resolution."

36. S. Ahmed, *The Cultural Politics of Emotion*, 49.

37. Spivak, *The Postcolonial Critic*, 125.

38. Butler, "Endangered/Endangering," 17, 16, 17, 16.

39. Ibid., 19, 21, 20.

40. S. Ahmed, "Affective Economies," 119, 124, 127, 119, 131.

41. Ibid., 123, 135.

42. Ibid., 128, 126.

43. Cross-faith and interfaith dialogues are part of this mission; see IndiaExpress Bureau, "U.S. Sikhs."

44. For example, the documentary *Mistaken Identity: Sikhs in America* is billed as a film that shows "a white American, the young student Amanda Gesine, trying to demystify the enigma of Sikh Americans while sharing the hopes and desires of Americans from all ethnic backgrounds who seek to close ranks against bigotry and hatred. Amanda plays the host and investigative journalist in a search to discover her Sikh American neighbours." Here, Sikhs are made out to be exotic creatures devoid of any modernist traits: a sense of their "enigma" speaking to Orientalist fantasies. In short, the mistaken identity line of reasoning articulates a fantasy about cultural difference that behaves as if racism did not exist. Asians in Media, "Award Winning Documentary."

45. Massumi adds, "Call that 'something recognizable' a quality (or property)"; *Parables for the Virtual*, 60–61.

46. Saldanha, "Reontologising Race," 13, 18.

47. Interestingly, all three authors—Butler, Ahmed, and Saldanha—read Fanon's work in order to make their divergent arguments. Perhaps pending is some thought on the potential of a rereading of Fanon through Massumi's work (or better yet, a rereading of Massumi through Fanon's work).

48. Saldanha, "Reontologising Race," 10, 20, 19.

49. Kalra, "Locating the Sikh *Pagh*," 77, 82, 84.

50. On the history of British colonial fascination with Sikh turbans, see Axel, *The Nation's Tortured Body*, especially "The Maharaja's Glorious Body" (39–78) on the travels to Britain of Maharaja Duleep Singh, the "last Sikh ruler of Punjab" (39). Axel traces the emergence of the Sikh subject in the mid- to late nineteenth century within the "colonial scene of surrender" (41), marked predominantly by the visual identification of a Sikh male turbaned body (42). This visual recognition produces the Sikh turbaned male as a regulatory figure and the Sikh subject par excellence, yet simultaneously produces this subject as "a figure of subjection to the [British] Crown" (49). Axel's historical analysis demonstrates that the "image of the male Sikh body became increasingly translocal" (63), cleaving and collapsing various male Sikh bodies: sardars, Amritdharis, and the tortured body.

51. Massumi, *Parables for the Virtual*, 95.

52. Deleuze and Guattari, *A Thousand Plateaus*, 88.

53. Taussig, *Mimesis and Alterity*.

54. May Joseph, "Old Routes," 46. On racial melancholia, see Eng and Han, "A Dialogue."

55. Deleuze and Guattari, *A Thousand Plateaus*, 492.

56. Chow, "Writing in the Realm of the Senses," ii.

57. Foucault, "*Society Must Be Defended*," 254, 255.

58. Massumi, *Parables for the Virtual*, 14.

59. Sikhs, in particular men, have become fodder for renewed anti-Sikh sentiment even from purportedly progressive factions of South Asian communities. The South Asian novelist Bharati Mukherjee, criticized for her deplorable generalizations about non-Hindus and acclaimed for her portrayals of immigrant acculturation (as appears, for example, in *Jasmine*), claimed in an interview on May 2, 2003, with Bill Moyers that Sikhs had established "sleeper terrorist cells" across the United States and Canada; *NOW with Bill Moyers*. Her efforts to transpose the anxiety attached to the vocabulary of terror of the al-Qaeda network are bolstered by her accusation later in the interview that since 9/11, Sikhs have been conducting terrorist fundraising efforts in mosques on a transnational scale. In this puzzling conflation of Sikh temples of worship with Muslim mosques, Mukherjee's outrageous statements would be hilarious if she were not considered such an exemplar of model minority discourses, her novels being immensely and widely popular among South Asian American and (white) liberal readers. Her conduct is consistent with her literary depictions of Punjabi Sikhs, Sikh men in particular, as militant religious fanatics, inherently violent, hypermasculine, "lecherous, dirty, and uncultured, especially when they [drink], and they [drink] all the time" (see *Wife*, as one case in point); in contrast, the Hindu male subject masquerades as the secular subject, as the central, indeed paradigmatic Indian subject. The Sikh Mediawatch and Resource Task Force responded to the interview by writing a letter to Moyers: "In fact, the Sikh community harbors no enmity towards the United States or Canada, nor are Sikhs raising money for any terrorist campaigns. There are no Sikh 'sleeper terrorist cells'"; "Interview with Bharati Mukherjee." This example demonstrates the intricately bound natures of Hindu and American nationalisms: the most rigorous refutation of Hindu nationalism can best (and perhaps only) be achieved through an announcement of loyalty and allegiance to the United States. For the feminized turban wearer, the convergence of vitriolic U.S. heteronormative patriotism and the deepening entrenchment of Hindu nationalist politics both in India and the diaspora render Sikhs and Muslims doubly vulnerable. The online transcript of the interview is now preceded by a statement that an "editing error" resulted in "misunderstanding and confusion," and that Mukherjee did not wish to imply "that she believes that Sikhs were involved in fundraising activities in support of the terrorism activities of 9/11." This change to the transcript, which inserts "[Muslim terrorists]" into the interview before Mukherjee's claims about terrorist fundraising, is the result of SMART's activities; see Sikh Mediawatch and Resource Taskforce, "PBS Producer Recognizes Error."

60. Massumi, *Parables for the Virtual*, 139.

61. Gladwell, "Troublemakers," 42.

62. Ibid.

63. H. Campbell, "Beyond Militarism," 31.

64. As such, the *Thind* case foreshadows, through its disciplinary apparatus, the proliferation of detention technologies; indeed, the spaces of citizenship inclusion offered through liberal multicultural model minority discourses operate both as spaces of dissent and extensions of hypervisible detention cells—that is to say, detention is no longer only a disciplinary apparatus of isolation but most insidiously distributed

control within the public sphere. Thanks to Amit Rai for a synthesis of citizenship as a form of detention.

65. Turbaned individuals in multicultural America have often been referred to as "towel heads" and "rag heads"; U.S. Congressman James Cooksey (R-LA) called them "diapers." See McKinney, "Cooksey." See also Sikh Mediawatch and Resources Taskforce, "SMART Calls for Action," where SMART initiates a national letter-writing and telephone campaign protesting Cooksey's remarks.

66. Butler, interview.

67. Deleuze, *Negotiations*, 181.

68. Rai, untitled paper presented at "Beyond Biopolitics."

69. Massumi, untitled paper presented at "Beyond Biopolitics."

70. As an example: In *Hitman 2: Silent Assassin*, a videogame released in 2002 by Eidos Interactive, Sikh and Dalit characters are teamed together to battle a Western hero. The Orientalist game takes the player to Punjab, India, where one site of bloodshed is a Sikh temple of worship, a gurdwara: "A magnificent, ancient gurdwara (Sikh temple)—complete with marble inlays, glazed tiles, filigree partitions, priceless old wall paintings and gold domes—is flanked by a qila (old fort) and protected by high walls as well as fanatical believers—in front, a maze of small shops and bangalas (small houses) gives evidence of riches and prosperity in this otherwise poverty stricken remote region of Punjab in Northern India. Relentless loos (hot dry winds that blow across the plains of North India during summer) keeps this little oasis isolated from the outside world. A Sikh uprising in this region in the mid 80's was ruthlessly cracked down on by government issued troops, and many innocents were killed—ever since, no outsider has dared venture into this territory for fear of reprisals"; quoted in SikhNet, "Please Sign Hitman 2 Video Petition." What the video game enables goes far beyond the representational dilemma addressed by Sikh advocacy groups, who argue that violence begets violence and "negative" media representation must be eradicated and supplanted with educational representation. The Sikh Coalition writes: "Hitman 2 sends messages to youth engaged with the game plot that killing people who look different and killing in general is a celebrated value in today's society. These dangerous notions perpetuate intolerance amongst people in a very multicultural global village"; "Video Game by Eidos Interactive." However, in effect the simulation of terrorist warfare allows for an extension of the counterterrorism imaginary, a production of the docile patriot as indispensable to the war on terrorism not simply through the forces of disciplinary surveillance but through combat and attack itself, beyond postmodern time-space compression, through the collapsing of speed, time, place, and virtual and material corporealities. As many critical theorists have argued, these images do not simply do the work of representation—reflection and (re)production—but they also function as weapons of war, as intrinsic to the very perpetuation, experience, and maintenance of war; see Butler, "Contingent Foundations," 11; Mitchell, "The War of Images." It is through this activity of simulated death that the bias crime perpetrator's alibi of mistaken identity is revealed as fallacious. This experience of the game is supported by proliferating technologies of voyeuristic participation, where Hollywood, the Internet, blogs, CNN, airplane simulations, terrorist rap videos, photo-shopped cartoon strips all

engage in verisimilitudes of absence and presence, pretenses and concealments, and have been developed in tandem with media technologies used in military combat: GIS, satellite surveillance photography, radar, sonar, electronic battlefield, military training simulations, for example, airplane simulators such as F-Stealth, Apache; videogames such as *Battlefield 1942*. See also the simulation by Gonzalo Frasca, *September 12th: A Toy World*. In what Horace Campbell names the "armaments culture," this conjoining of the entertainment industry and military establishments has deep roots: military consultants are used for the film and television industries to "simulate situations that emotionally tie citizens to the ideology and practices of militarism"; corporate alliances between the Pentagon, Hollywood, and Silicon Valley abound; "Beyond Militarism," 28. See also M. Parenti, *Make-Believe Media*; Der Derian, *Virtuous War*; also see Information Technology, War and Peace Project, *InfoTechWarPeace*. Indeed, the language of video simulation, the target that is the blip on the screen, is part and parcel of the vernacular of the military.

conclusion

A very preliminary version of this conclusion appeared as "Queer Times, Queer Assemblages," in *Social Text* 23, no. 3–4 84–85 (fall–winter 2005): 121–40.

1. Scott, "Gender," 46.
2. Chow, *The Age of the World Target*, 66–69.
3. See Deleuze, *Negotiations*, 182.
4. Alarcón, "The Theoretical Subject(s)," 361.
5. Foucault, *"Society Must Be Defended,"* 252–53; Chow, *The Protestant Ethnic*, 7.
6. One trenchant example can be found in the recent Katrina debates regarding the relation of African Americans to the category "refugee." While this debate raged on, many missed what was really at stake: not what those displaced from the Gulf Coast hurricanes were to be named, but where to put them, that is, where to dispose of them. Thus the juridical differences in the status of citizens versus refugees became potent fodder for obscuring or masking the real connections being made through the conjoining of African Americans and other black populations to refugees, that is, the construction of populations of "human waste" (Bauman, *Wasted Lives*), of the living dying, or of those occupying spaces of deferred death, the connection of refugee, evacuee, detainee. "Without papers" takes on a new intonation here.
7. Clough, *The Affective Turn*; Massumi, *Parables for the Virtual*; Hardt, "Affective Labor"; Hardt and Negri, *Empire*; Parisi, *Abstract Sex*; De Landa, *Intensive Science*; Muñoz, "Feeling Brown"; S. Ahmed, *The Cultural Politics of Emotions*; Sedgwick, *Touching Feeling*; Cvetkovich, *An Archive of Feelings*.
8. Spivak, "Can the Subaltern Speak?"
9. Massumi, *Parables for the Virtual*, 35.
10. Muñoz, "Feeling Brown," 70, 67–79.
11. Rai, untitled paper presented at "Beyond Biopolitics."
12. Wilson, *Neural Geographies*, 15.
13. As an important exception see Elizabeth Grosz's earlier work: *Volatile Bodies* and *Space, Time, and Perversion*. An incisive article by Miriam Fraser, "What Is the Matter

of Feminist Criticism?,'" sketches out the work of other important theorists debate whom I have been unable to incorporate due to time and space const Karen Barad, Vicky Kirby, and Pheng Cheah. She also gestures to the formativ of Donna Haraway.

14. For examples of this work, see McRuer, "Compulsory Able-Bodiedness," and "Composing Bodies"; Chinn, "Feeling Her Way"; Clare, "Stolen Bodies"; Shildrick, "Queering Performativity."

15. Saldanha, "Reontologising Race," 18, 22, 20–21.

16. Wilson, *Neural Geographies*, 3.

17. Parisi, *Abstract Sex*, 1, 102, 99.

18. Clough, *Autoaffection*, 135.

19. Edelman, *No Future*, 4.

20. Ibid., 17.

21. Deleuze and Guattari, *A Thousand Plateaus*, 8.

22. I have had many incredible conversations with Patricia Clough about assemblages in specific and Deleuzian philosophy in general. I can only hope to convey a small part of what I have learned from her here.

23. Massumi, *Parables for the Virtual*, 3, 3–4.

24. Ibid., 5, 10, 6, 8.

25. Jagose, *Inconsequence*, x, xi, 145, 144.

26. Massumi, *Parables for the Virtual*, 8, 7–8.

27. Ibid., 8, 9, 15.

28. Spivak, "Practical Politics."

29. Hardt, "The Withering of Civil Society," 32.

30. Parisi, *Abstract Sex*, 37.

31. Weizman, "Walking through Walls."

32. This is not to disavow or minimize the important interventions that intersectional theorizing makes possible and continues to stage, or the feminist critical spaces that gave rise to intersectional analyses. For examples of this work and fairly comprehensive review essays, see K. W. Crenshaw, "Mapping the Margins"; Combahee River Collective, "A Black Feminist Statement"; Lorde, *Sister Outsider*; Stasiulis, "Intersectional Feminist Theorizing"; McCall, "The Complexity of Intersectionality"; Blackwell and Naber, "Intersectionality."

33. Hage, "'Comes a Time We Are All Enthusiasm,'" 66–67. Hage extends his observation in the epigraph to elucidate why many leftist factions have resisted embracing the Palestinian cause: "The violent resistance of the Palestinian people stands in the way between them (the leftists) and their radicalisms. The sooner the Palestinians swap the bombs for bottles of whiskey or gin, the better. Then, the radical leftists can become truly radical and outraged about the conditions of the Palestinian people without violently disrupting their leftism" (82).

34. Ibid., 77, 74, 77.

35. Mbembe, "Necropolitics," 12, 36.

36. Spivak, "Class and Culture in Diaspora."

37. Ramachandran, "Women Suicide Bombers"; *Guardian*, "'I Made the Ring.'"

38. Spivak, "Terror," 96–97.

39. For an interesting collection of short essays that attempt to subvert and deconstruct the problematic replay of these binaries of resistance/complicity, martyr/perpetrator, life/death in regard to female militancy in general and female suicide bombers in specific, see *to kill, to die: female contestations on gender and political violence*: Hilla Dayan, "Poisoned Cats and Angels of Death"; Julie V. G. Rajan, "Subversive Visibility and Political Agency"; and an interview with Drucilla Cornell, "Ethical Feminism and the Call of the Other (Woman)."

40. C. J. Cohen, "Punks, Bulldaggers."

41. Foucault, *The History of Sexuality*.

references

Abu-Lughod, Lila. "Do Muslim Women Really Need Saving? Anthropological Reflections on Cultural Relativism and its Others." *American Anthropologist* 104, no. 3 (September 2002): 783–90.

Adam, Barry D. "The Defense of Marriage Act and American Exceptionalism: The 'Gay Marriage' Panic in the United States." *Journal of the History of Sexuality* 12, no. 2 (April 2003): 259–76.

Afary, Janet, and Kevin B. Anderson. *Foucault and the Iranian Revolution: Gender and the Seductions of Islamism.* Chicago: University of Chicago Press, 2005.

Agamben, Giorgio. *Homo Sacer: Sovereign Power and Bare Life.* Translated by Daniel Heller-Roazen. Stanford: Stanford University Press, 1998.

——. *The State of Exception.* Translated by Kevin Attell. Chicago: University of Chicago Press, 2005.

Ahmad, Muneer. "Homeland Insecurity: Racial Violence the Day after September 11." *Social Text* 20, no. 3 72 (fall 2002): 101–15.

Ahmed, Sara. "Affective Economies." *Social Text* 22, no. 2 79 (summer 2004): 117–39.

——. *The Cultural Politics of Emotion.* London: Routledge, 2005.

Ahmed, Rashmee Z. "Sikh Forced to Take Off Turban." *Times of India,* January 22, 2004. http://timesofindia.indiatimes.com (accessed June 21, 2006).

Alam, Faisal. "Gay Media's Failure to Accurately Report Stories Adds to Growing Islamophobia and Hatred towards Islamic World." August 1, 2005. http://www.ukgay news.org.uk (accessed September 9, 2006).

——. "Remembering September 11th as a Queer Muslim." *The Gully,* September 11, 2002. http://www.thegully.com (accessed June 11, 2006).

Alarcón, Norma. "The Theoretical Subject(s) of *This Bridge Called My Back* and Anglo-American Feminism." In *Making Face, Making Soul/Haciendo Caras: Creative and Critical Perspectives by Feminists of Color,* edited by Gloria Anzaldúa, 356–69. San Francisco: Aunt Lute Foundation Books, 1990.

Alexander, M. Jacqui. "Erotic Autonomy as a Politics of Decolonization: An Anatomy of Feminist and State Practice." In *Feminist Genealogies, Colonial Legacies, Democratic Futures,* edited by Chandra Talpade Mohanty and M. Jacqui Alexander, 63–100. New York: Routledge, 1996.

——. "Not Just (Any)*Body* Can Be a Citizen: The Politics of Law, Sexuality and Postcoloniality in Trinidad and Tobago and the Bahamas." *Feminist Review* 48 (autumn 1994): 5–23.

——. *Pedagogies of Crossing: Meditations on Feminism, Sexual Politics, Memory, and the Sacred.* Durham: Duke University Press, 2005.

Al-Fatiha. "Al-Fatiha." Updated June 2006. www.al-fatiha.org (accessed June 10, 2006).

——. "Al-Fatiha Calls for a Second Day of Action against Egypt." Press release. November 3, 2001. Republished at Sodomy Laws, World Laws, Egypt, www.sodomylaws.org (accessed June 13, 2006).

——. "LGBTQ Muslims Condemn Terrorist Attack: Warn of Repercussions against Arabs and Muslims." September 12, 2001. Reprinted in *PFLAG-Cleveland Newsletter*, November 2001. http://www.pflagcleveland.org (accessed June 13, 2006).

——. "LGBTQ Muslims Express Concerns about Infringements on Civil Liberties." Press release. October 27, 2001. http://www.peaceresponse.org (accessed February 19, 2003; no longer available).

——. "Queer Rights Leaders to Address War against Iraq." Press release. November 6, 2002. http://www.q.co.za (accessed June 13, 2006).

Al-Fatiha Foundation. "Al-Fatiha Condemns Sexual Humiliation of Iraqi Detainees." Press release. May 10, 2004. http://ukgaynews.org.uk (accessed June 19, 2006).

Ali, Kecia. "Special Focus: Islam: Same-Sex Sexual Activity and Lesbian and Bisexual Women." *The Feminist Sexual Ethics Project*, Brandeis University. December 10, 2002. http://www.brandeis.edu (accessed June 11, 2006).

Al Jazeera. "Hersh: U.S. GIs Sodomised Iraqi Boys." July 19, 2004. http://english.aljazeera.net (accessed June 19, 2006).

——. "Israeli Interrogator Was at Abu Ghraib." July 3, 2004. http://english.aljazeera.net (accessed June 19, 2006).

Allen, Charlotte. "Return of the Guy." *Women's Quarterly* 12, no. 3 (January 2002): [unpaged].

Allen, Dan. "Falwell from Grace." *The Advocate*, October 23, 2001, 15.

Alliance of South Asians Taking Action. "Press Release: ASATA Condemns World Trade Center Attacks and Anti-Arab Sentiments." September 12, 2001. http://www.asata.org (accessed June 21, 2006).

American Civil Liberties Union. "Surveillance." April 29, 2004. http://www.aclu.org (accessed June 26, 2006).

——. *Worlds Apart: How Deporting Immigrants after 9/11 Tore Families Apart and Shattered Communities*. December 2004. http://www.aclu.org (accessed June 26, 2006).

American Immigration Law Foundation. "Targets of Suspicion: The Impact of Post-9/11 Policies on Muslims, Arabs and South Asians in the United States." *Immigration Policy in Focus* 3. 2 (May 2004). http://www.ailf.org (accessed June 26, 2006).

American Immigration Lawyers Association. "The 107th Congress: A Legislative and Regulatory Overview." AILA Issue Papers. 2002. http://www.aila.org (accessed June 27, 2005).

Amnesty International. "United States of America: Amnesty International's Concerns Regarding Post September 11 Detentions in the USA." May 14, 2002. http://web.amnesty.org (accessed June 27, 2005).

——. "USA Amnesty International's Supplementary Briefing to the UN Committee against Torture." May 3, 2006. http://web.amnesty.org (accessed June 20, 2006).

——. "USA: Pattern of Brutality and Cruelty—War Crimes at Abu Ghraib." Press release. May 7, 2006. http://www.amnestyusa.org (accessed June 19, 2006).

Amnesty International USA et al. "Statement of Principles." November 1, 2001. http://www.crlp.org (accessed June 10, 2006).

Anderson, Jon Lee. "Letter from Afghanistan: After the Revolution." *New Yorker*, January 28, 2002, 62–69.

Andreas, Peter. "Redrawing the Line: Borders and Security in the 21st Century." *International Security* 28, no. 2 (fall 2003): 78–111.

Anonymous. "Renting Wombs." *Antipode: A Radical Journal of Geography* 34, no. 5 (November 2002): 864–73.

Anti-Defamation League. "ADL Offers Reward in Attack on Sikh." May 23, 2003. http://www.adl.org (accessed June 21, 2006).

Aravosis, John. "9/11 Fund to Discriminate against Gays." *Lesbian News* 7, no. 9 (April 2002): 23–24.

Arensen, Karen W. "The Supreme Court: Affirmative Action; Impact on Universities Will Range from None to a Lot." *New York Times*, June 25, 2003, A22.

Armitage, John. "Militarized Bodies: An Introduction." *Body and Society* 9, no. 4 (December 2003): 1–12.

Arondekar, Anjali. "Border/Line Sex: Queer Postcolonialities and How Race Matters outside the United States." *Interventions: International Journal of Postcolonial Studies* 7, no. 2 (2005): 236–50.

——. "Without a Trace: Sexuality and the Colonial Archive." *Journal of the History of Homosexuality* 14, no. 1–2 (2005): 10–18.

Asher, Jon ben. "War Concerns May Impact 'Cairo-52' Trial." *PlanetOut News*, September 24, 2001. http://www.planetout.com (accessed June 13, 2006).

Asians in Media. "Award Winning Documentary on Sikh Hate-Crime Comes to London." *Asians in Media Magazine*, March 29, 2004. http://www.asiansinmedia.org (accessed June 23, 2006).

Associated Press. "Anti-Arab Incidents Hike Number of Hate Crimes in Mass." September 25, 2002. LexisNexis (accessed June 21, 2006).

——. "FBI to Investigate Killing of Egyptian Grocery Store Owner as Hate Crime." September 17, 2001. LexisNexis (accessed June 21, 2006).

——. "Gay Partners of Sept. 11 Victims May Face Tangles over Benefits." December 4, 2001. http://multimedia.belointeractive.com (accessed June 12, 2006).

——. "A Look at Convictions in Abu Ghraib Cases." September 26, 2005. LexisNexis (accessed June 21, 2006).

——. "Man Sentenced to Death Receives 36 Years in Prison." October 15, 2003. LexisNexis (accessed June 22, 2006).

——. "Sikh Shot At in Hate Crime Case." *The Tribune* (India), May 21, 2003. http://www.tribuneindia.com (accessed June 22, 2006).

——. "Sikhs Coping with Apparent Hate Crime." Casa Grande Valley Newspapers, Inc. May 22, 2003. http://www.zwire.com (accessed June 21, 2006).

ASWAT—Palestinian Gay Women. "Parade to the Wall: World Pride under Occupation." *ColorLife!* (Summer 2005): 1, 4.

Audre Lorde Project. "About the Project." n.d. http://alp.org (accessed June 26, 2006).

Audre Lorde Project, *Communities at a Crossroads: U.S. Right Wing Policies and Lesbian, Gay, Bisexual, Two Spirit and Transgender Immigrants of Color in New York City*. New York: Audre Lorde Project, 2004.

Audre Lorde Project and American Friends Service Committee. "Community Groups

Rally against War." *Gay City News*, (February 21–27, 2003). http://www.gaycitynews
.com (accessed June 13, 2006).

Audre Lorde Project and the LGBT Unit of the American Friends Service Committee. "An Open Letter to Lesbian Gay Bisexual Two-Spirit and Transgender People of Color Communities Opposing War." January 27, 2003. http://www.alp.org (accessed June 13, 2006).

Axel, Brian Keith. "The Diasporic Imaginary." *Public Culture* 14, no. 2 (May 2002): 411–28.

———. *The Nation's Tortured Body: Violence, Representation, and the Formation of a Sikh "Diaspora."* Durham: Duke University Press, 2001.

Bacchetta, Paola. "Rescaling Transnational 'Queerdom': Lesbian and 'Lesbian' Identitary-Positionalities in Delhi in the 1980s." *Antipode: A Radical Journal of Geography* 34, no. 5 (November 2002): 947–73.

Badgett, M. V. Lee. "Beyond Biased Samples: Challenging the Myths on the Economic Status of Lesbians and Gay Men." In *Homo Economics: Capitalism, Community, and Lesbian and Gay Life*, edited by Amy Gluckman and Betsy Reed, 65–72. New York: Routledge, 1997.

Barnard, Ian. *Queer Race: Cultural Interventions in the Racial Politics of Queer Theory.* New York: Peter Lang, 2004.

Barrett, Jon. "This Is Mark Bingham." *The Advocate*, January 22, 2002, 41–46.

Basu, Amrita, Paula Giddings, Inderpal Grewal, et al. "Creating an Archive: September 11: A Feminist Archive." *Meridians* 2, no. 2 (spring 2002): 250–315.

Baudrillard, Jean. "The Mind of Terrorism." Paper presented at the European Graduate School, July 11, 2005. http://www.egs.edu (accessed June 12, 2006).

Bauman, Zygmunt. *Wasted Lives: Modernity and its Outcasts.* Cambridge, Mass.: Polity Press, 2004.

BBC News. "Obituary: Pim Fortuyn." May 6, 2002. http://news.bbc.co.uk (accessed June 25, 2005).

Belkin, Aaron, and Melissa Sheridan Embser-Herbert. "A Modest Proposal: Privacy as a Flawed Rationale for the Exclusion of Gays and Lesbians in the U.S. Military." *International Security* 27, no. 2 (fall 2002): 178–97.

Bendersky, Ari. " 'Cairo 52' Trial Ends: Controversies Go On." *PlanetOut News and Politics*, October 17, 2001. http://www.planetout.com (accessed June 13, 2006).

———. "San Francisco Honors Mark Bingham." *PlanetOut News*, September 6, 2002. http://www.planetout.com (accessed June 13, 2006).

Benjamin, Walter. *Reflections.* Edited by Peter Demetz. Translated by Edmund Jephcott. New York: Schoken Books, 1986.

———. "Theses on the Philosophy of History." In *Illuminations.* Edited by Hannah Arendt. Translated by Harry Zohn, 253–64. New York: Schoken Books, 1969.

Berger, Anne-Emmanuelle. "The Newly Veiled Woman: Irigaray, Specularity, and the Islamic Veil." *Diacritics* 28, no. 1 (spring 1998): 93–119.

Berlant, Lauren. "Intimacy." *Critical Inquiry* 24. 2 (winter 1998): 281–88.

———. *The Queen of America Goes to Washington City: Essays on Sex and Citizenship.* Durham: Duke University Press, 1997.

Berlant, Lauren, and Michael Warner. "Sex in Public." *Critical Inquiry* 24, no. 2 (winter 1998): 547–66.

Bernstein, Nina. "2 Men Charge Abuse in Arrests after 9/11 Terror Attack." *New York Times*, May 3, 2004, B1.

Bersani, Leo. "Is the Rectum a Grave?" *October* 43 (winter 1987): 197–222.

Besen, Wayne. "A True American Hero." September 19, 2005. http://www.waynebesen .com (accessed June 12, 2006).

Bhattacharjee, Ananya. "The Public/Private Mirage: Mapping Homes and Undomesticating Violence Work in the South Asian Immigrant Community." In *Feminist Genealogies, Colonial Legacies, Democratic Futures*, edited by M. Jacqui Alexander and Chandra Talpade Mohanty, 308–29. New York: Routledge, 1997.

Binnie, Jon. "Trading Places: Consumption, Sexuality, and the Production of Queer Space." In *Mapping Desires: Geographies of Sexualities*, edited by David Bell and Gill Valentine, 182–99. New York: Routledge, 1995.

Bishnoi, Rati. "Hate Crimes Rise from Ashes of September 11 Attacks." *National NOW Times* (spring 2002). http://www.now.org (accessed June 21, 2006).

Black Is . . . Black Ain't: A Personal Journey through Black Identity. Produced and directed by Marlon Riggs. 88 min. California Newsreel, San Francisco, 1995.

Black Radical Congress. "Terror Attacks of September 11, 2001." September 13, 2001. http://www.monthlyreview.org (accessed June 10, 2006).

Blackwell, Maylei, and Nadine Naber. "Intersectionality in an Era of Globalization: The Implications of the UN World Conference against Racism for Transnational Feminist Practices." *Meridians: Feminism, Race, Transnationalism* 2, no. 2 (2002): 237–48.

Bloom, Steve, et al. "An Open Letter to Activists Concerning Racism in the Anti-War Movement." Colorado Campaign for Middle East Peace. February 13, 2003. http:// www.ccmep.org (accessed June 28, 2005).

Boone, Joseph A. "Vacation Cruises, or, The Homoerotics of Orientalism." *PMLA* 110, no. 1 (January 1995): 89–107.

Borneman, John. "Genital Anxiety." *Anthropological Quarterly* 75, no. 1 (winter 2002): 129–37.

Boston Globe. "Spotlight Investigation: Abuse in the Catholic Church." *Boston Globe* online. Updated April 30, 2006. http://www.boston.com (accessed June 25, 2006).

Bourke, Joanna. "Torture as Pornography." *Guardian* (London), May 7, 2004, 6.

Boykin, Keith. "Life after Lawrence-Garner." August 11, 2003. http://www.keithboykin .com (accessed June 25, 2006). Originally published as "Lawrence and LGBT African Americans," *Gay City News*, August 8–14, 2003. http://www.gaycitynews.com (accessed June 25, 2006).

Bradford, Tom. "Re: Hate Crimes against Sikh Community." Posting. September 14, 2001. http://lists.xml.org (accessed June 21, 2006).

Bradley, John R. "Saudi Gays Flaunt New Freedoms: 'Straights Can't Kiss in Public or Hold Hands Like Us.'" *The Independent*, February 20, 2004, 34.

Brady, Mary Pat. *Extinct Lands, Temporal Geographies: Chicana Literature and the Urgency of Space*. Durham: Duke University Press, 2002.

Brandeis University. International Students and Scholars Office. "National Security Entry-Exit Registration System (NSEERS)." Updated January 2004. http://www.brandeis.edu (accessed June 26, 2006).

Brody, Reed. "What about the Other Secret U.S. Prisons?" Opinion. *International Herald Tribune*, May 3, 2004, 8.

Bronski, Michael. "Gay Goes Mainstream." *Boston Phoenix*, January 16–23, 2003. http://www.bostonphoenix.com (accessed 13 May 2006).

Brooke, Aslan. "Clear Violation." Originally in *Frontiers Newsmagazine*. Reposted October 26, 2001. http://www.sldn.org (accessed June 13, 2006).

Brothers and Others. Produced by Baraka Productions, Nicolas Rossier, and Trilby MacDonald. Directed by Nicolas Rossier. 54 min. Arab Film Distribution, Seattle, 2002.

Brown, Bill. "The Dark Wood of Postmodernity (Space, Faith, Allegory)." *PMLA* 120, no. 3 (May 2005): 734–50.

Brown, Janelle. "A Coalition of Hope." *Ms.*, spring 2002, 65–76.

Buchanan, Wyatt. "Broad Opposition to World Pride in Jerusalem." *San Francisco Chronicle*, July 26, 2006, A2.

Bull, Chris. " 'Don't Ask, Don't Tell' Goes to War." *The Advocate*, December 4, 2001, 45–46, 48.

——. "Gay, Muslim, and Scared." *The Advocate*, October 23, 2001, 54.

Bumiller, Elizabeth. "First Lady to Speak about Afghan Women." *New York Times*, November 16, 2001, B2.

Bunting, Madeleine. "Women and War: While the Media's Response to the Destruction in America Has Been Deafening, the Voices of Women Have Grown Strangely Quiet." *Guardian* (London), September 20, 2001, 19.

Busbach, Tom. "Military Readies to Suspend Gay Discharges." *PlanetOut News*, September 19, 2001. http://www.planetout.com (accessed June 12, 2006).

Butler, Judith. "Contingent Foundations: Feminism and the Question of 'Postmodernism.' " In *Feminists Theorize the Political*, edited by Judith Butler and Joan Scott, 3–21. New York: Routledge, 1992.

——. "Endangered/Endangering: Schematic Racism and White Paranoia." In *Reading Rodney King, Reading Urban Uprising*, edited by Robert Gooding-Williams, 15–22. New York: Routledge, 1993.

——. "Explanation and Exoneration, or What We Can Hear." *Social Text* 20, no. 3 72 (fall 2002): 177–88.

——. *Gender Trouble: Feminism and the Subversion of Identity*. New York: Routledge, 1990.

——. "Global Violence, Sexual Politics." In *Queer Ideas: The David R. Kessler Lectures in Lesbian and Gay Studies*, edited by CLAGS, 199–214. New York: Feminist Press of the City University of New York, 2003.

——. "Is Kinship Always Already Heterosexual?" *differences: A Journal of Feminist Cultural Studies* 13, no. 1 (spring 2002): 14–44.

——. *Precarious Life: The Power of Mourning and Violence*. New York: Verso, 2004.

——. "Sexual Inversions." In *Foucault and the Critique of Institution*, edited by John D. Caputo and Mark Yount, 81–98. University Park: Pennsylvania State University Press, 1993.

Califia, Pat. *Public Sex: The Culture of Radical Sex*. San Francisco: Cleis Press, 2000.

Campbell, Horace. "Beyond Militarism and Terrorism in the Biotech Century: Toward a Culture of Peace and Transformation beyond Militarism." *Radical History Review* 2003, no. 85 (winter 2003): 24–36.

Campbell, Nancy D. "Technologies of Suspicion: Coercion and Compassion in Postdisciplinary Surveillance Regimes." *Surveillance and Society* 2, no. 1 (March 2004): 78–92. http://www.surveillance-and-society.org (accessed June 26, 2006).

Cantú, Jr., Lionel, and Eithne Luibhéid, eds. *Queer Migrations: Sexuality, U.S. Citizenship, and Border Crossings*. Minneapolis: University of Minnesota Press, 2005.

Carby, Hazel. "A Strange and Bitter Crop: The Spectacle of Torture." November 10, 2004. http://www.opendemocracy.net (accessed June 14, 2006).

Carnes, Tony. "Wooing the Faithful." September 28, 2004. http://www.christianity today.com (accessed June 15, 2005).

Center for Constitutional Rights. "CCR Files Lawsuit against Private Contractors for Torture Conspiracy." June 9, 2004. http://www.ccr-ny.org (accessed June 19, 2006).

Chari, Sharad. "F 9/11, a View from South Africa." *Environment and Planning D: Society and Space* 22, no. 6 (2004): 907–10.

Chasin, Alexandra. *Selling Out: The Lesbian and Gay Movement Goes to Market*. New York: Palgrave Macmillan, 2000.

Chatterjee, Partha. "The Nationalist Resolution of the Women's Question." In *Recasting Women: Essays in Indian Colonial History*, edited by Kumkum Sangari and Sudesh Vaid, 233–53. New Brunswick, N.J.: Rutgers University Press, 1990.

Chauncey, George. " 'What Gay Studies Taught the Court': The Historians' Amicus Brief in *Lawrence v. Texas*." *GLQ: A Journal of Gay and Lesbian Studies* 10, no. 3 (August 2004): 509–538.

Chhibber, Kavita. "Sikh Lives: The Sikh American Experience As Told by Those Who Lived It." n.d. http://www.kavitachhibber.com (accessed June 23, 2006).

Chibbaro, Lou, Jr. "New Afghan Rulers Better for Gays?" *Washington Blade*, December 21, 2001. Republished n.d. http://www.sodomylaws.org (accessed June 13, 2006).

Chinn, Sarah E. "Feeling Her Way: Audre Lorde and the Power of Touch." *GLQ: A Journal of Lesbian and Gay Studies* 9, no. 1–2 (2003): 181–204.

Chow, Rey. *The Age of the World Target: Self-Referentiality in War, Theory, and Comparative Work*. Durham: Duke University Press, 2006.

——. *The Protestant Ethnic and the Spirit of Capitalism*. New York: Columbia University Press, 2002.

——. "Writing in the Realm of the Senses: Introduction." *differences: A Journal of Feminist Cultural Studies* 11, no. 2 (1999): i–ii.

Clare, Eli. "Stolen Bodies, Reclaimed Bodies: Disability and Queerness." *Public Culture* 13, no. 3 (fall 2001): 359–65.

Clinton, Kate. " 'In Memoriam': Excerpts of Remarks by Kate Clinton." October 1, 2001. http://www.glaad.org (accessed June 13, 2006).

Clough, Patricia Ticineto. "The Affective Turn." *Theory, Culture, and Society*, forthcoming.

——. *Autoaffection: Unconscious Thought in the Age of Teletechnology*. Minneapolis: University of Minnesota Press, 2000.

——, organizer. "Beyond Biopolitics: State Racism and the Politics of Life and Death." Conference at the CUNY Graduate Center, New York, March 17–18, 2006.

——. "Future Matters: Technoscience, Global Politics, and Cultural Criticism." *Social Text* 22, no. 3 80 (fall 2004): 1–23.

Clough, Patricia Ticineto, ed. with Jean Halley. *The Affective Turn: Toward Theorizing the Social*. Durham: Duke University Press, 2007.

CNN. "Bauer Compares Vermont Gay Rights Decision to Terrorism." December 27, 1999. http://archives.cnn.com (accessed June 10, 2006).

——. "Hate Crimes Reports Up in Wake of Terrorist Attacks." September 17, 2001. http:// archives.cnn.com (accessed June 21, 2006).

——. "New Jersey Governor Quits, Comes Out as Gay." August 12, 2004. http://www .militaryarticles.com (accessed August 24, 2005; no longer available, printout on file with author).

Cogswell, Kelly. "Torture and America: So This Is Us." *The Gully*, May 13, 2004. http:// www.thegully.com (accessed June 19, 2006).

Cohen, Cathy J. *The Boundaries of Blackness: AIDS and the Breakdown of Black Politics.* Chicago: University of Chicago Press, 1999.

——. "Punks, Bulldaggers, and Welfare Queens: The Radical Potential of Queer Politics?" *GLQ: A Journal of Lesbian and Gay Studies* 3, no. 4 (1997): 437–65.

Cohen, Richard. "The Mary Cheney Flap: A Gaffe vs. Ignorance." Editorial. *Washington Post*, October 19, 2004, A23.

Collar, Julia. "Responding to Sexual Stereotypes of Fundamentalist and Charismatic Leaders in Religious Studies." November 1, 2005. http://prs.heacademy.ac.uk (accessed June 12, 2006).

Combahee River Collective. "A Black Feminist Statement." In *The Black Feminist Reader*, edited by Joy James and Tracy Denean Sharpley-Whiting, 261–70. Malden, Mass.: Blackwell, 2000.

Community Marketing, Inc. "'A Place for Us,' 2001: Tourism Industry Opportunities in the Gay and Lesbian Market." *Sixth Annual Gay and Lesbian Travel Survey.* http:// www.communitymarketinginc.com (accessed June 13, 2006).

Corcoran, Patrick. "Ego Tourism: 'Homebody/Kabul' Explores Life in Afghanistan, but Western Interests Still Prevail." Review of *Homebody/Kabul*, by Tony Kushner. Mark Taper Forum, Los Angeles. *Los Angeles City Beat*, October 9, 2003. http://www.lacity beat.com (accessed June 12, 2006).

Cornell, Drucilla. "Ethical Feminism and the Call of the Other (Woman): An Interview with Drucilla Cornell." In *to kill, to die: female contestations on gender and political violence*, edited by Hilla Dayan, 14–15. Special publication for Women's International Day. New York: New School University, March 2004.

——. "The New Political Infamy and the Sacrilege of Feminism." *Metaphilosophy* 35, no. 3 (April 2004): 313–29.

Council on American-Islam Relations. "Muslims Meet with FBI on Radiation Monitoring." January 11, 2006. http://www.cairchicago.org (accessed May 21, 2006).

Coyle, Hugh. "Terrorism Nothing New to Us." *Out in the Mountains* 6, no. 3 (April 1991). www.mountainpridemedia.org (accessed June 13, 2006).

Crea, Joe. "Gay Sex Used to Humiliate Iraqis." *Washington Blade Online*, May 7, 2004. http://www.washblade.com (accessed June 14, 2006).

Crenshaw, Kimberlé Williams. "Mapping the Margins: Intersectionality, Identity Politics, and Violence against Women of Color." *Stanford Law Review* 43, no. 6 (June 1991): 1241–99.

Crenshaw, Martha. "The Causes of Terrorism." *Comparative Politics* 13, no. 4 (July 1981): 379–99.

Cruz-Malave, Arnoldo, and Martin F. Manalansan IV, eds. *Queer Globalizations: Citizenship and the Afterlife of Colonialism.* New York: New York University Press, 2002.

Curry, Michael R. "The Profiler's Question and the Treacherous Traveler: Narratives of Belonging in Commercial Aviation." *Surveillance and Society* 1, no. 4 (December 2003): 475–99. http://www.surveillance-and-society.org (accessed June 30, 2006).

Curtis, Christopher. "Gay Bar Bomber Eric Rudolph Sentenced to Life." July 18, 2005. http://www.gay.com (accessed June 12, 2006).

Cushman, Thomas. "A Conversation with Veena Das on Religion and Violence, Suffering and Language." *Hedgehog Review* 6, no. 1 (spring 2004), http://www.virginia.edu/iasc/hedgehog.html (accessed April 28, 2006).

Cvetkovich, Ann. *An Archive of Feelings: Trauma, Sexuality, and Lesbian Public Cultures*. Durham: Duke University Press, 2003.

——. "Queer Feelings." *Center for Lesbian and Gay Studies (CLAGS) Newsletter* 11, no. 3 (fall 2001): 1, 4.

Cyphers, Amber L. "Discharged Gay Linguist Speaks at Annual SLDN Event." Service-members Legal Defense Network. May 15, 2003. http://www.sldn.org (accessed June 13, 2006).

Dahir, Mubarak. "Gay Imam Will Reach Out to Gay and Lesbian Muslims." *Temenos*, September 6, 2004. http://www.temenos.net (accessed June 11, 2006).

——. "Gay Sex and Prison Torture in Iraq War." Opinion. *New York Blade*, May 14, 2004. http://newyorkblade.com (accessed June 19, 2006).

——. "Our Heroes." *The Advocate*, October 9, 2001. http://advocate.com (accessed June 12, 2006).

——. "Our Heroes." *The Advocate*, October 23, 2001. http://advocate.com (accessed June 12, 2006).

——. "Proud of 'Intolerance.'" *Windy City Times*, September 30, 2003. http://www.windycitytimes.com (accessed June 11, 2006).

——. "Queer and Muslim." *San Francisco Pride Official Magazine*, 2002, 91–93.

——. "Stop Using Gay 'Liberation' as a War Guise." *Windy City Times*, April 23, 2003. http://www.windycitymediagroup.com (accessed June 13, 2006).

Danner, Mark. *Torture and Truth: America, Abu Ghraib, and the War on Terror*. New York: New York Review Books, 2004.

Dao, James, and Paul Von Zielbauer, with Fox Butterfield. "Abuse Charges Bring Anguish in Unit's Home." *New York Times*, May 6, 2004, A1.

Dawn. "35pc of Deported from U.S. Are Pakistanis." July 28, 2003. http://www.dawn.com (accessed June 26, 2006).

Dayan, Hilla. "Poisoned Cats and Angels of Death: Israeli and Palestinian Female Suicide Bombers." In *to kill, to die: female contestations on gender and political violence*, edited by Hilla Dayan, 9–12. Special publication for Women's International Day. New York: New School University, March 2004.

Deb, Trishala, and Rafael Mutis. "Smoke and Mirrors: Abu Ghraib and the Myth of Liberation." *ColorLife!* Summer 2004, 1, 4–7. http://www.alp.org (accessed June 14, 2006).

Deer, Patrick, moderator. "Iraq and Postcoloniality." Roundtable held at the 2005 Left Forum, CUNY Graduate Center, New York City, April 15–17, 2005.

Defert, Daniel. "'Popular Life' and Insurance Technology." In *The Foucault Effect: Studies in Governmentality*, edited by Graham Burchell, Colin Gordon, and Peter Miller, 211–34. Chicago: University of Chicago Press, 1991.

De Landa, Manuel. *Intensive Science and Virtual Philosophy*. London: Continuum, 2002.

——. *War in the Age of Intelligent Machines*. New York: Zone Books, 1991.

Deleuze, Gilles. *Negotiations: 1972–1990*. Translated by Martin Joughin. New York: Columbia University Press, 1997.

Deleuze, Gilles, and Félix Guattari. *A Thousand Plateaus: Capitalism and Schizophrenia*. Translated by Brian Massumi. Minneapolis: University of Minnesota Press, 1987.

deMause, Lloyd. "The Childhood Origins of Terrorism." In *The Emotional Life of Nations*, 39–48. New York: Other Press, 2002.

D'Emilio, John. "Capitalism and Gay Identity." In *Powers of Desire: The Politics of Sexuality*, edited by Ann Snitow, Christine Stansell, and Sharon Thompson, 100–113. New York: Monthly Review Press, 1983.

Der Derian, James. *Virtuous War: Mapping the Military-Industrial-Media-Entertainment Network*. Boulder, Colo.: Westview Press, 2001.

de Rosa, Mary. "Privacy in an Age of Terror." *Washington Quarterly* 26, no. 3 (summer 2003): 27–41.

Derrida, Jacques. *Specters of Marx: The State of Debt, the Work of Mourning, and the New International*. Translated by Peggy Kamuf. New York: Routledge, 1994.

Desai, Poulomi, and Parminder Sekhon. *Red Threads: The South Asian Queer Connection in Photographs*. London: Diva Books, 2003.

Desis Rising Up and Moving. "About DRUM." n.d. http://www.drumnation.org (accessed June 26, 2006).

DiGiacomo, Robin. "Hate Leaflets Don't Sway WorldPride Resolve." July 11, 2006. http://www.gay.com (accessed September 5, 2006).

"Do the Handicapped Go to Hell?" *South Park*. Written and directed by Trey Parker. Comedy Central. July 19, 2000, episode 410.

Donohue, Pete. "TA Edict Spurs Turban Tussle." *New York Daily News*, June 24, 2004, 39.

DontAmend.com and The Equality Campaign, Inc. 2004. http://www.dearmary.com (accessed June 26, 2006).

Dotinga, Randy. "Despite Emergency, Gays Can't Give Blood." *PlanetOut News*, September 13, 2001. http://www.planetout.com (accessed June 12, 2006).

——. "Navy Photo Shows Antigay Slur on Bomb." *PlanetOut News and Politics*, October 12, 2001. http://www.planetout.com (accessed June 13, 2006).

Douglas, Carol Anne. "NWSA Looks at September 11 and the War on Terrorism." *Off Our Backs* 32, no. 9–10 (September 2002): 10–15, 45–48.

Dow, Mark. "The New Secret War against Immigrants." Editorial. *Gotham Gazette*, January 30, 2002. http://www.gothamgazette.com (accessed September 6, 2006).

Drinkwater, Gregg. "Bi-national Couples Face More Restrictions." *PlanetOut News*, October 1, 2001. http://www.planetout.com (accessed June 12, 2006).

Driscoll, Mark. "Reverse Postcoloniality." *Social Text* 22, no. 1 78 (spring 2004): 59–84.

Duggan, Lisa. "Beyond Blood." *Center for Lesbian and Gay Studies (CLAGS) Newsletter* 11, no. 3 (fall 2001): 1–2.

——. Excerpt from *The End of Marriage: The War over the Future of State Sponsored Love*. Berkeley: University of California Press, forthcoming.

——. "Holy Matrimony!" *The Nation*, March 15, 2004, 14–19.

——. "The New Homonormativity: The Sexual Politics of Neoliberalism." In *Materializ-*

ing Democracy: Toward a Revitalized Cultural Politics, edited by Russ Castronovo and Dana Nelson, 175–94. Durham: Duke University Press, 2002.

Eakin, Emily. "Ideas and Trends: All Roads Lead to D.C." New York Times, March 31, 2002, sec. 4, p. 4.

Earls, Meg. "Stressors in the Lives of GLBTQ Youth." Transitions 14, no. 2 (June 2002): 3–4, 19. http://www.advocatesforyouth.org (accessed June 25, 2006).

Easterbrook, Gregg. "Whatever It Takes." New Republic online. May 17, 2006. http://www.tnr.com (accessed June 19, 2006).

Economist. "A Business in Search of Customers." September 29, 2001, 61–62.

Edelman, Lee. No Future: Queer Theory and the Death Drive. Durham: Duke University Press, 2004.

Ehrenreich, Barbara. "A Mystery of Misogyny." The Progressive 65, no. 12 (December 2001): 12–13.

———. "Prison Abuse: Feminism's Assumptions Upended." Opinion. Los Angeles Times, May 16, 2004, M1.

Eisenstein, Zillah. "Feminisms in the Aftermath of September 11." Social Text 20, no. 3 72 (fall 2002): 79–99.

———. "Sexual Humiliation, Gender Confusion and the Horrors at Abu Ghraib." Posting. June 21, 2004. http://lists.portside.org (accessed June 13, 2006).

Empire State Pride Agenda. "NY State Crime Victims Board Extends Equal Benefits to Surviving Domestic Partners of Homicide Victims." Press release. October 17, 2002. http://www.prideagenda.org (accessed June 12, 2006).

Eng, David L. "Transnational Adoption and Queer Diasporas." Social Text 21, no. 3 76 (fall 2003): 1–37.

———. "The Value of Silence." Center for Lesbian and Gay Studies (CLAGS) Newsletter 11, no. 3 (fall 2001): 7, 9.

Eng, David L., Judith Halberstam, and José Esteban Muñoz, eds. "What's Queer about Queer Studies Now?" Special issue of Social Text 23, no. 3–4 84–85 (fall–winter 2005).

Eng, David L., and Shinhee Han. "A Dialogue on Racial Melancholia." In Loss: The Politics of Mourning, edited by David L. Eng and David Kazanjian, 343–71. Berkeley: University of California Press, 2003.

Eng, David L., and Alice Y. Hom. "Q and A: Notes on a Queer Asian America." In Q and A: Queer in Asian America, edited by David L. Eng and Alice Y. Hom, 1–21. Philadelphia: Temple University Press, 1998.

Ettelbrick, Paula. Open letter. July 29, 2005. http://pageoneq.com (accessed September 9, 2006).

European Court of Human Rights. Dudgeon v. The United Kingdom, Series A, no. 45 (1981). Publications of the European Court of Human Rights, Series A, v. 45. Strasbourg: Greffe de la Cour, Conseil de l'Europe, 1982.

Fanon, Frantz. Black Skins, White Masks. Translated by Contance Farrington. New York: Grove Press Books, 1967.

———. A Dying Colonialism. Translated by Haakon Chevalier. New York: Grove Press, 1965.

Fears, Daryl. "Draft Bill Stirs Debate over the Military, Race and Equity." Washington Post, February 4, 2003, A3.

Feingold, Russ. "Statement on the Discharge of Gay Linguists from the Military." GLBT

Information Center. February 27, 2003. http://www.thinkingink.com (accessed June 13, 2006).

Fejes, Fred, and Ron Lennon. "Defining the Lesbian/Gay Community? Market Research and the Lesbian/Gay Press." *Journal of Homosexuality* 39, no. 1 (2000): 25–42.

Fellner, Jamie. "Prisoner Abuse: How Different Are U.S. Prisons?" Commentary. Human Rights Watch. May 14, 2004. http://hrw.org (accessed June 20, 2006).

Feminist Majority Foundation. "Eve Ensler's Tribute to Afghan Women Is a Sold Out Success at Madison Square Garden." February 12, 2001. http://feminist.org (accessed June 11, 2006).

Ferguson, Roderick. *Aberrations in Black: Towards a Queer of Color Critique*. Minneapolis: University of Minnesota Press, 2003.

Fiol-Matta, Licia. *A Queer Mother for the Nation: The State and Gabriela Mistral*. Minneapolis: University of Minnesota Press, 2002.

Fortier, Anne-Marie. "Making Home: Queer Migrations and Motions of Attachment." In *Uprootings/Regroundings: Questions of Home and Migration*, edited by Sarah Ahmed, Claudia Castaneda, and Anne-Marie Fortier, 115–36. New York: Berg, 2003.

Foucault, Michel. *The History of Sexuality: An Introduction*. Vol. 1. Translated by Robert Hurley. New York: Vintage Books, 1990.

——. *The Order of Things: An Archaeology of Human Sciences*. Translated from the French. New York: Vintage Books, 1994.

——. *"Society Must Be Defended": Lectures at the College de France, 1975–1976*. Translated by David Macey. New York: Picador, 2003.

Frameline. "I Exist: Voices from the Lesbian and Gay Middle Eastern Community." 26th San Francisco International Gay and Lesbian Film Festival. 2002. http://www.frame line.org (accessed June 11, 2006).

Franke, Katherine M. "The Domesticated Liberty of *Lawrence v. Texas*." *Columbia Law Review* 104, no. 5 (June 2004): 1399–426.

——. "Putting Sex to Work." *Denver University Law Review* 75, no. 4 (1998): 1138–80.

Frasca, Gonzalo. *September 12th: A Toy World*. Videogame. www.newsgaming.com (accessed June 23, 2006).

Fraser, Mariam. "What Is the Matter of Feminist Criticism?" *Economy and Society* 31, no. 4 (November 2002): 606–25.

Freeman, Elizabeth. "Time Binds, or, Erotohistoriography." *Social Text* 23, no. 3–4 84–85 (fall–winter 2005): 57–68.

Freedman, Ina. "'Jerusalem Will Be No More Holy If Gays Are Distanced from It.'" *Jerusalem Report*, August 7, 2006, 64.

Frieden, Terry. "Ashcroft Meets with Muslim, Arab Leaders." October 16, 2001. http://archives.cnn.com (accessed June 22, 2006).

Friedman, Thomas L. "Restoring Our Honor." Editorial. *New York Times*, May 6, 2004, A35.

Frist, Bill. "Safe at Home: A Family Survival Guide." In *When Every Moment Counts: What You Need to Know about Bioterrorism from the Senate's Only Doctor*, 21–48. New York: Rowman and Littlefield, 2002.

Fuoco, Michael A., and Cindi Lash. "A Long Way from Obscurity." *Pittsburgh Post-Gazette*, May 14, 2004, A1.

Furuhashi, Yoshie. "A 'Clash of Civilizations,' Sending Pink Sparks Flying?" Critical Montages. Posted June 8, 2004. http://montages.blogspot.com (accessed June 17, 2005).

———. "Orientalist Torture." Critical Montages. Posted June 6, 2004. http://montages.blogspot.com (accessed June 19, 2006).

Garden State Sikh Association. "Flier: Sikhs Are Not Muslims." n.d., on file with the author.

———. "Our Fellow Americans and President Bush Need Our Support to Win the War against Terrorism." September 2001, on file with the author.

———. "Post–September 11th Flier." n.d., on file with the author.

———. "Press Release." September 14, 2001, on file with the author.

Gardiner, Sean. "Sikh Wants End to Turban Ban." March 11, 2002. http://www.sikhcoalition.org (accessed June 21, 2006). Originally published in *Newsday*, March 11, 2002.

Garry, Joan M. "GLAAD Statement Regarding Oct. 11 Associated Press Photo." October 12, 2001. http://www.glaad.org (accessed May 13, 2006).

Gay and Lesbian Alliance against Defamation. "Heroes and Victims of 9-11-01." n.d. http://www.glaad.org (accessed June 12, 2006).

Gay City News. "An Emerging Debate about War." February 21–27, 2003. http://www.gaycitynews.com (accessed June 13, 2006).

Gay.com UK. "Gay Muslims Condemn U.S. Attacks." *PlanetOut News*, September 12, 2001. http://www.planetout.com (accessed June 14, 2005).

———. "U.K. Faith Leaders Unite, Urge Tolerance." *PlanetOut News and Politics*, September 26, 2004. http://www.planetout.com (accessed June 14, 2005).

Gay Today and Lambda Legal Defense Fund. "Government Keeps Door Open for Survivors of 9/11 Victims." December 27, 2001. http://gaytoday.badpuppy.com (accessed June 12, 2006).

Gephardt, Richard A. "Gephardt Statement on the Day of National Prayer and Remembrance and on the Need for Tolerance." News from the House Democratic Leader, September 14, 2001. Posted September 14, 2001. http://www.sikh-atlanta.org (accessed June 21, 2006).

Gerber, Judy. "Activists Mobilize against War, Racism." *PlanetOut News and Politics*, September 27, 2001. http://www.planetout.com (accessed June 13, 2006).

Ghani, Mariam, and Chitra Ganesh. *How Do You See the Disappeared? A Warm Database*. May 2004. http://turbulence.org (accessed June 27, 2005).

Ghent, Bill. "Tragedy Changed Gay Climate." *National Journal*, January 12, 2002, 104.

Ghoussoub, Mai. "Abu Ghraib: I Do Not Know Where to Look for Hope." May 10, 2004. http://www.opendemocracy.net (accessed June 19, 2006).

Gibson-Graham, J. K. *The End of Capitalism (As We Knew It): A Feminist Critique of Political Economy*. London: Blackwell, 1996.

Gilliom, John. "Resisting Surveillance." *Social Text* 23, no. 2 83 (summer 2005): 71–83.

Gilson, Dave. "America's Laziest Fascist." *Salon.com*, May 20, 2004. http://dir.salon.com (accessed June 26, 2006).

Gladwell, Malcolm. "Troublemakers: What Pit Bulls Can Teach Us about Profiling." *New Yorker*, January 1, 2006. http://www.newyorker.com (accessed March 5, 2007).

Goldberg, Michelle. "Is This Play Illegal?" Review of *"I'm Gonna Kill the President": A Federal Offense*, written and directed by Hieronymus Bang. Brooklyn, New York. *Salon.com*, October 29, 2003. http://dir.salon.com (accessed June 14, 2006).

Goldman, David. "Gay Muslims," *Southern Voice*, August 19, 1999. Republished n.d. http://www.flameout.org (accessed June 11, 2006).

Goldstein, Joshua. "John Wayne and GI Jane," *Christian Science Monitor*, January 10, 2002, 11.

Goldstein, Richard. "Butching Up for Victory." *The Nation*, January 26, 2004, 11–14.

——. "Stuff Happens! Don't Call It Torture. It's Just a Broomstick up the Butt." *Village Voice* online, May 5, 2004. http://www.villagevoice.com (accessed June 19, 2006).

Göle, Nilüfer. "Close Encounters: Islam, Modernity and Violence." *interdisciplines*, January 1, 2004. http://www.interdisciplines.com (accessed January 8, 2004). Previously published in *Understanding September 11*, edited by Craig Calhoun, Paul Price, and Ashley Timmer, 332–44. New York: Norton, 2002.

Goodstein, Laurie, and Tamar Lewin. "Victims of Mistaken Identity, Sikhs Pay a Price for Turbans." *New York Times*, September 19, 2001, A1.

Gopinath, Gayatri. "Bollywood Spectacles: Queer Diasporic Critique in the Aftermath of 9/11." *Social Text* 23, no. 3–4 84–85 (fall–winter 2005): 157–69.

——. *Impossible Desires: Queer Diasporas and South Asian Public Cultures*. Durham: Duke University Press, 2005.

Gordon, Avery. *Ghostly Matters: Haunting and the Sociological Imagination*. Minneapolis: University of Minnesota Press, 1997.

Gordon, Daniel. "Moralism, the Fear of Social Chaos: The Dissent in *Lawrence* and the Antidotes of Vermon and *Brown*." *Texas Journal on Civil Liberties and Civil Rights* 9, no. 1 (winter 2003): 1–21.

Gorton, Don. "Gay Rights in the Clash of Civilizations." *Gay and Lesbian Review* 8, no. 6 (January/February 2002): 16–17.

Graham, Stephen. "Postmortem City: Towards an Urban Geopolitics." *City* 8, no. 2 (July 2004): 165–96.

Greenberg, Karen J., and Joshua L. Dratel, eds. *The Torture Papers: The Road to Abu Ghraib*. New York: Cambridge University Press, 2005.

Gregory, Derek. *The Colonial Present: Afghanistan, Palestine, Iraq*. Oxford: Blackwell, 2004.

Grewal, Inderpal. *Transnational America: Feminisms, Diasporas, Neoliberalisms*. Durham: Duke University Press, 2005.

Grier, Miles Parks. "Having Their Cake . . . and Outlawing It, Too: How the War on Terror Expands Racial Profiling by Pretending to Erase It." *Politics and Culture*, 2006. http://aspen.conncoll.edu (accessed September 6, 2006).

Griffin, Michael. "The Taleban: Repressed Homosexuality?" *Times* (London), October 5, 2001. http://www.freerepublic.com (accessed June 29, 2006).

Grosz, Elizabeth. *Space, Time, and Perversion: Essays on the Politics of Bodies*. New York: Routledge, 1995.

——. *Volatile Bodies: Toward a Corporeal Feminism*. Bloomington: Indiana University Press, 1994.

Guardian. "'I Made the Ring from a Bullet and the Pin of a Hand Grenade.'" January 26, 2001. http://www.guardian.co.uk (accessed June 27, 2006).

Hage, Ghassan. "'Comes a Time We Are All Enthusiasm': Understanding Palestinian Suicide Bombers in Times of Exighophobia." *Public Culture* 15, no. 1 (winter 2003): 65–89.

Halberstam, Judith. *In a Queer Time and Place: Transgender Bodies, Subcultural Lives*. New York: New York University Press, 2005.

Halbfinger, David M. "Veteran Battles Charge He's Soft on Defense." *New York Times*, October 28, 2002, A22.

Halley, Janet. "Reasoning about Sodomy: Act and Identity in and after Bowers v. Hardwick." *Virginia Law Review* 79 (October 1993): 1721–80.

Hamad, Claudette Shwiry, ed. "Appendix: Hate-Based Incidents September 11–October 10, 2001." Arab American Institute Foundation Report, prepared for the United States Commission on Civil Rights. October 11, 2001. http://www.thememoryhole.org (accessed June 1, 2006).

Hanashiro, Robert. "Hate Crimes Born Out of Tragedy Create Victims." *USAToday.com*, September 11, 2002. www.usatoday.com (accessed June 22, 2006).

Hansen, Mark. "Digitizing the Racialized Body, or The Politics of Universal Address." *SubStance: A Review of Theory and Literary Criticism* 33, no. 2 (2004): 107–33.

Haraway, Donna. *The Companion Species Manifesto: Dogs, People, and Significant Otherness*. Chicago: Prickly Paradigm Press, 2003.

Harding, Luke. "The Other Prisoners." *Guardian* (London), May 20, 2004, 10.

Hardisty, Jean, and Amy Gluckman. "The Hoax of 'Special Rights': The Right Wing's Attack on Gay Men and Lesbians." In *Homo Economics: Capitalism, Community, and Lesbian and Gay Life*, edited by Amy Gluckman and Betsy Reed, 209–22. New York: Routledge, 1997.

Hardt, Michael. "Affective Labor." *boundary 2* 26, no. 2 (summer 1999): 89–100.

———. "The Withering of Civil Society." In *Deleuze and Guattari: New Mappings in Politics, Philosophy and Culture*, edited by Eleanor Kaufman and Kevin Jon Heller, 23–39. Minneapolis: University of Minnesota Press, 1998.

Hardt, Michael, and Antonio Negri. *Empire*. Cambridge, Mass.: Harvard University Press, 2000.

Hart, Lynda. *Fatal Women: Lesbian Sexuality and the Mark of Aggression*. Princeton: Princeton University Press, 1994.

Hartley Film Foundation. "In the Name of Allah." Updated February 28, 2006. http://www.hartleyfoundation.org (accessed June 12, 2006).

Hassner, Pierre. "The United States: The Empire of Force or the Force of Empire." *Chaillot Papers* no. 54. Paris: Institute for Security Studies, European Union, 2002: 46. http://www.iss-eu.org (accessed June 11, 2006).

Hawley, John C., ed. *Postcolonial and Queer Theories: Intersections and Essays*. Westport, Conn.: Greenwood Press, 2001.

———, ed. *Postcolonial, Queer: Theoretical Intersections*. Albany: State University of New York Press, 2001.

Hayes, Jarrod. *Queer Nations: Marginal Sexualities in the Maghreb*. Chicago: University of Chicago Press, 2000.

Haykel, Bernard. "Implications of Photographs Inside Prison in Iraq," *The Charlie Rose Show*. Public Broadcasting System, May 3, 2004.

Hays, Matthew. "Act of Faith: A Film on Gays and Islam." *New York Times*, November 2, 2004, late ed., E3.

Healy, Patrick. "3 Indians Attacked on Street and the Police Call It Bias." *New York Times*, August 5, 2003, B3.

Henry, Alice. "Trouble and Strife: Feminist Perspectives after September 11." *Off Our Backs* 32, no. 11–12 (November 2002): 50–53.

Herbert, Bob. "America's Abu Ghraibs." *New York Times*, May 31, 2004, A17.

Hersh, Seymour M. "Chain of Command." *New Yorker*, May 17, 2004, 38–43.

——. "The Gray Zone." *New Yorker*, May 24, 2004, 38–44.

——. "Implications of Photographs inside Prison in Iraq." *The Charlie Rose Show*. Public Broadcasting System, May 3, 2004.

——. "Torture at Abu Ghraib." *New Yorker*, April 30, 2004. http://www.newyorker.com (accessed June 25, 2006).

——. "Torture at Abu Ghraib." *New Yorker*, May 10, 2004, 42–47.

——. "Torture at Abu Ghraib." n.d. http://www.globalpolicy.org (accessed June 25, 2006).

——. "Torture at Abu Ghraib." n.d. http://www.notinourname.net (accessed June 25, 2006).

——. "Torture at Abu Ghraib." n.d. http://www.november.org (accessed June 25, 2006).

——. "The U.S.A.'s Abu Ghraib Torture Scandal." May 1, 2004. http://www.uslabor againstwar.org (accessed June 25, 2006).

Hess, Gary R. "The Forgotten Asian Americans: The East Indian Community in the United States." In *The History and Immigration of Asian Americans*, edited by Franklin Ng, 106–26. New York: Garland, 1998.

Hier, Sean P. "Probing the Surveillant Assemblage: On the Dialectics of Surveillance Practices as Processes of Social Control." *Surveillance and Society* 1, no. 3 (June 2003): 399–411. http://www.surveillance-and-society.org (accessed June 30, 2006).

Hilton, Isabel. "Torture: Who Gives the Orders?" May 13, 2004. http://www.opendemo cracy.net (accessed June 19, 2006).

Hirshkind, Charles, and Saba Mahmood. "Feminism, the Taliban, and Politics of Counter-Insurgency." *Anthropological Quarterly* 75, no. 2 (spring 2002): 339–54.

Horne, Alistair. *A Savage War of Peace*. London: Pan Books, 2002.

Howard, John. *Men Like That: A Southern Queer History*. Chicago: University of Chicago Press, 2001.

——. "The Talk of the Country: Revisiting Accusation, Murder, and Mississippi, 1895." In *Queer Studies: An Interdisciplinary Reader*, edited by Robert J. Corber and Steven Valocchi, 142–58. Malden, Mass.: Blackwell, 2003.

Howe, Marvine. "Sikh Leaders in U.S. Voicing Fear of Becoming Scapegoats." *New York Times*, June 29, 1985, sec. 1, p. 3.

Howell, Sally, and Andrew Shryock. "Cracking Down on Diaspora: Arab Detroit and America's 'War on Terror.'" *Anthropological Quarterly* 76, no. 3 (summer 2003): 443–62.

Hudson, Rex A. *The Sociology and Psychology of Terrorism: Who Becomes a Terrorist and Why?* Federation of American Scientists. Report prepared at request of Federal Research Division of the Library of Congress, September 1999. www.fas.org (accessed June 13, 2006).

Human Rights Campaign Foundation. "Florida's Gay Adoption Ban." n.d. http://www .hrc.org (accessed June 25, 2006).

——. "Second-Parent/Stepparent Adoption Laws in the U.S." Fact sheet. 2006. http:// www.hrc.org (accessed June 25, 2006).

——. "Secretary Rice Urged to Condemn Execution of Gay Iranian Teens." Press release. July 22, 2005. http://www.hrc.org (accessed September 9, 2006).

Human Rights First. "End Torture Now." Updated May 19, 2006. http://www.human rightsfirst.org (accessed June 20, 2006).

Human Rights Watch. "Dutch Officials Should Not Force Choice between Silence and Death." March 8, 2006. http://hrw.org (accessed September 9, 2006).

——. *Guantanamo: Detainee Accounts.* October 26, 2004. http://hrw.org (accessed June 26, 2006).

——. "Stop Hate Crimes Now." September 21, 2001. http://www.hrw.org (accessed June 21, 2006).

——. "The United States' 'Disappeared': The CIA's Long-Term 'Ghost Detainees.' " Briefing paper. October 2004. http://www.hrw.org (accessed June 27, 2005).

——. "United States: Locked Away: Immigration Detainees in Jails in the United States." September 1998. http://www.hrw.org (accessed June 27 2005).

Humm, Andy. "The Rights of Same-Sex Partners." *Gotham Gazette*, June 24, 2002. http://www.gothamgazette.com (accessed June 13, 2006).

Hunter, Nan. "Sexual Orientation and the Paradox of Heightened Scrutiny." *Michigan Law Review* 102, no. 7 (June 2004): 1528–54.

Hyndman, Jennifer. "Beyond Either/Or: A Feminist Analysis of September 11th." *ACME: An International E-Journal for Critical Geographies* 2, no. 1 (2003): 1–13. http://www.acme-journal.org (accessed June 11, 2006).

Ide, Reed. Editorial. *Passport Magazine*, October 2001, 3.

Independent Centre for Strategic Studies and Analysis. "About Us." 2003. http://icssa.org (accessed June 25, 2006).

IndiaExpress Bureau. "U.S. Sikhs." August 10, 2002. www.religionnewsblog.com (accessed June 22, 2006).

——. "U.S. Sikhs' Initiative to End Hate-Crime." August 9, 2002. http://www.indiaexpress.com (accessed March 18, 2004; no longer available). Republished August 10, 2002. http://www.religionnewsblog.com (accessed June 21, 2006).

Indo-Asian News Service. "White Hate Groups Target U.S. Sikhs." *Times of India* online, December 12, 2003. http://timesofindia.indiatimes.com (accessed March 21, 2004; no longer available).

Information Technology, War and Peace Project. *InfoTechWarPeace*. Watson Institute for International Studies, Brown University. www.infopeace.org (accessed June 23, 2006).

International Initiative for Justice. *Threatened Existence: A Feminist Analysis of the Genocide in Gujarat.* December 2003. http://www.onlinevolunteers.org (accessed June 19, 2006).

In the Name of Allah. "In the Name of Allah." n.d. http://www.inthenameofallah.net (accessed July 5, 2005).

Ireland, Doug. "Global Protests July 19 to Commemorate Hanging of 2 Iranian Teens." June 28, 2006. http://direland.typepad.com (accessed September 9, 2006).

Isherwood, Charles. "Shades of Abu Ghraib, and of Fleet Street, Too." Review of *Guardians*, by Peter Morris. Culture Project, New York. *New York Times*, April 13, 2006, sec. 2A, p. 5.

IslamOnline and News Agencies. "Pakistani Grocer Shot Dead in Texas." *IslamOnline.net*, September 16, 2001. http://www.islam-online.net (accessed June 21, 2006).

Iyer, Deepa. "A Community on the Front Lines: Pushing Back the Rising Tide of Anti-Immigrant Policy Since September 11th." *Subcontinental* 3, no. 1 (autumn 2003): 35–53. http://www.thesubcontinental.org (accessed June 26, 2006).

Jachimowicz, Maia, and Ramah McKay. "'Special Registration' Program." *Migration Information Source*, April 1, 2003. http://www.migrationinformation.org (accessed June 26, 2006).

Jacinto, Leela. "Muslim Blacklisting? American Muslims Accuse Banks and Other Financial Institutions of Discrimination." June 11, 2003. http://abcnews.go.com (originally accessed July 8, 2003; no longer available, printout on file with author).

Jacques, Cheryl, C. Dixon Osburn, and A. J. Rogue. "Fighting for Freedom." Human Rights Campaign. Press release. May 28, 2004. http://www.hrc.org (accessed June 19, 2006).

Jagose, Annamarie. *Inconsequence: Lesbian Representation and the Logic of Sexual Sequence.* Ithaca, N.Y.: Cornell University Press, 2002.

———. *Queer Theory: An Introduction.* New York: New York University Press, 1997.

Jakobsen, Janet. "Can Homosexuals End Western Civilization As We Know It? Family Values in a Global Economy." In *Queer Globalizations: Citizenship and the Afterlife of Colonialism*, edited by Arnoldo Cruz-Malave and Martin Manalansan IV, 49–70. New York: New York University Press, 2002.

Jannah.org. "Muslim Victims of Terrorist Attacks and Continuing Hate Crimes." September 22, 2001. http://www.jannah.org (accessed June 22, 2006).

Jay, Gregory. "White Out: Race and Nationalism in American Studies." *American Quarterly* 55, no. 4 (December 2003): 781–95.

Jehl, Douglas, and Eric Schmitt. "The Military: In Abuse, a Portrayal of Ill-Prepared, Overwhelmed G.I.'s." *New York Times*, May 9, 2004, sec. 1, p. 1.

Jewett, Christina. "Army Rules Deter Sikhs from Joining." *Sacramento Bee*, February 27, 2004, A1.

Johnson, Paul. "Frank Attacks Bush's Silence on Egypt Trial." *PlanetOut News and Politics*, December 24, 2001. http://www.planetout.com (accessed June 13, 2006).

———. "Group: Egypt Using War to Hide Abuses." *PlanetOut News and Politics*, October 12, 2001. http://www.planetout.com (accessed June 13, 2006).

———. "Military Gay Linguist Firings Escalate." April 16, 2003. http://365gay.com (accessed May 12, 2006; no longer available).

Joseph, May. "Old Routes, Mnemonic Traces." *UTS Review* 6, no. 2 (November 2000): 44–56.

Joseph, Miranda. *Against the Romance of Community.* Minneapolis: University of Minnesota Press, 2002.

Joseph, Nicola. "9-11, from a Different Perspective: Interview with Nawal El Sadaawi and Sherif Hetata." *Women in Action*, no. 1 (2002). http://www.isiswomen.org (accessed June 11, 2006).

Journal Star. "The Aftermath of the Abu Ghraib Abuse." Editorial. September 28, 2005. http://pjstar.com (accessed March 4, 2006).

Kalra, Virinder S. "Locating the Sikh Pagh." *Sikh Formations: Religion, Culture, Theory* 1, no. 1 (June 2005): 75–92.

Kalra, Virinder S., Raminder Kaur, and John Hutnyk. *Diaspora and Hybridity.* London: Sage, 2005.

Kammen, Michael. "The Problem of American Exceptionalism: A Reconsideration." *American Quarterly* 45, no. 1 (March 1993): 1–43.

Kaplan, Amy. "Violent Belongings and the Question of Empire Today: Presidential Address to the American Studies Association, October 17, 2003." *American Quarterly* 56, no. 1 (March 2004): 1–18.

Kaplan, Danny. *Brothers and Others in Arms: The Making of Love and War in Israeli Combat Units.* New York: Harrington Park Press, 2002.

Kaplan, David E. "Exclusive: Nuclear Monitoring of Muslims Done without Search Warrants." *U.S. News and World Report* online, December 22, 2005. http://www.usnews.com (accessed May 21, 2006).

Katyal, Sonia. "Exporting Identity." *Yale Journal of Law and Feminism* 14, no. 1 (spring 2002): 97–157.

———. "Sexuality and Sovereignty: The Global Limits and Possibilities of Lawrence." *William and Mary Bill of Rights Law Journal* 14 (2006): 1429–87.

Kaur, Jasbir, and The Sikh Sentinel. "State Department Tells School Children Sikhs Are Terrorists." *Sikh Sentinel*, July 23, 2003. http://www.sikhsentinel.com (accessed June 21, 2006).

Kazanjian, David. *The Colonizing Trick: National Culture and Imperial Citizenship in Early America.* Minneapolis: University of Minnesota Press, 2003.

Kazmi, Laila. "Shame." May 13, 2004. http://www.opendemocracy.net (accessed June 19, 2006).

Kennedy, Dan. "Media Log." *Boston Pheonix* online, May 3, 2004. http://www.bostonphoenix.com (accessed June 26, 2006).

Kerman, Dan. "Military Gay Discharges Spiked in 2001." *PlanetOut News and Politics*, March 14, 2002. http://www.planetout.com (accessed June 13, 2006).

Khalsa, Ek Ong Kaar Kaur. "Re: State Department Tells School Children, Sikhs Are Terrorists." Posting. September 4, 2003. http://www.sikhnet.com (accessed June 21, 2006).

Khalsa, Gurumustuk Singh. "President and Congress Sign into Law Support for Sikh Americans." Posting. October 31, 2001. http://www.sikhnet.com (accessed June 21, 2006).

Khan, Surina. "Bombing Afghanistan: Breeding More Terror?" Interview by Tim Kingston. *San Francisco Frontiers*, November 15, 2001. Republished n.d. http://www.globalgayz.com (accessed June 13, 2006).

———. "Surina Khan, a Pakistani Advocate for Gay and Lesbian Human Rights Shares Her Thoughts about America's War on Terror." Interview by Michael Bronski. *Boston Phoenix*, October 18–25, 2001. http://www.bostonphoenix.com (accessed June 13, 2006).

———. "Who Pays the Price of War?" *Gay and Lesbian Review* 8, no. 6 (January/February 2002): 14–16.

Khouri, Rami. "Abu Ghraib in the Arab Mirror." October 19, 2004. http://www.opendemocracy.net (accessed June 19, 2006).

Kim, Richard. "Sodomy for Some." *The Nation*, May 19, 2003, 6.

———. "Witness to an Execution." *The Nation*, August 7, 2005. http://www.thenation.com (accessed September 9, 2006).

Kim, Ryan. "Attacked for Art, S.F. Gallery to Close: Backers Rally after Violent Responses to Painting of Tortured Iraqis." *San Francisco Chronicle*, May 30, 2004, B2.

Kimmel, Michael. "Gender, Class, and Terrorism." *Chronicle of Higher Education*, February 8, 2002, B11–B12.

Kirkland, Michael. "Analysis: The Changing Face of Terror." *Washington Times* online, August 3, 2004. http://www.washtimes.com (accessed August 24, 2004; no longer available).

Knickmeyer, Ellen. "Vice Creeps Back to Kandahar." *Guardian Unlimited*, February 22, 2002. http://www.guardian.co.uk (accessed June 11, 2006).

Knippenberg, Joseph M. "The Long and Winding Road: George W. Bush and the African-American Churches." Editorial. Ashbrook Center for Public Affairs at Ashland University, October 2004. http://www.ashbrook.org (accessed August 23, 2005).

Knopp, Larry. "Sexuality and Urban Space: A Framework for Analysis." In *Mapping Desires: Geographies of Sexualities*, edited by David Bell and Gill Valentine, 149–63. New York: Routledge, 1995.

Kobayashi, Audrey, and Brian Ray. "Placing American Emigration to Canada in Context." *Migration Information Source*. Migration Policy Institute. January 1, 2005. http://www.migrationinformation.org (accessed June 26, 2006).

Koshy, Susan. "Morphing Race into Ethnicity: Asian Americans and Critical Transformations of Whiteness." *boundary 2* 28, no. 1 (February 2001): 153–94.

Kong, Deborah. "Arabs, Muslims, and Sikhs Report Sporadic Hate Crimes as War Continues." March 28, 2003. LexisNexis (accessed June 21, 2006).

KRAC.com. "Man Accused of Sikh Hate Crime Apologizes: Accused Says It Was an Act of 'Senseless Patriotism.'" September 18, 2001. http://www.krac.com (accessed June 21, 2006).

LaBarbera, Peter. "Columnist: Traitor's Dad Was Homosexual Adulterer." Concerned Women for America. January 10, 2002. http://www.cultureandfamily.org (accessed June 13, 2006).

"A Ladder to Heaven." *South Park*. Written and directed by Trey Parker. Comedy Central. November 6, 2002, episode 612.

Lawrence v. Texas 2003 U.S. LEXIS 5013 (2003).

LeCarré, John. "A War We Cannot Win." *The Nation*, November 19, 2001, 15–17.

Lee, Becky. "The Wars We Are Still Fighting." *ColorLife!* Spring 2004, 1, 4–7. http://www.alp.org (accessed June 13, 2006).

Lee, JeeYeun. "Toward a Queer Korean American Diasporic History." In *Q and A: Queer in Asian America*, edited by David L. Eng and Alice Y. Hom, 185–209. Philadelphia: Temple University Press, 1998.

Leonard, Autumn, Tomás Aguilar, Mike Prokosch, and Dara Silverman. "Organizing after September 11." *Dollars and Sense: The Magazine of Economic Justice*, no. 240 (March–April 2002). http://www.dollarsandsense.org (accessed June 13, 2006).

Leonard, Christina, Jim Walsh, Charles Kelly, and Lindsey Collom. "Sikhs Voice Outrage over Mesa Hate Killing." *Arizona Republic* online, September 18, 2001. http://www.azcentral.com (accessed June 22, 2006).

Lerner, Sharon. "What Women Want: Feminists Agonize over War in Afghanistan." *Village Voice*, November 6, 2001, 53–55.

Lest We Forget. Produced by Jason DaSilva and Roopa De Choudhury. Directed by Jason DaSilva. 57 min. Third World Newsreel, New York, N.Y. 2003.

Letellier, Parick. "Egyptians Decry 'Gay' Abuse in Iraq: LGBT Groups Hit Out at 'Torture' Confusion." *PlanetOut News and Politics*, May 17, 2004. http://icq.planetout.com (accessed June 19, 2006).

———. "Poll: Overwhelming Support for Gays in the Military." *PlanetOut News*, December 30, 2003. http://www.planetout.com (accessed June 13, 2006).

Lianos, Michalis. "Social Control after Foucault." Translated by David Wood and Michalis Lianos. *Surveillance and Society* 1, no. 3 (June 2003): 412–30. http://www.surveillance-and-society.org (accessed June 30, 2006).

Library, University of California, Berkeley. *Echoes of Freedom: South Asian Pioneers in California, 1899–1965*. Online exhibition. Curated by Suzanne McMahon. Updated October 3, 2001. http://www.lib.berkeley.edu (accessed June 23, 2006).

Limbaugh, Rush. Posting. May 4, 2004. www.rushlimbaugh.com (accessed May 20, 2004; no longer available).

Lisotta, Christopher. "Los Angeles Reports Rise in Hate Crimes." *PlanetOut News and Politics*, September 10, 2002. http://www.planetout.com (accessed June 13, 2006).

Livingstone, Ken, et al. "The Fight against Oppression and Islamophobia." Letter. *Guardian* (London), September 30, 2004, 27.

Long, Scott. "Debating Iran." *Gay City News*, July 27–August 2, 2006. http://www.gaycitynews.com (accessed September 9, 2006).

———. "HRW Letter to Minister Verdonk." March 8, 2006. http://hrw.org (accessed September 9, 2006).

Lorde, Audre. *Sister Outsider: Essays and Speeches*. Trumansburg, N.Y.: Crossing Press, 1984.

Losurdo, Domenico. "Preemptive War, Americanism, and Anti-Americanism." *Metaphilosophy* 35, no. 3 (April 2004): 365–85.

Luibhéid, Eithne. *Entry Denied: Controlling Sexuality at the Border*. Minneapolis: University of Minnesota Press, 2002.

Lunsing, Wim. "Islam Versus Homosexuality? Some Reflections on the Assassination of Pim Fortuyn." *Anthropology Today* 19, no. 2 (April 2003): 19-21.

Luongo, Michael T. "Eroticism among Kabul's Warriors." *Gay City News*, April 29–May 5, 2004. http://www.gaycitynews.com (accessed June 13, 2006).

———. "Follow-up Interview with Michael Luongo on His Return from 'Gay Afghanistan': On Afghani Male Intimacy and Sex." Interview by Globalgayz.com. July 2004. http://www.globalgayz.com (accessed June 11, 2006).

———. "Links to Some of My Work." n.d. http://www.michaelluongo.com (accessed June 11, 2006).

———. "WorldPride: Notes from Jerusalem." August 12, 2006. http://www.gay.com (accessed September 6, 2006).

Lyon, David. "Editorial. Surveillance Studies: Understanding Visibility, Mobility and the Phenetic Fix." *Surveillance and Society* 1, no. 1 (2002): 1–7. http://www.surveillance-and-society.org (accessed June 25, 2006).

MacDonald, Heather. "What We Don't Know *Can* Hurt Us." *City Journal* 14, no. 2 (spring 2004): 14–31.

MacKinnon, Catherine A. "State of Emergency." *Women's Review of Books* 19, no. 6 (March 2002): 7–8.

MAHA. "A Message from Iran." *Gay City News*, August 10–16, 2006. http://www.gaycit ynews.com (accessed September 9, 2006).

Mahabir, Karen, and Raghuram Vadarevu. "A Cultural Torment: False Report Underscores Pressures on Young Sikhs." March 14, 2004. http://www.sikhcoalition.org (accessed August 28, 2006). Originally published in *The Record*, March 14, 2004.

Mahmood, Cynthia Keppley. *Fighting for Faith and Nation: Dialogues with Sikh Militants.* Philadephia: University of Pennsylvania Press, 1996.

Mahmood, Saba. *Politics of Piety: The Islamic Revival and the Feminist Subject.* Princeton: Princeton University Press, 2004.

Maira, Sunaina. "Youth Culture, Citizenship, and Globalization: South Asian Muslim Youth in the United States after September 11th." *Comparative Studies of South Asia, Africa, and the Middle East* 24, no. 1 (2004): 219–31.

Mamdani, Mahmood. *Good Muslim, Bad Muslim: America, the Cold War, and the Roots of Terror.* New York: Three Leaves Press, 2005.

Manalansan, Martin F., IV. *Global Divas: Filipino Gay Men in the Diaspora.* Durham: Duke University Press, 2003.

——. "Race, Violence, and Neoliberal Spatial Politics." *Social Text* 23, no. 3–4 84–85 (fall/ winter): 141–55.

Mangat, Satwinder. "Hate Crimes against Sikh Community." Posting. September 14, 2001. http://lists.xml.org (accessed June 21, 2006).

Manji, Irshad. "America's Wild West." Op-Ed. *Los Angeles Times*, May 1, 2005. http:// www.latimes.com (accessed June 11, 2006).

Maran, Rita. *Torture: The Role of Ideology in the French-Algerian War.* New York: Praeger, 1989.

Margasak, Larry. "FBI Monitors Radiation Levels at Muslim Sites without Warrants." December 23, 2005. LexisNexis (accessed May 21, 2006).

Mariner, David. "NLGTF Not a Win without War Coalition Member." January 30, 2003. http://www.gaylinkcontent.com (accessed June 13, 2006). Originally published in *Temenos: The Progressive Lesbian, Gay, Bisexual, Trans, Intersex (LGBTI) Community Online*, January 30, 2003, www.temenos.net.

——. "NGLTF Response to Temenos Article." Queers for Peace and Justice discussion group e-mail, October 1, 2003. http://groups.yahoo.com (accessed June 13, 2006).

Marks, Alexandra. "In This War, American Women Shed Role as 'Doves.'" *Christian Science Monitor*, November 6, 2001, 1.

Martin, Douglas. "As Indian's Ranks in Canada Grow, Old Conflicts Are Also Transplanted." *New York Times*, June 26, 1985, A11.

Massad, Joseph. "Re-Orienting Desire: The Gay International and the Arab World." *Public Culture* 14. 2 (May 2002): 361–85.

Massumi, Brian. *Parables for the Virtual: Movement, Affect, Sensation.* Durham: Duke University Press, 2002.

——. Untitled paper presented at "Beyond Biopolitics: State Racism and the Politics of Life and Death" conference, The Graduate Center, City University of New York, March 17, 2006.

Maxwell, Richard. "Surveillance: Work, Myth, and Policy." *Social Text* 23, no. 2 83 (summer 2005): 1–19.

Mayer, Jane. "Q&A: Torture by Proxy." Interview by Amy Davidson. *New Yorker*, February 8, 2005. http://www.newyorker.com (accessed June 19, 2006).

Mbembe, Achille. "Necropolitics." Translated by Libby Meintjes. *Public Culture* 15, no. 1 (winter 2003): 11–40.

——. *On the Postcolony*. Translated by A. M. Berrett, Janet Roitman, Murray Last, and Steven Rendall. Berkeley: University of California Press, 2001.

McCall, Leslie. "The Complexity of Intersectionality." *Signs: Journal of Women, Culture, and Society* 30, no. 3 (2005): 1771–800.

McCauley, C. R., and M. E. Segal. "Social Psychology of Terrorist Groups." In *Group Processes and Intergroup Relations*, edited by C. Hendrick, 231–256. Vol. 9 of *Annual Review of Social and Personality Psychology*. Beverly Hills, Calif.: Sage, 1987.

McClintock, Anne. *Imperial Leather: Race, Gender, and Sexuality*. New York: Routledge, 1995.

McKinney, Joan. "Cooksey: Expect Racial Profiling." *The Advocate* (Baton Rouge), September 19, 2001, B-1, B-2.

McRuer, Robert. "Composing Bodies; or, De-Composition: Queer Theory, Disability Studies, and Alternative Corporealities." *Journal of Advanced Composition* 24 (2004): 47–78.

——. "Compulsory Able-Bodiedness and Queer/Disabled Existence." In *Disability Studies: Enabling the Humanities*, edited by Sharon L. Snyder, Brenda Jo Brueggemann, and Rosemarie Garland-Thomson, 88–99. New York: Modern Language Association of America, 2002.

McWhorter, Ladelle. "Sex, Race, and Biopower: A Foucauldian Genealogy." *Hypatia: A Journal of Feminist Philosophy* 19, no. 3 (summer 2003): 38–62.

Media Matters for America. "Limbaugh on Torture of Iraqis: U.S. Guards Were 'Having a Good Time,' Blow[ing] off Some Steam.'" May 5, 2006. http://mediamatters.org (accessed June 14, 2006).

Menchaca, Paul. "Sikh Community Outraged in Wake of Woodside Hate Crime." *Queens Chronicle* online, August 7, 2003. http://www.zwire.com (accessed June 21, 2006).

Merom, Gil. "Israel's National Security and the Myth of Exceptionalism." *Political Science Quarterly* 114, no. 3 (autumn 1999): 409–34.

Metropolitan Community Churches. "A Call for Peaceful Resolution to Conflict with Iraq." News release. September 30, 2002. http://www.mcchurch.org (accessed June 13, 2006).

Milbank, Dana, and Emily Wax. "Bush Visits Mosque to Forestall Hate Crimes." *Washington Post*, September 18, 2001, A1.

MilitaryArticles.com. "Abu Ghraib: The Root of the Problem." Posting by Ace Fumigators. May 11, 2004. http://www.militaryarticles.com (accessed August 24, 2005; no longer available, printout on file with author).

Miller, Elizabeth. "An Open Letter to the Editors of Ms. Magazine." Middle Eastern Affairs Conference, Pittsburg State University International Studies Program. April 20, 2002. http://www.pittstate.edu (accessed June 11, 2006).

Miller, Judith. "Hunting bin Laden: Interview." *Frontline*. Public Broadcasting System, September 12, 2001. www.pbs.org (accessed June 13, 2006).

Minwalla, Framji. "Tony Kushner's *Homebody/Kabul*: Staging History in a Post-colonial World." *Theater* 33, no. 1 (winter 2003): 29–43.

Mitchell, W. J. T. "The War of Images." *University of Chicago Magazine* 94. 2 (December 2001). http://magazine.uchicago.edu (accessed June 23, 2006).

Mohanty, Chandra Talpade. "Under Western Eyes: Feminist Scholarship and Colonial Discourse." *Feminist Review*, no. 30 (autumn 1988): 61–88.

Monroe, Irene. "Justice Begins in the Bedroom." *The Witness*, July 21, 2003. http://thewitness.org (accessed June 25, 2006).

Moore, Patrick. "Gay Sexuality Shouldn't Become a Torture Device." *Newsday*, May 7, 2004, A51.

Morcos, Rauda. "Queering Palestinian Solidarity Activism." Posted June 6, 2004. http://montages.blogspot.com (accessed June 12, 2006).

Morgan, Robin. *The Demon Lover: The Roots of Terrorism*. New York: Washington Square Press, 1989.

Mosco, Vincent. *The Digital Sublime: Myth, Power, and Cyberspace*. Cambridge, Mass.: MIT Press, 2004.

Mukherjee, Bharati. *NOW with Bill Moyers*. Public Broadcasting System. May 2, 2003. Transcript available at http://www.pbs.org (accessed June 23, 2006).

——. *Jasmine*. New York: Grove Press, 1989.

——. *Wife*. New York: Fawcett Crest, 1975.

Muñoz, José Esteban. *Disidentifications: Queers of Color and the Performance of Politics*. Minneapolis: University of Minnesota Press, 1999.

——. "Feeling Brown: Ethnicity and Affect in Ricardo Bracho's *The Sweetest Hangover (and Other STDs)*," *Theater Journal* 52, no. 1 (March 2000): 67–79.

——. "A Forum on Theatre and Tragedy In the Wake of September 11, 2001." *Theatre Journal* 54. 1 (March 2002): 122–23.

Musbach, Tom. "Gay Politicos Unite over Survivor Benefits." *PlanetOut News*, November 26, 2001. http://www.planetout.com (accessed June 12, 2006).

——. "Group Warns Bush: AIDS Is Security Issue." March 13, 2002. http://www.gay.com (accessed June 13, 2006).

——. "Navy Refuses to Discharge Gay Member." September 24, 2002. http://www.gay.com (accessed June 13, 2006).

——. "Sen. McCain Pays Tribute to Mark Bingham." *PlanetOut News and Politics*, September 24, 2001. http://www.planetout.com (accessed June 13, 2006).

Mustikhan, Ahmar. "Group Fights for Palestinian Gays' Safety." *PlanetOut News and Politics*, April 4, 2003. http://www.planetout.com (accessed June 15, 2005).

Musto, Michael. "Alien vs. Predator: What the McGreevey Mess Means for Closets, Corruption, and Casting Couches." *Village Voice*, August, 24, 2004, 1, 28.

Myslik, W. "Renegotiating the Social/Sexual Identities of Places: Gay Communities as Safe Havens or Sites of Resistance?" In *BodySpace: Destabilizing Geographies of Gender and Sexuality*, edited by Nancy Duncan, 156–69. New York: Routledge, 1996.

Naim, Tahir. "SABA: South Asians Being Targeted in Wake of Attack." E-mail forwarded to author. Received September 13, 2001.

Najmabadi, Afsaneh. *Women with Mustaches and Men without Beards: Gender and Sexual Anxieties of Iranian Modernity*. Berkeley: University of California Press, 2005.

Nanda, Tanmaya Kumar. "Sikhs Become Targets of Ire in New York." *rediff.com*, U.S. ed., September 12, 2001. http://www.rediff.com (accessed June 21, 2006).

Nast, Heidi J. "Prologue: Crosscurrents." In "Queer Patriarchies, Queer Racisms, International." Special issue of *Antipode* 34, no. 5 (November 2002): 835–44.

——. "Queer Patriarchies, Queer Racisms, International." Special issue of *Antipode: A Radical Journal of Geography* 34, no. 5 (November 2002): 874–909.

——. ed. "Queer Patriarchies, Queer Racisms, International." Special issue of *Antipode* 34, no. 5 (November 2002).

National Center for Lesbian Rights. "National Center for Lesbian Rights Hails Supreme Court Decision Striking Texas Sodomy Statute: Background Information: How Sodomy Laws Have Been Used As a Weapon of Discrimination against Lesbians." Press release. June 2003. http://www.nclrights.org (accessed June 25, 2006).

National Coalition of Anti-Violence Programs. *Anti-Lesbian, Gay, Bisexual and Transgender Violence in 2002: A Report of the National Coalition of Anti-Violence Programs.* Preliminary ed., 2003. http://www.avp.org (accessed June 13, 2006).

National Gay and Lesbian Task Force. " 'Anti-Gay Groups Active in Massachusetts: A Closer Look' Exposes Broad Reactionary Agenda of Anti-Gay Groups Working against Marriage Equality." March 11, 2004. http://www.thetaskforce.org (accessed June 10, 2006).

——. "Response to Recent False Allegations Regarding NGLTF's Position against the War." Press release. January 30, 2003. http://www.thetaskforce.org (accessed June 13, 2006).

NBC News. "U.S. Army Report on Iraqi Prisoner Abuse." *Nightly News with Brian Williams.* May 4, 2004. http://www.msnbc.msn.com (accessed June 19, 2006).

Neumayr, George. "The Abu Ghraib Collection." *American Spectator* online, May 12, 2004. http://www.spectator.org (accessed June 19, 2006).

Newindpress. "Sher-e-Punjab Sponsors 92-Year-Old Sikh for NY Marathon." September 26, 2003. http://www.saldef.org (accessed June 22, 2006).

New York Advisory Committee. "Panel Summaries." In *Civil Rights Implications of Post-September 11 Law Enforcement Practices in New York.* A report prepared for the U.S. Commission on Civil Rights. March 2004. http://www.usccr.gov (accessed June 26, 2006).

New York City Association of Homeless and Street-Involved Youth Organizations. "State of the City's Homeless Youth Report 2003." Empire State Coalition of Youth and Family Services. 2003. http://www.empirestatecoalition.org (accessed June 25, 2006).

New York Times. "A Million Votes for Dead Man." May 22, 2002, A14.

NewsPlanet Staff. "Breaking News: London Bombing!" *PlanetOut News and Politics*, April 29, 1999. http://www.planetout.com (accessed June 12, 2006).

——. "London Gay Bar Bombed." *PlanetOut News*, April 30, 1999. http://www.planetout.com (accessed June 12, 2006).

Nieves, Evelyn, and Ann Scott Tyson. "Fewer Gays Being Discharged Since 9/11: 'Don't Ask' Ousters at Lowest Level Yet." *Washington Post*, February 12, 2005, A1.

Niranjana, Tejaswini. *Mobilizing India: Women, Music and Migration between India and Trinidad.* Durham: Duke University Press, 2006.

Nolan, Clancy. "Patriotic Pride." *Independent Weekly*, September 26, 2001. http://www.indyweek.com (accessed June 13, 2006).

No Pride in Occupation. "No Pride in Occupation." n.d. www.nopridewithoutpalestinians.org (accessed June 12, 2006).

OMB Watch. "Anti-Terrorism Bill Could Impact Nonprofits." November 14, 2001. http://www.ombwatch.org (accessed June 21, 2006).

"Osama bin Laden Has Farty Pants." *South Park.* Written and directed by Trey Parker. Comedy Central. November 7, 2001, episode 509.

Osborne, Duncan. "Mashad Hangings Anniversary Marked in Midtown Vigil." *Gay City News,* July 20–26, 2006. http://www.gaycitynews.com (accessed September 9, 2006).

———. "Pentagon Uses Gay Sex as Tool of Humiliation." *Gay City News,* May 13–17, 2004. http://www.gaycitynews.com (accessed June 19, 2006).

OutRage! "Muslim Cleric Says: Death to Gays and Jews." Press release. July 9, 2004. www.outrage.nabumedia.com (accessed June 15, 2005; no longer available). Republished July 9, 2004. http://www.indymedia.org.uk (accessed June 12, 2006).

———. "Press Photos." http://outrage.nabumedia.com (accessed July 14, 2005; no longer available). Republished http://www.petertatchel.net (accessed June 12, 2006).

———. Press release. http://outrage.nabumedia.com (accessed July 14, 2005; no longer available, printout on file with author).

———. "Terrorist Danger to Gay Venues; 'Increase Security,' Urges OutRage!" Press release. July 18, 2005. http://outrage.nabumedia.com (accessed 30 August 2005; no longer available). Republished July 26, 2005. http://haganah.org.il (accessed June 12, 2006).

Oxford English Dictionary, s.v. "sodomy." http://dictionary.oed.com (accessed June 25, 2006).

Painter, George. "The Sensibilities of Our Forefathers: The History of Sodomy Laws in the United States: Introduction." n.d. http://www.sodomylaws.org (accessed June 25, 2006).

Palumbo-Lui, David. "Multiculturalism Now: Civilization, National Identity, and Difference before and after September 11th." *boundary 2* 29, no. 2 (June 2002): 109–27.

Parasuram, T. V. "Indian Embassy Condemns Attacks on Sikhs." *rediff.com,* U.S. ed., September 14, 2001. http://www.rediff.com (accessed June 22, 2006).

Parenti, Christian. *The Soft Cage: Surveillance in America.* New York: Basic Books, 2003.

Parenti, Michael. *Make-Believe Media: The Politics of Entertainment.* New York: St. Martin's Press, 1992.

Parisi, Luciana. *Abstract Sex: Philosophy, Biotechnology and the Mutations of Desire.* New York: Continuum, 2004.

Patel, Geeta. "Homely Housewives Run Amok: Lesbians in Marital Fixes." *Public Culture* 16, no. 1 (winter 2004): 131–57.

Patton, Cindy, and Benigno Sanchez-Eppler, eds. *Queer Diasporas.* Durham: Duke University Press, 2000.

Pease, Donald. "The Global Homeland State: Bush's Biopolitical Settlement." *boundary 2* 30, no. 3 (fall 2003): 1–18.

Pellegrini, Ann. "Commodity Capitalism and Transformations in Gay Identity." In *Queer Globalizations: Citizenship and the Afterlife of Colonialism,* edited by Arnaldo Cruz-Malave and Martin Manalansan IV, 134–45. New York: New York University Press, 2002.

People's Law Dictionary, s.v. "sodomy." http://dictionary.law.com (accessed June 25, 2006).

Perez, Hiram. "You Can Have My Brown Body and Eat It, Too!" *Social Text* 23, no. 3–4 84–85 (fall–winter 2005): 171–91.

Perry, Troy D. "A Pastoral Statement from Metropolitan Community Churches." Toronto Metropolitan Community Churches, Office of the MCC Moderator. May 2004. http://www.mcctoronto.com (accessed June 19, 2006).

Petchesky, Rosalind. "Phantom Towers." Paper presented at CUNY Hunter College, New York, October 2001.

Peterson, V. Spike. "Sexing Political Identities: Nationalism as Heterosexism." *International Feminist Journal of Politics* 1, no. 1 (June 1999): 34–65.

Phelan, Shane. *Sexual Strangers: Gays, Lesbians, and Dilemmas of Citizenship*. Philadelphia: Temple University Press, 2001.

Phillips, Richard. "Writing Travel and Mapping Sexuality: Richard Burton's Sotadic Zone." In *Writes of Passage: Reading Travel Writing*, edited by James S. Duncan and Derek Gregory, 70–91. New York: Routledge, 1999.

PlanetOut Network. "Amsterdam Police Vow to Combat Hate Crimes." *PlanetOut News and Politics*, June 10, 2005. http://www.planetout.com (accessed June 12, 2006).

Post, Jerrold. "Rewarding Fire with Fire? Effects of Retaliation on Terrorist Group Dynamics." In *Contemporary Trends in World Terrorism*, edited by Anat Kurz, 103–15. New York: Praeger, 1987.

——. "Terrorist Psycho-logic: Terrorist Behavior as a Product of Psychological Forces." In *Origins of Terrorism: Psychologies, Ideologies, Theologies, States of Mind*, edited by Walter Reich, 25–42. Cambridge, England: Cambridge University Press, 1990.

Povinelli, Elizabeth A. "Notes on Gridlock: Genealogy, Intimacy, Sexuality." *Public Culture* 14, no. 1 (winter 2002): 215–38.

Powell, Michael. "An Exodus Grows in Brooklyn: 9/11 Still Rippling through Pakistani Neighborhood." *Washington Post*, May 29, 2003, A1.

Pradhan, Avanti A. "The Mourning After: Sikh Americans' Cultural Awareness Campaign Following 9/11." *SAGAR: A South Asian Graduate Research Journal* 9 (fall 2002): 79–94.

Price, Deb. "Black Supporters of Gays Ignored." *Detroit News*, January 12, 2004. Reposted at http://www.hrc.org (accessed June 25, 2006).

Priest, Dana, and Joe Stephens. "Secret World of U.S. Interrogation: Long History of Tactics in Overseas Prisons Is Coming to Light." *Washington Post*, May 11, 2004, A1.

"Primary Sources: The Torture Debate." *New Yorker*, February 8, 2005. http://www.newyorker.com (accessed July 13, 2005).

"Probably." *South Park*. Written and directed by Trey Parker. Comedy Central. July 26, 2000, episode 411.

Puar, Jasbir Kaur, ed. "Queer Tourism: Geographies of Globalization." Special issue of *GLQ: A Journal of Lesbian and Gay Studies* 8, no. 1–2 (2002).

——. "Transnational Configurations of Desire: The Nation and Its White Closets." In *The Making and Unmaking of Whiteness*, edited by Birgit Brander Rasmussen, Irene J. Nexica, Eric Klinenberg, and Matt Wray, 167–83. Durham: Duke University Press, 2001.

Puar, Jasbir K., and Amit S. Rai. "Monster, Terrorist, Fag: The War on Terrorism and the Production of Docile Patriots." *Social Text* 20, no. 3 72 (fall 2002): 117–48.

——. "The Remaking of a Model Minority: Perverse Projectiles under the Specter of (Counter)Terrorism." *Social Text* 22, no. 3 80 (fall 2004): 75–104.

Puar, Jasbir Kaur, Dereka Rushbrook, and Louisa Schein, eds. "Sexuality and Space: Queering Geographies of Globalization." Special issue of *Environment and Planning D: Society and Space* 21, no. 4 (August 2003).

Purewal, Sukhjit. "Threats, Snide Remarks Worsen the Pain of Bay Area Muslims." *rediff.com*, U.S. ed., September 12, 2001. http://www.rediff.com (accessed June 21, 2006).

Purnick, Joyce. "Transit Rules? Scratch Head, Covered or Not." *New York Times*, June 10, 2004, B1.

Qidwai, Minhaj. "Abu-Ghrayb: Reminder of Inept Ummah." Independent Centre for Strategic Studies and Analysis. May 29, 2004. http://icssa.org (accessed June 25, 2006).

Queer Jihad. "About Queer Jihad." Updated January 10, 2003. http://www.well.com (accessed June 11, 2006).

——. "Queer Jihad." Updated August 7, 2005. http://www.well.com (accessed June 11, 2006).

Queers for Peace and Justice. "LGBT Call to Action for an Anti War Pride—please endorse, please forward." Forwarded e-mail, received by author, June 13, 2003. On file with author.

Quinn, Andrew. "Gay Muslims Come Out in S.F. Pride Parade," *PlanetOut News and Politics*, June 25, 2001. http://www.planetout.com (accessed June 11, 2006).

Quittner, Jeremy. "New Hurdles for Survivors." *The Advocate*, February 5, 2002, 13.

Qureshi, Emram. "Misreading *The Arab Mind*." *Boston Globe*, May 30, 2004, D1.

Radical Women and Freedom Socialist Party, "We're Here, We're Queer, We're Gonna Stop the War Machine!" Flier, disseminated fall 2001, on file with author.

Rai, Amit. "Patriotism and the Muslim Citizen in Hindi Films." *Harvard Asia Quarterly* 7, no. 3 (summer 2003). http://www.asiaquarterly.com (accessed June 21, 2006).

——. Untitled paper presented at "Beyond Biopolitics: State Racism and the Politics of Life and Death" conference, The Graduate Center, City University of New York, March 17, 2006.

Rajan, Julie V. G. "Subversive Visibility and Political Agency: The Case of the Palestinian Female Suicide Bombers." In *to kill, to die: female contestations on gender and political violence*, edited by Hilla Dayan, 12–13. Special publication for Women's International Day. New York: New School University, March 2004.

Ramachandran, Sudha. "Women Suicide Bombers Defy Israel." *Asia Times Online*, October 25, 2003. http://www.atimes.com (accessed June 27, 2006).

Rauchway, Eric. "More Means Different: Quantifying American Exceptionalism." *Reviews in American History* 30, no. 3 (September 2002): 504–16.

Rawls, Philip. "Riley Administration Changes Rules on Head Scarves." February 20, 2004. LexisNexis (accessed June 22, 2006).

Reddy, Chandan. "Asian Diasporas, Neoliberalism, and Family: Reviewing the Case for Homosexual Asylum in the Context of Family Rights." *Social Text* 23, no. 3–4 84–85 (fall–winter 2005): 101–19.

Reilly, Kristie. "Warning! You Are Being Watched: Reading This Magazine in Public May Result in Questioning by the FBI." *In These Times*, September 19, 2003. http://www.inthesetimes.com (accessed June 26, 2006).

Rejali, Darius. "A Long-Standing Trick of the Torturer's Art." Opinion. *Seattle Times*, May 14, 2004. http://seattletimes.nwsource.com (accessed June 19, 2006).

——. *Torture and Modernity: Self, Society and State in Modern Iran*. Boulder, Colo.: Westview Press, 1994.

Reuters. "Nigerian Man Sentenced to Stoning for Gay Sex." July 9, 2005. http://www.abc .net.au (accessed September 9, 2006).

Reynolds, Maura. "Kandahar's Lightly Veiled Homosexual Habits." *Los Angeles Times*, April 3, 2002. http://www.latimes.com (accessed June 11, 2006).

Rich, Frank. "The War's Lost Weekend." *New York Times*, May 9, 2004, sec. 2, p. 1.

Richard, Diane. "War and Sex." *Contemporary Sexuality* 36, no. 1 (January 2002): 1, 4–6.

Riley, John. "How War Imperils the Fight against AIDS." *Gay City News*, February 21–27, 2003. http://www.gaycitynews.com (accessed June 13, 2006).

Rimer, Sara. "Pakistanis Unperturbed by U.S. Raid on Residence." *New York Times*, November 17, 2001, B8.

Rimer, Sara, and Karen W. Arensen. "Top Colleges Take More Blacks, but Which Ones?" *New York Times*, June 24, 2004, A1.

Rising Up: The Alams. Produced and directed by Konrad Aderer. 11 min. Third World Newsreel, New York, N.Y. 2005.

Robson, Ruthann. "The Missing Word in *Lawrence v. Texas*." *Cardozo Women's Law Journal* 10, no. 2 (winter 2004): 397–410.

Roche, Timothy, Brian Bennet, Anne Berryman, Hilary Hylton, Siobhan Morrissey, and Amany Radwan. "The Making of John Walker Lindh." *Time*, October 7, 2002, 44–54.

Rodriguez, Juana María. *Queer Latinidad: Identity Practices, Discursive Spaces*. New York: New York University Press, 2003.

Root, Nathan. "Accenture Faces Daunting Task with US-VISIT Contract." June 9, 2004. http://www.insideid.com (accessed September 6, 2006).

Roots in the Sand. Produced and directed by Jayasri Mujamdar Hart. 57 min. National Asian American Telecommunications Association (now Center for Asian American Media), San Francisco, 1998.

Rosendall, Richard J. "No Excuses for Iran." Independent Gay Forum: Forging a Gay Mainstream. July 27, 2006. http://www.indegayforum.org (accessed September 9, 2006).

Roth, Thomas. "Welcoming Remarks." Presented at International Gay and Lesbian Tourism Association annual conference, Los Angeles, March, 4, 2002.

Rothenberg, Tamar. "'And She Told Two Friends': Lesbians Creating Urban Social Space." In *Mapping Desires: Geographies of Sexualities*, edited by David Bell and Gill Valentine, 165–81. New York: Routledge, 1995.

Rowe, John Carlos. "Edward Said and American Studies." *American Quarterly* 56, no. 1 (March 2004): 33–47.

Roy, Arundhati. "The Algebra of Infinite Justice: As the U.S. Prepares to Wage a New Kind of War, Arundhati Roy Challenges the Instinct for Vengeance." *Guardian* (London), September 29, 2001, 1.

Roy, Sandip. "Banks Allegedly Blacklisting Muslims: Civil Liberties Digest." July 2, 2003. http://news.pacificnews.org (accessed July 15, 2005).

——. "Can Gay Marriage Protect Europe from Subway Bombers?" July 13, 2005. http:// news.pacificnews.org (accessed July 14, 2005).

Rubenstein, Diane. "Did You Pack Your Bags Yourself? Governmentality after 9/11." *CR: The New Centennial Review* 3, no. 2 (summer 2003): 303–31.

Rubin, Gayle. "Thinking Sex: Notes for a Radical Theory of the Politics of Sexuality." In *The Lesbian and Gay Studies Reader*, edited by Henry Abelove, Michele Aina Barale, and David M. Halperin, 3–44. New York: Routledge, 1993.

Ruskola, Teemu. "Gay Rights vs. Queer Theory: What Is Left of Sodomy after *Lawrence v. Texas*." *Social Text* 23, no. 3–4 84–85 (fall–winter 2005): 235–49.

Russ, Hilary. "Leave Home without It." *City Limits Monthly*, May 2003. http://www.city limits.org (accessed July 15, 2005).

Ryan, Caitlin, and Donna Futterman. *Lesbian and Gay Youth: Care and Counseling*. New York: Columbia University Press, 1998.

Sacks, Oliver. "Speed: Aberrations of Time and Movement." *New Yorker*, August 23, 2004, 60–69.

Sadownick, Douglas, Chris Kilbourne, and Wendell Jones. "War Fever and Gay Resistance." *Gay and Lesbian Review* 8, no. 6 (January/February 2002): 26–27.

Said, Edward. "The Essential Terrorist." In *Blaming the Victims: Spurious Scholarship and the Palestine Question*, edited by Edward Said and Christopher Hitchens, 149–58. New York: Verso, 1988.

——. "Islam and the West Are Inadequate Banners." Comment. *Observer*, September 16, 2001. http://observer.guardian.co.uk (accessed June 10, 2006).

——. *Orientalism*. New York: Vintage Books, 1979.

Sakhuja, Vijay. "Terrorism and Tourism." Institute of Peace and Conflict Studies, no. 699. February 17, 2002. http://www.ipcs.org (accessed June 13, 2006).

Saldanha, Arun. "Reontologising Race: The Machinic Geography of Phenotype." *Environment and Planning D: Society and Space* 24, no. 1 (2006): 9–24.

Salter, Sunny. Review of *"I'm Gonna Kill the President": A Federal Offense*, written and directed by Hieronymus Bang, Brooklyn, New York, *Theater Journal* 56, no. 3 (October 2004): 513–14.

Sánchez-Eppler, Benigno, and Cindy Patton. "Introduction: With a Passport out of Eden." In *Queer Diasporas*, edited by Cindy Patton and Benigno Sánchez-Eppler, 1–14. Durham: Duke University Press, 2000.

Sanders, Eli. "Understanding Turbans." Illustrated by Paul Schmid. *Seattle Times*, September 27, 2001, E1.

Schaffer, Kay, and Sidonie Smith, eds. "Personal Effects." Special issue of *Biography: An Interdisciplinary Quarterly* 27, no. 1 (winter 2004).

Scheer, Robert. "Homophobia and Apple Pie." *Los Angeles Times*, July 20, 2004. www.latimes.com (accessed June 15, 2005).

Schindler, Paul. "Gay Linguist Discharges Continue." *Gay City News*, April 18–24, 2003. http://www.gaycitynews.com (accessed June 13, 2006).

Schmitt, Eric, and Kate Zernike. "Iraq Abuse Trial Is Again Limited to Lower Ranks." *New York Times*, March 23, 2006, A1.

Schneider, William. Reporting for *Insight*, CNN. May 5, 2004. http://transcripts.cnn.com (accessed June 19, 2006).

Sciolino, Elaine. "Next Target in the French Headgear Debate: The Bandana." *New York Times*, January 20, 2004. http://www.nytimes.com (accessed June 21, 2006).

Scott, Joan Wallach. *Gender and the Politics of History*. Rev. ed. New York: Columbia University Press, 1999.

Scroggins, Deborah. "The Dutch-Muslim Culture War." *Nation*, June 27, 2005, 21–25.

Section for the Study of Islam. "Statement from the Steering Committee and Members, Section for the Study of Islam: Statement from Scholars of the Islamic Religion." September 17, 2001. http://groups.colgate.edu (accessed June 10, 2006).

Sedgwick, Eve Kosofsky. *Touching Feeling: Affect, Pedagogy, Performativity*. Durham: Duke University Press, 2003.

Seidman, Steven. "Identity and Politics in a 'Postmodern' Gay Culture: Some Historical and Conceptual Notes." In *Fear of a Queer Planet: Queer Politics and Social Theory*, edited by Michael Warner, 105–42. Minneapolis: University of Minnesota Press, 1993.

Servicemembers Legal Defense Network. "Conduct Unbecoming: The 8th Annual Report on 'Don't Ask, Don't Tell.'" March 14, 2002. http://www.sldn.org (accessed June 13, 2006).

Shah, Nayan. "Between 'Oriental Depravity' and 'Natural Degenerates': Spatial Borderlands and the Making of Ordinary Americans." *American Quarterly* 57, no. 3 (September 2005): 703–25.

——. "Perversity, Contamination and the Dangers of Queer Domesticity." In *Queer Studies: An Interdisciplinary Reader*, edited by Robert J. Corber and Stephen Valocchi, 121–41. Oxford: Blackwell, 2003.

——. "Policing Privacy, Migrants, and the Limits of Freedom." *Social Text* 23, no. 3–4 84–85 (fall–winter 2005): 275–84.

Shah, Svati P., and Rebecca Young. "A 'Morning After Prescription': Remembering Abu Ghraib." *SAMAR Magazine Online* 18 (fall 2004). http://www.samarmagazine.org (accessed June 19, 2006).

Shanker, Thom, and Jacques Steinberg. "Bush Voices 'Disgust' at Abuse of Iraqi Prisoners." *New York Times*, May 1, 2004, A1.

Sharma, Parvez. "Manufacturing Dissent." *Center for Lesbian and Gay Studies (CLAGS) Newsletter*, fall 2004, 5.

Sheffer, Doron, and Efrat Weiss. "Violence Erupts at Gay Pride Parade." June 30, 2005. http://www.ynetnews.com (accessed June 12, 2006).

Shenon, Philip, and Robin Toner. "Immigrant Arrests, 75 in Custody Following Terror Attack Can Be Held Indefinitely." *New York Times*, September 19, 2001, A1, B7.

Shildrick, Margrit. "Queering Performativity: Disability after Deleuze." *Scan: Journal of Media Arts Culture* 1, no. 3 (November 2004). http://scan.net.au (accessed August 31, 2006).

Shrader, Esther, and Elizabeth Shogren. "Officials Clash on Roles at Prison." *Los Angeles Times*, May 12, 2004, A1.

Shukla, Sandhya. *India Abroad: Diasporic Cultures of Postwar America and England*. Princeton: Princeton University Press, 2003.

Sikh.org. http://www.sikh.org (accessed January 18, 2001; no longer available).

Sikh American Legal Defense and Education Fund. "Alabama Discriminatory Driver's License Policy Overturned." February 20, 2002. http://www.saldef.org (accessed June 21, 2006).

Sikh Coalition. "Allow Turbaned Sikhs to Serve as Officers in the NYPD." Online petition to Mayor Michael R. Bloomberg and the NYPD. n.d. http://www.petitiononline.com (accessed June 21, 2006).

——. "Coalition Continues to Defend Sikh's Rights to Practice Their Faith: Case Profile: Harvinder Kaur, Overland Park, KS." n.d. http://www.sikhcoalition.org (accessed June 22, 2006).

——. "Measure Supporting Sikh Americans Becomes Law: Law States: 'The Civil Rights and Civil Liberties of All Americans, Including Sikh Americans, Should Be Protected.'" Press release. n.d. http://www.sikhcoalition.org (accessed June 21, 2006).

——. "Please Participate in Candle Night Vigil." Posting to Sikhupdate Yahoo group, December 7, 2001. http://groups.yahoo.com (accessed June 22, 2006).

——. "Press Packet: New Jersey Sikh Civil Rights and Civic Engagement Initiative." December 9, 2003. www.sikhcoalition.org (accessed June 21, 2006).

——. "Resolution on Hate Crimes against Sikh-Americans: Congressional Briefing Package." September 28, 2001. http://www.sikhcoalition.org (accessed June 22, 2006).

——. *Sikhs*. Microsoft PowerPoint presentation. n.d. http://www.sikhcoalition.org (accessed June 23, 2006).

——. "Video Game by Eidos Interactive Depicts Racist Violence." n.d. http://www.sikh coalition.org (accessed June 23, 2006).

——. "Your Rights and Avenues of Action As a Victim of Airport Profiling." Fact sheet. n.d. http://www.sikhcoalition.org (accessed June 23, 2006).

Sikh Council on Religion and Education. "About Us." n.d. http://www.sikhcouncilusa .org (accessed June 22, 2006).

Sikh Mediawatch and Resource Task Force. "Airport Security and Your Rights As an Airline Passenger." October 3, 2001. http://www.saldef.org (accessed June 23, 2006).

——. "Interview with Bharati Mukherjee Aired on May 2, 2003." May 20, 2003. http:// www.saldef.org (accessed June 23, 2006).

——. "Multi-Jurisdiction Meeting Held to Address California Sikh Cab Driver Shootings." Press release. July 24, 2003. http://www.saldef.org (accessed June 22, 2006).

——. "PBS Producer Recognizes Error in Bharati Mukherjee's Comments." Press release. August 11, 2003. http://www.saldef.org (accessed June 23, 2006).

——. "Sikh Americans Denounce the Terrorist Attack, Ask Americans to Unite." Press release. September 12, 2001. http://www.saldef.org (accessed June 22, 2006).

——. "SMART Calls for Action against Cooksey." Press release. September 20, 2001. http: //www.saldef.org (accessed June 23, 2006).

——. "SMART Encourages Community Members to Educate Local Airport Security Personnel about Sikhs." November 16, 2001. http://sikhnet.com (accessed November 17, 2001).

——. "SMART Initiates Airport Educational Campaign, Requests Community Involvement." November 16, 2001. http://sikhnet.com (accessed November 17, 2001).

Sikh Mediawatch and Resource Task Force, Sikh-Sewa (N.Y.), Sikh Youth Federation of North America, United Sikhs in Service of America, Sikh Heresy Regulation Board, Sikh Network, Sikh Sisterhood, and Columbia University Sikhs. "Americans of Sikhs [*sic*] Extraction Caution Indian Prime Minister." Posting to Sikhupdates Yahoo group, September 19, 2001. http://groups.yahoo.com (accessed June 22, 2006).

SikhNet. "Attack on America." November 16, 2001. http://www.Sikhnet.com (accessed June 23, 2006).

——. "Federal Aviation Administration to Ensure New Security Procedures That Preserve

and Respect the Civil Rights of All Americans." November 19, 2001. http://www.Sikh
net.com (accessed June 22, 2006).

———. "Please Sign Hitman 2 Video Petition: Sikh Organizations Unite against Racism:
International Outcry against Video Game Linking Sikhs and Dalits to Terror." October
16, 2002. http://www.sikhnet.com (accessed June 23, 2006).

———. "Sikh Representatives Meet U.S. Congressional Leaders." 2001. http://www.sikh
net.com (accessed June 22, 2006).

SikhNet, Sikh American Association, Sikh Coalition, Sikh Council on Religion and Edu-
cation, Sikh Mediawatch and Resource Taskforce, and The Sikh Communications
Council. "Sikhs Respond to Representative Saxby Chambliss Bigoted Comments."
Press release. December 22, 2001. http://www.sikhnet.com (accessed June 22, 2006).

SikhWomen.com. "U.S. Department of Transporation (DOT) Turban Policy." Fact sheet
and memorandum. May 2, 2002. http://www.sikhwomen.com (accessed June 23,
2006).

Simo, Ana. "Civic Life and Death in the Gay Apple." *The Gully*, October 31, 2001. http://
www.thegully.com (accessed June 13, 2006).

Simon, Bart. "The Return of Panopticism: Supervision, Subjection and the New Surveillance." *Surveillance and Society* 3, no. 1 (2005): 1–20. http://www.surveillance-and-
society.org (accessed June 25, 2006).

Singh, Amarajit. "Are Kashmiri Sikhs Next on India's Hit List—Again?" *Khalistan Calling*
newsletter, August 7, 2001. http://www.khalistan-affairs.org (accessed June 22, 2001).

———. "35 Sikhs Murdered on March 20, 2000 in Indian Occupied Kashmir: Fingerprints
of Indian Intelligence Agencies All Over the Gruesome Massacre of Sikh Innocents."
March 22, 2000. http://www.khalistan-affairs.org (accessed June 22, 2006).

Siu, Jack. "Sept. 11 Aftermath Hurts AIDS Funding." *PlanetOut News*, November 21, 2001.
http://www.planetout.com (accessed June 13, 2006).

Skier, Stephanie. "Western Lenses on Male Same-Sex Relationality in Pashtun Afghanistan." *queer* (spring 2004): 11–22. http://www.queer-journal.com (accessed June 11,
2006).

Smeal, Eleanor. "Special Message from the Feminist Majority on the Taliban, Osama bin
Laden, and Afghan Women." September 18, 2001. http://feminist.org (accessed June
11, 2006).

Smith, Chris S. "Kandahar Journal. Shh, It's an Open Secret: Warlords and Pedophilia."
New York Times, February 21, 2002, A4.

Smith, Rhonda. "More Acceptance for Gay Muslims Since 9/11." *Washington Blade*, April
5, 2002. Republished http://www.globalgayz.com (accessed June 11, 2006).

SodomyLaws.org. "*Lawrence & Garner v. State of Texas*." Updated April 13, 2006. http://
www.sodomylaws.org (accessed June 25, 2006).

Solomon, Alisa. "Insisting on Inquiry." *Center for Lesbian and Gay Studies (CLAGS) Newsletter* 11, no. 3 (fall 2001): 1.

Somerville, Siobhan B. "Queer *Loving*." *GLQ: A Journal of Lesbian and Gay Studies* 11, no. 3
(June 2005): 335–70.

———. *Queering the Color Line: Race and the Invention of Homosexuality in American Culture*.
Durham: Duke University Press, 2000.

———. "Sexual Aliens and the Racialized State: A Queer Reading of the 1952 U.S. Immigration and Nationality Act." In *Queer Migrations: Sexuality, U.S. Citizenship, and Border Crossings*, edited by Eithne Luibhéid and Lionel Cantú Jr., 75–91. Minneapolis: University of Minnesota Press, 2005.

Sontag, Susan. *Regarding the Pain of Others*. New York: Farrar, Straus and Giroux, 2002.

——. "Regarding the Torture of Others." *New York Times Magazine*, May 23, 2004, 24–27.

——. "Talk of the Town." *New Yorker*, September 24, 2001, 32.

South Asians against Police Brutality and Racism. "Not in Our Name: An Anti-Detention Testimonial." *SAMAR: South Asian Magazine for Action and Reflection* no. 15 (summer/fall 2002). http://www.samarmagazine.org (accessed June 27, 2005).

"South Park Is Gay!" *South Park*. Written and directed by Trey Parker. Comedy Central. October 22, 2003, episode 708.

Spiegel, Peter. "No Contractors Facing Abu Ghraib Abuse Charges." *Financial Times* (London), August 9, 2005, 6.

Spivak, Gayatri Chakravorty. "Can the Subaltern Speak? Speculations on Widow Sacrifice." *Wedge* 7–8 (winter/spring 1985): 120–30.

——. "Class and Culture in Diaspora." Keynote address at "Translating Class, Altering Hospitality" conference, Leeds University, England, June 22, 2002.

——. "Globalicities: Terror and Its Consequences," *CR: The New Centennial Review* 4, no. 1 (spring 2004): 73–94.

——. *The Postcolonial Critic: Interviews, Strategies, Dialogues*. Edited by Sara Harasym. New York: Routledge, 1990.

——. "Scattered Speculations on the Question of Value." In *In Other Worlds: Essays in Cultural Politics*, 154–75. New York: Routledge, 1988.

——. "Terror: A Speech after 9-11." *boundary 2* 31, no. 2 (summer 2004): 81–111.

Stalder, Felix. "Opinion: Privacy Is Not the Antidote to Surveillance." *Surveillance and Society* 1, no. 1 (September 2002): 120–24. http://www.surveillance-and-society.org (accessed June 26, 2006).

Stasiulis, Daiva. "Intersectional Feminist Theorizing." In *Race and Ethnic Relations in Canada*, edited by Peter S. Li, 347–97. Oxford: Oxford University Press, 1999.

Stephen, Chris. "Startled Marines Find Afghan Men All Made Up to See Them." *Scotsman*, May 24, 2002, 15.

Stern, Jessica. "Dreaded Risks and the Control of Biological Weapons." *International Security* 27, no. 3 (winter 2002–2003): 89–123.

——. "Holy Avengers." *Financial Times* (London), June 12, 2004, 14.

Stolba, Christine. "Feminists Go to War." *Women's Quarterly*, January 1, 2002, [unpaged].

Stoler, Ann Laura. *Race and the Education of Desire: Foucault's History of Sexuality and the Colonial Order of Things*. Durham: Duke University Press, 1995.

Stout, David. "Rumsfeld Offers Apology for Abuse of Iraqi Prisoners." *New York Times*, May 7, 2004. http://www.nytimes.com (accessed June 30, 2006).

Street, Richard Steven. *Beasts of the Field: A Narrative History of California Farmworkers 1769–1913*. Stanford: Stanford University Press, 2004.

Suan, Tara. "Suspension for Ceremonial Knives Slices Religious Rights." *Daily Californian*, September 2, 1994, 1, 7.

Suburban Emergency Management Project. "SEMP Biot #128: What Is 'Prison Islam'?" October 27, 2004. http://www.semp.us (accessed June 26, 2006).

Sullivan, Andrew. "Daily Dish." May 4, 2006. http://www.andrewsullivan.com (accessed June 19, 2006).

——. "Decent Exposure." Review of *The Trouble with Islam*, by Irshad Manji. *New York Times*, January 25, 2004, sec. 7, p. 10.

——. "Islamists versus Gays." Republished at Watch: Covering the War on Terror. July 20, 2005. http://watch.windsofchange.net (accessed September 9, 2006). Originally published July 20, 2005, at AndrewSullivan.com.

Swapan, Ashfaque. "South Asian Reporters Help Present Community's Stories." *India-West*, October 4, 2001. Republished October 4, 2001. http://www.sree.net (accessed June 22, 2006).

Takaki, Ronald. *Strangers from a Different Shore: A History of Asian Americans*. New York: Back Bay Books, 1989.

Talvi, Silja J. A. "Round Up: INS 'Special Registration' Ends in Mass Arrests." *In These Times*, January 17, 2003. http://www.inthesetimes.com (accessed March 4, 2007).

Targeting the Turban: Sikh Americans after September 11. Directed by Valerie Kaur Brar. Preliminary edit, in possession of author. Stanford University, forthcoming.

Tatchell, Peter. "Iran—10 Arabs Face Execution: Tehran Is a Racist State, as well as a Homophobic One." Tatchell Rights Fund, August 3, 2006. http://www.petertatchell.net (accessed September 9, 2006).

——. "Islamic Fundamentalism in Britain: Peter Tatchell Warns That Muslim Fundamentalists Are a Growing Threat to Gay Human Rights in Britain." 1995. http://www.petertatchell.net (accessed June 12, 2006). Originally published in *Gay Times*, October 1995.

——. "The New Dark Ages: Peter Tatchell Documents the Global Threat of Islamic Fundamentalism," 1995. http://www.petertatchell.net (accessed June 12, 2006).

——. "Peter Tatchell: Gay and Human Rights Campaigns." n.d. http://www.petertatchell.net (accessed June 1, 2006).

——. "Peter Tatchell Human Rights Fund." n.d. http://www.tatchellrightsfund.org (accessed June 1, 2006).

——. "The Rise of Islamic Fundamentalism in Britain." Press release. April 10, 1998. http://outrage.nabumedia.com (accessed June 15, 2005; now unavailable).

Taussig, Michael. *Mimesis and Alterity: A Particular History of the Senses*. New York: Routledge, 1993.

Thacker, Eugene. *The Global Genome: Biotechnology, Politics, and Culture*. Cambridge, Mass.: MIT Press, 2005.

TheGully.com. "Why Queers Were Silent." *The Gully*, October 31, 2001. http://www.thegully.com (accessed June 13, 2006).

Third World Gay Revolution (New York City). "What We Want, What We Believe." In *Out of the Closets: Voices of Gay Liberation*, edited by Karla Jay and Allan Young, 363–67. New York: New York University Press, 1992.

Thompson, Celso A. "Message from the IGLTA President." *IGLTA Today* newsletter, November 2001. http://iglta.org (accessed December 15, 2001; no longer available).

Thomsen, Scott. "Arizona Man Accused of Killing Sikh: 'I'm an American!'" September 28, 2001. LexisNexis (accessed June 1, 2006).

ThreeSources.com. "From Iraq." Posting by jk. March 22, 2005. http://www.threesources.com (accessed June 25, 2006).

Tiger, Lionel. "Is Manliness Really Back in Favor?" Interview with Charlotte Hayes. *Women's Quarterly* 12, no. 3 (January 2002): [unpaged].

——. "Rogue Males." *Guardian* (London) October 2, 2001, 8.

Times of India. "Sporadic Violence against Ethnic Minorities." September 14, 2001. http://timesofindia.indiatimes.com (accessed June 22, 2006).

Toensing, Chris, ed. "Sexuality, Suppression and the State." Special issue of *Middle East Report* 230 (spring 2004).

Toolis, Kevin. "Rise of the Terrorist Professors." *New Statesman,* June 14, 2004, 26–27.

Trinquier, Roger. *Modern Warfare.* New York: Praeger, 1964.

Under Attack: Arab, Muslim and South Asian Communities Since September 11th. Documentary audio CD. Produced by Sarah Olson. 30 min. Not in Our Name, Oakland, Calif. 2004.

United News of India. "U.S. Senator Kerry Apologizes to Sikhs." Free Republic, February 10, 2004. http://209.157.64.201 (accessed June 21, 2006).

United Press International. "U.S. Muslims Protest FBI Radiation Scans." December 29, 2005. LexisNexis (accessed May 21, 2006).

United States v. Bhagat Singh Thind, 1923 U.S. LEXIS 2544 (1923).

U.S. Department of Homeland Security. U.S. Immigration and Customs Enforcement. "Changes to National Security Entry/Exit Registration System (NSEERS)." Fact sheet. December 1, 2003. http://www.ice.gov (accessed June 26, 2006).

U.S. Department of State. Bureau of International Information Programs. USINFO. "National Security Entry-Exit Registration System." June 5, 2002. http://usinfo.state.gov (accessed June 26, 2006).

——. Bureau of International Information Programs. USINFO. "Response to Terrorism—U.S. Department of State." Updated June 2006. http://usinfo.state.gov (accessed June 10, 2006).

——. Bureau of Public Affairs. *Curriculum Materials: Terrorism: A War without Borders.* September 2002. http://future.state.gov (accessed June 21, 2006).

U.S. Department of Transportation. Federal Aviation Administration. "Guidance for Screeners and Other Security Personnel." n.d. http://www.sikhcoalition.org (accessed June 23, 2006).

Valentine, Gill. "(Re)Negotiating the 'Heterosexual Street.'" In *BodySpace: Destabilizing Geographies of Gender and Sexuality,* edited by Nancy Duncan, 146–55. New York: Routledge, 1996.

Vanita, Ruth, ed. *Queering India: Same-Sex Love and Eroticism in Indian Culture and Society.* New York: Routledge, 2002.

Varnell, Paul. "Why Gays Should Support the Iraq War." *Gay City News,* February 21–27, 2003. http://www.gaycitynews.com (accessed June 13, 2006).

Vimalassery, Manu. "Passports and Pink Slips: Immigration and Labor after 9/11." *SAMAR: South Asian Magazine for Action and Reflection* no. 15 (summer/fall 2002). http://www.samarmagazine.org (accessed June 27, 2005).

Visible Collective. *Disappeared in America.* www.disappearedinamerica.org (accessed June 26, 2006).

Vogler, Candance. "Sex and Talk." *Critical Inquiry* 24, no. 2 (winter 1998): 328–65.

Volpp, Leti. "The Citizen and the Terrorist." *UCLA Law Review* 49, no. 5 (June 2002): 1575–600.

Wald, Matthew L. "Widespread Radioactivity Monitoring Is Confirmed." *New York Times*, December 24, 2005, A1.

Warner, Michael. "Publics and Counter Publics." *Public Culture* 14, no. 1 (winter 2002): 49–90.

——. *The Trouble with Normal: Sex, Politics, and the Ethics of Queer Life*. Cambridge, Mass.: Harvard University Press, 2000.

Washington Post. "Sworn Statements by Abu Ghraib Detainees." January 16–21, 2004. http://www.washingtonpost.com (accessed June 20, 2006).

Weinraub, Bernie. "Subdued Patriotism Replaces Glitter as Television Finally Presents Its Emmys." *New York Times*, November 5, 2001, A9.

Weinstein, MaxZine. "Gay Press Says: 'God Bless GLBT America.'" *RFD*, no. 108 (winter 2001/2002): 15.

Weizman, Eyal. "The Politics of Verticality." April 24–May 2, 2002. http://www.open democracy.net (accessed June 26, 2006).

——. "Walking through Walls: Soldiers As Architects in the Israeli-Palestinian Conflict." *Radical Philosophy*, no. 136 (2006): 8–22.

White House. *National Strategy for Combating Terrorism*. 2003. http://www.whitehouse .gov (accessed June 13, 2006).

Wilchins, Riki. "Airport Insecurity." *The Advocate*, June 25, 2003, 136. Reprinted at Gender Public Advocacy Coalition. http://www.gpac.org (accessed June 13, 2006).

Wilcox, Barbara. "WorldPride Denied Parade Permit." July 21, 2006. http://www.gay .com (accessed September 6, 2006).

Wilson, Elizabeth A. *Neural Geographies: Feminism and the Microstructure of Cognition*. New York: Routledge, 1998.

Wilson, Robert. Executive Director's Report. October 1, 2001. http://iglta.com (accessed December 15, 2001).

Wockner, Rex. "The Wockner Wire." Opinion. *PlanetOut News and Politics*, August 30, 2002. http://www.planetout.com (accessed June 12, 2006).

Wood, David. "Editorial: Foucault and Panopticism Revisited." *Surveillance and Society* 1, no. 3 (2003): 234–39. http://www.surveillance-and-society.org (accessed June 25, 2006).

Wyman, Hastings. "Capital Letters: Highlighting the Q in Iraq." *Letters from Camp Rehoboth*, October 18, 2002. http://www.camprehoboth.com (accessed June 13, 2006).

Young, Iris Marion. "Feminist Reactions to the Contemporary Security Regime." *Hypatia: A Journal of Feminist Philosophy* 18, no. 1 (winter 2003): 223–31.

Yuskaev, Timur, and Matt Weiner. "Secular and Religious Rights: Ban the Croissant!" Opinion. *International Herald Tribune*, December 19, 2003, 8.

Zeesil, Leah. "Jerusalem WorldPride Smaller Than Expected." *Windy City Times*, August 16, 2006. http://www.windycitytimes.com (accessed September 6, 2006).

Zernike, Kate, Michael Moss, and James Risen. "Accused Soldier Paints Scene of Eager Mayhem at Iraqi Prison." *New York Times*, May 14, 2006, A1.

Zinn, Howard. "The Power and the Glory: Myths of American Exceptionalism." *Boston Review: A Political and Literary Forum* 30, no. 3–4 (summer 2005). http://bostonre view.net (accessed June 11, 2006).

Žižek, Slavoj. "Between Two Deaths: The Culture of Torture." *London Review of Books*, June 3, 2004. http://www.lrb.co.uk (accessed March 5, 2007).

——. *Welcome to the Desert of the Real: Five Essays on September 11 and Related Dates*. New York: Verso, 2002.

——. "What Rumsfeld Doesn't Know That He Knows about Abu Ghraib." *In These Times*, May 21, 2004, 32.

Zupan, Cheryl, and Kelly Peters. "Anti-War Protest in Ann Arbor: LGBTs Highly Vocal at Event." *Between the Lines News*, March 27, 2003. http://www.pridesources.com (accessed June 13, 2006).

Index

141; diaspora and, 170–75; identity and, 204–6, 215; modernity and, 74–76, 222; necropolitics and, 32–36; as regulatory, 11–24, 140, 199, 200; as transgression, 22–23, 174, 205. *See also* Liberalism: queerness and; Nation: queerness and; Race: linked to sexuality

Queers for Peace and Justice, 44, 246 n. 25

Queer studies: xiv, 35, 93–94, 163; affect and, 174, 206–7

Quinn, Andrew, 234 n. 29

Race, 31–32, 44–45, 92, 158, 176; as assemblage, 192–96, 210; biopolitics and, 35, 194–95; "Don't Ask, Don't Tell" policy and, 1–2, 232 n. 2; ethnicity and, 25–28; fear and, 184–89; gay marriage and, 29–30; heteronormativity and, 30, 34, 40–41, 63; linked to sexuality, 38–39, 117–21, 125, 218, 221–22; nation and, 30, 47, 145, 173; visual and, 183–89. *See also* Ascendancy of whiteness; Queerness: cleaved from race; Whiteness

Racialization, xi–xiii, 132–33, 140; of religion, 38, 119, 160–61

Racism: biopolitics and, 194–95; of gay communities, 28, 75; gay epithets and, 43, 73; of South Asians, 133; state, 26, 35, 133, 158–59

Rai, Amit S., 208, 277 n. 24, 282–83 n. 64

Rape, 110; capitalism and, 47, 249 n. 34; prisoners and, 97–98, 101

Rejali, Darius M., 82, 102, 104

Religion, 13–15, 93: as pathological, 55–56, 59; race and, 13, 38, 119, 160–61

Rendition, 87

Representation, xiv, 152, 172, 188, 199, 201, 213, 215; affect and, 104, 107, 112, 194, 204–9, 221

Repression. *See* Sexuality: repression of

Repressive hypothesis (Foucault), 9, 14, 34, 93, 140

Reproduction: of nation, 77, 126; queerness and, 210–11

Resistance, 23–24, 220

Revolutionary Association of the Women of Afghanistan (RAWA), 6–7, 231 n. 16

Riggs, Marlon, 131

Rimer, Sara, 268 n. 104

Robertson, Pat, 40

Roque, Francisco Silva, 166, 271 n. 3

Roth, Thomas, 62

Roy, Arundhati, 72, 231 n. 16

Rubin, Gayle, 97

Rumsfeld, Donald, 79

Sacks, Oliver, xxi–xxii

Sadomasochism, 71, 79, 90

Sadownick, Douglas, 242 n. 11

Said, Edward, 39, 52–53, 75, 84, 94, 231 n. 16

Saldanha, Arun, 189–90, 193, 209–10, 211

Sallat, Salah Edine, 102, *103*

SAMAR, 267 n. 89

Santorum, Rick, 77–78

Sarkar, Vinanti: *Mistaken Identity: Sikhs in America*, 186, 281 n. 44

Saudi Arabia, 72

Savage, Michael, 139

Scientia sexualis (Foucault), 74–76. See also *Ars erotica*

Scott, Joan, 204

Scroggins, Deborah, 236 n. 52

Secularism, 55, 59, 60; queer, 13–15, 17

Sedgwick, Eve Kosofsky, xix–xx, 206

Segal, M. E., 54

Sensation, 171–73, 177, 207–8. *See also* Affect

September 11, 2001, 40, 71–72, 129, 133; bereavement funds, 41, 240–41 n. 9; business and, 64–66, 150; temporality and, xviii, 69, 230–31 n. 15

Serra, Richard, 102, *103*

Sex, 160, 210

Sexism. *See* Misogyny

Sexuality, 87–88, 195–96, 206, 211, 220, 230 n. 9: linked to race, 38–39, 117–21, 125, 218, 221–22; nation and, 47, 98–100; power and, 112–13; repression of, 83–84, 91–92, 94–95, 138–40. *See also* Muslims: sexuality of

ontogenesis and, 214; paranoid, xix–xx; preemptive, 154–55, 183–85; queer, 76, 217–18

Terminology: sexuality and, 230 n. 9

Terrorism, 37–40, 43, 67, 119; family and, 52, 56–58; pyramid/network models of, 52, 73, 85, 250 n. 41; queerness and, xxiii–xxiv, 75, 169; studies, 52–56, 84

Terrorist: look-alikes, 52, 119, 136, 151, 175, 194; patriot vs., 38, 76–77, 198

Testimonials: of U.S. prisoners/detainees, 110–11, 143, 145–46, 148, 267 n. 89

Thacker, Eugene, 151, 159–60, 239 n. 84

Thind, Bhagat Singh, *176*; *United States v.*, 176–78, 276 n. 22, 282 n. 64

Thomas, Kendall, 118

Thompson, Celso A., 65

Tide of turbans, 275 n. 19, 275–76 n. 20

Tin, Louis-George, x

Titan Corporation, 84–85

Tolerance, 71, 73, 137. *See also* United States: as sexually tolerant

Toolis, Kevin, 55–56, 250 n. 51

Torture, 81–82, 112–13; gay sex as, 97–98, 111, 140–41; masculinity and 86–87, 91–92, 98–100; Muslim body and, 85–87, 96; techniques of, 84–85, 102, 104, 254–55 n. 3.

Tourism: gay and lesbian, 62–67, 252 n. 71, 252 n. 74

Transnationalism, 16, 51, 67; kinship and, 61–62, 148

Transportation Security Agency, 155

Turbans, 275 n. 19, 275–76 n. 20, 279 n. 31, 280 n. 34; assemblage and, 174, 192–94; becoming and, 187, 192, 194; as objects of violence, 149, 166–67, 179–80; queerness and, 169; tradition and, 174, 181–82; visual and, 167, 274 n. 10, 281 n. 50

United Nations, xiii, 79

United States, 77, 145; imperialism and, 1–2, 8, 37, 69, 72, 79, 116, 140, 221; psychic health of, 67, 80–81; as sexually toler-ant, 69, 88, 94–95, 98, 111, 131

United States v. Bhagat Singh Thind, 176–78, 276 n. 22, 282 n. 64

Urbanity, 66, 69–70

USA PATRIOT Act, xxvi, 26, 78, 116; race and, 92, 142, 266–67 n. 81

Varnell, Paul, 248–49 n. 31

Veiling: France and, 180; as symbol of oppression, 59, 102–3, 173, 181

Verkouw, Deborah, 241 n. 10

Victimization, 60; Abu Ghraib and, 80, 89, 96; gays and, 43–44, 95; Sikhs and, 182, 202

"Vietnam," 102, *103*, 104, *105*

Violence, 24, 56, 75, 109; blackness and, 183–86; gender and; 89–90; as sociality, 81–82, 90. *See also* Hate crimes

Visible Collective, *134–35*, *144*, 265 n. 67, 286 n. 97

Visual, 107, 125, 180; race and, 175, 183–89; turbans and, 167, 274 n. 10, 281 n. 50

Volpp, Leti, 38

Walter McCarren Immigration and Natu-ralization Act, 119

Warner, Michael, 47

Weizman, Eyal, 152, 154, 215–16

Welfare, 124, 237 n. 69

Welfare Reform Act, 28, 78

Whiteness, 22, 78, 126, 208; as queer norm, 76, 95, 118, 128, 131, 141. *See also* Ascendancy of whiteness; Queerness: cleaved from race

Wilson, Elizabeth A., 208–9

Wilson, Robert, 64

Winfrey, Oprah, 6

Women, 60, 89, 126; private and, 124; as suicide bombers, 220, 286 n. 39; tradi-tion and, 98, 174, 182, 195, 280 n. 35; violence and, 90. *See also* Femininity

World Pride 2006, 16–17, 235 n. 40

World Sikh Syndicate, *201*

Žižek, Slavoj, 85, 104, 108–9, 113, 257 n. 13

JASBIR K. PUAR is an associate professor of Women's and Gender Studies
at Rutgers University.

Library of Congress Cataloging-in-Publication Data
Puar, Jasbir K.
Terrorist assemblages : homonationalism in
queer times / Jasbir K. Puar.
p. cm.(Next wave: new directions in women's studies)
Includes bibliographical references and index.
ISBN 978-0-8223-4094-2 (cloth : alk. paper)
ISBN 978-0-8223-4114-7 (pbk. : alk. paper)
1. Homosexuality—Political aspects.
2. Terrorism—Social aspects.
I. Title.   HQ76.25.P83 2007
306.76′6090511—dc22
2007017112